★ ★ ★

GILBERT HERNANDEZ
BLOOD OF
PALOMAR

W9-CDD-209

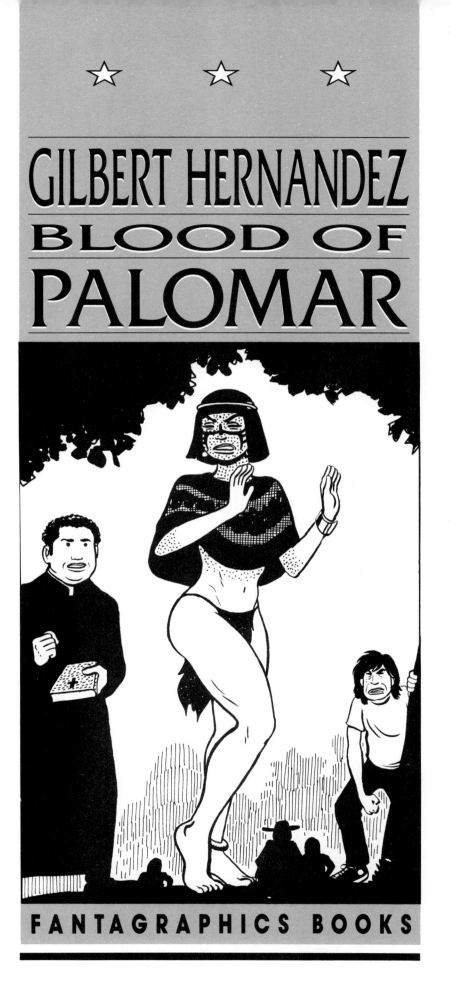

GILBERT HERNANDEZ
BLOOD OF PALOMAR

FANTAGRAPHICS BOOKS

FANTAGRAPHICS BOOKS
7563 Lake City Way N.E.
Seattle, WA 98115

Editor: Gary Groth
Art Director: Roberta Gregory
Front cover colored by Jim Woodring
Back cover colored by G. Hernandez; seps by Roberta Gregory

The comics herein are © 1987, 1988 Gilbert Hernandez.
This edition is copyright © 1989 Fantagraphics Books, Inc.

NOTE: "Human Diastrophism" has been substantially altered by the
author from its initial appearance in Love and Rockets #21-26.

All rights reserved. Permission to excerpt or reproduce material
for reviews or notices must be obtained from Fantagraphics
Books, Inc., at 7563 Lake City Way N.E., Seattle, WA 98115

First Fantagraphics Books edition: December, 1989.
1 3 5 7 9 10 8 6 4 2

ISBN (soft): 1-56097-005-7. ISBN (hard): 1-56097-006-5.
Printed in Singapore through Palace Press.

CONTENTS

Welcome to Palomar
1

Sugar and Spikes
3

Space Case
6

Heraclio's Burden
10

The Cast of Characters
of "Human Diastrophism"
12

Human Diastrophism
13

Cover Gallery and Chapter Headings
119

FANTAGRAPHICS BOOKS

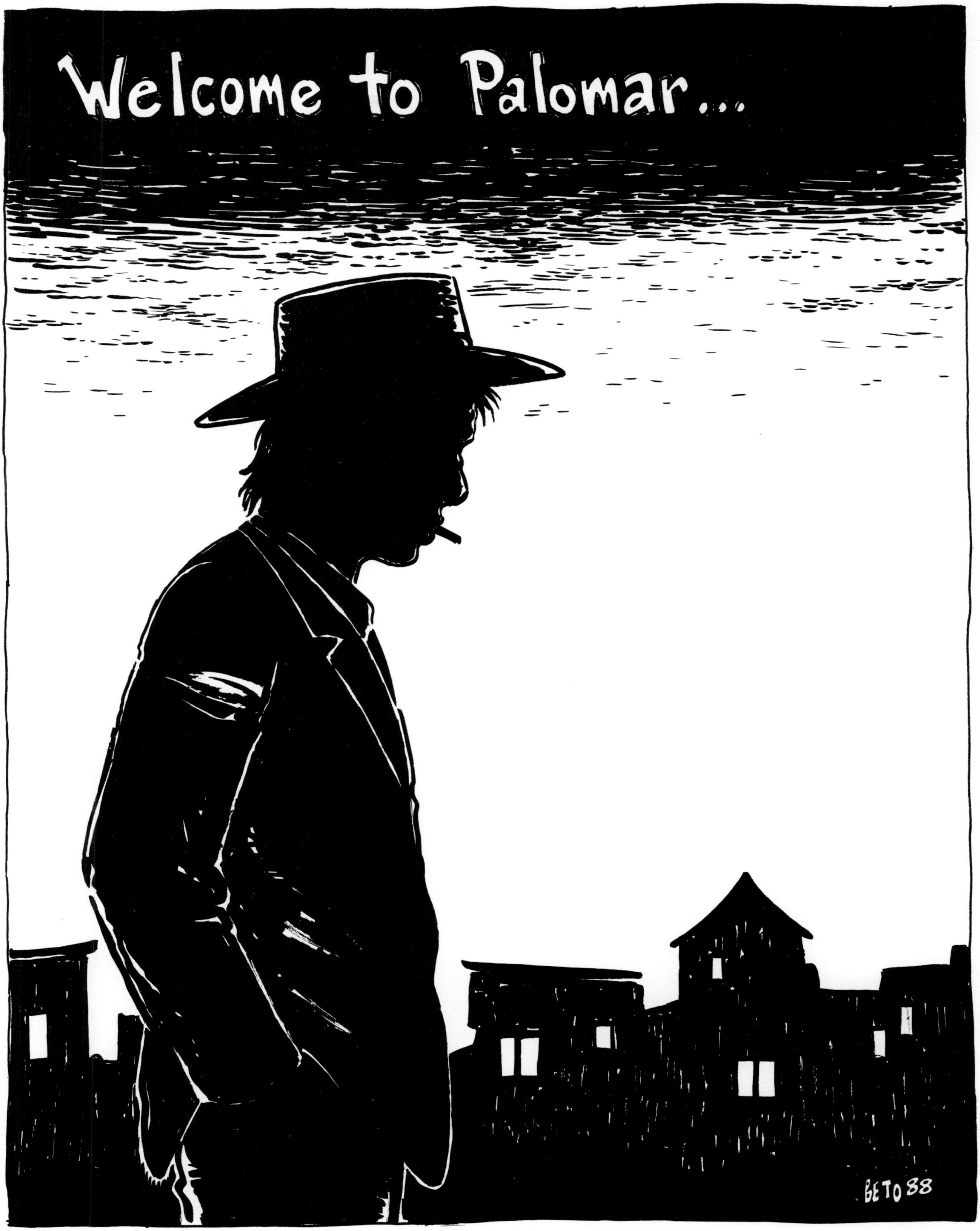
Welcome to Palomar...
BETO 88

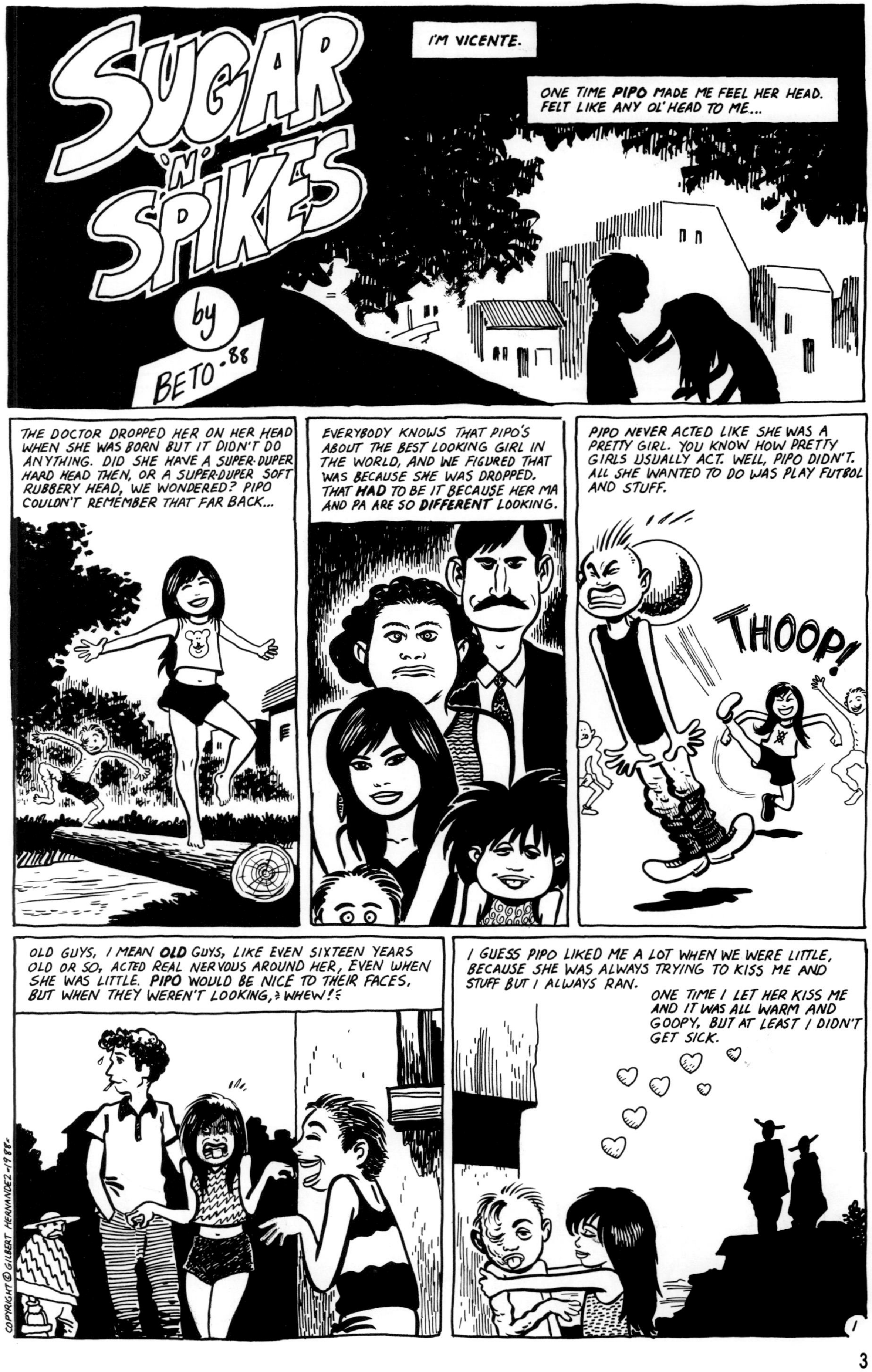
SUGAR 'N' SPIKES
by BETO-88
I'M VICENTE.
ONE TIME PIPO MADE ME FEEL HER HEAD. FELT LIKE ANY OL' HEAD TO ME...
THE DOCTOR DROPPED HER ON HER HEAD WHEN SHE WAS BORN BUT IT DIDN'T DO ANYTHING. DID SHE HAVE A SUPER-DUPER HARD HEAD THEN, OR A SUPER-DUPER SOFT RUBBERY HEAD, WE WONDERED? PIPO COULDN'T REMEMBER THAT FAR BACK...
EVERYBODY KNOWS THAT PIPO'S ABOUT THE BEST LOOKING GIRL IN THE WORLD, AND WE FIGURED THAT WAS BECAUSE SHE WAS DROPPED. THAT HAD TO BE IT BECAUSE HER MA AND PA ARE SO DIFFERENT LOOKING.
PIPO NEVER ACTED LIKE SHE WAS A PRETTY GIRL. YOU KNOW HOW PRETTY GIRLS USUALLY ACT. WELL, PIPO DIDN'T. ALL SHE WANTED TO DO WAS PLAY FUTBOL AND STUFF.
THOOP!
OLD GUYS, I MEAN OLD GUYS, LIKE EVEN SIXTEEN YEARS OLD OR SO, ACTED REAL NERVOUS AROUND HER, EVEN WHEN SHE WAS LITTLE. PIPO WOULD BE NICE TO THEIR FACES, BUT WHEN THEY WEREN'T LOOKING, WHEW!
COPYRIGHT © GILBERT HERNANDEZ-1988-
I GUESS PIPO LIKED ME A LOT WHEN WE WERE LITTLE, BECAUSE SHE WAS ALWAYS TRYING TO KISS ME AND STUFF BUT I ALWAYS RAN.
ONE TIME I LET HER KISS ME AND IT WAS ALL WARM AND GOOPY, BUT AT LEAST I DIDN'T GET SICK.
1

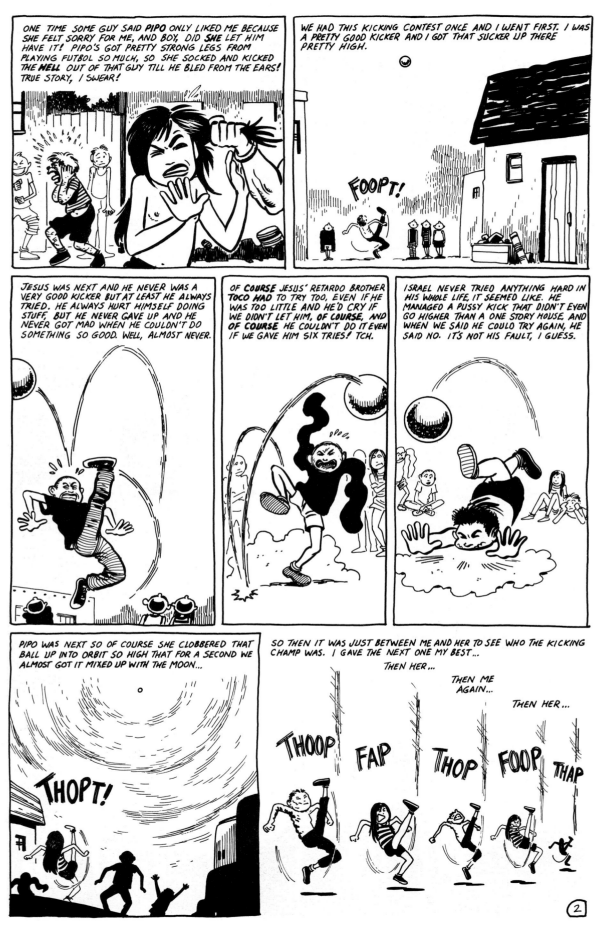

ONE TIME SOME GUY SAID **PIPO** ONLY LIKED ME BECAUSE SHE FELT SORRY FOR ME, AND BOY, DID **SHE** LET HIM HAVE IT! PIPO'S GOT PRETTY STRONG LEGS FROM PLAYING FUTBOL SO MUCH, SO SHE SOCKED AND KICKED **THE HELL** OUT OF THAT GUY TILL HE BLED FROM THE EARS! TRUE STORY, I SWEAR!

WE HAD THIS KICKING CONTEST ONCE AND I WENT FIRST. I WAS A PRETTY GOOD KICKER AND I GOT THAT SUCKER UP THERE PRETTY HIGH.

FOOPT!

JESUS WAS NEXT AND HE NEVER WAS A VERY GOOD KICKER BUT AT LEAST HE ALWAYS TRIED. HE ALWAYS HURT HIMSELF DOING STUFF, BUT HE NEVER GAVE UP AND HE NEVER GOT MAD WHEN HE COULDN'T DO SOMETHING SO GOOD. WELL, ALMOST NEVER.

OF **COURSE** JESUS' RETARDO BROTHER **TOCO HAD** TO TRY TOO, EVEN IF HE WAS TOO LITTLE AND HE'D CRY IF WE DIDN'T LET HIM, **OF COURSE**, AND **OF COURSE** HE COULDN'T DO IT EVEN IF WE GAVE HIM SIX TRIES! TCH.

ISRAEL NEVER TRIED ANYTHING HARD IN HIS WHOLE LIFE, IT SEEMED LIKE. HE MANAGED A PUSSY KICK THAT DIDN'T EVEN GO HIGHER THAN A ONE STORY HOUSE, AND WHEN WE SAID HE COULD TRY AGAIN, HE SAID NO. IT'S NOT HIS FAULT, I GUESS.

PIPO WAS NEXT SO OF COURSE SHE CLOBBERED THAT BALL UP INTO ORBIT SO HIGH THAT FOR A SECOND WE ALMOST GOT IT MIXED UP WITH THE MOON...

THOPT!

SO THEN IT WAS JUST BETWEEN ME AND HER TO SEE WHO THE KICKING CHAMP WAS. I GAVE THE NEXT ONE MY BEST... THEN HER... THEN ME AGAIN... THEN HER...

THOOP FAIP THOP FOOP THAP

②

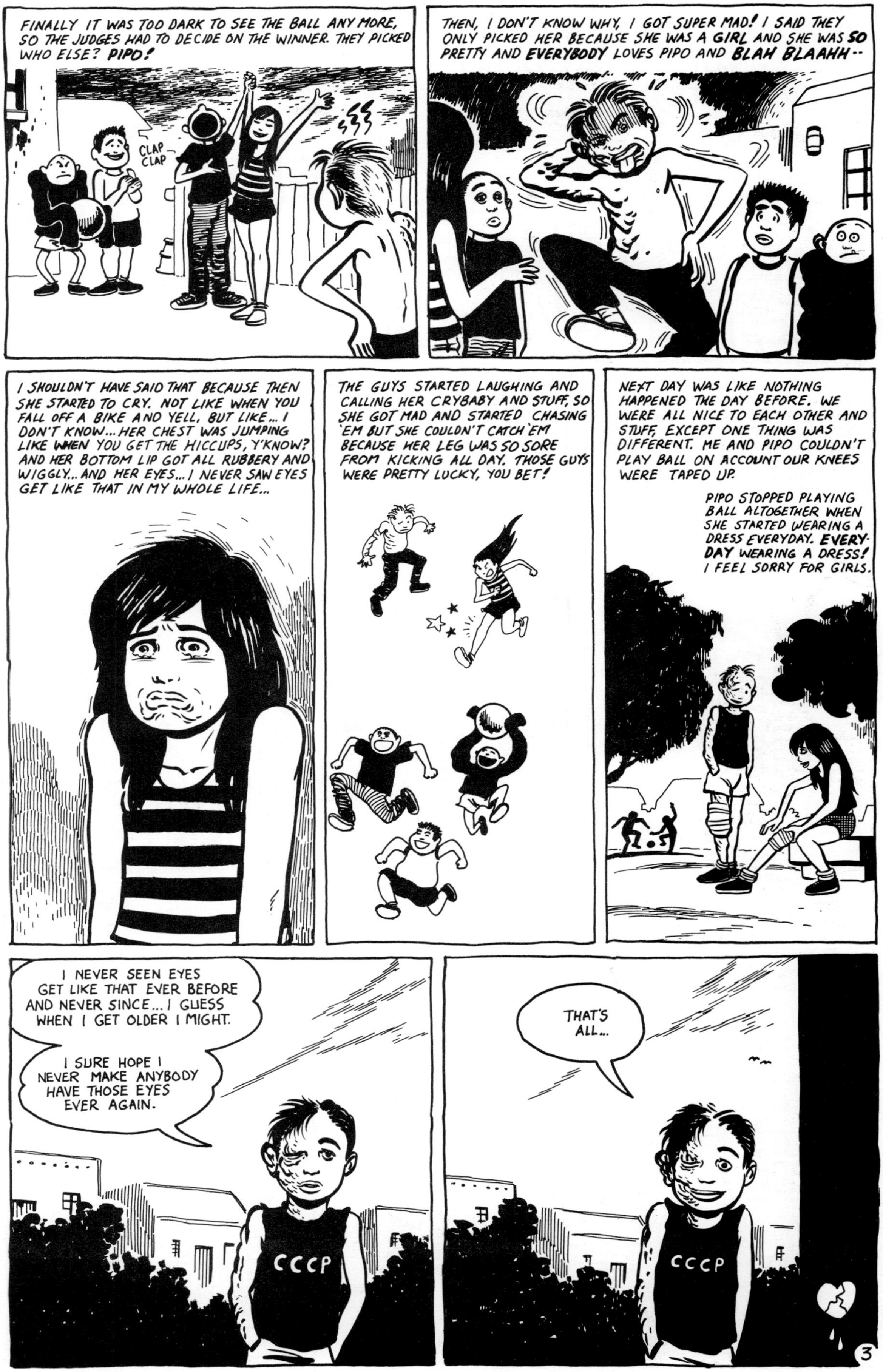
FINALLY IT WAS TOO DARK TO SEE THE BALL ANY MORE, SO THE JUDGES HAD TO DECIDE ON THE WINNER. THEY PICKED WHO ELSE? PIPO!
CLAP CLAP
THEN, I DON'T KNOW WHY, I GOT SUPER MAD! I SAID THEY ONLY PICKED HER BECAUSE SHE WAS A GIRL AND SHE WAS SO PRETTY AND EVERYBODY LOVES PIPO AND BLAH BLAAHH--
I SHOULDN'T HAVE SAID THAT BECAUSE THEN SHE STARTED TO CRY. NOT LIKE WHEN YOU FALL OFF A BIKE AND YELL, BUT LIKE... I DON'T KNOW... HER CHEST WAS JUMPING LIKE WHEN YOU GET THE HICCUPS, Y'KNOW? AND HER BOTTOM LIP GOT ALL RUBBERY AND WIGGLY... AND HER EYES... I NEVER SAW EYES GET LIKE THAT IN MY WHOLE LIFE...
THE GUYS STARTED LAUGHING AND CALLING HER CRYBABY AND STUFF, SO SHE GOT MAD AND STARTED CHASING 'EM BUT SHE COULDN'T CATCH 'EM BECAUSE HER LEG WAS SO SORE FROM KICKING ALL DAY. THOSE GUYS WERE PRETTY LUCKY, YOU BET!
NEXT DAY WAS LIKE NOTHING HAPPENED THE DAY BEFORE. WE WERE ALL NICE TO EACH OTHER AND STUFF, EXCEPT ONE THING WAS DIFFERENT. ME AND PIPO COULDN'T PLAY BALL ON ACCOUNT OUR KNEES WERE TAPED UP.
PIPO STOPPED PLAYING BALL ALTOGETHER WHEN SHE STARTED WEARING A DRESS EVERYDAY. EVERY-DAY WEARING A DRESS! I FEEL SORRY FOR GIRLS.
I NEVER SEEN EYES GET LIKE THAT EVER BEFORE AND NEVER SINCE... I GUESS WHEN I GET OLDER I MIGHT.
I SURE HOPE I NEVER MAKE ANYBODY HAVE THOSE EYES EVER AGAIN.
CCCP
THAT'S ALL...
CCCP
3

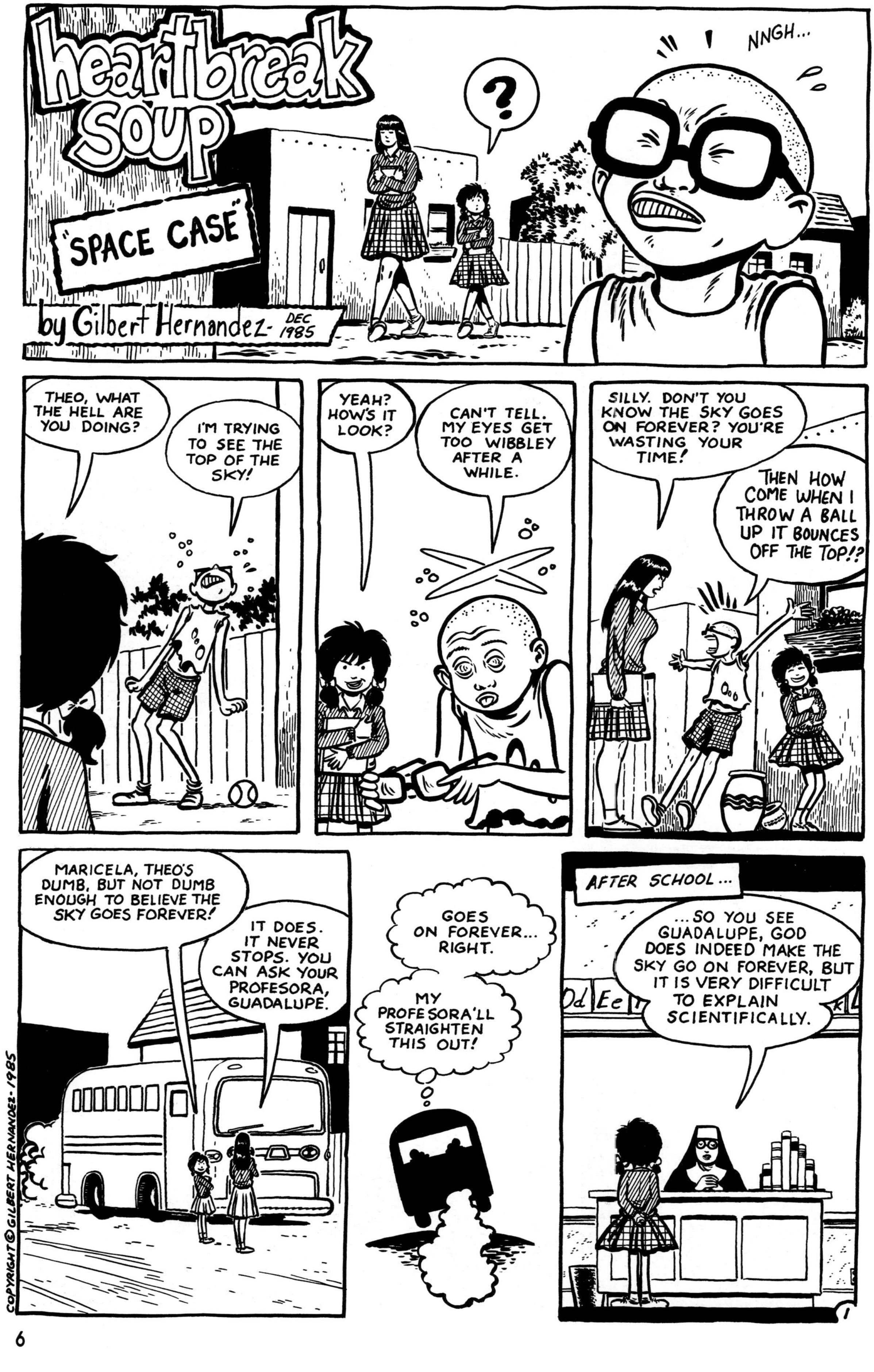
heartbreak soup
"SPACE CASE"
by Gilbert Hernandez- DEC 1985
?
NNGH...
THEO, WHAT THE HELL ARE YOU DOING?
I'M TRYING TO SEE THE TOP OF THE SKY!
YEAH? HOW'S IT LOOK?
CAN'T TELL. MY EYES GET TOO WIBBLEY AFTER A WHILE.
SILLY. DON'T YOU KNOW THE SKY GOES ON FOREVER? YOU'RE WASTING YOUR TIME!
THEN HOW COME WHEN I THROW A BALL UP IT BOUNCES OFF THE TOP!?
MARICELA, THEO'S DUMB, BUT NOT DUMB ENOUGH TO BELIEVE THE SKY GOES FOREVER!
IT DOES. IT NEVER STOPS. YOU CAN ASK YOUR PROFESORA, GUADALUPE.
GOES ON FOREVER... RIGHT.
MY PROFESORA'LL STRAIGHTEN THIS OUT!
AFTER SCHOOL...
...SO YOU SEE GUADALUPE, GOD DOES INDEED MAKE THE SKY GO ON FOREVER, BUT IT IS VERY DIFFICULT TO EXPLAIN SCIENTIFICALLY.
1

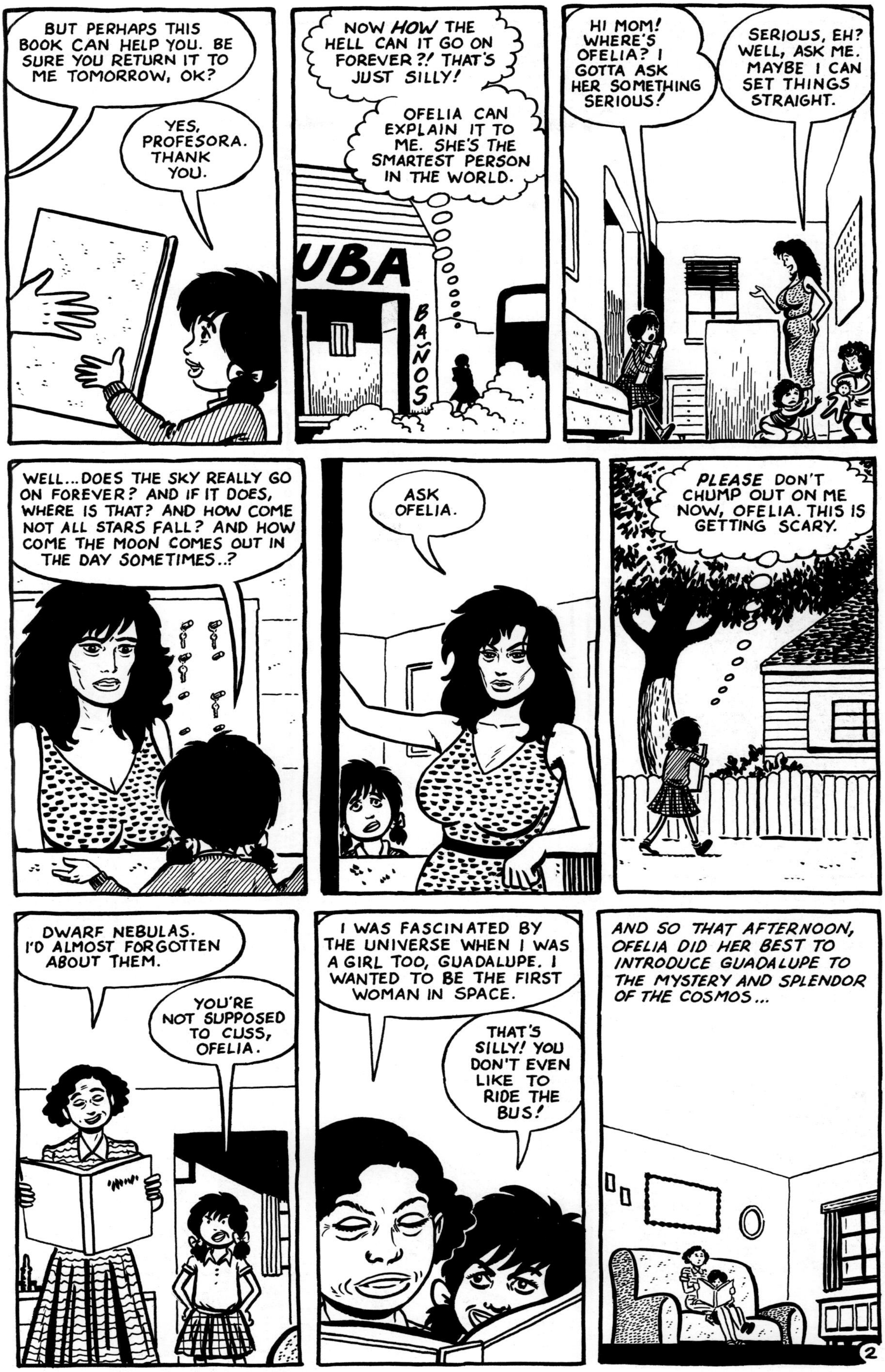
BUT PERHAPS THIS BOOK CAN HELP YOU. BE SURE YOU RETURN IT TO ME TOMORROW, OK?
YES, PROFESORA. THANK YOU.
NOW HOW THE HELL CAN IT GO ON FOREVER?! THAT'S JUST SILLY!
OFELIA CAN EXPLAIN IT TO ME. SHE'S THE SMARTEST PERSON IN THE WORLD.
UBA
BAÑOS
HI MOM! WHERE'S OFELIA? I GOTTA ASK HER SOMETHING SERIOUS!
SERIOUS, EH? WELL, ASK ME. MAYBE I CAN SET THINGS STRAIGHT.
WELL... DOES THE SKY REALLY GO ON FOREVER? AND IF IT DOES, WHERE IS THAT? AND HOW COME NOT ALL STARS FALL? AND HOW COME THE MOON COMES OUT IN THE DAY SOMETIMES..?
ASK OFELIA.
PLEASE DON'T CHUMP OUT ON ME NOW, OFELIA. THIS IS GETTING SCARY.
DWARF NEBULAS. I'D ALMOST FORGOTTEN ABOUT THEM.
YOU'RE NOT SUPPOSED TO CUSS, OFELIA.
I WAS FASCINATED BY THE UNIVERSE WHEN I WAS A GIRL TOO, GUADALUPE. I WANTED TO BE THE FIRST WOMAN IN SPACE.
THAT'S SILLY! YOU DON'T EVEN LIKE TO RIDE THE BUS!
AND SO THAT AFTERNOON, OFELIA DID HER BEST TO INTRODUCE GUADALUPE TO THE MYSTERY AND SPLENDOR OF THE COSMOS...
2

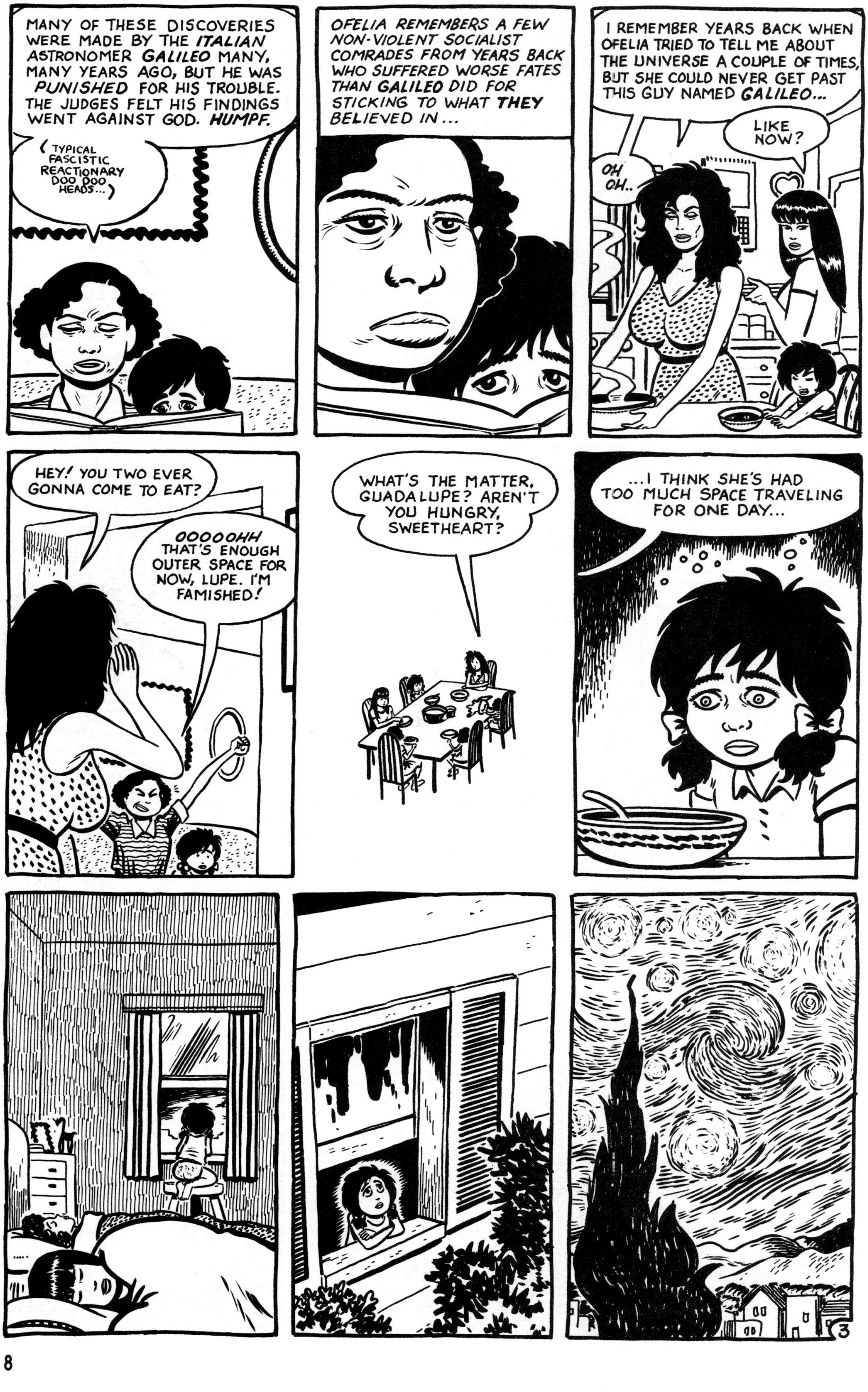
MANY OF THESE DISCOVERIES WERE MADE BY THE ITALIAN ASTRONOMER GALILEO MANY, MANY YEARS AGO, BUT HE WAS PUNISHED FOR HIS TROUBLE. THE JUDGES FELT HIS FINDINGS WENT AGAINST GOD. HUMPF.
(TYPICAL FASCISTIC REACTIONARY DOO DOO HEADS...)
OFELIA REMEMBERS A FEW NON-VIOLENT SOCIALIST COMRADES FROM YEARS BACK WHO SUFFERED WORSE FATES THAN GALILEO DID FOR STICKING TO WHAT THEY BELIEVED IN...
I REMEMBER YEARS BACK WHEN OFELIA TRIED TO TELL ME ABOUT THE UNIVERSE A COUPLE OF TIMES, BUT SHE COULD NEVER GET PAST THIS GUY NAMED GALILEO...
OH OH..
LIKE NOW?
HEY! YOU TWO EVER GONNA COME TO EAT?
OOOOOHH THAT'S ENOUGH OUTER SPACE FOR NOW, LUPE. I'M FAMISHED!
WHAT'S THE MATTER, GUADALUPE? AREN'T YOU HUNGRY, SWEETHEART?
...I THINK SHE'S HAD TOO MUCH SPACE TRAVELING FOR ONE DAY...
3

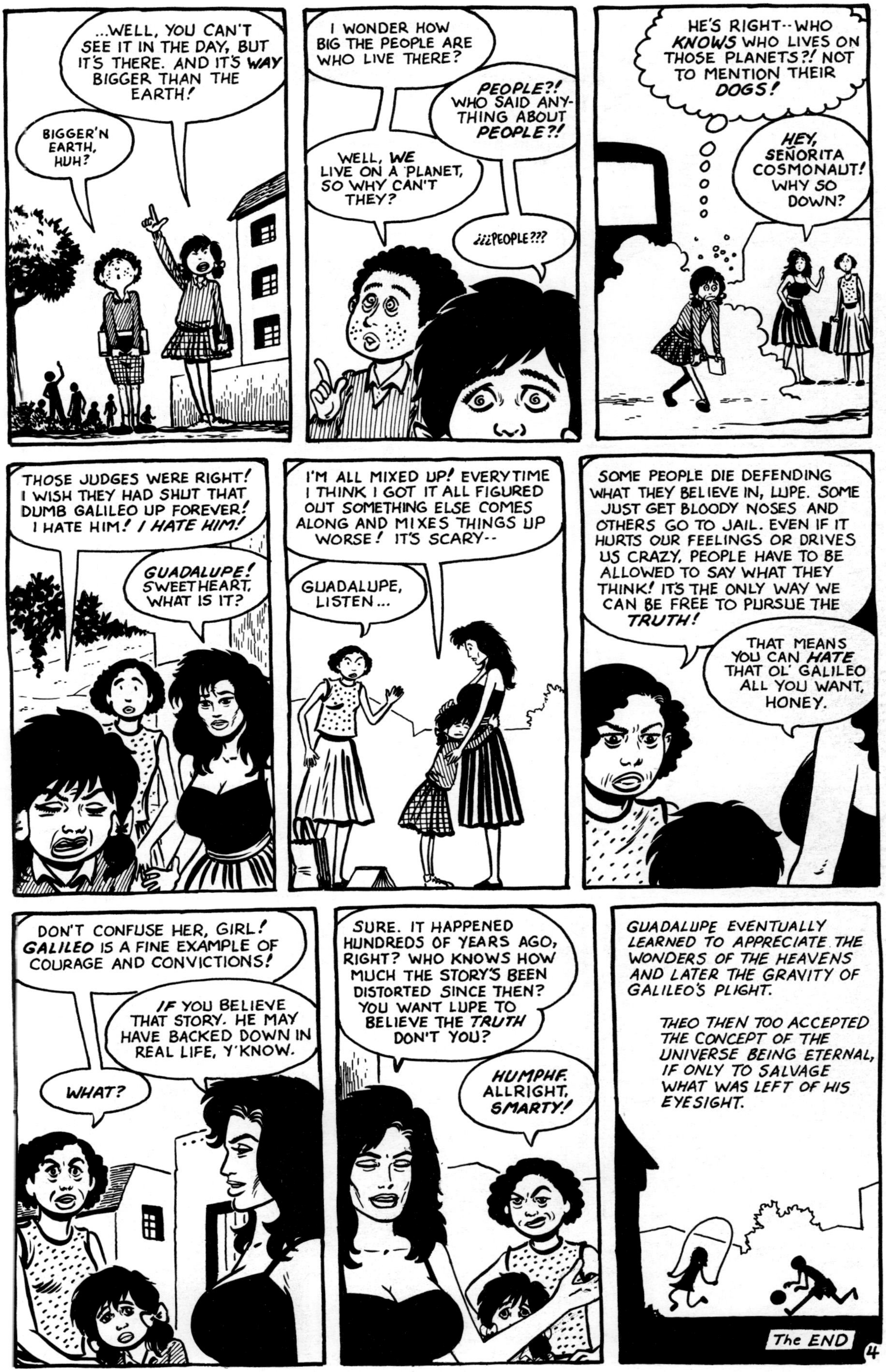
...WELL, YOU CAN'T SEE IT IN THE DAY, BUT IT'S THERE. AND IT'S WAY BIGGER THAN THE EARTH!
BIGGER'N EARTH, HUH?
I WONDER HOW BIG THE PEOPLE ARE WHO LIVE THERE?
PEOPLE?! WHO SAID ANY-THING ABOUT PEOPLE?!
WELL, WE LIVE ON A PLANET, SO WHY CAN'T THEY?
¿¿¿PEOPLE???
HE'S RIGHT--WHO KNOWS WHO LIVES ON THOSE PLANETS?! NOT TO MENTION THEIR DOGS!
HEY, SEÑORITA COSMONAUT! WHY SO DOWN?
THOSE JUDGES WERE RIGHT! I WISH THEY HAD SHUT THAT DUMB GALILEO UP FOREVER! I HATE HIM! I HATE HIM!
GUADALUPE! SWEETHEART, WHAT IS IT?
I'M ALL MIXED UP! EVERYTIME I THINK I GOT IT ALL FIGURED OUT SOMETHING ELSE COMES ALONG AND MIXES THINGS UP WORSE! IT'S SCARY--
GUADALUPE, LISTEN...
SOME PEOPLE DIE DEFENDING WHAT THEY BELIEVE IN, LUPE. SOME JUST GET BLOODY NOSES AND OTHERS GO TO JAIL. EVEN IF IT HURTS OUR FEELINGS OR DRIVES US CRAZY, PEOPLE HAVE TO BE ALLOWED TO SAY WHAT THEY THINK! IT'S THE ONLY WAY WE CAN BE FREE TO PURSUE THE TRUTH!
THAT MEANS YOU CAN HATE THAT OL' GALILEO ALL YOU WANT, HONEY.
DON'T CONFUSE HER, GIRL! GALILEO IS A FINE EXAMPLE OF COURAGE AND CONVICTIONS!
IF YOU BELIEVE THAT STORY. HE MAY HAVE BACKED DOWN IN REAL LIFE, Y'KNOW.
WHAT?
SURE. IT HAPPENED HUNDREDS OF YEARS AGO, RIGHT? WHO KNOWS HOW MUCH THE STORY'S BEEN DISTORTED SINCE THEN? YOU WANT LUPE TO BELIEVE THE TRUTH DON'T YOU?
HUMPHF. ALLRIGHT, SMARTY!
GUADALUPE EVENTUALLY LEARNED TO APPRECIATE THE WONDERS OF THE HEAVENS AND LATER THE GRAVITY OF GALILEO'S PLIGHT.
THEO THEN TOO ACCEPTED THE CONCEPT OF THE UNIVERSE BEING ETERNAL, IF ONLY TO SALVAGE WHAT WAS LEFT OF HIS EYESIGHT.
The END
4

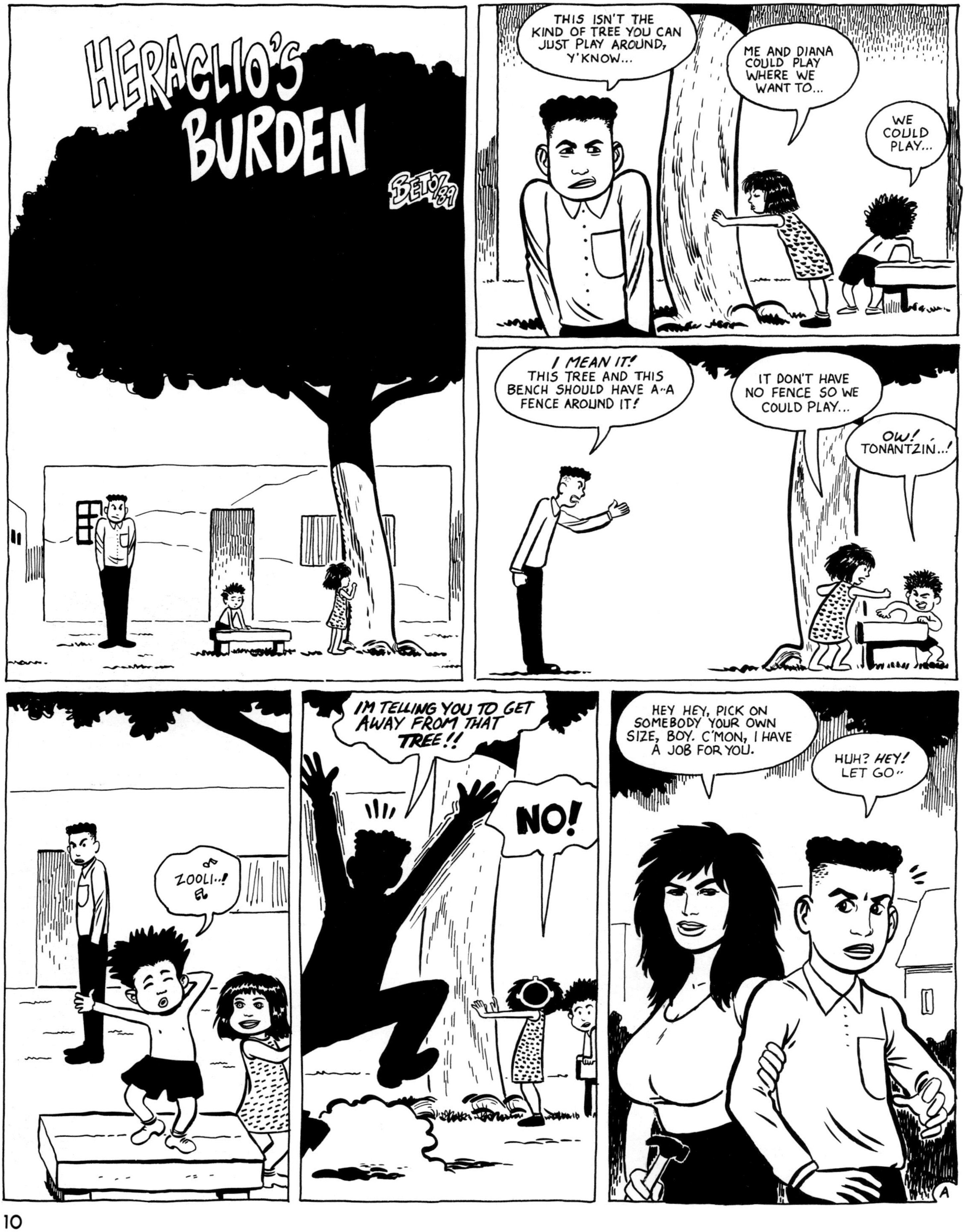
HERACLIO'S BURDEN
BETO '89
THIS ISN'T THE KIND OF TREE YOU CAN JUST PLAY AROUND, Y'KNOW...
ME AND DIANA COULD PLAY WHERE WE WANT TO...
WE COULD PLAY...
I MEAN IT! THIS TREE AND THIS BENCH SHOULD HAVE A··A FENCE AROUND IT!
IT DON'T HAVE NO FENCE SO WE COULD PLAY...
OW! TONANTZIN...!
ZOOLI..!
I'M TELLING YOU TO GET AWAY FROM THAT TREE!!
NO!
HEY HEY, PICK ON SOMEBODY YOUR OWN SIZE, BOY. C'MON, I HAVE A JOB FOR YOU.
HUH? HEY! LET GO··
A

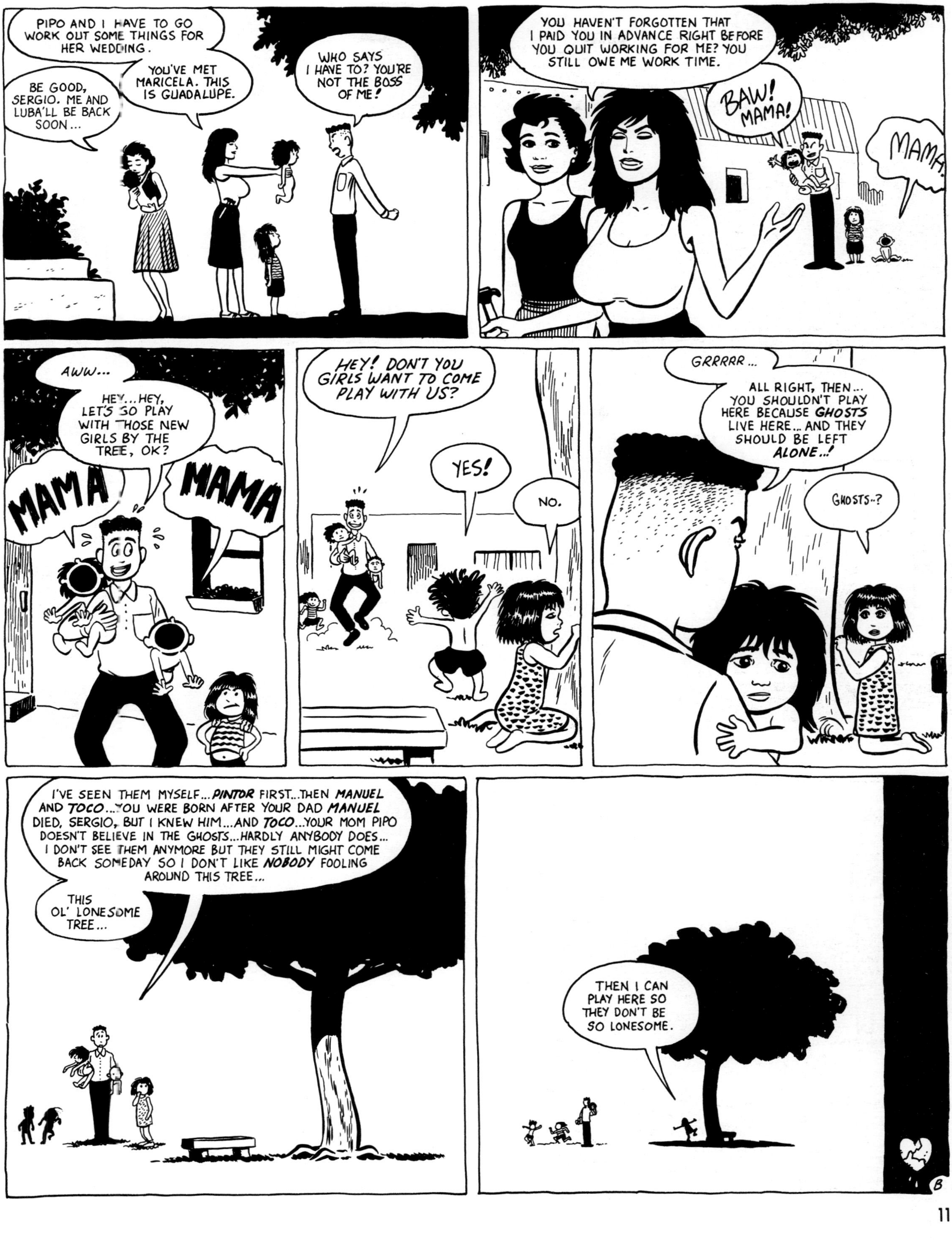
PIPO AND I HAVE TO GO WORK OUT SOME THINGS FOR HER WEDDING.
BE GOOD, SERGIO. ME AND LUBA'LL BE BACK SOON...
YOU'VE MET MARICELA. THIS IS GUADALUPE.
WHO SAYS I HAVE TO? YOU'RE NOT THE BOSS OF ME!
YOU HAVEN'T FORGOTTEN THAT I PAID YOU IN ADVANCE RIGHT BEFORE YOU QUIT WORKING FOR ME? YOU STILL OWE ME WORK TIME.
BAW! MAMA!
MAMA.
AWW...
HEY...HEY, LET'S GO PLAY WITH THOSE NEW GIRLS BY THE TREE, OK?
MAMA
MAMA
HEY! DON'T YOU GIRLS WANT TO COME PLAY WITH US?
YES!
NO.
GRRRRR...
ALL RIGHT, THEN... YOU SHOULDN'T PLAY HERE BECAUSE GHOSTS LIVE HERE... AND THEY SHOULD BE LEFT ALONE..!
GHOSTS..?
I'VE SEEN THEM MYSELF... PINTOR FIRST...THEN MANUEL AND TOCO...YOU WERE BORN AFTER YOUR DAD MANUEL DIED, SERGIO, BUT I KNEW HIM...AND TOCO...YOUR MOM PIPO DOESN'T BELIEVE IN THE GHOSTS...HARDLY ANYBODY DOES... I DON'T SEE THEM ANYMORE BUT THEY STILL MIGHT COME BACK SOMEDAY SO I DON'T LIKE NOBODY FOOLING AROUND THIS TREE...
THIS OL' LONESOME TREE...
THEN I CAN PLAY HERE SO THEY DON'T BE SO LONESOME.
B

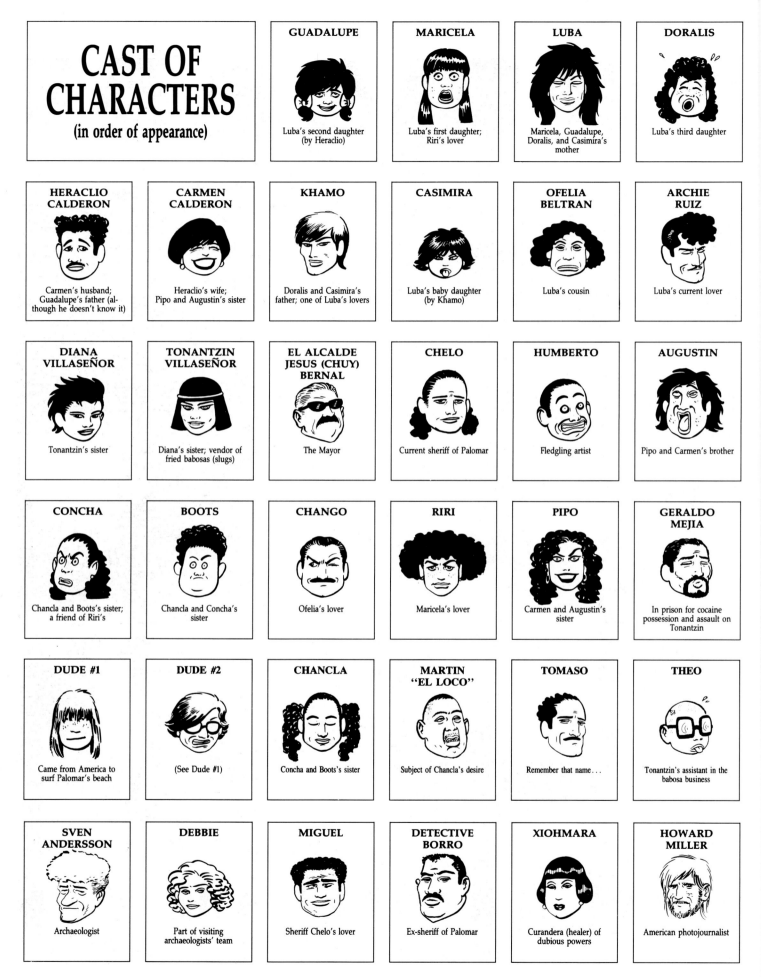

CAST OF CHARACTERS
(in order of appearance)

GUADALUPE

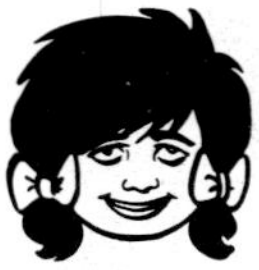

Luba's second daughter (by Heraclio)

MARICELA

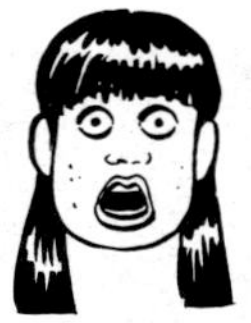

Luba's first daughter; Riri's lover

LUBA

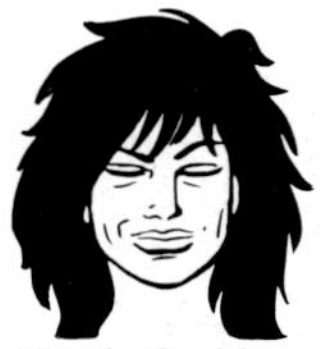

Maricela, Guadalupe, Doralis, and Casimira's mother

DORALIS

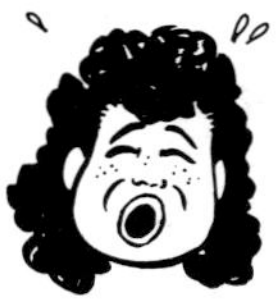

Luba's third daughter

HERACLIO CALDERON

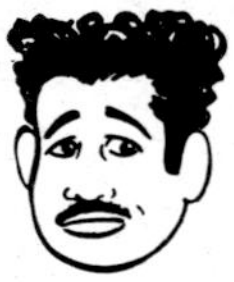

Carmen's husband; Guadalupe's father (although he doesn't know it)

CARMEN CALDERON

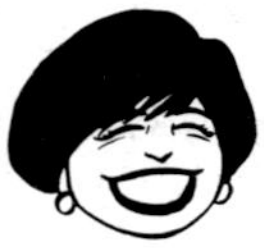

Heraclio's wife; Pipo and Augustin's sister

KHAMO

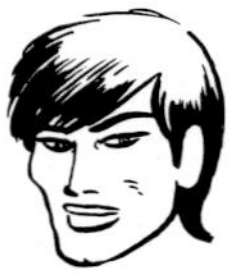

Doralis and Casimira's father; one of Luba's lovers

CASIMIRA

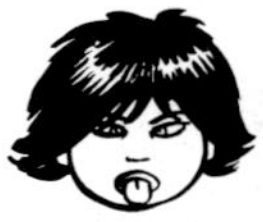

Luba's baby daughter (by Khamo)

OFELIA BELTRAN

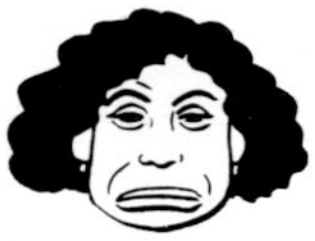

Luba's cousin

ARCHIE RUIZ

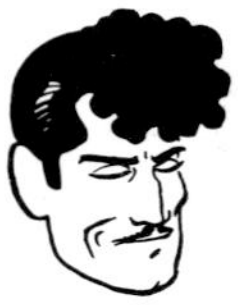

Luba's current lover

DIANA VILLASEÑOR

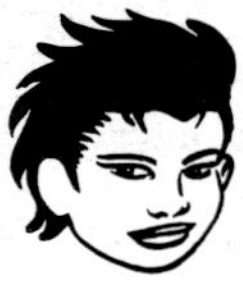

Tonantzin's sister

TONANTZIN VILLASEÑOR

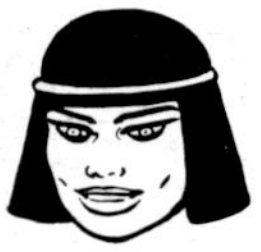

Diana's sister; vendor of fried babosas (slugs)

EL ALCALDE JESUS (CHUY) BERNAL

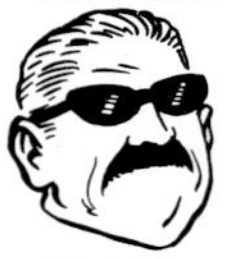

The Mayor

CHELO

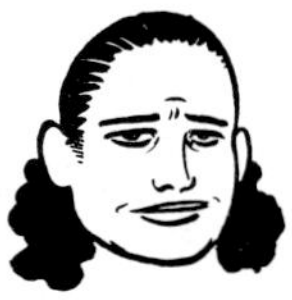

Current sheriff of Palomar

HUMBERTO

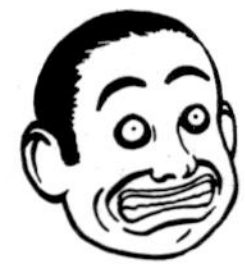

Fledgling artist

AUGUSTIN

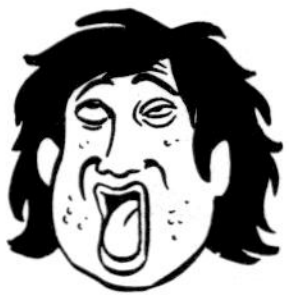

Pipo and Carmen's brother

CONCHA

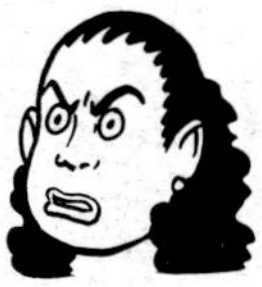

Chancla and Boots's sister; a friend of Riri's

BOOTS

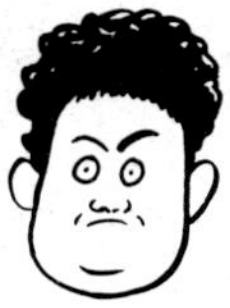

Chancla and Concha's sister

CHANGO

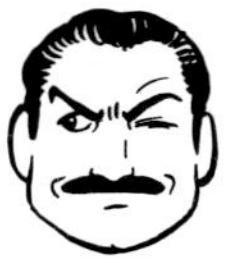

Ofelia's lover

RIRI

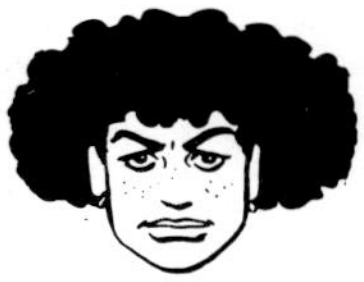

Maricela's lover

PIPO

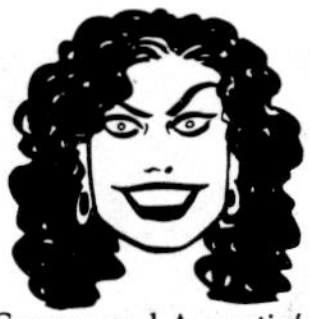

Carmen and Augustin's sister

GERALDO MEJIA

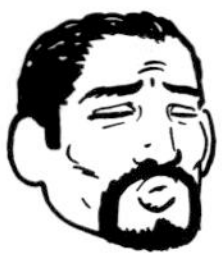

In prison for cocaine possession and assault on Tonantzin

DUDE #1

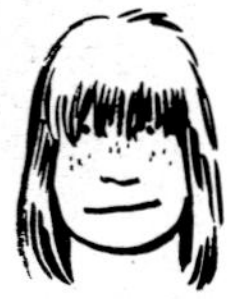

Came from America to surf Palomar's beach

DUDE #2

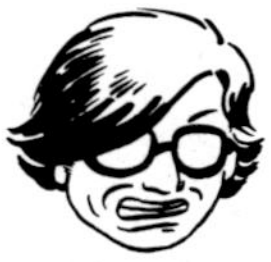

(See Dude #1)

CHANCLA

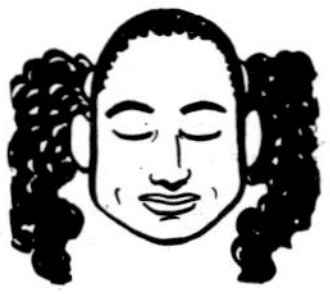

Concha and Boots's sister

MARTIN "EL LOCO"

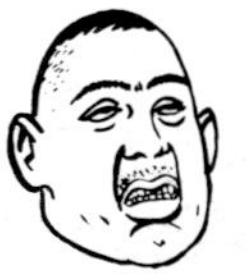

Subject of Chancla's desire

TOMASO

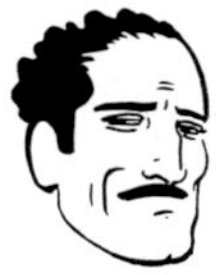

Remember that name...

THEO

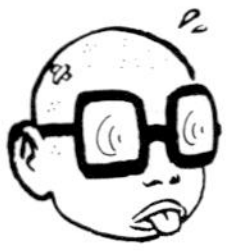

Tonantzin's assistant in the babosa business

SVEN ANDERSSON

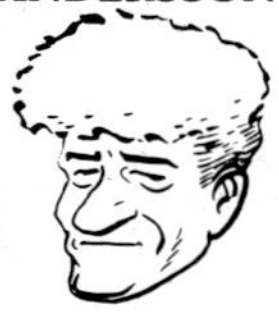

Archaeologist

DEBBIE

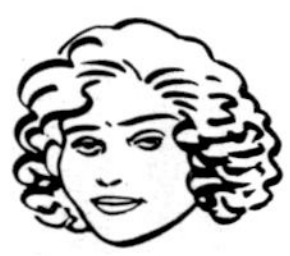

Part of visiting archaeologists' team

MIGUEL

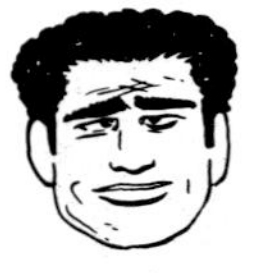

Sheriff Chelo's lover

DETECTIVE BORRO

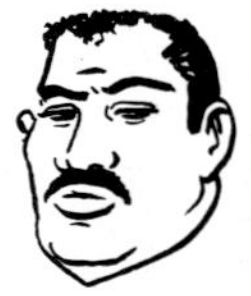

Ex-sheriff of Palomar

XIOHMARA

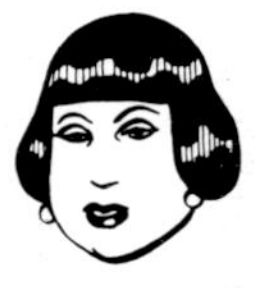

Curandera (healer) of dubious powers

HOWARD MILLER

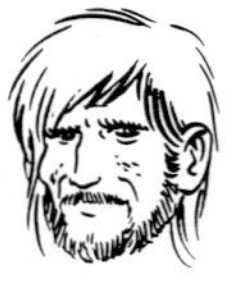

American photojournalist

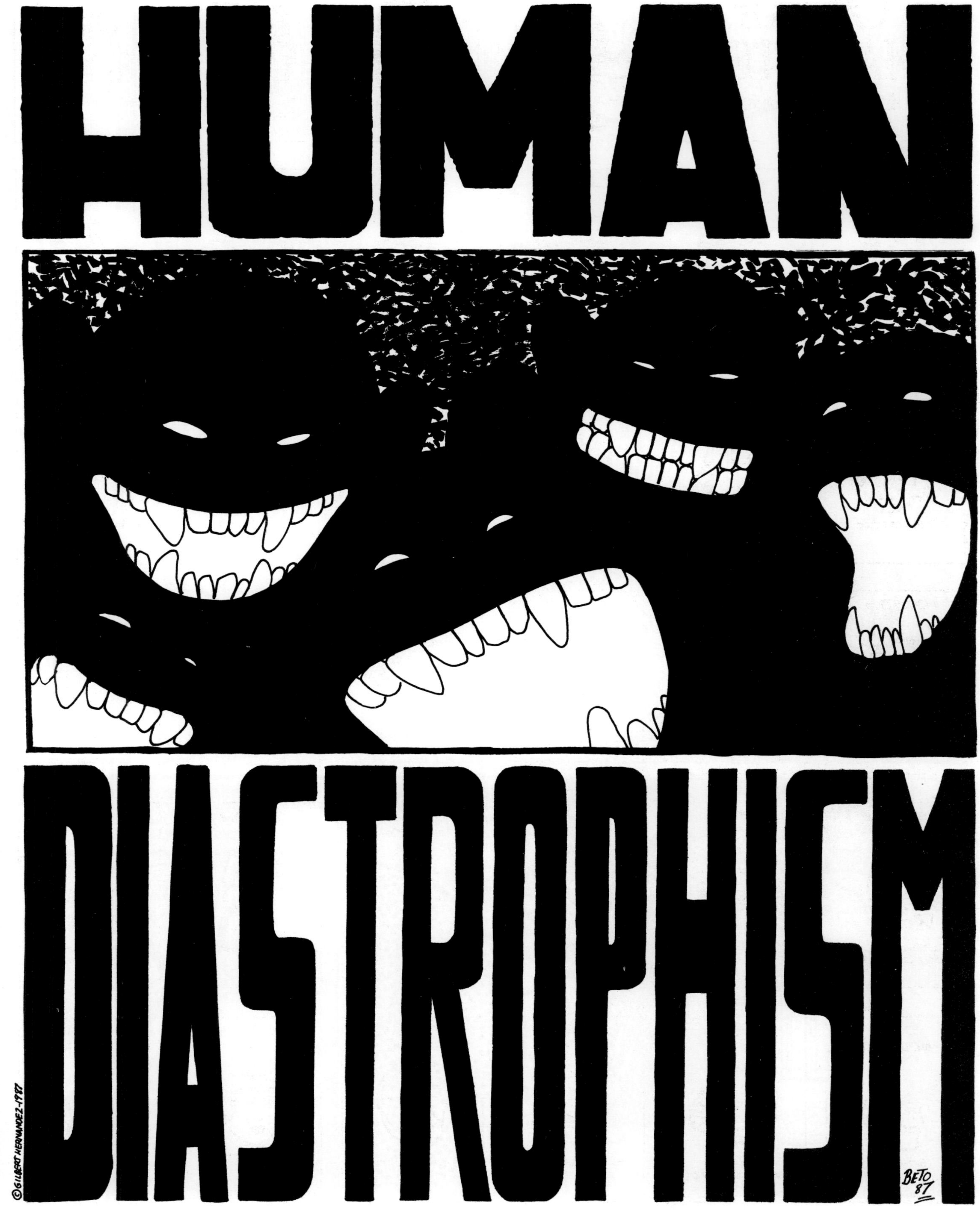
HUMAN
DIASTROPHISM
©GILBERT HERNANDEZ-1987
BETO 87

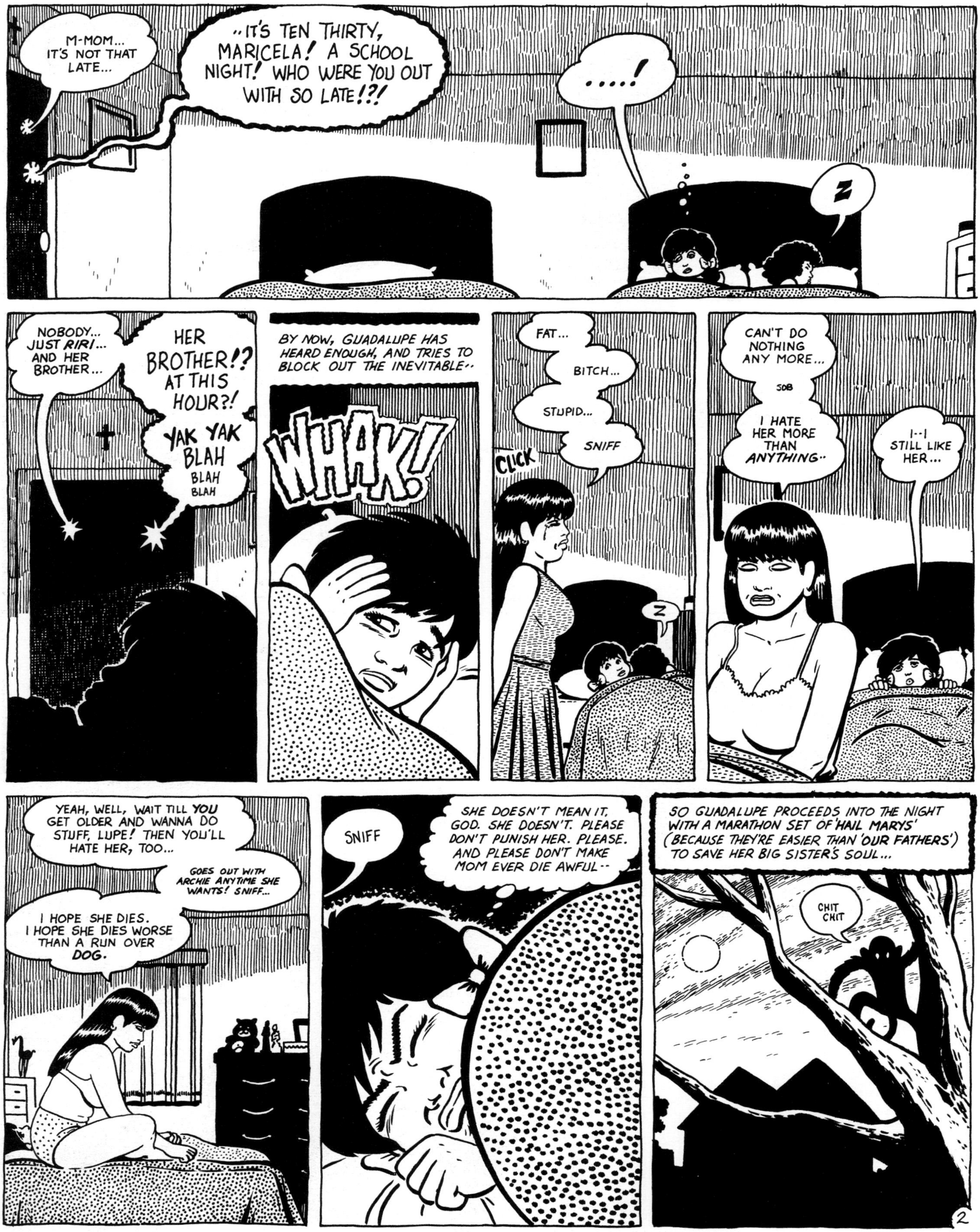
M-MOM... IT'S NOT THAT LATE...
..IT'S TEN THIRTY, MARICELA! A SCHOOL NIGHT! WHO WERE YOU OUT WITH SO LATE!?!
....!
Z
NOBODY... JUST RIRI... AND HER BROTHER...
HER BROTHER!? AT THIS HOUR?!
YAK YAK BLAH BLAH BLAH
BY NOW, GUADALUPE HAS HEARD ENOUGH, AND TRIES TO BLOCK OUT THE INEVITABLE..
WHAK!
CLICK
FAT...
BITCH...
STUPID...
SNIFF
Z
CAN'T DO NOTHING ANY MORE...
SOB
I HATE HER MORE THAN ANYTHING..
I--I STILL LIKE HER...
YEAH, WELL, WAIT TILL YOU GET OLDER AND WANNA DO STUFF, LUPE! THEN YOU'LL HATE HER, TOO...
GOES OUT WITH ARCHIE ANYTIME SHE WANTS! SNIFF...
I HOPE SHE DIES. I HOPE SHE DIES WORSE THAN A RUN OVER DOG.
SNIFF
SHE DOESN'T MEAN IT, GOD. SHE DOESN'T. PLEASE DON'T PUNISH HER. PLEASE. AND PLEASE DON'T MAKE MOM EVER DIE AWFUL--
SO GUADALUPE PROCEEDS INTO THE NIGHT WITH A MARATHON SET OF 'HAIL MARYS' (BECAUSE THEY'RE EASIER THAN 'OUR FATHERS') TO SAVE HER BIG SISTER'S SOUL...
CHIT CHIT
2

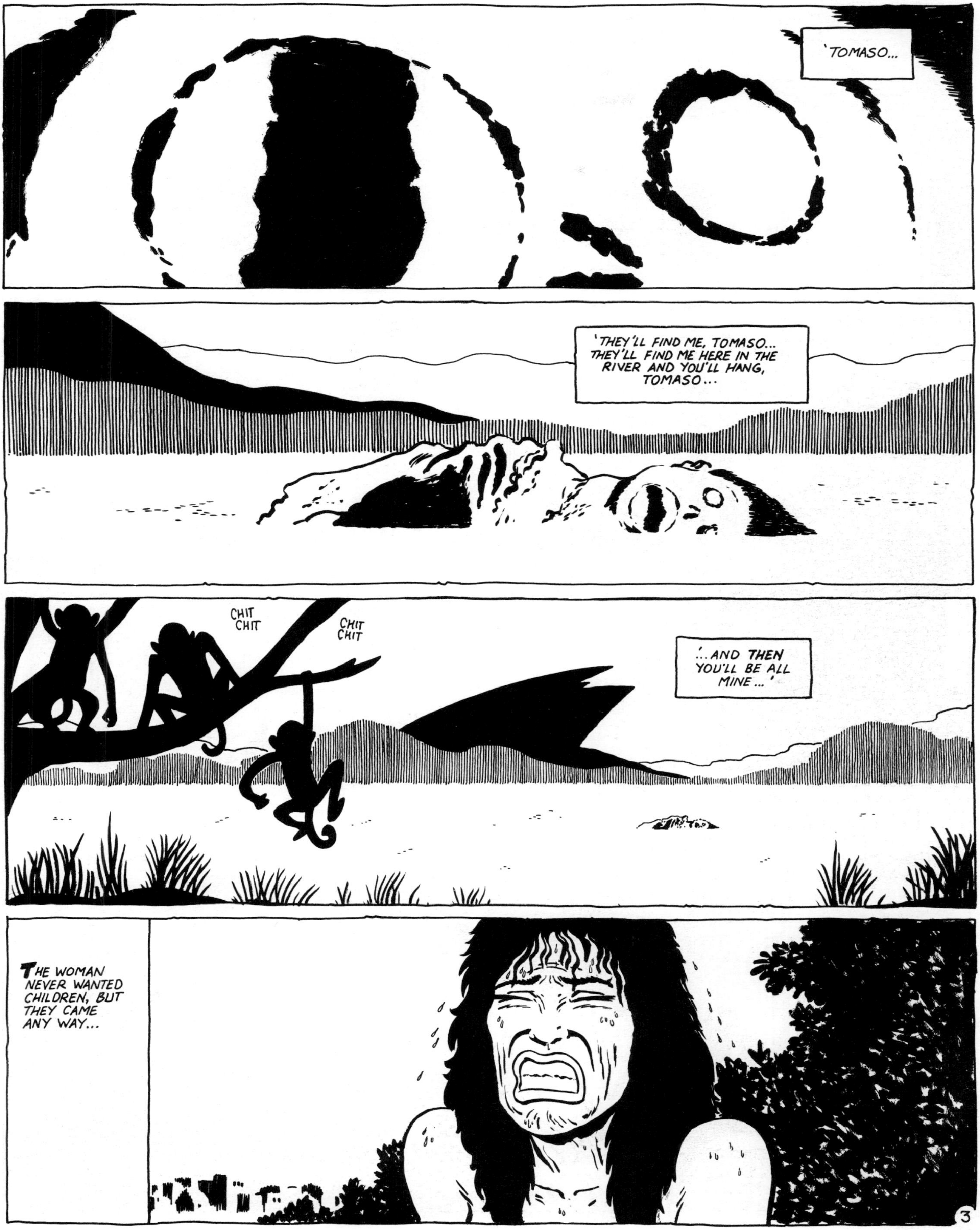
'TOMASO...
'THEY'LL FIND ME, TOMASO... THEY'LL FIND ME HERE IN THE RIVER AND YOU'LL HANG, TOMASO...
CHIT CHIT
CHIT CHIT
'...AND THEN YOU'LL BE ALL MINE...'
THE WOMAN NEVER WANTED CHILDREN, BUT THEY CAME ANY WAY...
3

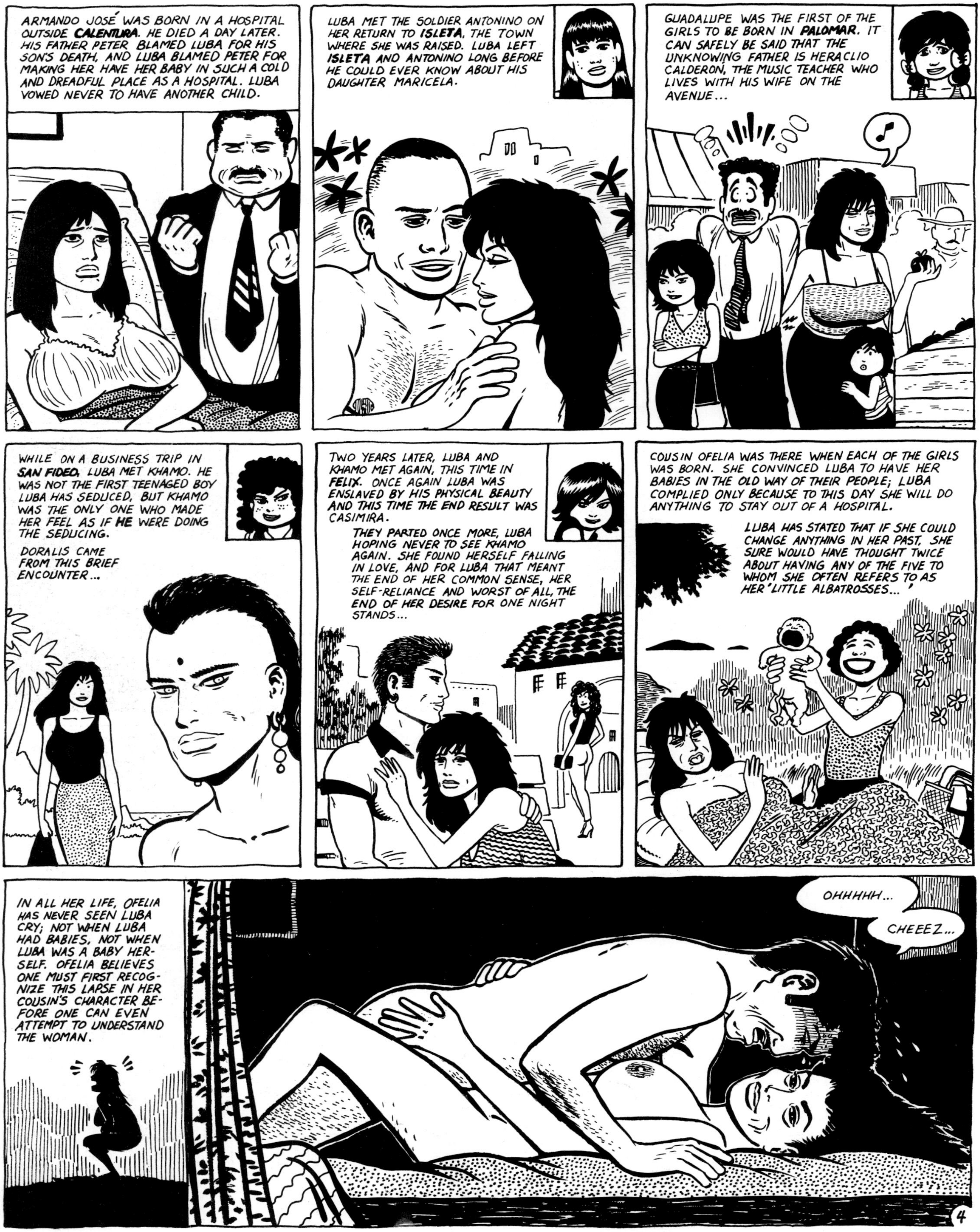
ARMANDO JOSÉ WAS BORN IN A HOSPITAL OUTSIDE CALENTURA. HE DIED A DAY LATER. HIS FATHER PETER BLAMED LUBA FOR HIS SON'S DEATH, AND LUBA BLAMED PETER FOR MAKING HER HAVE HER BABY IN SUCH A COLD AND DREADFUL PLACE AS A HOSPITAL. LUBA VOWED NEVER TO HAVE ANOTHER CHILD.
LUBA MET THE SOLDIER ANTONINO ON HER RETURN TO ISLETA, THE TOWN WHERE SHE WAS RAISED. LUBA LEFT ISLETA AND ANTONINO LONG BEFORE HE COULD EVER KNOW ABOUT HIS DAUGHTER MARICELA.
GUADALUPE WAS THE FIRST OF THE GIRLS TO BE BORN IN PALOMAR. IT CAN SAFELY BE SAID THAT THE UNKNOWING FATHER IS HERACLIO CALDERON, THE MUSIC TEACHER WHO LIVES WITH HIS WIFE ON THE AVENUE...
WHILE ON A BUSINESS TRIP IN SAN FIDEO, LUBA MET KHAMO. HE WAS NOT THE FIRST TEENAGED BOY LUBA HAS SEDUCED, BUT KHAMO WAS THE ONLY ONE WHO MADE HER FEEL AS IF HE WERE DOING THE SEDUCING.
DORALIS CAME FROM THIS BRIEF ENCOUNTER...
TWO YEARS LATER, LUBA AND KHAMO MET AGAIN, THIS TIME IN FELIX. ONCE AGAIN LUBA WAS ENSLAVED BY HIS PHYSICAL BEAUTY AND THIS TIME THE END RESULT WAS CASIMIRA.
THEY PARTED ONCE MORE, LUBA HOPING NEVER TO SEE KHAMO AGAIN. SHE FOUND HERSELF FALLING IN LOVE, AND FOR LUBA THAT MEANT THE END OF HER COMMON SENSE, HER SELF-RELIANCE AND WORST OF ALL, THE END OF HER DESIRE FOR ONE NIGHT STANDS...
COUSIN OFELIA WAS THERE WHEN EACH OF THE GIRLS WAS BORN. SHE CONVINCED LUBA TO HAVE HER BABIES IN THE OLD WAY OF THEIR PEOPLE; LUBA COMPLIED ONLY BECAUSE TO THIS DAY SHE WILL DO ANYTHING TO STAY OUT OF A HOSPITAL.
LUBA HAS STATED THAT IF SHE COULD CHANGE ANYTHING IN HER PAST, SHE SURE WOULD HAVE THOUGHT TWICE ABOUT HAVING ANY OF THE FIVE TO WHOM SHE OFTEN REFERS TO AS HER 'LITTLE ALBATROSSES...'
IN ALL HER LIFE, OFELIA HAS NEVER SEEN LUBA CRY; NOT WHEN LUBA HAD BABIES, NOT WHEN LUBA WAS A BABY HER-SELF. OFELIA BELIEVES ONE MUST FIRST RECOG-NIZE THIS LAPSE IN HER COUSIN'S CHARACTER BE-FORE ONE CAN EVEN ATTEMPT TO UNDERSTAND THE WOMAN.
OHHHHH...
CHEEEZ...
4

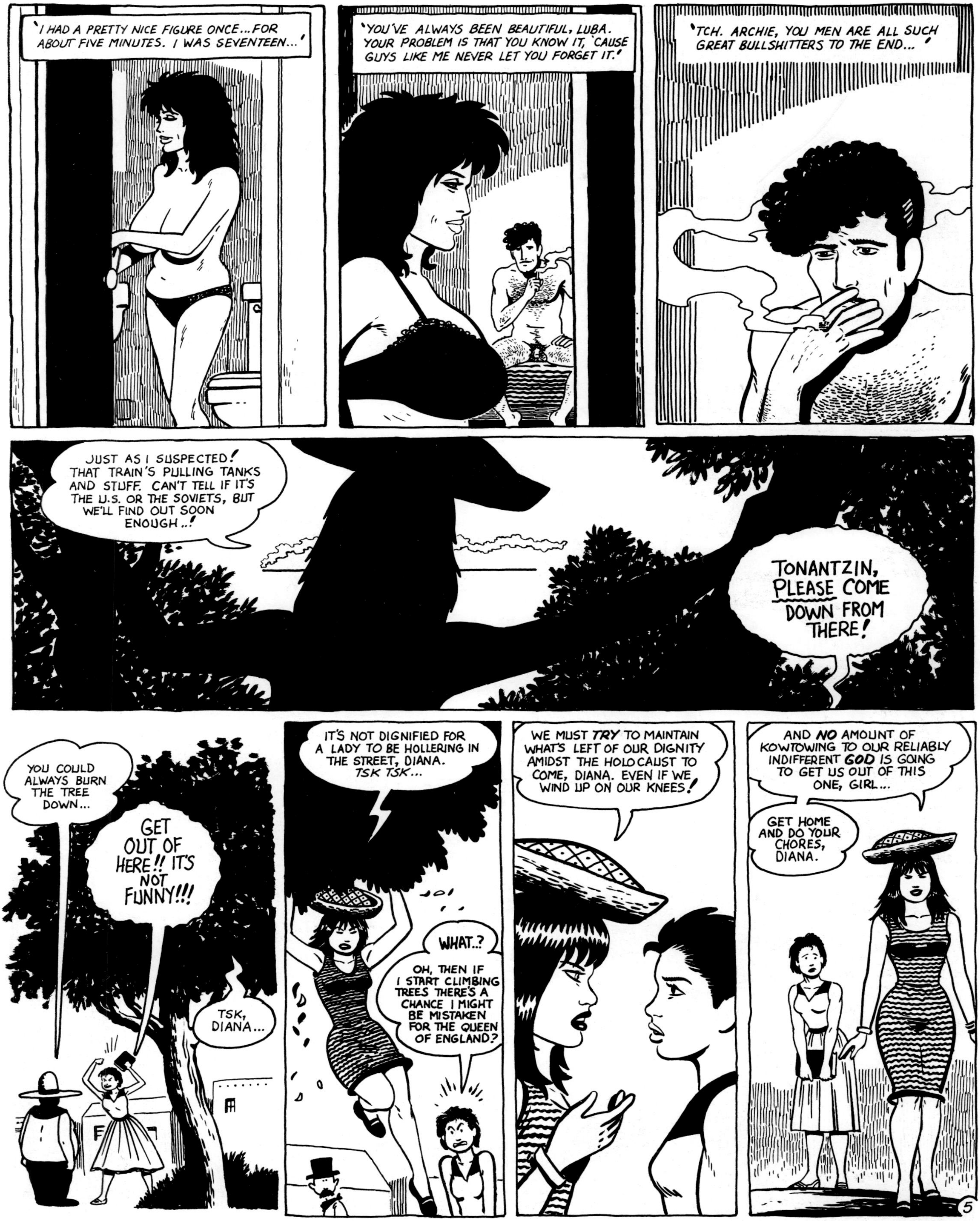
'I HAD A PRETTY NICE FIGURE ONCE...FOR ABOUT FIVE MINUTES. I WAS SEVENTEEN...'
'YOU'VE ALWAYS BEEN BEAUTIFUL, LUBA. YOUR PROBLEM IS THAT YOU KNOW IT, 'CAUSE GUYS LIKE ME NEVER LET YOU FORGET IT.'
'TCH. ARCHIE, YOU MEN ARE ALL SUCH GREAT BULLSHITTERS TO THE END...'
JUST AS I SUSPECTED! THAT TRAIN'S PULLING TANKS AND STUFF. CAN'T TELL IF IT'S THE U.S. OR THE SOVIETS, BUT WE'LL FIND OUT SOON ENOUGH..!
TONANTZIN, PLEASE COME DOWN FROM THERE!
YOU COULD ALWAYS BURN THE TREE DOWN...
GET OUT OF HERE!! IT'S NOT FUNNY!!!
TSK, DIANA...
IT'S NOT DIGNIFIED FOR A LADY TO BE HOLLERING IN THE STREET, DIANA. TSK TSK...
WHAT..?
OH, THEN IF I START CLIMBING TREES THERE'S A CHANCE I MIGHT BE MISTAKEN FOR THE QUEEN OF ENGLAND?
WE MUST TRY TO MAINTAIN WHAT'S LEFT OF OUR DIGNITY AMIDST THE HOLOCAUST TO COME, DIANA. EVEN IF WE WIND UP ON OUR KNEES!
AND NO AMOUNT OF KOWTOWING TO OUR RELIABLY INDIFFERENT GOD IS GOING TO GET US OUT OF THIS ONE, GIRL...
GET HOME AND DO YOUR CHORES, DIANA.
5

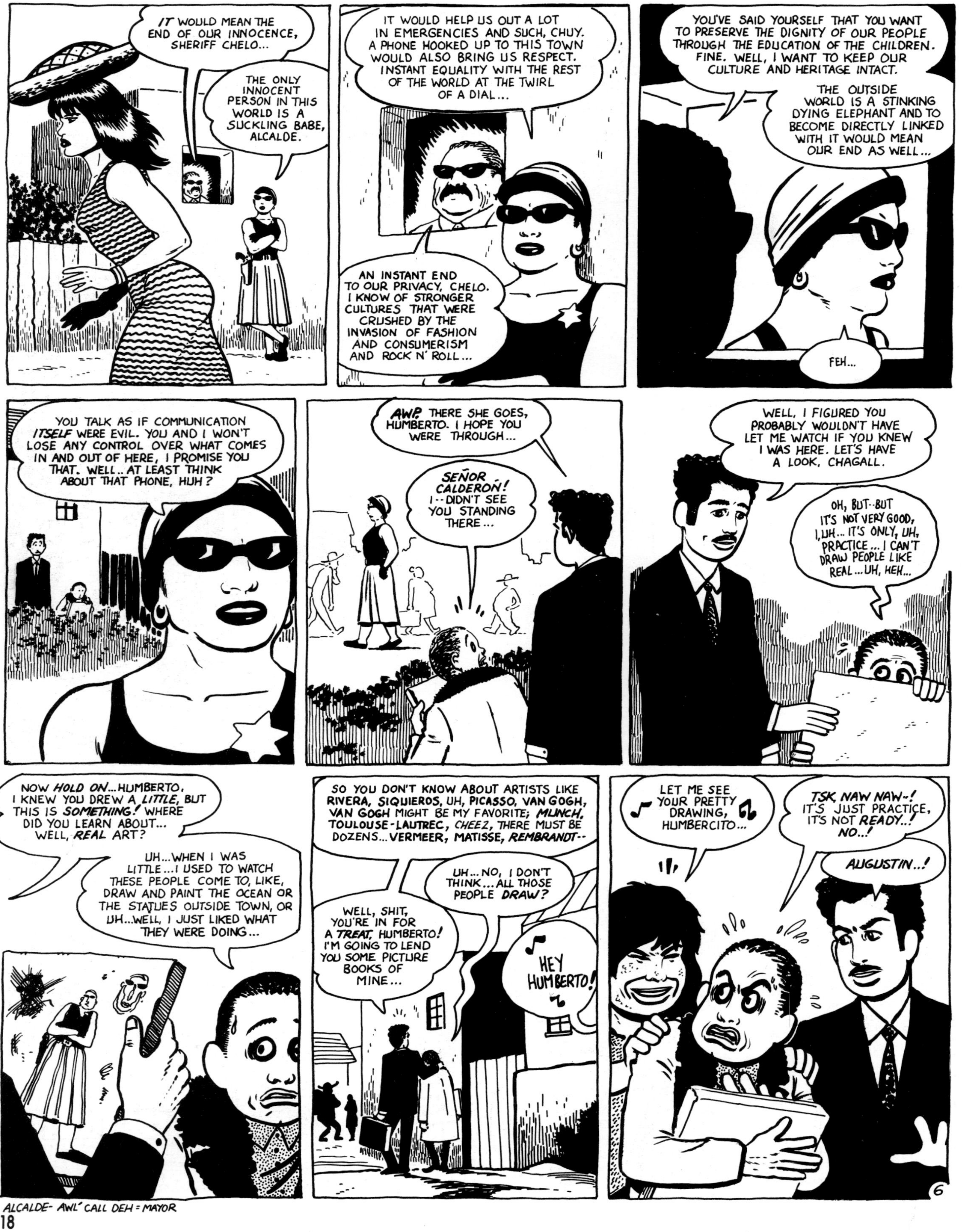
IT WOULD MEAN THE END OF OUR INNOCENCE, SHERIFF CHELO...
THE ONLY INNOCENT PERSON IN THIS WORLD IS A SUCKLING BABE, ALCALDE.
IT WOULD HELP US OUT A LOT IN EMERGENCIES AND SUCH, CHUY. A PHONE HOOKED UP TO THIS TOWN WOULD ALSO BRING US RESPECT. INSTANT EQUALITY WITH THE REST OF THE WORLD AT THE TWIRL OF A DIAL...
AN INSTANT END TO OUR PRIVACY, CHELO. I KNOW OF STRONGER CULTURES THAT WERE CRUSHED BY THE INVASION OF FASHION AND CONSUMERISM AND ROCK N' ROLL...
YOU'VE SAID YOURSELF THAT YOU WANT TO PRESERVE THE DIGNITY OF OUR PEOPLE THROUGH THE EDUCATION OF THE CHILDREN. FINE. WELL, I WANT TO KEEP OUR CULTURE AND HERITAGE INTACT.
THE OUTSIDE WORLD IS A STINKING DYING ELEPHANT AND TO BECOME DIRECTLY LINKED WITH IT WOULD MEAN OUR END AS WELL...
FEH...
YOU TALK AS IF COMMUNICATION ITSELF WERE EVIL. YOU AND I WON'T LOSE ANY CONTROL OVER WHAT COMES IN AND OUT OF HERE, I PROMISE YOU THAT. WELL.. AT LEAST THINK ABOUT THAT PHONE, HUH?
AWP. THERE SHE GOES, HUMBERTO. I HOPE YOU WERE THROUGH...
SEÑOR CALDERON! I--DIDN'T SEE YOU STANDING THERE...
WELL, I FIGURED YOU PROBABLY WOULDN'T HAVE LET ME WATCH IF YOU KNEW I WAS HERE. LET'S HAVE A LOOK, CHAGALL.
OH, BUT--BUT IT'S NOT VERY GOOD, I, UH... IT'S ONLY, UH, PRACTICE... I CAN'T DRAW PEOPLE LIKE REAL... UH, HEH...
NOW HOLD ON... HUMBERTO. I KNEW YOU DREW A LITTLE, BUT THIS IS SOMETHING! WHERE DID YOU LEARN ABOUT... WELL, REAL ART?
UH... WHEN I WAS LITTLE... I USED TO WATCH THESE PEOPLE COME TO, LIKE, DRAW AND PAINT THE OCEAN OR THE STATUES OUTSIDE TOWN, OR UH... WELL, I JUST LIKED WHAT THEY WERE DOING...
SO YOU DON'T KNOW ABOUT ARTISTS LIKE RIVERA, SIQUIEROS, UH, PICASSO, VAN GOGH, VAN GOGH MIGHT BE MY FAVORITE; MUNCH, TOULOUSE-LAUTREC, CHEEZ, THERE MUST BE DOZENS... VERMEER, MATISSE, REMBRANDT--
UH... NO, I DON'T THINK... ALL THOSE PEOPLE DRAW?
WELL, SHIT, YOU'RE IN FOR A TREAT, HUMBERTO! I'M GOING TO LEND YOU SOME PICTURE BOOKS OF MINE...
HEY HUMBERTO!
LET ME SEE YOUR PRETTY DRAWING, HUMBERCITO...
TSK, NAW NAW-! IT'S JUST PRACTICE, IT'S NOT READY..! NO..!
AUGUSTIN..!
6

ALCALDE- AWL' CALL DEH = MAYOR

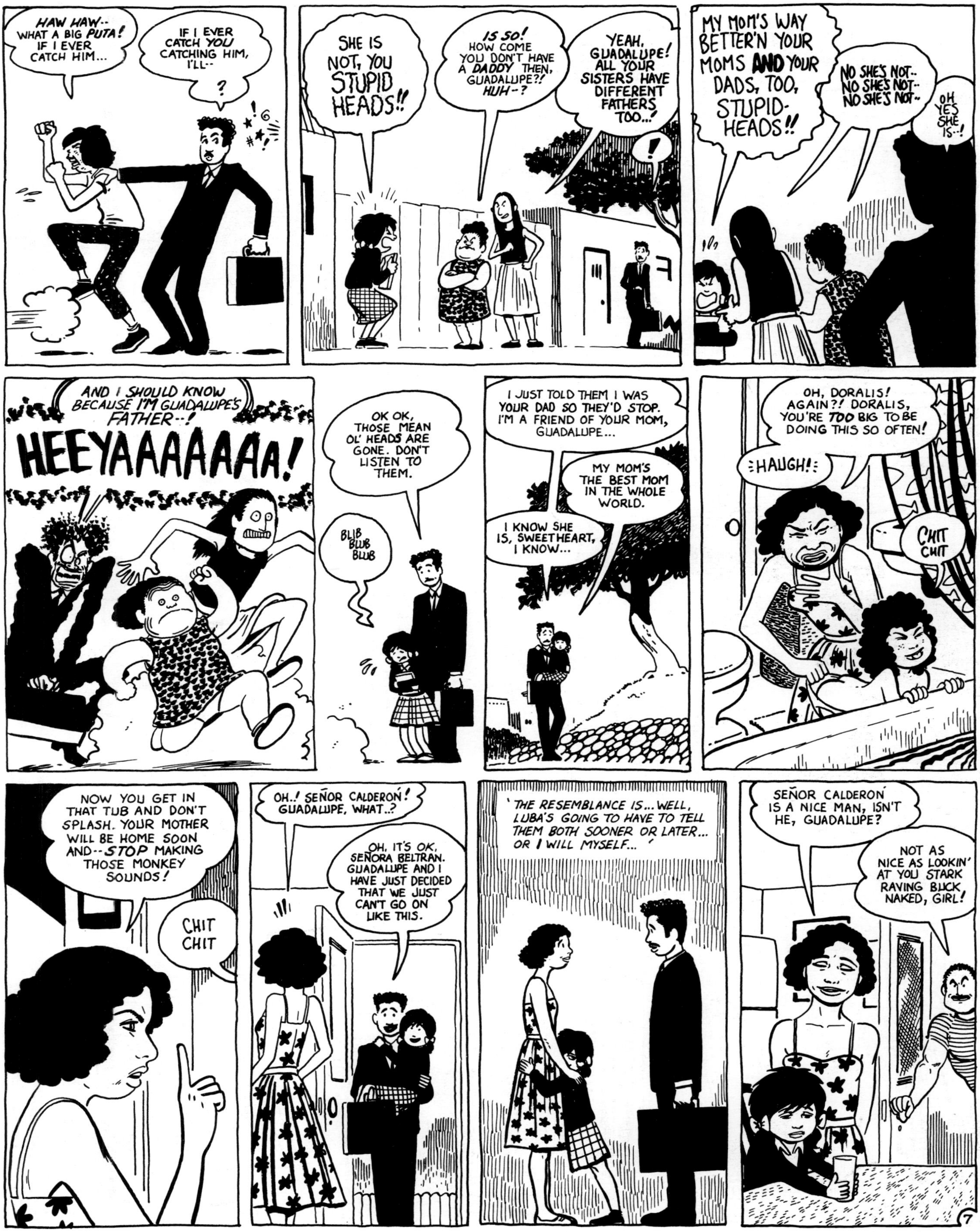
HAW HAW-- WHAT A BIG PUTA! IF I EVER CATCH HIM...
IF I EVER CATCH YOU CATCHING HIM, I'LL--
?
SHE IS NOT, YOU STUPID HEADS!!
IS SO! HOW COME YOU DON'T HAVE A DADDY THEN, GUADALUPE?! HUH--?
YEAH, GUADALUPE! ALL YOUR SISTERS HAVE DIFFERENT FATHERS TOO...!
!
MY MOM'S WAY BETTER'N YOUR MOMS AND YOUR DADS, TOO, STUPID-HEADS!!
NO SHE'S NOT-- NO SHE'S NOT-- NO SHE'S NOT--
OH YES SHE IS--!
AND I SHOULD KNOW BECAUSE I'M GUADALUPE'S FATHER--!
HEEYAAAAAAAA!
OK OK, THOSE MEAN OL' HEADS ARE GONE. DON'T LISTEN TO THEM.
BLIB BLUB BLUB
I JUST TOLD THEM I WAS YOUR DAD SO THEY'D STOP. I'M A FRIEND OF YOUR MOM, GUADALUPE...
MY MOM'S THE BEST MOM IN THE WHOLE WORLD.
I KNOW SHE IS, SWEETHEART, I KNOW...
OH, DORALIS! AGAIN?! DORALIS, YOU'RE TOO BIG TO BE DOING THIS SO OFTEN!
HAUGH!
CHIT CHIT
NOW YOU GET IN THAT TUB AND DON'T SPLASH. YOUR MOTHER WILL BE HOME SOON AND--STOP MAKING THOSE MONKEY SOUNDS!
CHIT CHIT
OH..! SEÑOR CALDERON! GUADALUPE, WHAT..?
OH, IT'S OK, SEÑORA BELTRAN. GUADALUPE AND I HAVE JUST DECIDED THAT WE JUST CAN'T GO ON LIKE THIS.
'THE RESEMBLANCE IS... WELL, LUBA'S GOING TO HAVE TO TELL THEM BOTH SOONER OR LATER... OR I WILL MYSELF...'
SEÑOR CALDERON IS A NICE MAN, ISN'T HE, GUADALUPE?
NOT AS NICE AS LOOKIN' AT YOU STARK RAVING BUCK NAKED, GIRL!
7

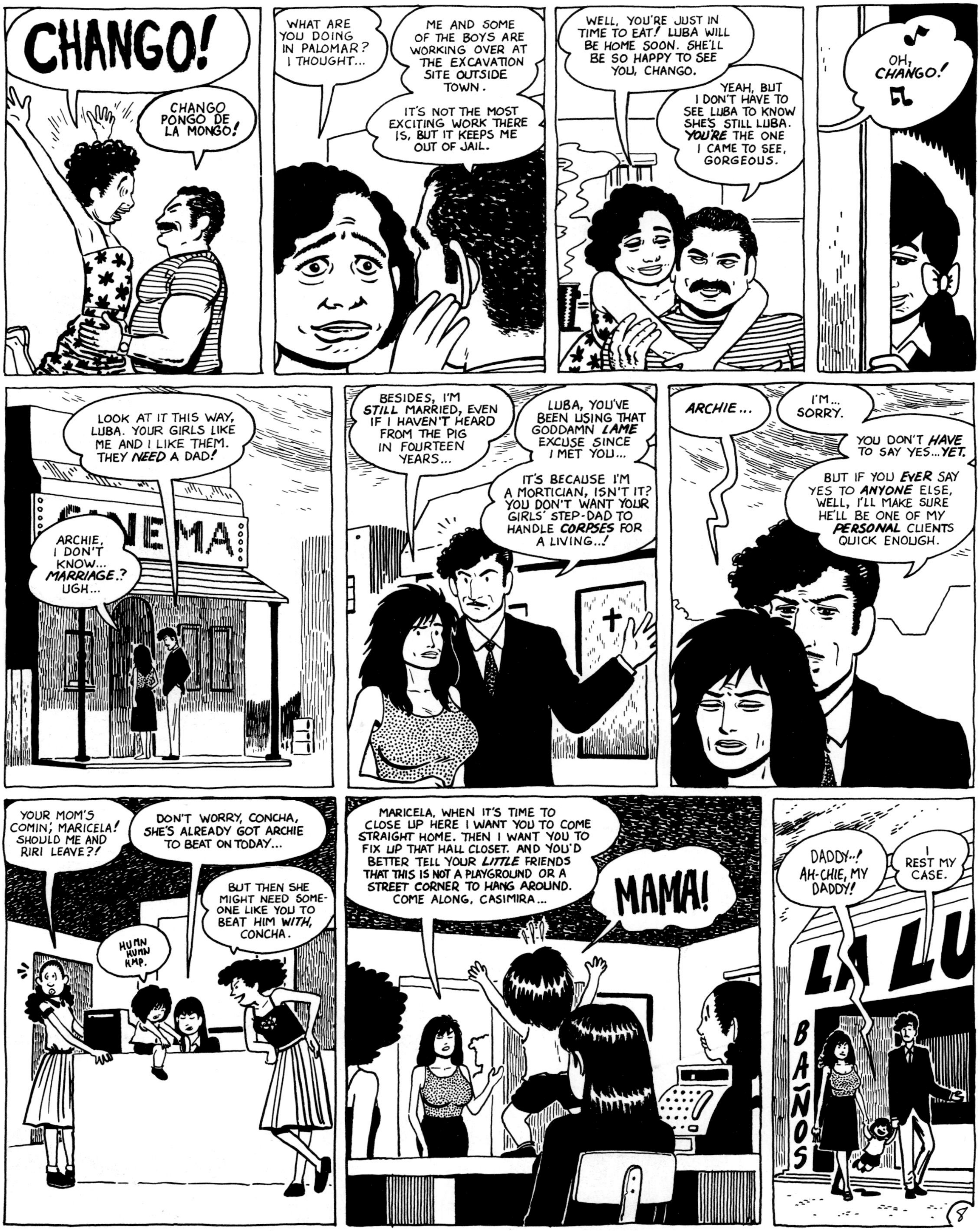
CHANGO!
CHANGO PONGO DE LA MONGO!
WHAT ARE YOU DOING IN PALOMAR? I THOUGHT...
ME AND SOME OF THE BOYS ARE WORKING OVER AT THE EXCAVATION SITE OUTSIDE TOWN.
IT'S NOT THE MOST EXCITING WORK THERE IS, BUT IT KEEPS ME OUT OF JAIL.
WELL, YOU'RE JUST IN TIME TO EAT! LUBA WILL BE HOME SOON. SHE'LL BE SO HAPPY TO SEE YOU, CHANGO.
YEAH, BUT I DON'T HAVE TO SEE LUBA TO KNOW SHE'S STILL LUBA. YOU'RE THE ONE I CAME TO SEE, GORGEOUS.
OH, CHANGO!
LOOK AT IT THIS WAY, LUBA. YOUR GIRLS LIKE ME AND I LIKE THEM. THEY NEED A DAD!
CINEMA
ARCHIE, I DON'T KNOW... MARRIAGE.? UGH...
BESIDES, I'M STILL MARRIED, EVEN IF I HAVEN'T HEARD FROM THE PIG IN FOURTEEN YEARS...
LUBA, YOU'VE BEEN USING THAT GODDAMN LAME EXCUSE SINCE I MET YOU...
IT'S BECAUSE I'M A MORTICIAN, ISN'T IT? YOU DON'T WANT YOUR GIRLS' STEP-DAD TO HANDLE CORPSES FOR A LIVING..!
ARCHIE...
I'M... SORRY.
YOU DON'T HAVE TO SAY YES...YET.
BUT IF YOU EVER SAY YES TO ANYONE ELSE, WELL, I'LL MAKE SURE HE'LL BE ONE OF MY PERSONAL CLIENTS QUICK ENOUGH.
YOUR MOM'S COMIN', MARICELA! SHOULD ME AND RIRI LEAVE?!
DON'T WORRY, CONCHA, SHE'S ALREADY GOT ARCHIE TO BEAT ON TODAY...
HUMN HUMN HMP.
BUT THEN SHE MIGHT NEED SOMEONE LIKE YOU TO BEAT HIM WITH, CONCHA.
MARICELA, WHEN IT'S TIME TO CLOSE UP HERE I WANT YOU TO COME STRAIGHT HOME. THEN I WANT YOU TO FIX UP THAT HALL CLOSET. AND YOU'D BETTER TELL YOUR LITTLE FRIENDS THAT THIS IS NOT A PLAYGROUND OR A STREET CORNER TO HANG AROUND. COME ALONG, CASIMIRA...
MAMA!
DADDY..! AH-CHIE, MY DADDY!
I REST MY CASE.
LA LU
BAÑOS
8

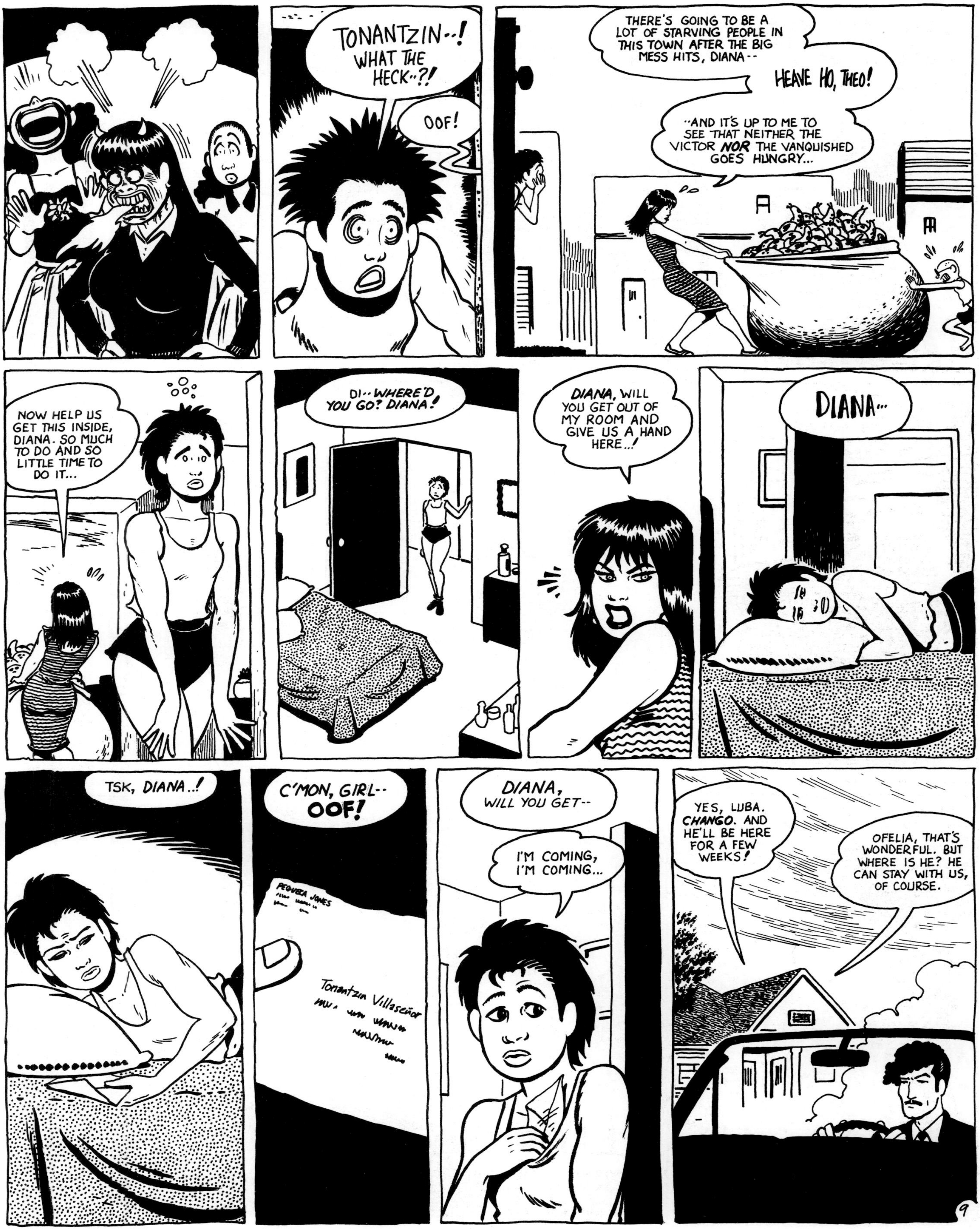
TONANTZIN--! WHAT THE HECK--?!
OOF!
THERE'S GOING TO BE A LOT OF STARVING PEOPLE IN THIS TOWN AFTER THE BIG MESS HITS, DIANA--
HEAVE HO, THEO!
--AND IT'S UP TO ME TO SEE THAT NEITHER THE VICTOR NOR THE VANQUISHED GOES HUNGRY...
NOW HELP US GET THIS INSIDE, DIANA. SO MUCH TO DO AND SO LITTLE TIME TO DO IT...
DI-- WHERE'D YOU GO? DIANA!
DIANA, WILL YOU GET OUT OF MY ROOM AND GIVE US A HAND HERE..!
DIANA...
TSK, DIANA..!
C'MON, GIRL-- OOF!
Tonantzin Villaseñor
DIANA, WILL YOU GET--
I'M COMING, I'M COMING...
YES, LUBA. CHANGO. AND HE'LL BE HERE FOR A FEW WEEKS!
OFELIA, THAT'S WONDERFUL. BUT WHERE IS HE? HE CAN STAY WITH US, OF COURSE.
9

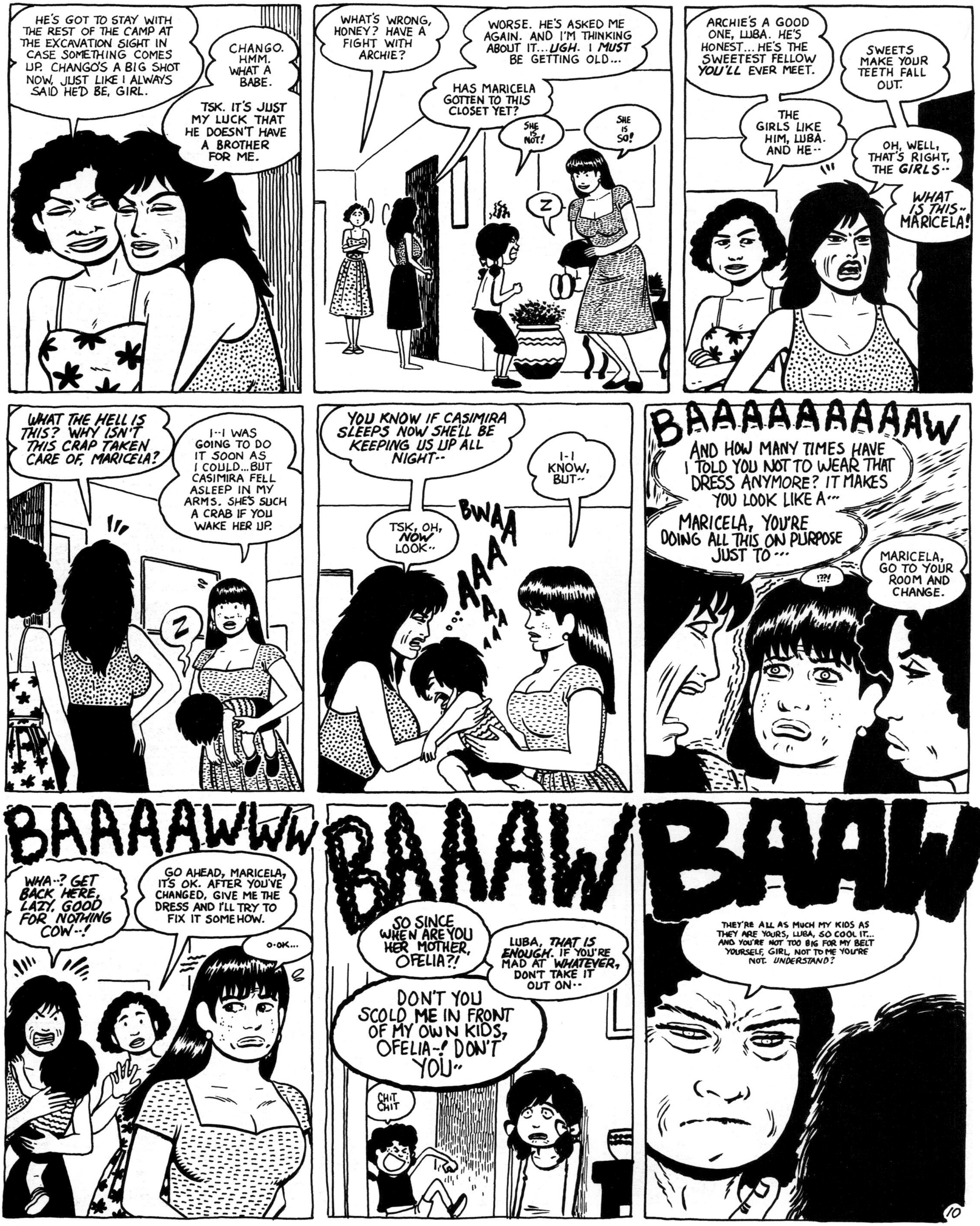
HE'S GOT TO STAY WITH THE REST OF THE CAMP AT THE EXCAVATION SIGHT IN CASE SOMETHING COMES UP. CHANGO'S A BIG SHOT NOW, JUST LIKE I ALWAYS SAID HE'D BE, GIRL.
CHANGO. HMM. WHAT A BABE.
TSK. IT'S JUST MY LUCK THAT HE DOESN'T HAVE A BROTHER FOR ME.
WHAT'S WRONG, HONEY? HAVE A FIGHT WITH ARCHIE?
WORSE. HE'S ASKED ME AGAIN. AND I'M THINKING ABOUT IT... UGH. I MUST BE GETTING OLD...
HAS MARICELA GOTTEN TO THIS CLOSET YET?
SHE IS NOT!
SHE IS SO!
Z
ARCHIE'S A GOOD ONE, LUBA. HE'S HONEST... HE'S THE SWEETEST FELLOW YOU'LL EVER MEET.
SWEETS MAKE YOUR TEETH FALL OUT.
THE GIRLS LIKE HIM, LUBA. AND HE--
OH, WELL, THAT'S RIGHT, THE GIRLS--
WHAT IS THIS-- MARICELA!
WHAT THE HELL IS THIS? WHY ISN'T THIS CRAP TAKEN CARE OF, MARICELA?
I--I WAS GOING TO DO IT SOON AS I COULD... BUT CASIMIRA FELL ASLEEP IN MY ARMS. SHE'S SUCH A CRAB IF YOU WAKE HER UP.
Z
YOU KNOW IF CASIMIRA SLEEPS NOW SHE'LL BE KEEPING US UP ALL NIGHT--
I-I KNOW, BUT--
TSK, OH, NOW LOOK--
BWAAAAAAAA
BAAAAAAAAAW
AND HOW MANY TIMES HAVE I TOLD YOU NOT TO WEAR THAT DRESS ANYMORE? IT MAKES YOU LOOK LIKE A---
MARICELA, YOU'RE DOING ALL THIS ON PURPOSE JUST TO---
!??!
MARICELA, GO TO YOUR ROOM AND CHANGE.
BAAAAWWW
WHA--? GET BACK HERE, LAZY, GOOD FOR NOTHING COW--!
GO AHEAD, MARICELA, IT'S OK. AFTER YOU'VE CHANGED, GIVE ME THE DRESS AND I'LL TRY TO FIX IT SOMEHOW.
O-OK...
BAAAW
SO SINCE WHEN ARE YOU HER MOTHER, OFELIA?!
LUBA, THAT IS ENOUGH. IF YOU'RE MAD AT WHATEVER, DON'T TAKE IT OUT ON--
DON'T YOU SCOLD ME IN FRONT OF MY OWN KIDS, OFELIA--! DON'T YOU--
CHIT CHIT
BAAW
THEY'RE ALL AS MUCH MY KIDS AS THEY ARE YOURS, LUBA, SO COOL IT... AND YOU'RE NOT TOO BIG FOR MY BELT YOURSELF, GIRL, NOT TO ME YOU'RE NOT. UNDERSTAND?
10

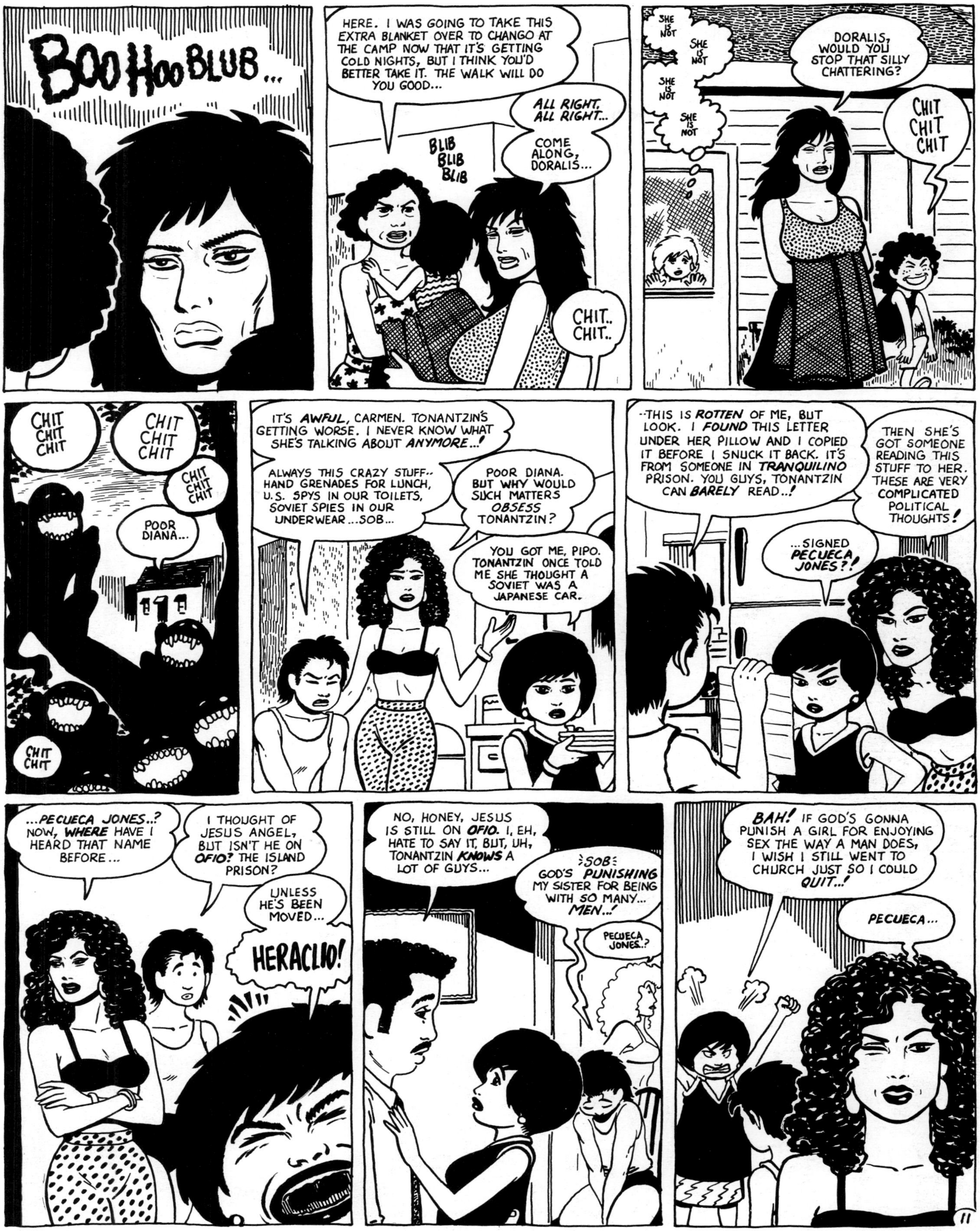

BOO HOO BLUB...
HERE. I WAS GOING TO TAKE THIS EXTRA BLANKET OVER TO CHANGO AT THE CAMP NOW THAT IT'S GETTING COLD NIGHTS, BUT I THINK YOU'D BETTER TAKE IT. THE WALK WILL DO YOU GOOD...
ALL RIGHT, ALL RIGHT...
BLIB BLIB BLIB
COME ALONG, DORALIS...
CHIT.. CHIT..
SHE IS NOT
SHE IS NOT
SHE IS NOT
SHE IS NOT
DORALIS, WOULD YOU STOP THAT SILLY CHATTERING?
CHIT CHIT CHIT
CHIT CHIT CHIT
CHIT CHIT CHIT
CHIT CHIT CHIT
POOR DIANA...
CHIT CHIT
IT'S AWFUL, CARMEN. TONANTZIN'S GETTING WORSE. I NEVER KNOW WHAT SHE'S TALKING ABOUT ANYMORE..!
ALWAYS THIS CRAZY STUFF.. HAND GRENADES FOR LUNCH, U.S. SPYS IN OUR TOILETS, SOVIET SPIES IN OUR UNDERWEAR...SOB...
POOR DIANA. BUT WHY WOULD SUCH MATTERS OBSESS TONANTZIN?
YOU GOT ME, PIPO. TONANTZIN ONCE TOLD ME SHE THOUGHT A SOVIET WAS A JAPANESE CAR.
--THIS IS ROTTEN OF ME, BUT LOOK. I FOUND THIS LETTER UNDER HER PILLOW AND I COPIED IT BEFORE I SNUCK IT BACK. IT'S FROM SOMEONE IN TRANQUILINO PRISON. YOU GUYS, TONANTZIN CAN BARELY READ..!
THEN SHE'S GOT SOMEONE READING THIS STUFF TO HER. THESE ARE VERY COMPLICATED POLITICAL THOUGHTS!
...SIGNED PECUECA JONES?!
...PECUECA JONES..? NOW, WHERE HAVE I HEARD THAT NAME BEFORE...
I THOUGHT OF JESUS ANGEL, BUT ISN'T HE ON OFIO? THE ISLAND PRISON?
UNLESS HE'S BEEN MOVED...
HERACLIO!
NO, HONEY, JESUS IS STILL ON OFIO. I, EH, HATE TO SAY IT, BUT, UH, TONANTZIN KNOWS A LOT OF GUYS...
SOB GOD'S PUNISHING MY SISTER FOR BEING WITH SO MANY... MEN..!
PECUECA JONES..?
BAH! IF GOD'S GONNA PUNISH A GIRL FOR ENJOYING SEX THE WAY A MAN DOES, I WISH I STILL WENT TO CHURCH JUST SO I COULD QUIT..!
PECUECA...
11

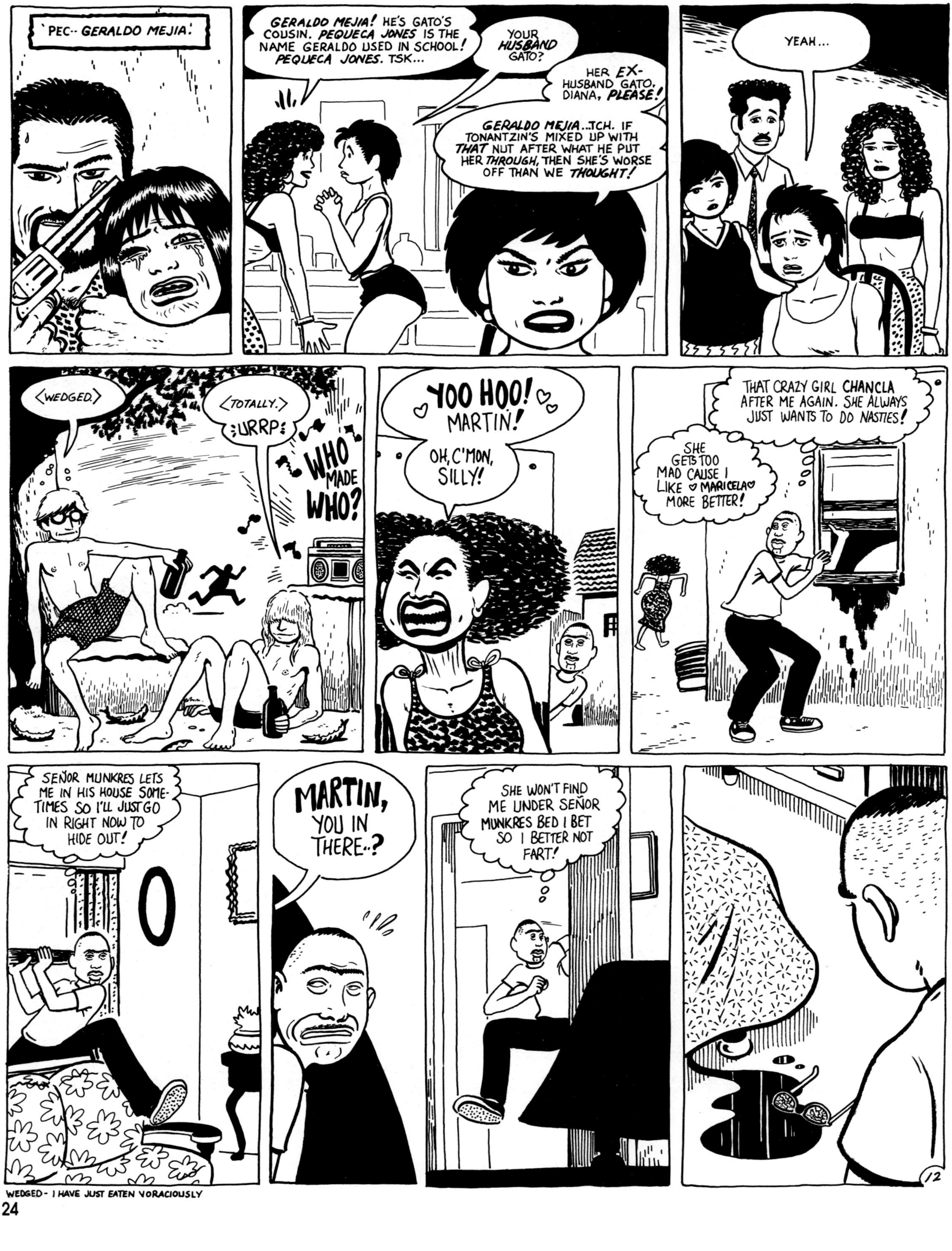
`PEC-- GERALDO MEJIA!
GERALDO MEJIA! HE'S GATO'S COUSIN. PEQUECA JONES IS THE NAME GERALDO USED IN SCHOOL! PEQUECA JONES. TSK...
YOUR HUSBAND GATO?
HER EX-HUSBAND GATO. DIANA, PLEASE!
GERALDO MEJIA...TCH. IF TONANTZIN'S MIXED UP WITH THAT NUT AFTER WHAT HE PUT HER THROUGH, THEN SHE'S WORSE OFF THAN WE THOUGHT!
YEAH...
<WEDGED.>
<TOTALLY.>
URRP
WHO MADE WHO?
YOO HOO! MARTIN!
OH, C'MON, SILLY!
THAT CRAZY GIRL CHANCLA AFTER ME AGAIN. SHE ALWAYS JUST WANTS TO DO NASTIES!
SHE GETS TOO MAD CAUSE I LIKE MARICELA MORE BETTER!
SEÑOR MUNKRES LETS ME IN HIS HOUSE SOMETIMES SO I'LL JUST GO IN RIGHT NOW TO HIDE OUT!
MARTIN, YOU IN THERE..?
SHE WON'T FIND ME UNDER SEÑOR MUNKRES BED I BET SO I BETTER NOT FART!
12

WEDGED - I HAVE JUST EATEN VORACIOUSLY

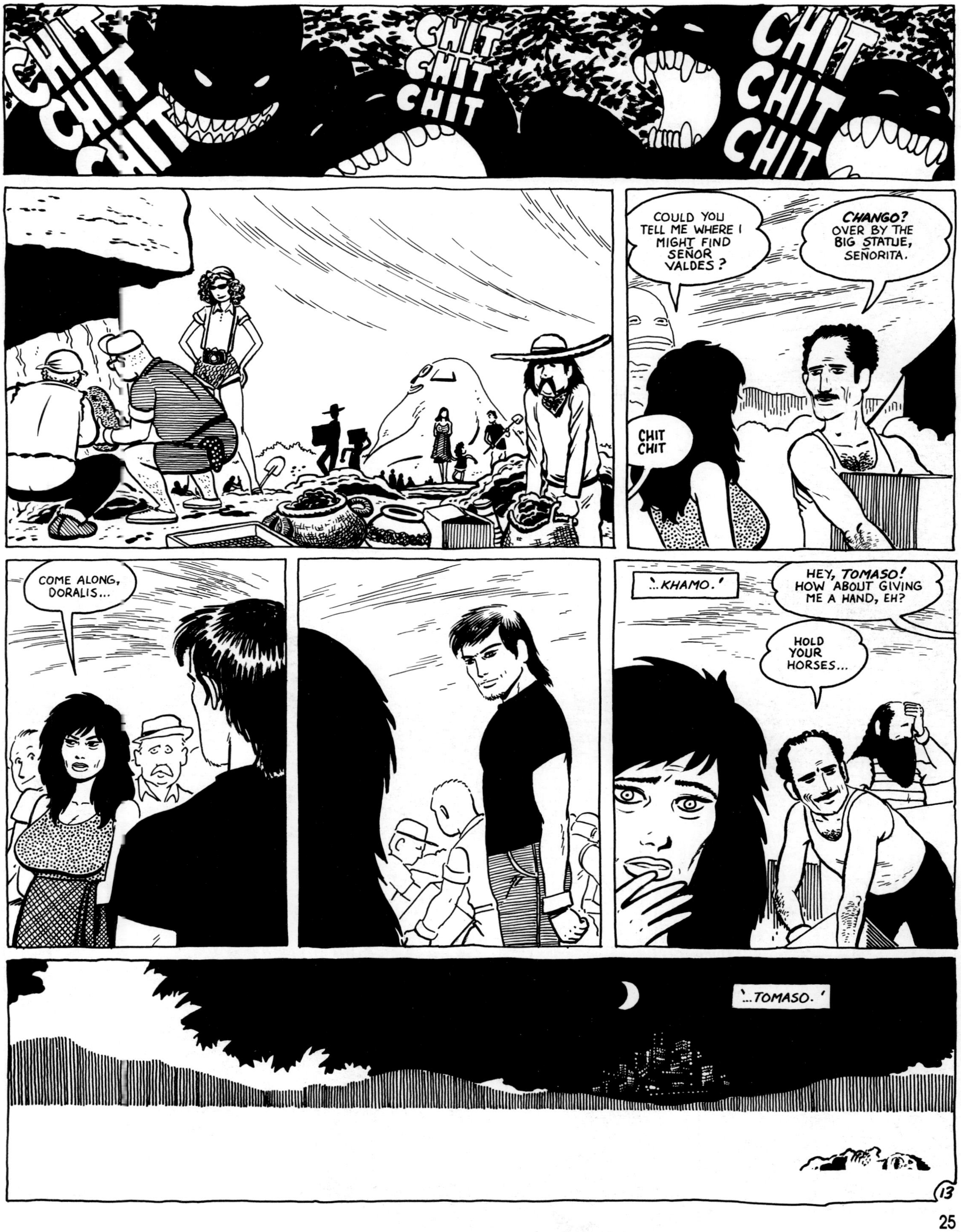
CHIT CHIT CHIT
CHIT CHIT CHIT
CHIT CHIT CHIT
COULD YOU TELL ME WHERE I MIGHT FIND SEÑOR VALDES?
CHANGO? OVER BY THE BIG STATUE, SEÑORITA.
CHIT CHIT
COME ALONG, DORALIS...
'...KHAMO.'
HEY, TOMASO! HOW ABOUT GIVING ME A HAND, EH?
HOLD YOUR HORSES...
'...TOMASO.'
13

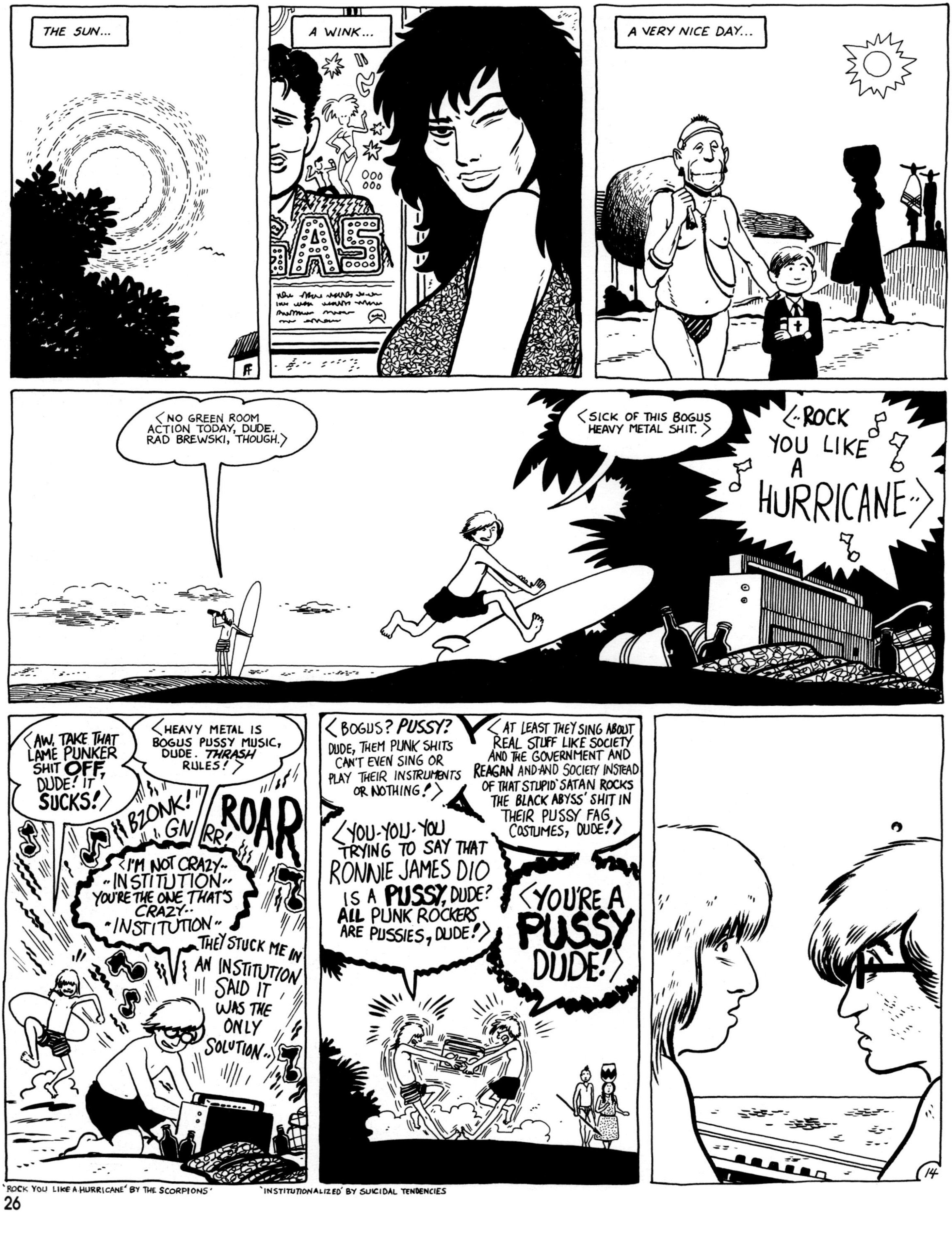
THE SUN...
A WINK...
A VERY NICE DAY...
<NO GREEN ROOM ACTION TODAY, DUDE. RAD BREWSKI, THOUGH.>
<SICK OF THIS BOGUS HEAVY METAL SHIT.>
<..ROCK YOU LIKE A HURRICANE..>
<AW, TAKE THAT LAME PUNKER SHIT OFF, DUDE! IT SUCKS!>
<HEAVY METAL IS BOGUS PUSSY MUSIC, DUDE. THRASH RULES!>
BZONK! GNRR! ROAR
<I'M NOT CRAZY.. ..INSTITUTION.. YOU'RE THE ONE THAT'S CRAZY.. ..INSTITUTION..
THEY STUCK ME IN AN INSTITUTION SAID IT WAS THE ONLY SOLUTION..>
<BOGUS? PUSSY? DUDE, THEM PUNK SHITS CAN'T EVEN SING OR PLAY THEIR INSTRUMENTS OR NOTHING!>
<AT LEAST THEY SING ABOUT REAL STUFF LIKE SOCIETY AND THE GOVERNMENT AND REAGAN AND-AND SOCIETY INSTEAD OF THAT STUPID 'SATAN ROCKS THE BLACK ABYSS' SHIT IN THEIR PUSSY FAG COSTUMES, DUDE!>
<YOU-YOU-YOU TRYING TO SAY THAT RONNIE JAMES DIO IS A PUSSY, DUDE? ALL PUNK ROCKERS ARE PUSSIES, DUDE!>
<YOU'RE A PUSSY DUDE!>
14

'ROCK YOU LIKE A HURRICANE' BY THE SCORPIONS'   'INSTITUTIONALIZED' BY SUICIDAL TENDENCIES

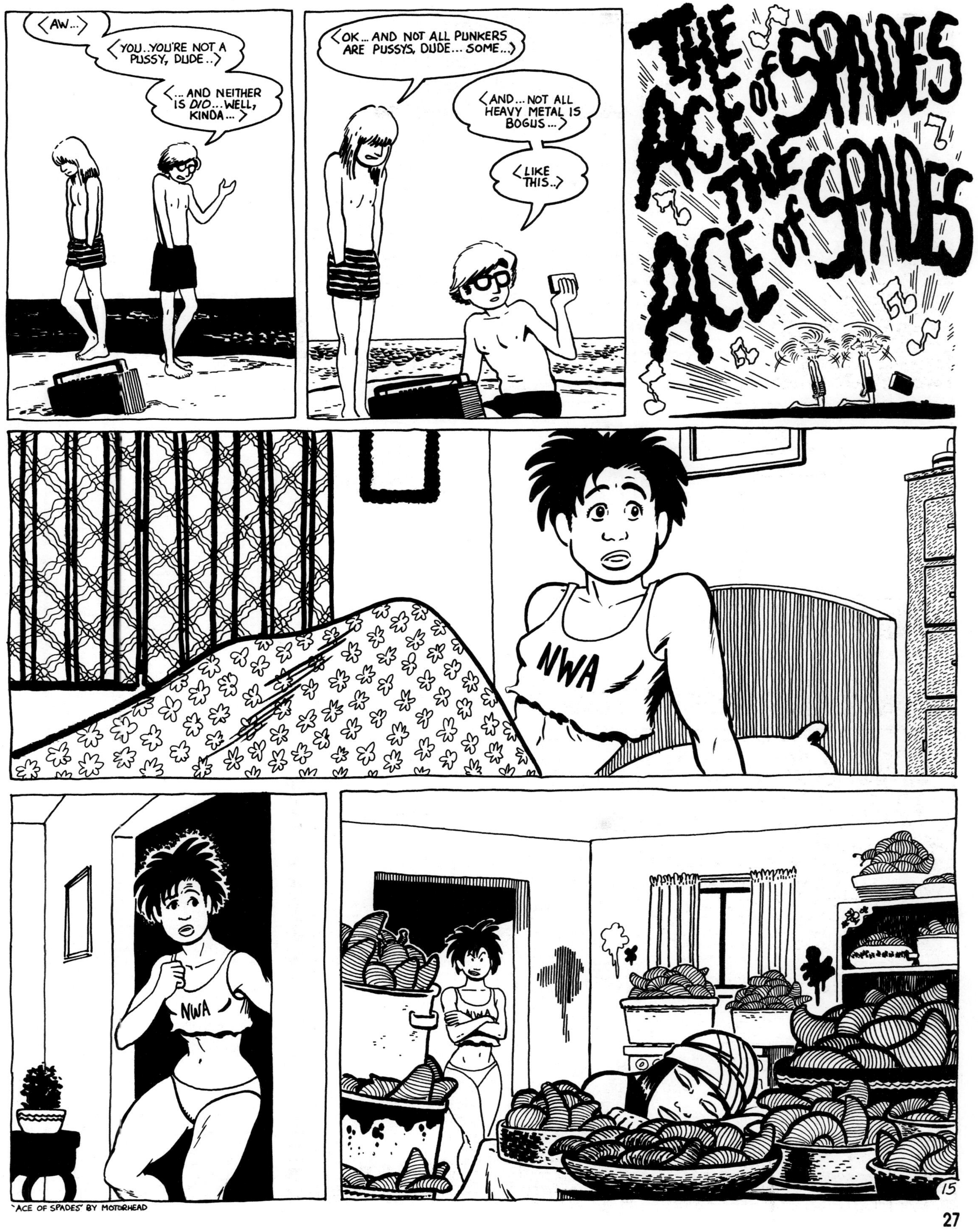

<AW...>
<YOU..YOU'RE NOT A PUSSY, DUDE..>
<...AND NEITHER IS DIO...WELL, KINDA...>
<OK... AND NOT ALL PUNKERS ARE PUSSYS, DUDE... SOME...>
<AND... NOT ALL HEAVY METAL IS BOGUS...>
<LIKE THIS..>
THE ACE of SPADES THE ACE of SPADES
NWA
NWA
NWA
15

'ACE OF SPADES' BY MOTORHEAD

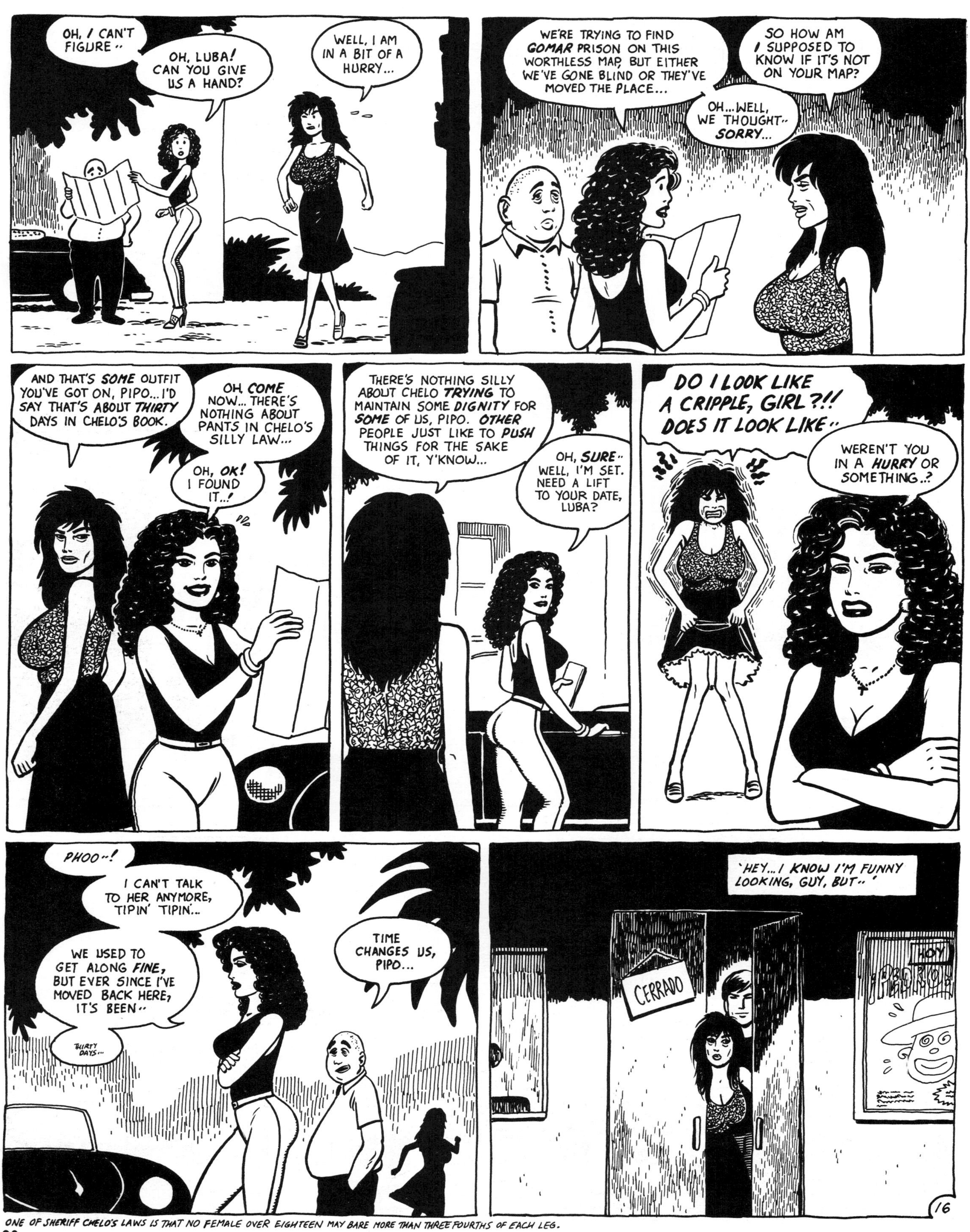
OH, I CAN'T FIGURE ..
OH, LUBA! CAN YOU GIVE US A HAND?
WELL, I AM IN A BIT OF A HURRY...
WE'RE TRYING TO FIND GOMAR PRISON ON THIS WORTHLESS MAP, BUT EITHER WE'VE GONE BLIND OR THEY'VE MOVED THE PLACE...
SO HOW AM I SUPPOSED TO KNOW IF IT'S NOT ON YOUR MAP?
OH...WELL, WE THOUGHT.. SORRY...
AND THAT'S SOME OUTFIT YOU'VE GOT ON, PIPO... I'D SAY THAT'S ABOUT THIRTY DAYS IN CHELO'S BOOK.
OH, COME NOW... THERE'S NOTHING ABOUT PANTS IN CHELO'S SILLY LAW...
OH, OK! I FOUND IT..!
THERE'S NOTHING SILLY ABOUT CHELO TRYING TO MAINTAIN SOME DIGNITY FOR SOME OF US, PIPO. OTHER PEOPLE JUST LIKE TO PUSH THINGS FOR THE SAKE OF IT, Y'KNOW...
OH, SURE.. WELL, I'M SET. NEED A LIFT TO YOUR DATE, LUBA?
DO I LOOK LIKE A CRIPPLE, GIRL?!! DOES IT LOOK LIKE..
WEREN'T YOU IN A HURRY OR SOMETHING..?
PHOO..!
I CAN'T TALK TO HER ANYMORE, TIPIN' TIPIN'...
WE USED TO GET ALONG FINE, BUT EVER SINCE I'VE MOVED BACK HERE, IT'S BEEN..
THIRTY DAYS...
TIME CHANGES US, PIPO...
`HEY... I KNOW I'M FUNNY LOOKING, GUY, BUT..'
CERRADO
HOY
16
ONE OF SHERIFF CHELO'S LAWS IS THAT NO FEMALE OVER EIGHTEEN MAY BARE MORE THAN THREE FOURTHS OF EACH LEG.

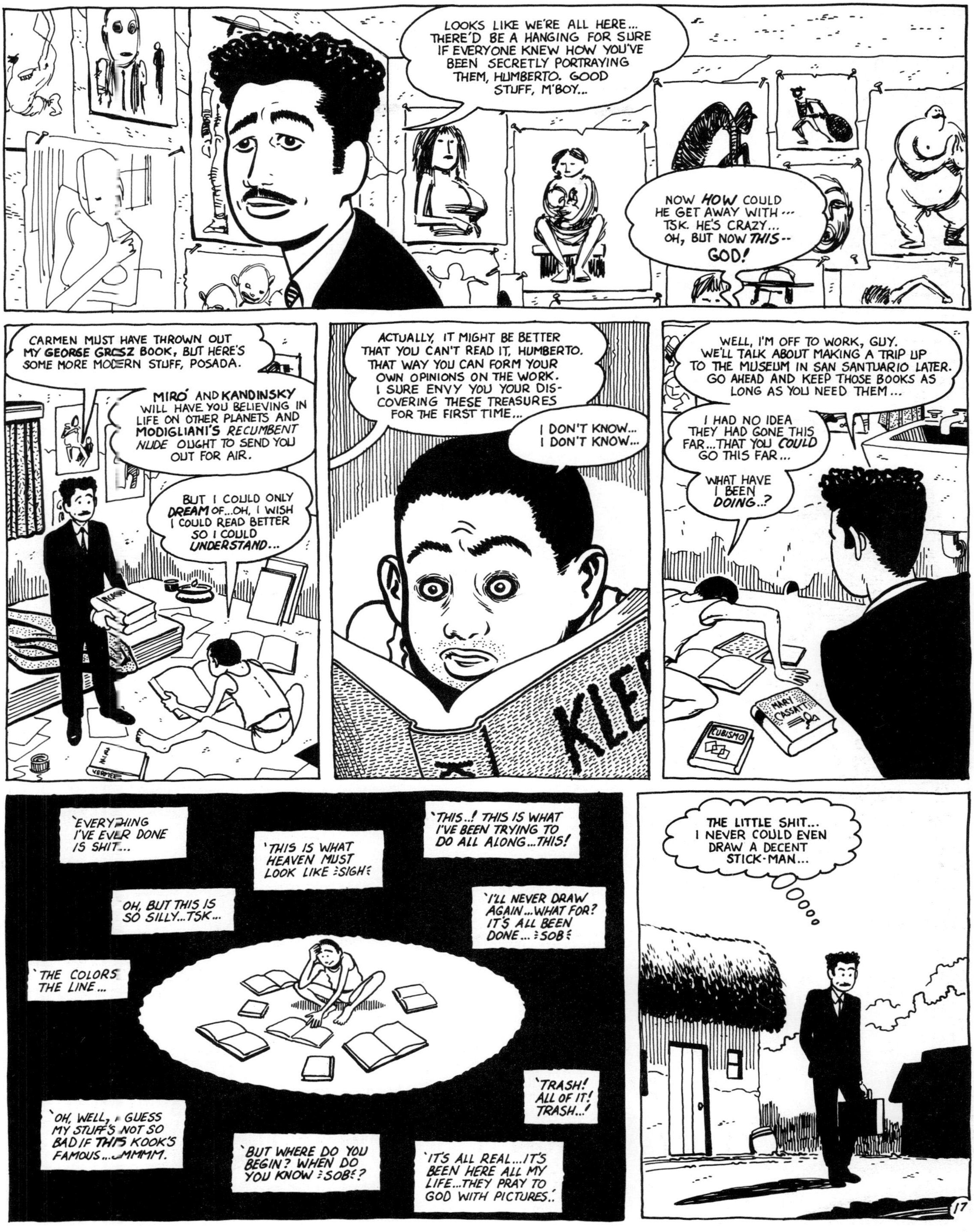
LOOKS LIKE WE'RE ALL HERE... THERE'D BE A HANGING FOR SURE IF EVERYONE KNEW HOW YOU'VE BEEN SECRETLY PORTRAYING THEM, HUMBERTO. GOOD STUFF, M'BOY...
NOW HOW COULD HE GET AWAY WITH... TSK. HE'S CRAZY... OH, BUT NOW THIS-- GOD!
CARMEN MUST HAVE THROWN OUT MY GEORGE GROSZ BOOK, BUT HERE'S SOME MORE MODERN STUFF, POSADA.
MIRÓ AND KANDINSKY WILL HAVE YOU BELIEVING IN LIFE ON OTHER PLANETS AND MODIGLIANI'S RECUMBENT NUDE OUGHT TO SEND YOU OUT FOR AIR.
BUT I COULD ONLY DREAM OF...OH, I WISH I COULD READ BETTER SO I COULD UNDERSTAND...
ACTUALLY, IT MIGHT BE BETTER THAT YOU CAN'T READ IT, HUMBERTO. THAT WAY YOU CAN FORM YOUR OWN OPINIONS ON THE WORK. I SURE ENVY YOU YOUR DISCOVERING THESE TREASURES FOR THE FIRST TIME...
I DON'T KNOW... I DON'T KNOW...
KLEE
WELL, I'M OFF TO WORK, GUY. WE'LL TALK ABOUT MAKING A TRIP UP TO THE MUSEUM IN SAN SANTUARIO LATER. GO AHEAD AND KEEP THOSE BOOKS AS LONG AS YOU NEED THEM...
I HAD NO IDEA THEY HAD GONE THIS FAR...THAT YOU COULD GO THIS FAR...
WHAT HAVE I BEEN DOING..?
MARY CASSATT
CUBISMO
'EVERYTHING I'VE EVER DONE IS SHIT...
'THIS IS WHAT HEAVEN MUST LOOK LIKE ⁝SIGH⁝
'THIS..! THIS IS WHAT I'VE BEEN TRYING TO DO ALL ALONG...THIS!
OH, BUT THIS IS SO SILLY...TSK...
'I'LL NEVER DRAW AGAIN...WHAT FOR? IT'S ALL BEEN DONE...⁝SOB⁝
'THE COLORS THE LINE...
'TRASH! ALL OF IT! TRASH...!
'OH, WELL, I GUESS MY STUFF'S NOT SO BAD IF THIS KOOK'S FAMOUS...MMMM.
'BUT WHERE DO YOU BEGIN? WHEN DO YOU KNOW ⁝SOB⁝?
'IT'S ALL REAL...IT'S BEEN HERE ALL MY LIFE...THEY PRAY TO GOD WITH PICTURES.'
THE LITTLE SHIT... I NEVER COULD EVEN DRAW A DECENT STICK-MAN...
17

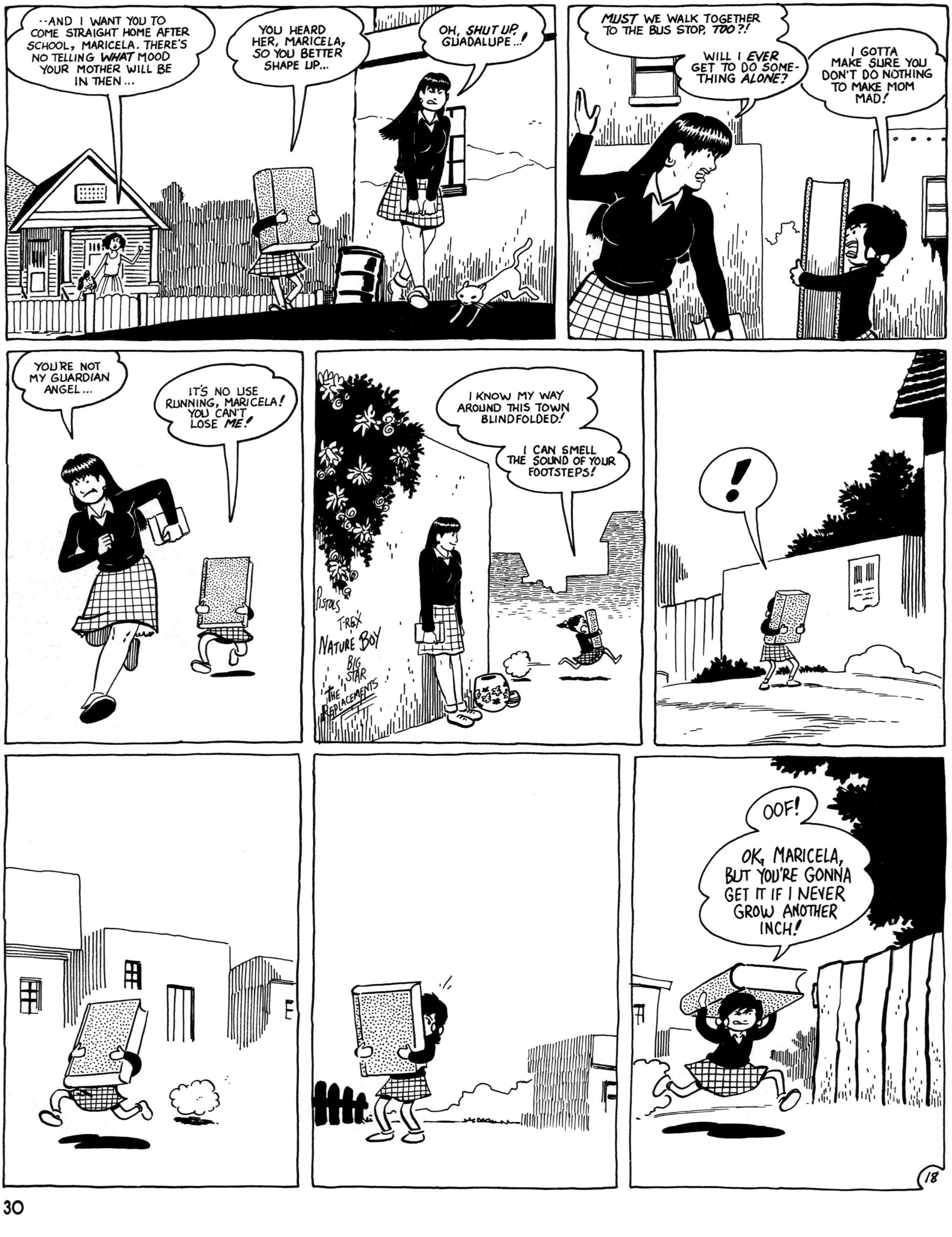
--AND I WANT YOU TO COME STRAIGHT HOME AFTER SCHOOL, MARICELA. THERE'S NO TELLING WHAT MOOD YOUR MOTHER WILL BE IN THEN...
YOU HEARD HER, MARICELA, SO YOU BETTER SHAPE UP...
OH, SHUT UP, GUADALUPE..!
MUST WE WALK TOGETHER TO THE BUS STOP, TOO?!
WILL I EVER GET TO DO SOMETHING ALONE?
I GOTTA MAKE SURE YOU DON'T DO NOTHING TO MAKE MOM MAD!
YOU'RE NOT MY GUARDIAN ANGEL...
IT'S NO USE RUNNING, MARICELA! YOU CAN'T LOSE ME!
I KNOW MY WAY AROUND THIS TOWN BLINDFOLDED!
I CAN SMELL THE SOUND OF YOUR FOOTSTEPS!
PISTOLS
T-REX
NATURE BOY
BIG STAR
THE REPLACEMENTS
!
OOF!
OK, MARICELA, BUT YOU'RE GONNA GET IT IF I NEVER GROW ANOTHER INCH!

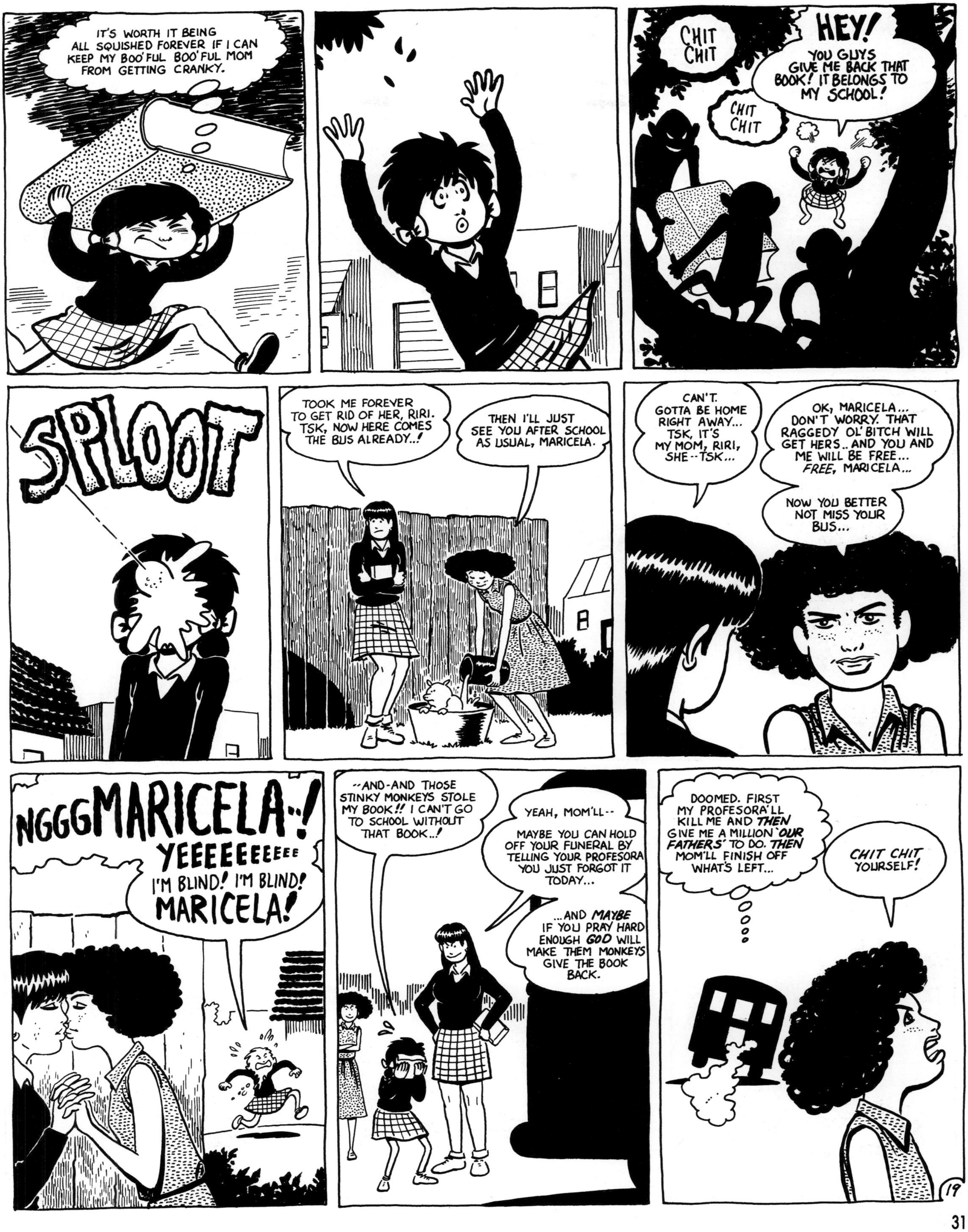
IT'S WORTH IT BEING ALL SQUISHED FOREVER IF I CAN KEEP MY BOO'FUL BOO'FUL MOM FROM GETTING CRANKY.
CHIT CHIT
HEY!
YOU GUYS GIVE ME BACK THAT BOOK! IT BELONGS TO MY SCHOOL!
CHIT CHIT
SPLOOT
TOOK ME FOREVER TO GET RID OF HER, RIRI. TSK, NOW HERE COMES THE BUS ALREADY..!
THEN I'LL JUST SEE YOU AFTER SCHOOL AS USUAL, MARICELA.
CAN'T. GOTTA BE HOME RIGHT AWAY... TSK, IT'S MY MOM, RIRI, SHE--TSK...
OK, MARICELA... DON'T WORRY. THAT RAGGEDY OL' BITCH WILL GET HERS.. AND YOU AND ME WILL BE FREE... FREE, MARICELA...
NOW YOU BETTER NOT MISS YOUR BUS...
NGGGMARICELA--!
YEEEEEEEEEE
I'M BLIND! I'M BLIND! MARICELA!
--AND-AND THOSE STINKY MONKEYS STOLE MY BOOK!! I CAN'T GO TO SCHOOL WITHOUT THAT BOOK..!
YEAH, MOM'LL--
MAYBE YOU CAN HOLD OFF YOUR FUNERAL BY TELLING YOUR PROFESORA YOU JUST FORGOT IT TODAY...
...AND MAYBE IF YOU PRAY HARD ENOUGH GOD WILL MAKE THEM MONKEYS GIVE THE BOOK BACK.
DOOMED. FIRST MY PROFESORA'LL KILL ME AND THEN GIVE ME A MILLION 'OUR FATHERS' TO DO. THEN MOM'LL FINISH OFF WHAT'S LEFT...
CHIT CHIT YOURSELF!
19

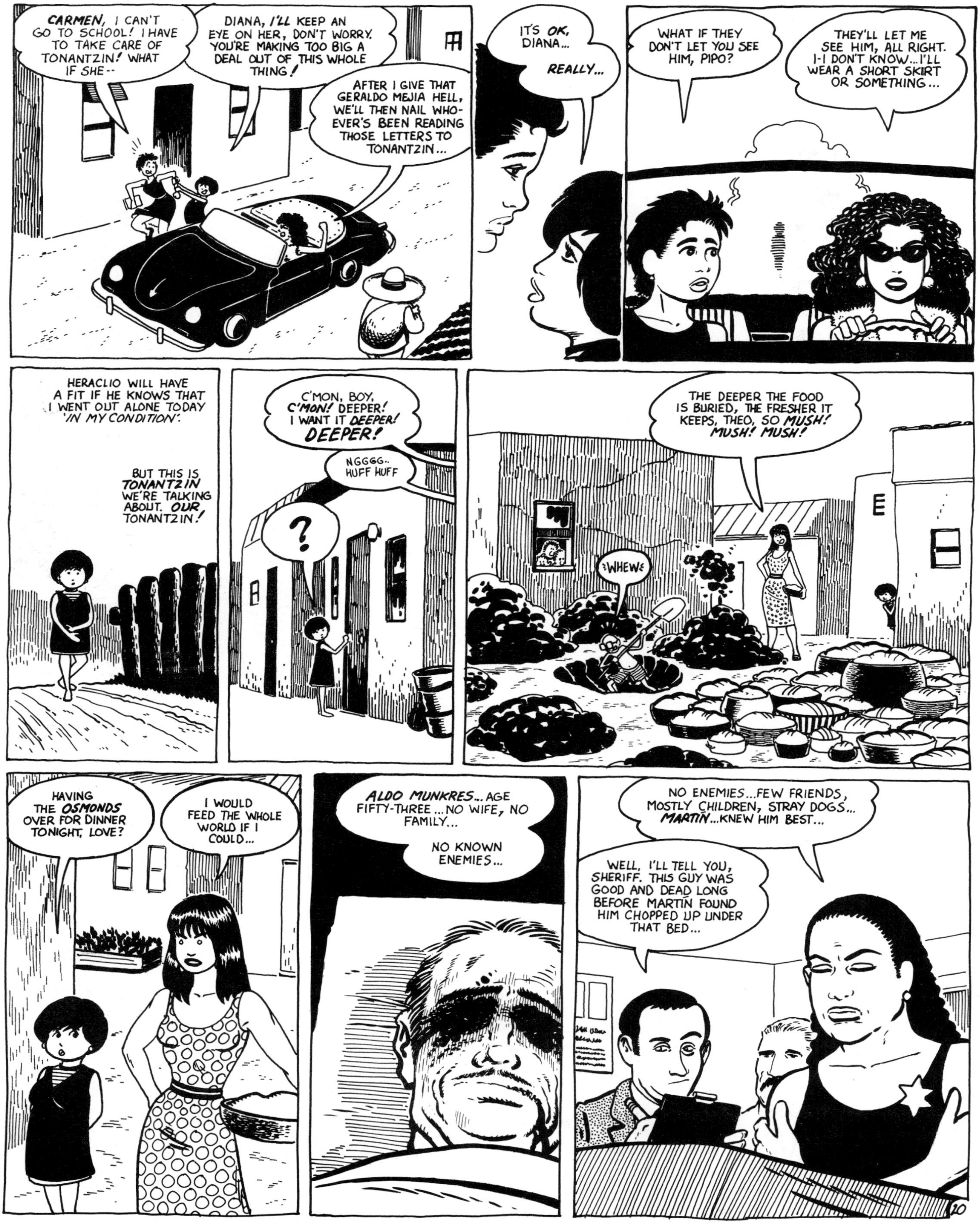
CARMEN, I CAN'T GO TO SCHOOL! I HAVE TO TAKE CARE OF TONANTZIN! WHAT IF SHE--
DIANA, I'LL KEEP AN EYE ON HER, DON'T WORRY. YOU'RE MAKING TOO BIG A DEAL OUT OF THIS WHOLE THING!
AFTER I GIVE THAT GERALDO MEJIA HELL, WE'LL THEN NAIL WHO-EVER'S BEEN READING THOSE LETTERS TO TONANTZIN...
IT'S OK, DIANA...
REALLY...
WHAT IF THEY DON'T LET YOU SEE HIM, PIPO?
THEY'LL LET ME SEE HIM, ALL RIGHT. I-I DON'T KNOW...I'LL WEAR A SHORT SKIRT OR SOMETHING...
HERACLIO WILL HAVE A FIT IF HE KNOWS THAT I WENT OUT ALONE TODAY 'IN MY CONDITION'.
BUT THIS IS TONANTZIN WE'RE TALKING ABOUT. OUR TONANTZIN!
C'MON, BOY, C'MON! DEEPER! I WANT IT DEEPER! DEEPER!
NGGGG.. HUFF HUFF
?
THE DEEPER THE FOOD IS BURIED, THE FRESHER IT KEEPS, THEO, SO MUSH! MUSH! MUSH!
WHEW
HAVING THE OSMONDS OVER FOR DINNER TONIGHT, LOVE?
I WOULD FEED THE WHOLE WORLD IF I COULD...
ALDO MUNKRES...AGE FIFTY-THREE...NO WIFE, NO FAMILY...
NO KNOWN ENEMIES...
NO ENEMIES...FEW FRIENDS, MOSTLY CHILDREN, STRAY DOGS... MARTÍN...KNEW HIM BEST...
WELL, I'LL TELL YOU, SHERIFF. THIS GUY WAS GOOD AND DEAD LONG BEFORE MARTÍN FOUND HIM CHOPPED UP UNDER THAT BED...
20

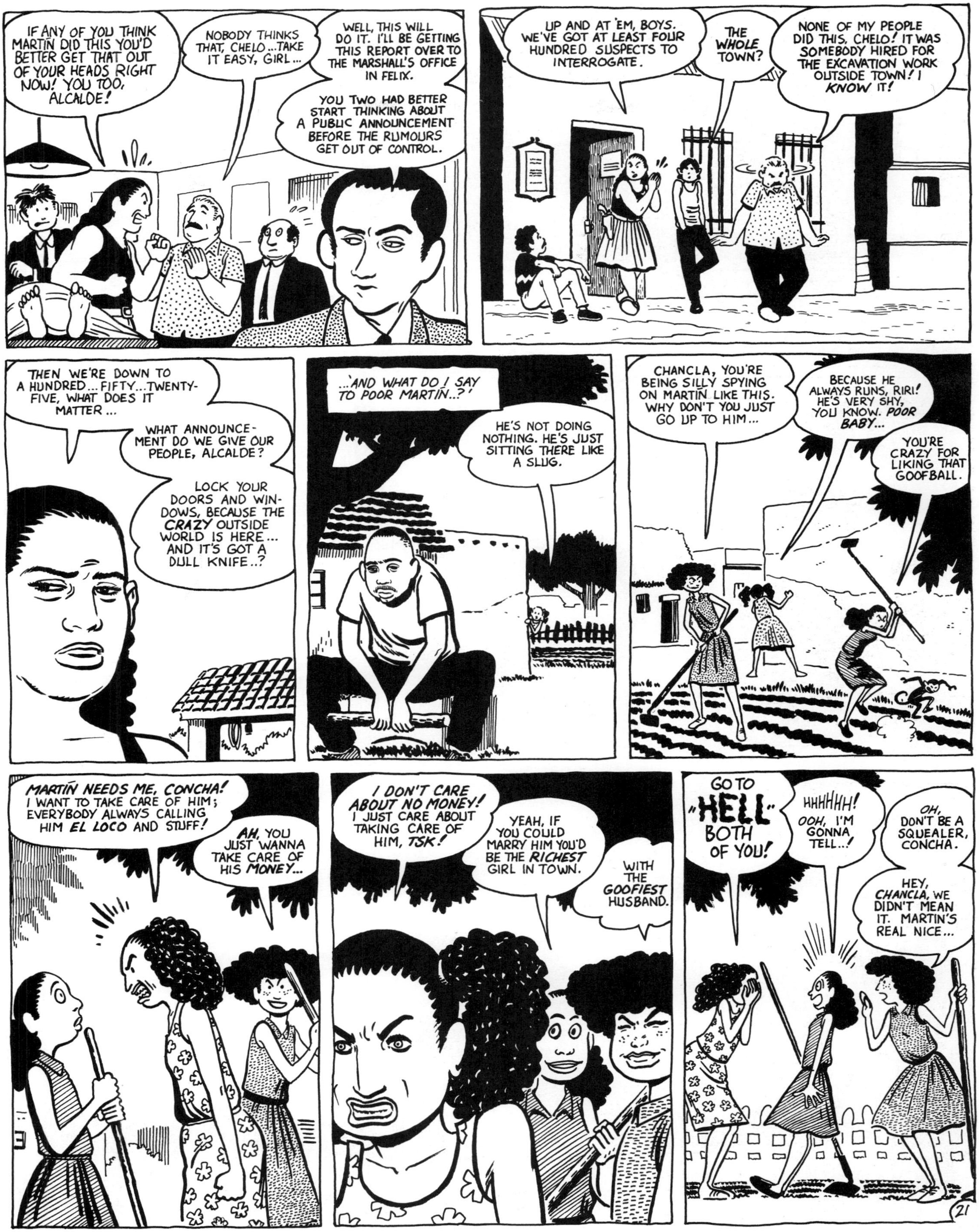

IF ANY OF YOU THINK MARTÍN DID THIS YOU'D BETTER GET THAT OUT OF YOUR HEADS RIGHT NOW! YOU TOO, ALCALDE!
NOBODY THINKS THAT, CHELO...TAKE IT EASY, GIRL...
WELL, THIS WILL DO IT. I'LL BE GETTING THIS REPORT OVER TO THE MARSHALL'S OFFICE IN FELIX.
YOU TWO HAD BETTER START THINKING ABOUT A PUBLIC ANNOUNCEMENT BEFORE THE RUMOURS GET OUT OF CONTROL.
UP AND AT 'EM, BOYS. WE'VE GOT AT LEAST FOUR HUNDRED SUSPECTS TO INTERROGATE.
THE WHOLE TOWN?
NONE OF MY PEOPLE DID THIS, CHELO! IT WAS SOMEBODY HIRED FOR THE EXCAVATION WORK OUTSIDE TOWN! I KNOW IT!
THEN WE'RE DOWN TO A HUNDRED... FIFTY... TWENTY-FIVE, WHAT DOES IT MATTER...
WHAT ANNOUNCE-MENT DO WE GIVE OUR PEOPLE, ALCALDE?
LOCK YOUR DOORS AND WIN-DOWS, BECAUSE THE CRAZY OUTSIDE WORLD IS HERE... AND IT'S GOT A DULL KNIFE..?
...'AND WHAT DO I SAY TO POOR MARTÍN..?'
HE'S NOT DOING NOTHING. HE'S JUST SITTING THERE LIKE A SLUG.
CHANCLA, YOU'RE BEING SILLY SPYING ON MARTÍN LIKE THIS. WHY DON'T YOU JUST GO UP TO HIM...
BECAUSE HE ALWAYS RUNS, RIRI! HE'S VERY SHY, YOU KNOW. POOR BABY...
YOU'RE CRAZY FOR LIKING THAT GOOFBALL.
MARTÍN NEEDS ME, CONCHA! I WANT TO TAKE CARE OF HIM; EVERYBODY ALWAYS CALLING HIM EL LOCO AND STUFF!
AH, YOU JUST WANNA TAKE CARE OF HIS MONEY...
I DON'T CARE ABOUT NO MONEY! I JUST CARE ABOUT TAKING CARE OF HIM, TSK!
YEAH, IF YOU COULD MARRY HIM YOU'D BE THE RICHEST GIRL IN TOWN.
WITH THE GOOFIEST HUSBAND.
GO TO "HELL" BOTH OF YOU!
HHHHHH! OOH, I'M GONNA TELL..!
OH, DON'T BE A SQUEALER, CONCHA.
HEY, CHANCLA, WE DIDN'T MEAN IT. MARTÍN'S REAL NICE...
21

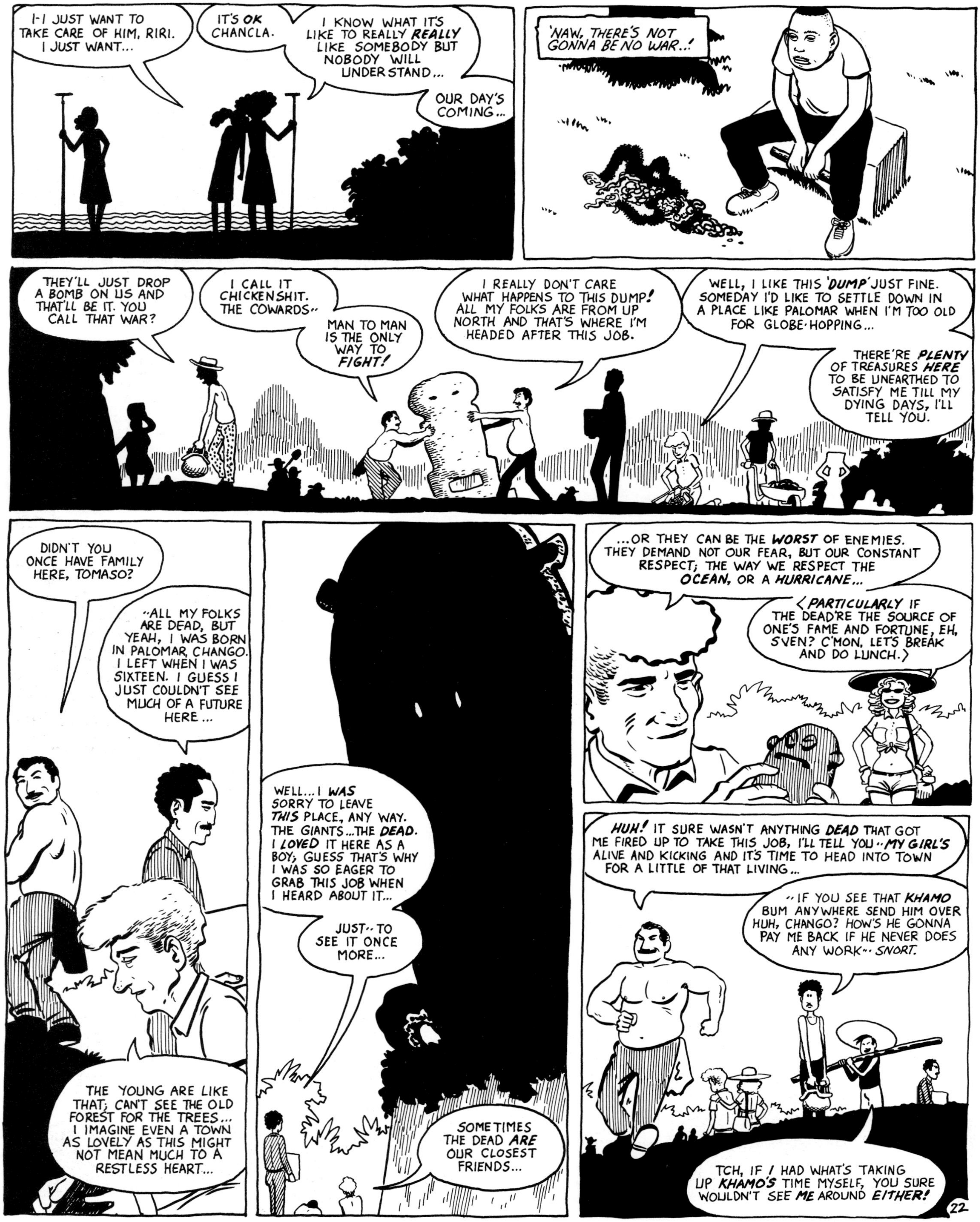

I-I JUST WANT TO TAKE CARE OF HIM, RIRI. I JUST WANT...
IT'S OK CHANCLA.
I KNOW WHAT IT'S LIKE TO REALLY REALLY LIKE SOMEBODY BUT NOBODY WILL UNDERSTAND...
OUR DAY'S COMING...
'NAW, THERE'S NOT GONNA BE NO WAR..!
THEY'LL JUST DROP A BOMB ON US AND THAT'LL BE IT. YOU CALL THAT WAR?
I CALL IT CHICKENSHIT. THE COWARDS..
MAN TO MAN IS THE ONLY WAY TO FIGHT!
I REALLY DON'T CARE WHAT HAPPENS TO THIS DUMP! ALL MY FOLKS ARE FROM UP NORTH AND THAT'S WHERE I'M HEADED AFTER THIS JOB.
WELL, I LIKE THIS 'DUMP' JUST FINE. SOMEDAY I'D LIKE TO SETTLE DOWN IN A PLACE LIKE PALOMAR WHEN I'M TOO OLD FOR GLOBE-HOPPING...
THERE'RE PLENTY OF TREASURES HERE TO BE UNEARTHED TO SATISFY ME TILL MY DYING DAYS, I'LL TELL YOU.
DIDN'T YOU ONCE HAVE FAMILY HERE, TOMASO?
..ALL MY FOLKS ARE DEAD, BUT YEAH, I WAS BORN IN PALOMAR, CHANGO. I LEFT WHEN I WAS SIXTEEN. I GUESS I JUST COULDN'T SEE MUCH OF A FUTURE HERE...
THE YOUNG ARE LIKE THAT; CAN'T SEE THE OLD FOREST FOR THE TREES... I IMAGINE EVEN A TOWN AS LOVELY AS THIS MIGHT NOT MEAN MUCH TO A RESTLESS HEART...
WELL... I WAS SORRY TO LEAVE THIS PLACE, ANY WAY. THE GIANTS... THE DEAD. I LOVED IT HERE AS A BOY; GUESS THAT'S WHY I WAS SO EAGER TO GRAB THIS JOB WHEN I HEARD ABOUT IT...
JUST.. TO SEE IT ONCE MORE...
SOMETIMES THE DEAD ARE OUR CLOSEST FRIENDS...
...OR THEY CAN BE THE WORST OF ENEMIES. THEY DEMAND NOT OUR FEAR, BUT OUR CONSTANT RESPECT; THE WAY WE RESPECT THE OCEAN, OR A HURRICANE...
<PARTICULARLY IF THE DEAD'RE THE SOURCE OF ONE'S FAME AND FORTUNE, EH, SVEN? C'MON, LET'S BREAK AND DO LUNCH.>
HUH! IT SURE WASN'T ANYTHING DEAD THAT GOT ME FIRED UP TO TAKE THIS JOB, I'LL TELL YOU.. MY GIRL'S ALIVE AND KICKING AND IT'S TIME TO HEAD INTO TOWN FOR A LITTLE OF THAT LIVING...
..IF YOU SEE THAT KHAMO BUM ANYWHERE SEND HIM OVER HUH, CHANGO? HOW'S HE GONNA PAY ME BACK IF HE NEVER DOES ANY WORK.. SNORT.
TCH, IF I HAD WHAT'S TAKING UP KHAMO'S TIME MYSELF, YOU SURE WOULDN'T SEE ME AROUND EITHER!
22

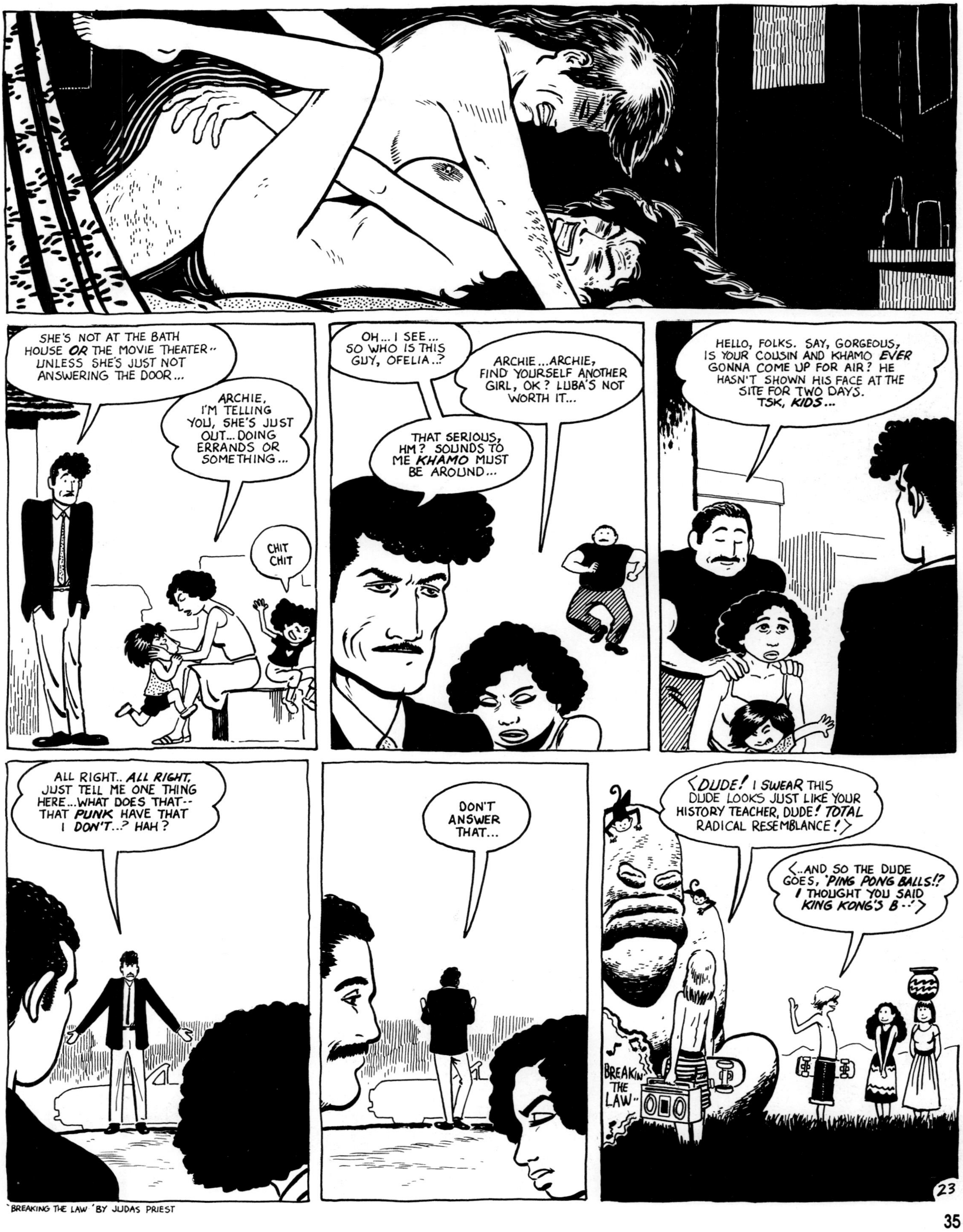
SHE'S NOT AT THE BATH HOUSE OR THE MOVIE THEATER.. UNLESS SHE'S JUST NOT ANSWERING THE DOOR...
ARCHIE, I'M TELLING YOU, SHE'S JUST OUT... DOING ERRANDS OR SOMETHING...
CHIT CHIT
OH... I SEE... SO WHO IS THIS GUY, OFELIA..?
THAT SERIOUS, HM? SOUNDS TO ME KHAMO MUST BE AROUND...
ARCHIE... ARCHIE, FIND YOURSELF ANOTHER GIRL, OK? LUBA'S NOT WORTH IT...
HELLO, FOLKS. SAY, GORGEOUS, IS YOUR COUSIN AND KHAMO EVER GONNA COME UP FOR AIR? HE HASN'T SHOWN HIS FACE AT THE SITE FOR TWO DAYS. TSK, KIDS...
ALL RIGHT.. ALL RIGHT, JUST TELL ME ONE THING HERE... WHAT DOES THAT-- THAT PUNK HAVE THAT I DON'T..? HAH?
DON'T ANSWER THAT...
<DUDE! I SWEAR THIS DUDE LOOKS JUST LIKE YOUR HISTORY TEACHER, DUDE! TOTAL RADICAL RESEMBLANCE!>
<..AND SO THE DUDE GOES, 'PING PONG BALLS!? I THOUGHT YOU SAID KING KONG'S B--'>
BREAKIN' THE LAW..
23

`BREAKING THE LAW' BY JUDAS PRIEST

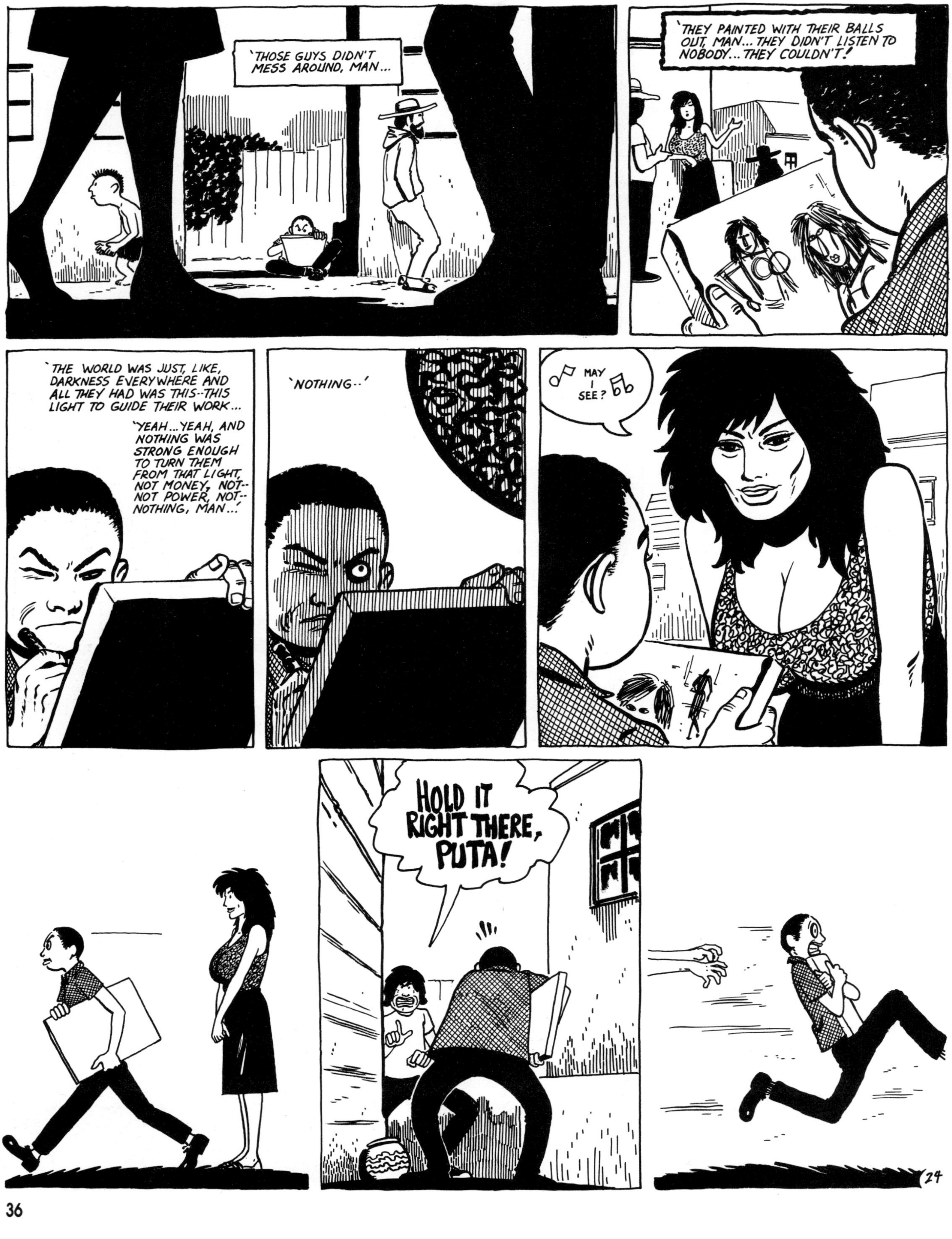
'THOSE GUYS DIDN'T MESS AROUND, MAN...
'THEY PAINTED WITH THEIR BALLS OUT, MAN... THEY DIDN'T LISTEN TO NOBODY... THEY COULDN'T!
'THE WORLD WAS JUST, LIKE, DARKNESS EVERYWHERE AND ALL THEY HAD WAS THIS--THIS LIGHT TO GUIDE THEIR WORK...
'YEAH... YEAH, AND NOTHING WAS STRONG ENOUGH TO TURN THEM FROM THAT LIGHT, NOT MONEY, NOT-- NOT POWER, NOT-- NOTHING, MAN...'
'NOTHING--'
MAY I SEE?
HOLD IT RIGHT THERE, PUTA!
24

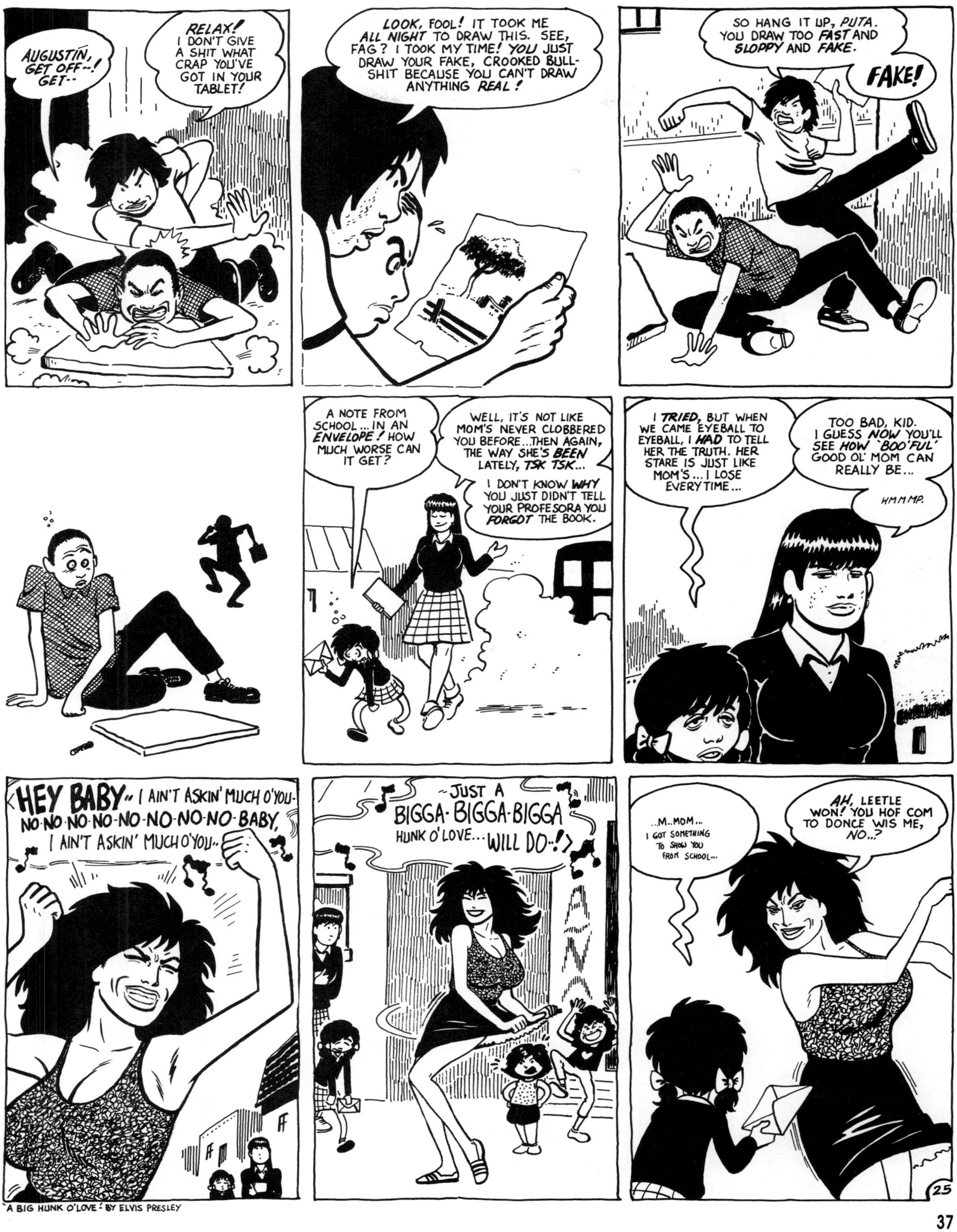
AUGUSTÍN, GET OFF--! GET--
RELAX! I DON'T GIVE A SHIT WHAT CRAP YOU'VE GOT IN YOUR TABLET!
LOOK, FOOL! IT TOOK ME ALL NIGHT TO DRAW THIS. SEE, FAG? I TOOK MY TIME! YOU JUST DRAW YOUR FAKE, CROOKED BULL-SHIT BECAUSE YOU CAN'T DRAW ANYTHING REAL!
SO HANG IT UP, PUTA. YOU DRAW TOO FAST AND SLOPPY AND FAKE.
FAKE!
A NOTE FROM SCHOOL... IN AN ENVELOPE! HOW MUCH WORSE CAN IT GET?
WELL, IT'S NOT LIKE MOM'S NEVER CLOBBERED YOU BEFORE...THEN AGAIN, THE WAY SHE'S BEEN LATELY, TSK TSK...
I DON'T KNOW WHY YOU JUST DIDN'T TELL YOUR PROFESORA YOU FORGOT THE BOOK.
I TRIED, BUT WHEN WE CAME EYEBALL TO EYEBALL, I HAD TO TELL HER THE TRUTH. HER STARE IS JUST LIKE MOM'S... I LOSE EVERYTIME...
TOO BAD, KID. I GUESS NOW YOU'LL SEE HOW 'BOO'FUL' GOOD OL' MOM CAN REALLY BE...
HMMMP.
HEY BABY.. I AIN'T ASKIN' MUCH O'YOU-
NO-NO-NO-NO-NO-NO-NO-NO-BABY,
I AIN'T ASKIN' MUCH O'YOU..
-JUST A
BIGGA-BIGGA-BIGGA
HUNK O' LOVE... WILL DO-!
..M..MOM... I GOT SOMETHING TO SHOW YOU FROM SCHOOL...
AH, LEETLE WON! YOU HOF COM TO DONCE WIS ME, NO..?
25
`A BIG HUNK O'LOVE' - BY ELVIS PRESLEY

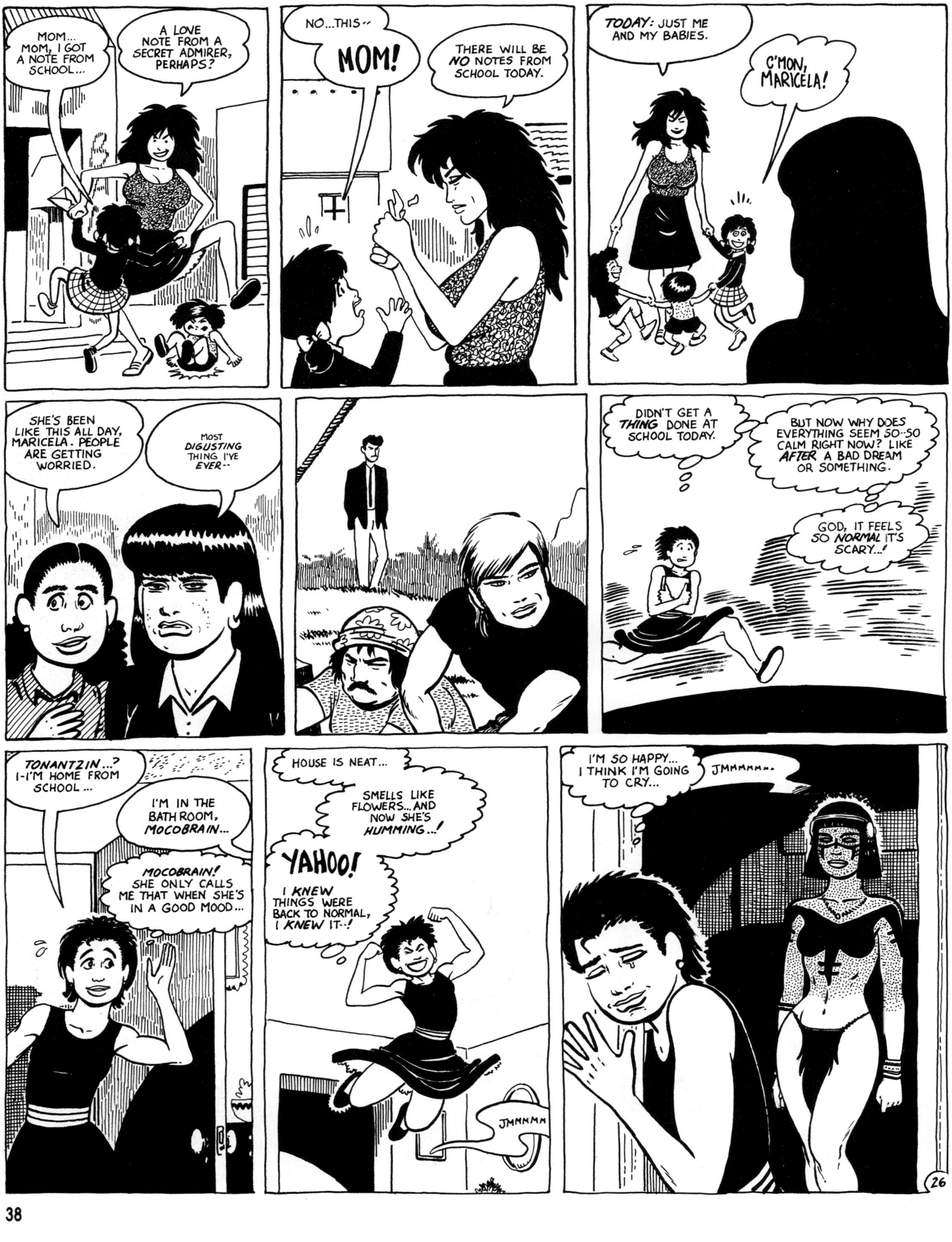
MOM... MOM, I GOT A NOTE FROM SCHOOL...
A LOVE NOTE FROM A SECRET ADMIRER, PERHAPS?
NO...THIS--
MOM!
THERE WILL BE NO NOTES FROM SCHOOL TODAY.
TODAY: JUST ME AND MY BABIES.
C'MON, MARICELA!
SHE'S BEEN LIKE THIS ALL DAY, MARICELA. PEOPLE ARE GETTING WORRIED.
MOST DIGUSTING THING I'VE EVER--
DIDN'T GET A THING DONE AT SCHOOL TODAY.
BUT NOW WHY DOES EVERYTHING SEEM SO--SO CALM RIGHT NOW? LIKE AFTER A BAD DREAM OR SOMETHING.
GOD, IT FEELS SO NORMAL IT'S SCARY...!
TONANTZIN...? I-I'M HOME FROM SCHOOL...
I'M IN THE BATH ROOM, MOCOBRAIN...
MOCOBRAIN! SHE ONLY CALLS ME THAT WHEN SHE'S IN A GOOD MOOD...
HOUSE IS NEAT...
SMELLS LIKE FLOWERS... AND NOW SHE'S HUMMING...!
YAHOO!
I KNEW THINGS WERE BACK TO NORMAL, I KNEW IT--!
JMMMMM
I'M SO HAPPY... I THINK I'M GOING TO CRY...
JMMMMMM..
26

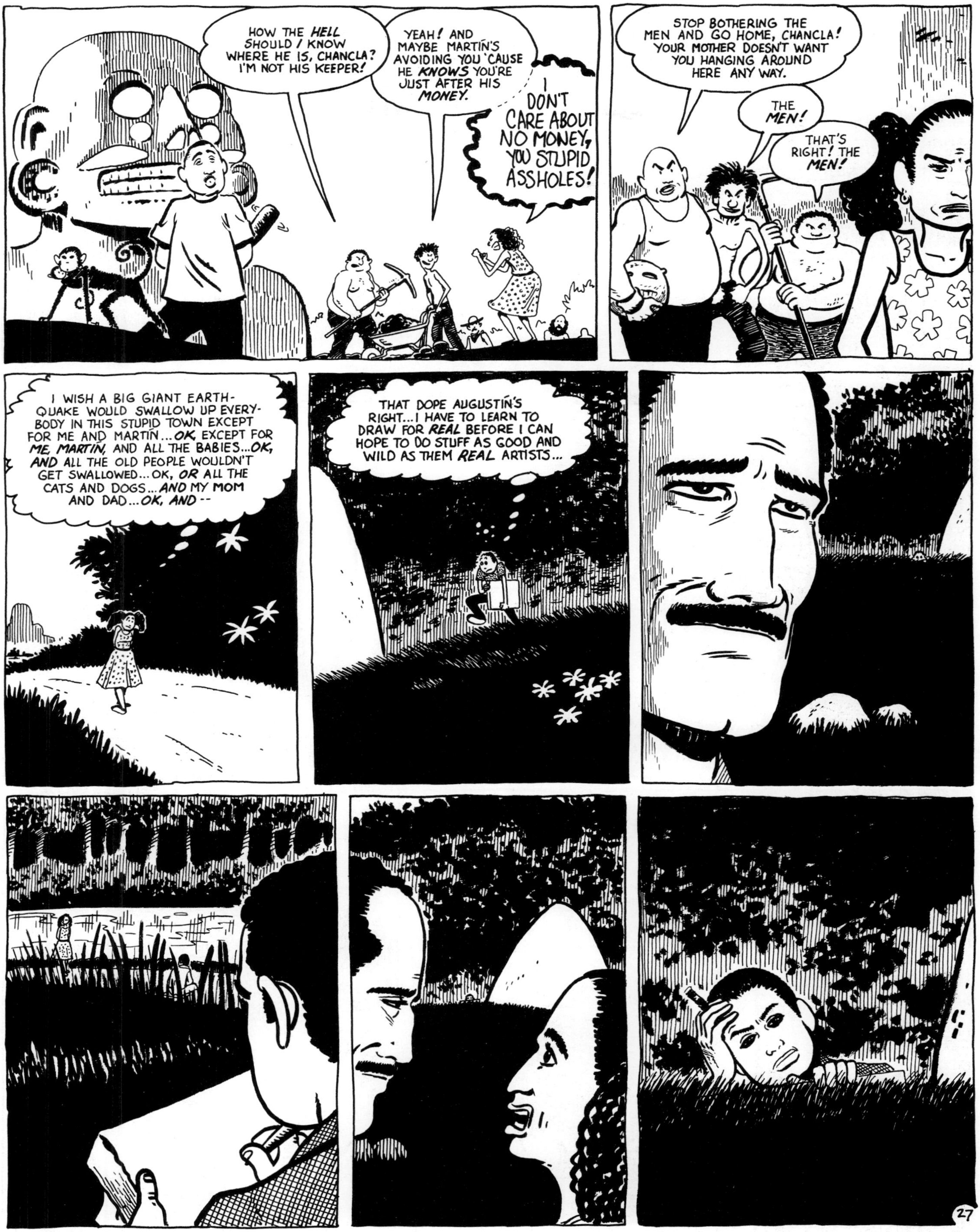
HOW THE HELL SHOULD I KNOW WHERE HE IS, CHANCLA? I'M NOT HIS KEEPER!
YEAH! AND MAYBE MARTÍN'S AVOIDING YOU 'CAUSE HE KNOWS YOU'RE JUST AFTER HIS MONEY.
I DON'T CARE ABOUT NO MONEY, YOU STUPID ASSHOLES!
STOP BOTHERING THE MEN AND GO HOME, CHANCLA! YOUR MOTHER DOESN'T WANT YOU HANGING AROUND HERE ANY WAY.
THE MEN!
THAT'S RIGHT! THE MEN!
I WISH A BIG GIANT EARTH-QUAKE WOULD SWALLOW UP EVERY-BODY IN THIS STUPID TOWN EXCEPT FOR ME AND MARTÍN...OK, EXCEPT FOR ME, MARTÍN, AND ALL THE BABIES...OK, AND ALL THE OLD PEOPLE WOULDN'T GET SWALLOWED...OK, OR ALL THE CATS AND DOGS...AND MY MOM AND DAD...OK, AND --
THAT DOPE AUGUSTÍN'S RIGHT...I HAVE TO LEARN TO DRAW FOR REAL BEFORE I CAN HOPE TO DO STUFF AS GOOD AND WILD AS THEM REAL ARTISTS...
27

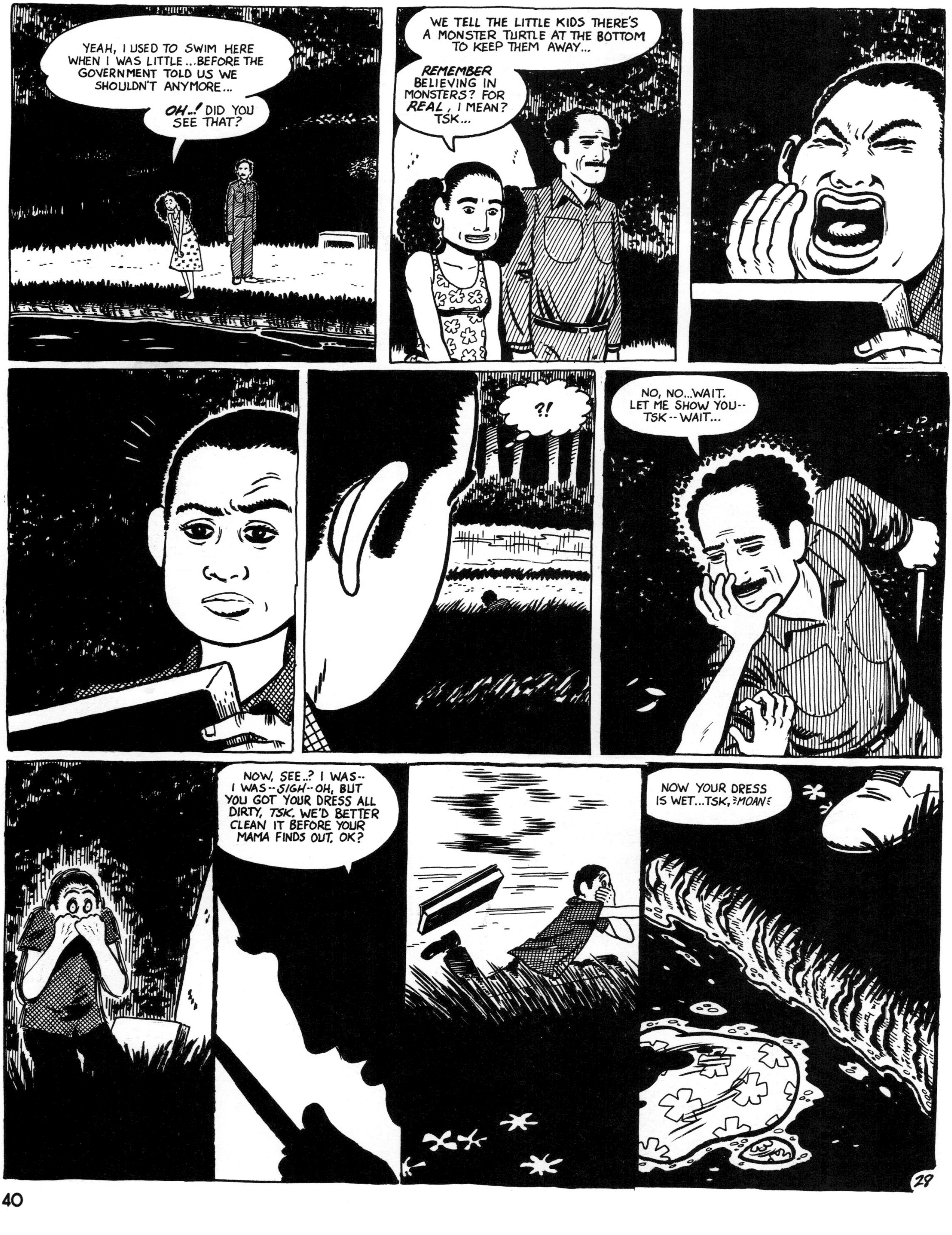
YEAH, I USED TO SWIM HERE WHEN I WAS LITTLE ...BEFORE THE GOVERNMENT TOLD US WE SHOULDN'T ANYMORE...
OH..! DID YOU SEE THAT?
WE TELL THE LITTLE KIDS THERE'S A MONSTER TURTLE AT THE BOTTOM TO KEEP THEM AWAY...
REMEMBER BELIEVING IN MONSTERS? FOR REAL, I MEAN? TSK...
?!
NO, NO...WAIT. LET ME SHOW YOU-- TSK--WAIT...
NOW, SEE..? I WAS-- I WAS--SIGH--OH, BUT YOU GOT YOUR DRESS ALL DIRTY, TSK. WE'D BETTER CLEAN IT BEFORE YOUR MAMA FINDS OUT, OK?
NOW YOUR DRESS IS WET...TSK, MOAN
28

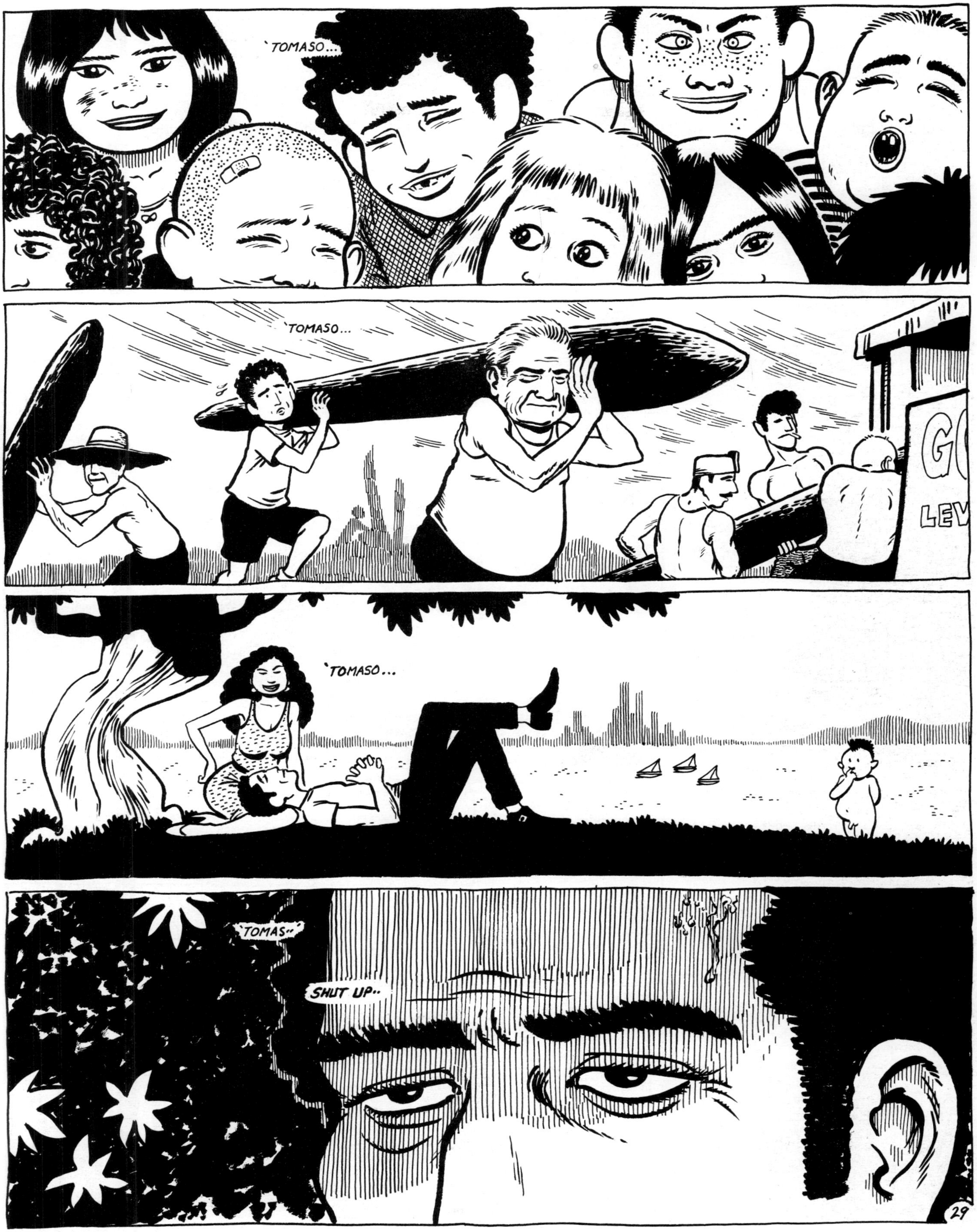
`TOMASO...
`TOMASO...
GO
LEV
`TOMASO...
`TOMAS..
SHUT UP..
29

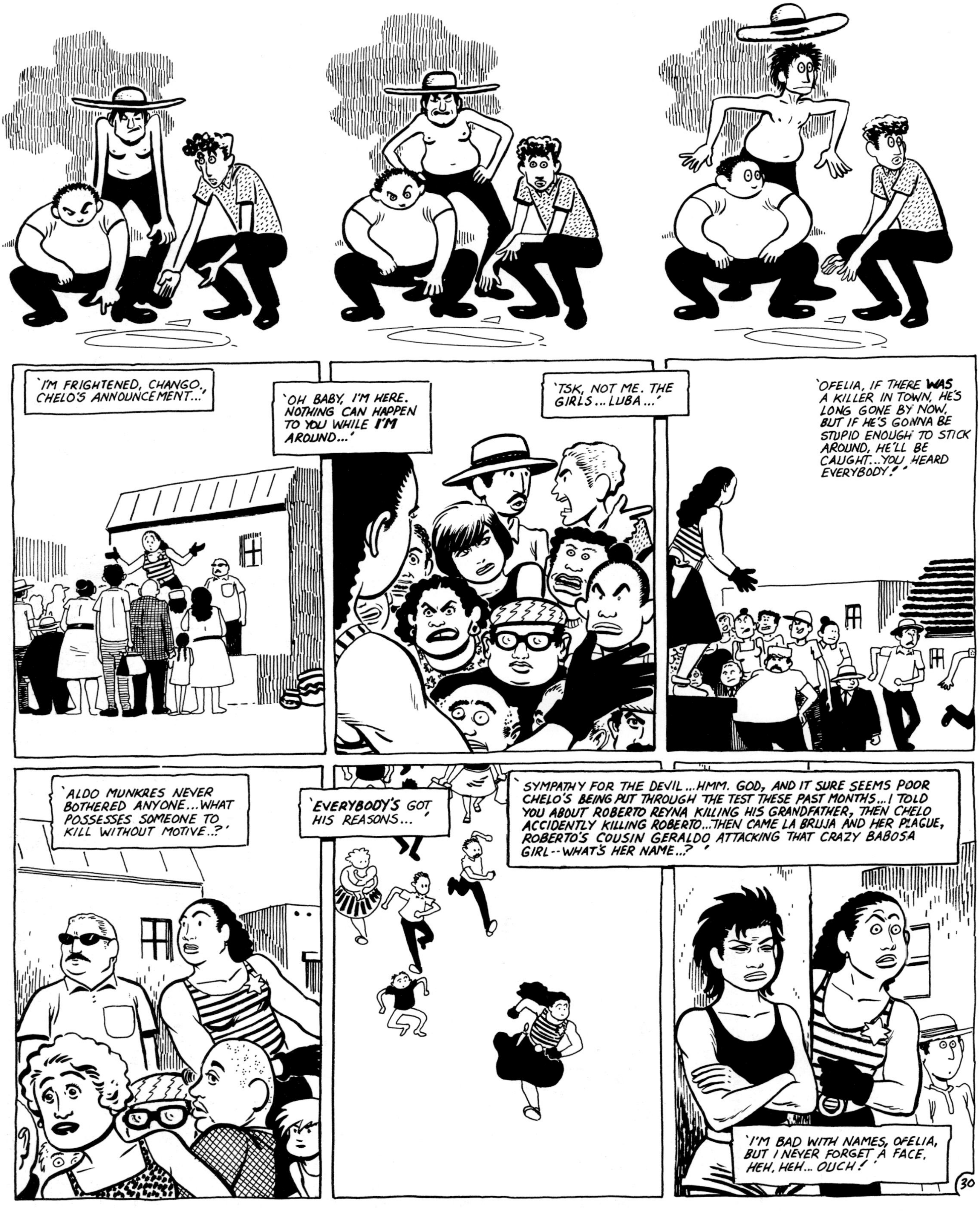
'I'M FRIGHTENED, CHANGO. CHELO'S ANNOUNCEMENT...'
'OH BABY, I'M HERE. NOTHING CAN HAPPEN TO YOU WHILE I'M AROUND...'
'TSK, NOT ME. THE GIRLS... LUBA...'
'OFELIA, IF THERE WAS A KILLER IN TOWN, HE'S LONG GONE BY NOW, BUT IF HE'S GONNA BE STUPID ENOUGH TO STICK AROUND, HE'LL BE CAUGHT... YOU HEARD EVERYBODY!'
'ALDO MUNKRES NEVER BOTHERED ANYONE... WHAT POSSESSES SOMEONE TO KILL WITHOUT MOTIVE..?'
'EVERYBODY'S GOT HIS REASONS...'
'SYMPATHY FOR THE DEVIL... HMM. GOD, AND IT SURE SEEMS POOR CHELO'S BEING PUT THROUGH THE TEST THESE PAST MONTHS... I TOLD YOU ABOUT ROBERTO REYNA KILLING HIS GRANDFATHER, THEN CHELO ACCIDENTLY KILLING ROBERTO... THEN CAME LA BRUJA AND HER PLAGUE, ROBERTO'S COUSIN GERALDO ATTACKING THAT CRAZY BABOSA GIRL--WHAT'S HER NAME..?'
'I'M BAD WITH NAMES, OFELIA, BUT I NEVER FORGET A FACE. HEH, HEH... OUCH!'
30

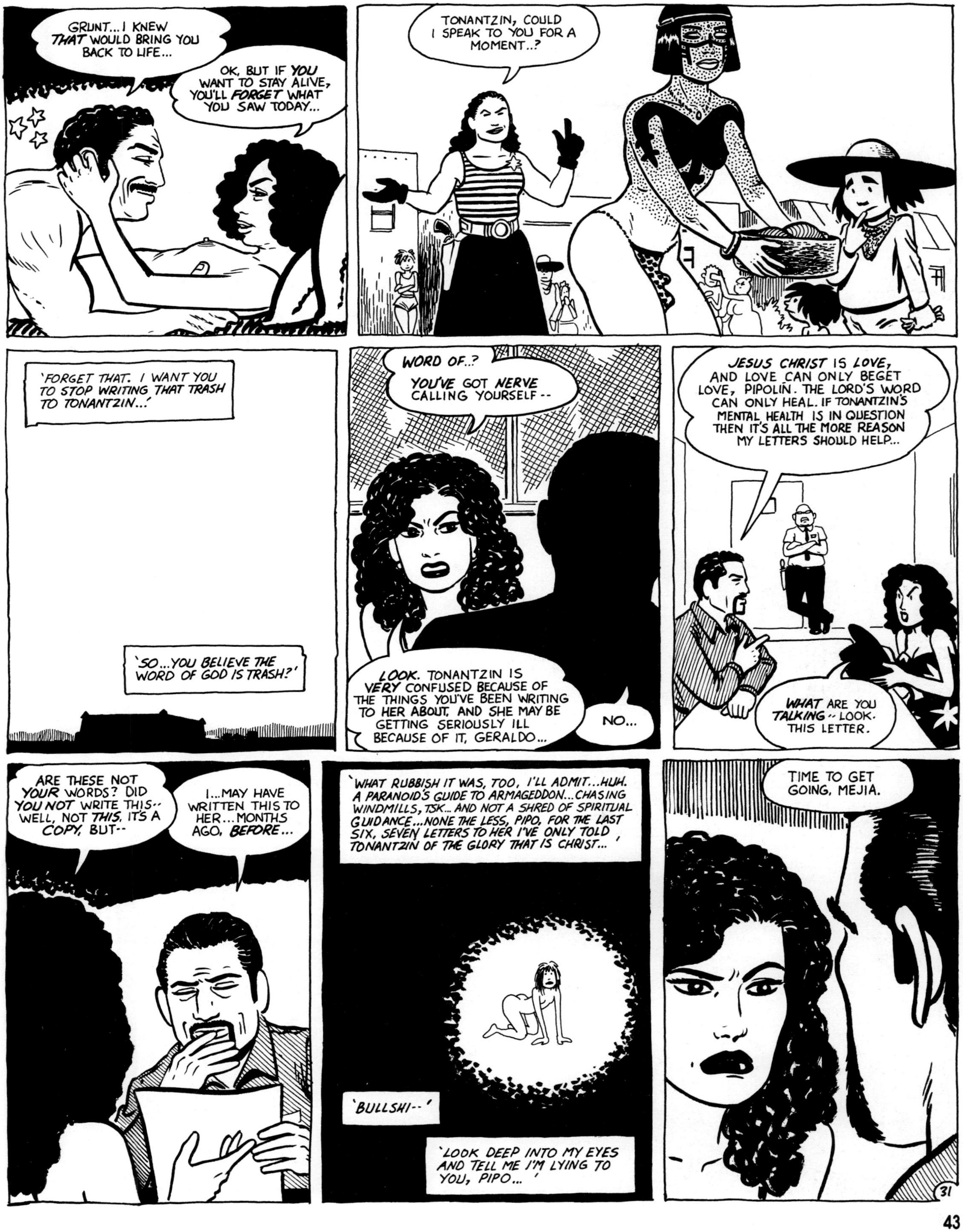

GRUNT... I KNEW THAT WOULD BRING YOU BACK TO LIFE...
OK, BUT IF YOU WANT TO STAY ALIVE, YOU'LL FORGET WHAT YOU SAW TODAY...
TONANTZIN, COULD I SPEAK TO YOU FOR A MOMENT..?
'FORGET THAT. I WANT YOU TO STOP WRITING THAT TRASH TO TONANTZIN...'
'SO... YOU BELIEVE THE WORD OF GOD IS TRASH?'
WORD OF..?
YOU'VE GOT NERVE CALLING YOURSELF --
LOOK. TONANTZIN IS VERY CONFUSED BECAUSE OF THE THINGS YOU'VE BEEN WRITING TO HER ABOUT, AND SHE MAY BE GETTING SERIOUSLY ILL BECAUSE OF IT, GERALDO...
NO...
JESUS CHRIST IS LOVE, AND LOVE CAN ONLY BEGET LOVE, PIPOLIN. THE LORD'S WORD CAN ONLY HEAL. IF TONANTZIN'S MENTAL HEALTH IS IN QUESTION THEN IT'S ALL THE MORE REASON MY LETTERS SHOULD HELP...
WHAT ARE YOU TALKING -- LOOK. THIS LETTER.
ARE THESE NOT YOUR WORDS? DID YOU NOT WRITE THIS -- WELL, NOT THIS, IT'S A COPY, BUT --
I... MAY HAVE WRITTEN THIS TO HER... MONTHS AGO, BEFORE...
'WHAT RUBBISH IT WAS, TOO, I'LL ADMIT... HUH. A PARANOID'S GUIDE TO ARMAGEDDON... CHASING WINDMILLS, TSK... AND NOT A SHRED OF SPIRITUAL GUIDANCE... NONE THE LESS, PIPO, FOR THE LAST SIX, SEVEN LETTERS TO HER I'VE ONLY TOLD TONANTZIN OF THE GLORY THAT IS CHRIST...'
'BULLSHI--'
'LOOK DEEP INTO MY EYES AND TELL ME I'M LYING TO YOU, PIPO...'
TIME TO GET GOING, MEJIA.
31

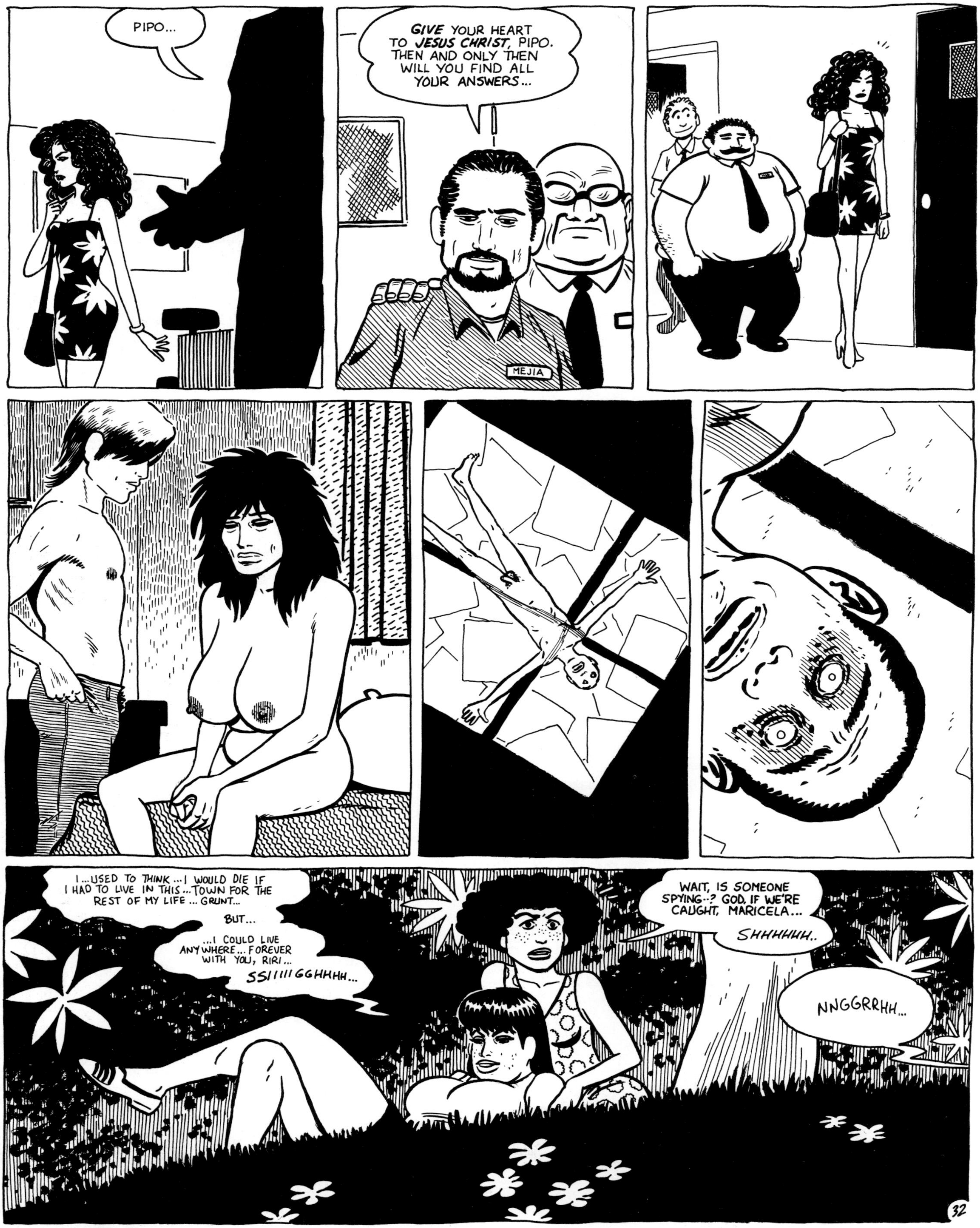
PIPO...
GIVE YOUR HEART TO JESUS CHRIST, PIPO. THEN AND ONLY THEN WILL YOU FIND ALL YOUR ANSWERS...
MEJIA
I...USED TO THINK...I WOULD DIE IF I HAD TO LIVE IN THIS...TOWN FOR THE REST OF MY LIFE...GRUNT...
BUT...
...I COULD LIVE ANYWHERE...FOREVER WITH YOU, RIRI...
SSIIIIIGGHHHH...
WAIT, IS SOMEONE SPYING--? GOD, IF WE'RE CAUGHT, MARICELA...
SHHHHHH..
NNGGRRHH...
32

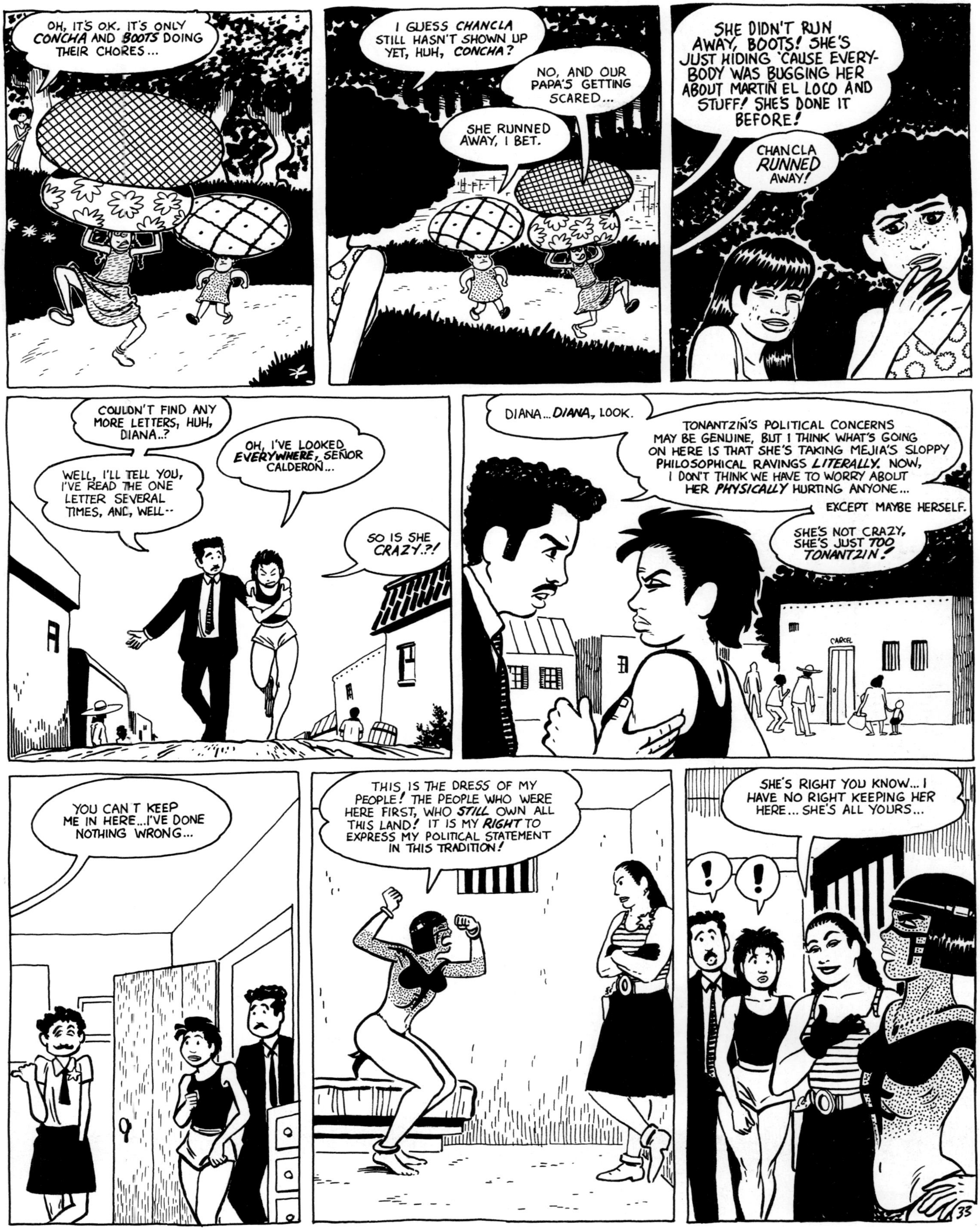
OH, IT'S O.K. IT'S ONLY CONCHA AND BOOTS DOING THEIR CHORES...
I GUESS CHANCLA STILL HASN'T SHOWN UP YET, HUH, CONCHA?
NO, AND OUR PAPA'S GETTING SCARED...
SHE RUNNED AWAY, I BET.
SHE DIDN'T RUN AWAY, BOOTS! SHE'S JUST HIDING 'CAUSE EVERY-BODY WAS BUGGING HER ABOUT MARTIN EL LOCO AND STUFF! SHE'S DONE IT BEFORE!
CHANCLA RUNNED AWAY!
COULDN'T FIND ANY MORE LETTERS, HUH, DIANA..?
OH, I'VE LOOKED EVERYWHERE, SEÑOR CALDERON...
WELL, I'LL TELL YOU, I'VE READ THE ONE LETTER SEVERAL TIMES, AND, WELL--
SO IS SHE CRAZY..?!
DIANA... DIANA, LOOK.
TONANTZIN'S POLITICAL CONCERNS MAY BE GENUINE, BUT I THINK WHAT'S GOING ON HERE IS THAT SHE'S TAKING MEJIA'S SLOPPY PHILOSOPHICAL RAVINGS LITERALLY. NOW, I DON'T THINK WE HAVE TO WORRY ABOUT HER PHYSICALLY HURTING ANYONE...
EXCEPT MAYBE HERSELF.
SHE'S NOT CRAZY, SHE'S JUST TOO TONANTZIN!
CARCEL
YOU CAN'T KEEP ME IN HERE...I'VE DONE NOTHING WRONG...
THIS IS THE DRESS OF MY PEOPLE! THE PEOPLE WHO WERE HERE FIRST, WHO STILL OWN ALL THIS LAND! IT IS MY RIGHT TO EXPRESS MY POLITICAL STATEMENT IN THIS TRADITION!
SHE'S RIGHT YOU KNOW... I HAVE NO RIGHT KEEPING HER HERE... SHE'S ALL YOURS...
!
!
33

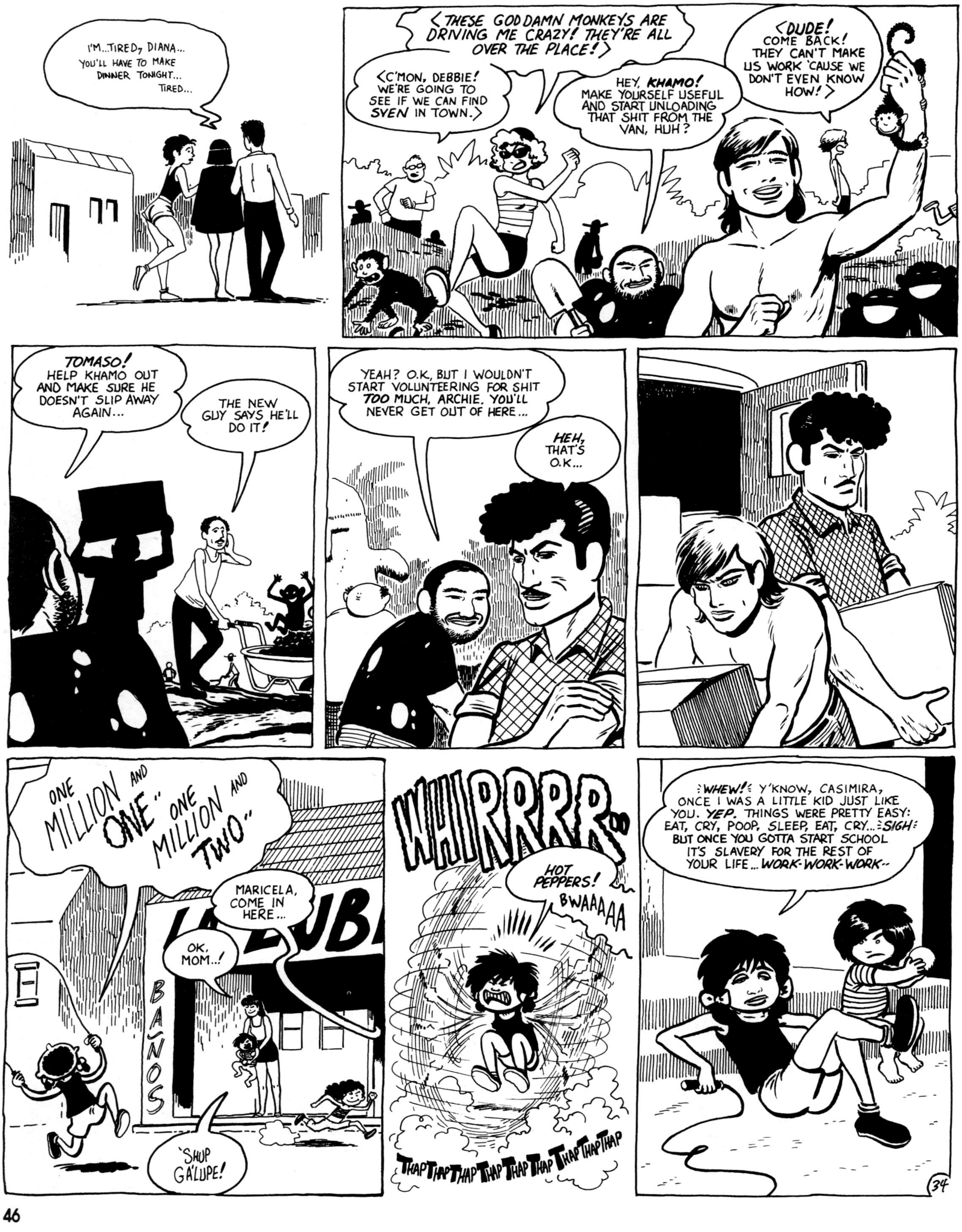
I'M...TIRED, DIANA... YOU'LL HAVE TO MAKE DINNER TONIGHT... TIRED...
<THESE GOD DAMN MONKEYS ARE DRIVING ME CRAZY! THEY'RE ALL OVER THE PLACE!>
<C'MON, DEBBIE! WE'RE GOING TO SEE IF WE CAN FIND SVEN IN TOWN.>
HEY, KHAMO! MAKE YOURSELF USEFUL AND START UNLOADING THAT SHIT FROM THE VAN, HUH?
<DUDE! COME BACK! THEY CAN'T MAKE US WORK 'CAUSE WE DON'T EVEN KNOW HOW!>
TOMASO! HELP KHAMO OUT AND MAKE SURE HE DOESN'T SLIP AWAY AGAIN...
THE NEW GUY SAYS HE'LL DO IT!
YEAH? O.K, BUT I WOULDN'T START VOLUNTEERING FOR SHIT TOO MUCH, ARCHIE. YOU'LL NEVER GET OUT OF HERE...
HEH, THAT'S O.K...
ONE MILLION AND ONE.. ONE MILLION AND TWO..
MARICELA, COME IN HERE...
OK, MOM..!
BAÑOS
'SHUP GA'LUPE!
WHIRRRR..
HOT PEPPERS!
BWAAAAAA
THAPTHAPTHAPTHAPTHAPTHAPTHAPTHAPTHAP
WHEW! Y'KNOW, CASIMIRA, ONCE I WAS A LITTLE KID JUST LIKE YOU. YEP. THINGS WERE PRETTY EASY: EAT, CRY, POOP, SLEEP, EAT, CRY... SIGH BUT ONCE YOU GOTTA START SCHOOL IT'S SLAVERY FOR THE REST OF YOUR LIFE... WORK-WORK-WORK..
34

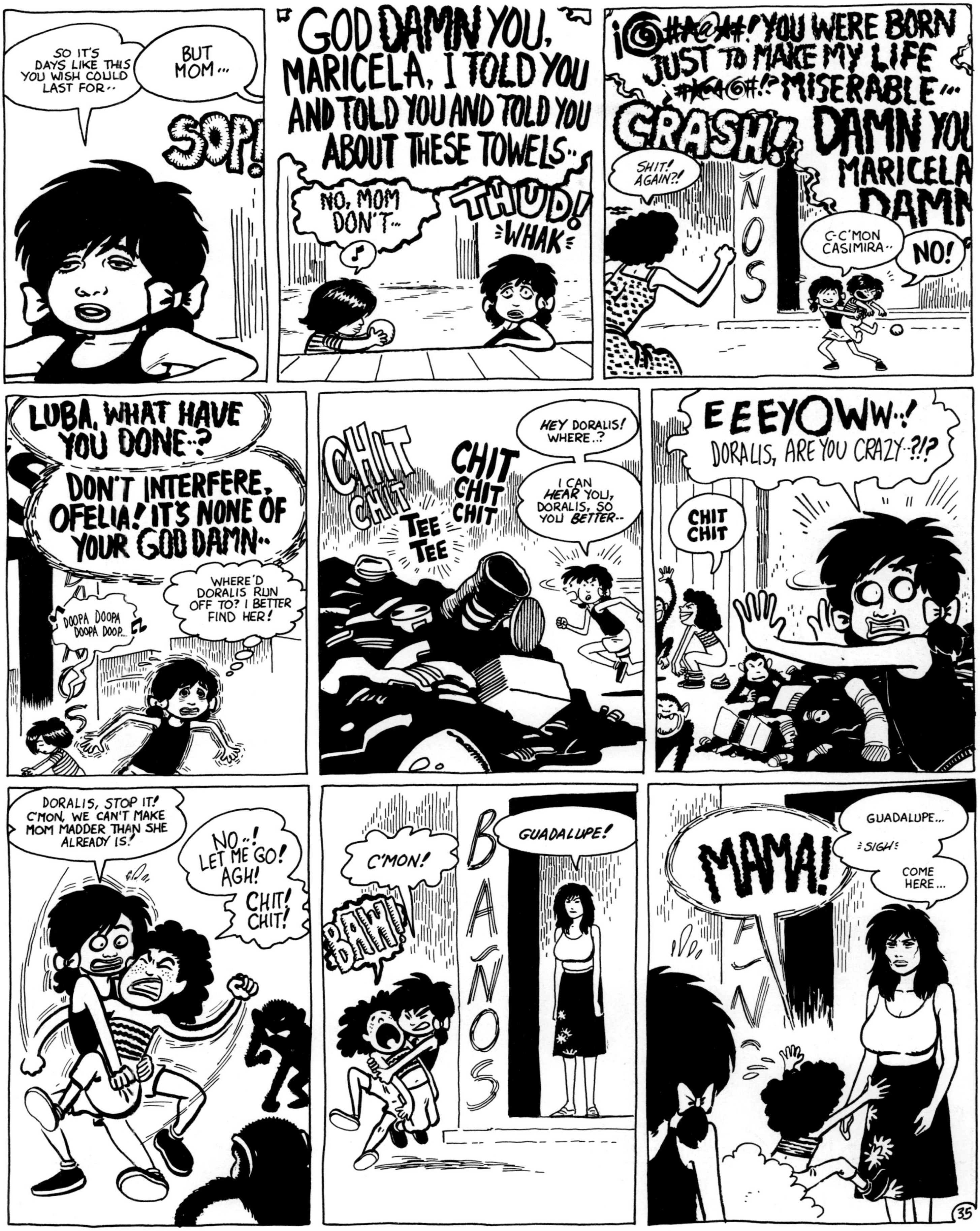
SO IT'S DAYS LIKE THIS YOU WISH COULD LAST FOR..
BUT MOM...
SOP!
"GOD DAMN YOU, MARICELA, I TOLD YOU AND TOLD YOU AND TOLD YOU ABOUT THESE TOWELS..
NO, MOM DON'T..
THUD!
WHAK
¡@#*@#!/ YOU WERE BORN JUST TO MAKE MY LIFE #*@#!? MISERABLE"...
CRASH!
DAMN YOU MARICELA DAMN
SHIT! AGAIN?!
C-C'MON CASIMIRA..
NO!
LUBA, WHAT HAVE YOU DONE..?
DON'T INTERFERE, OFELIA! IT'S NONE OF YOUR GOD DAMN..
WHERE'D DORALIS RUN OFF TO? I BETTER FIND HER!
DOOPA DOOPA DOOPA DOOP...
CHIT CHIT
TEE TEE
CHIT CHIT CHIT
HEY DORALIS! WHERE..?
I CAN HEAR YOU, DORALIS, SO YOU BETTER..
EEEYOWW..!
DORALIS, ARE YOU CRAZY..?!?
CHIT CHIT
DORALIS, STOP IT! C'MON, WE CAN'T MAKE MOM MADDER THAN SHE ALREADY IS!
NO..! LET ME GO! AGH!
CHIT! CHIT!
C'MON!
BAM!
GUADALUPE!
BAÑOS
MAMA!
GUADALUPE...
SIGH
COME HERE...
35

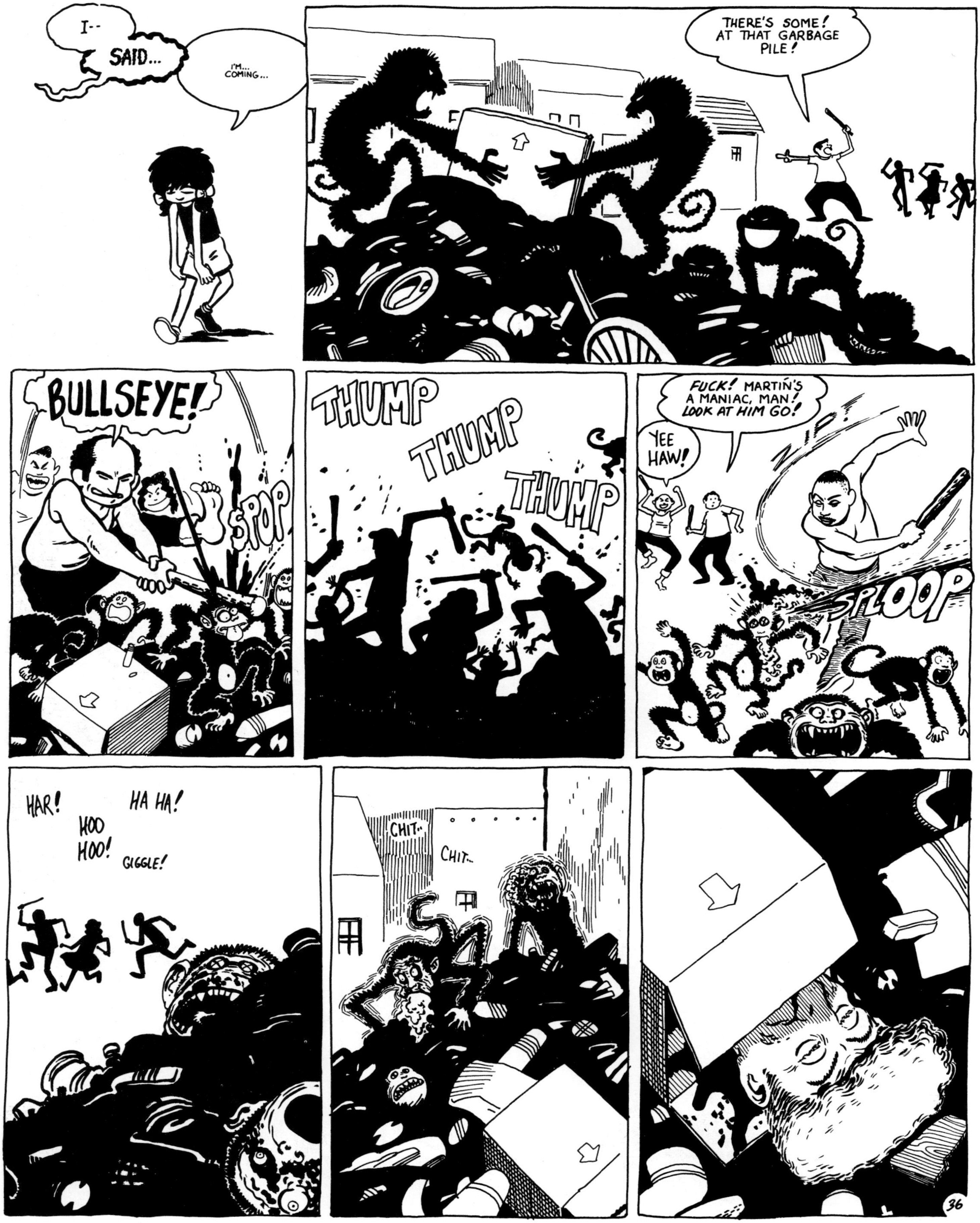
I--
SAID...
I'M... COMING...
THERE'S SOME! AT THAT GARBAGE PILE!
BULLSEYE!
SPOP
THUMP
THUMP
THUMP
FUCK! MARTÍN'S A MANIAC, MAN! LOOK AT HIM GO!
YEE HAW!
ZIP!
SPLOOP
HAR!
HOO HOO!
HA HA!
GIGGLE!
CHIT..
CHIT..
36

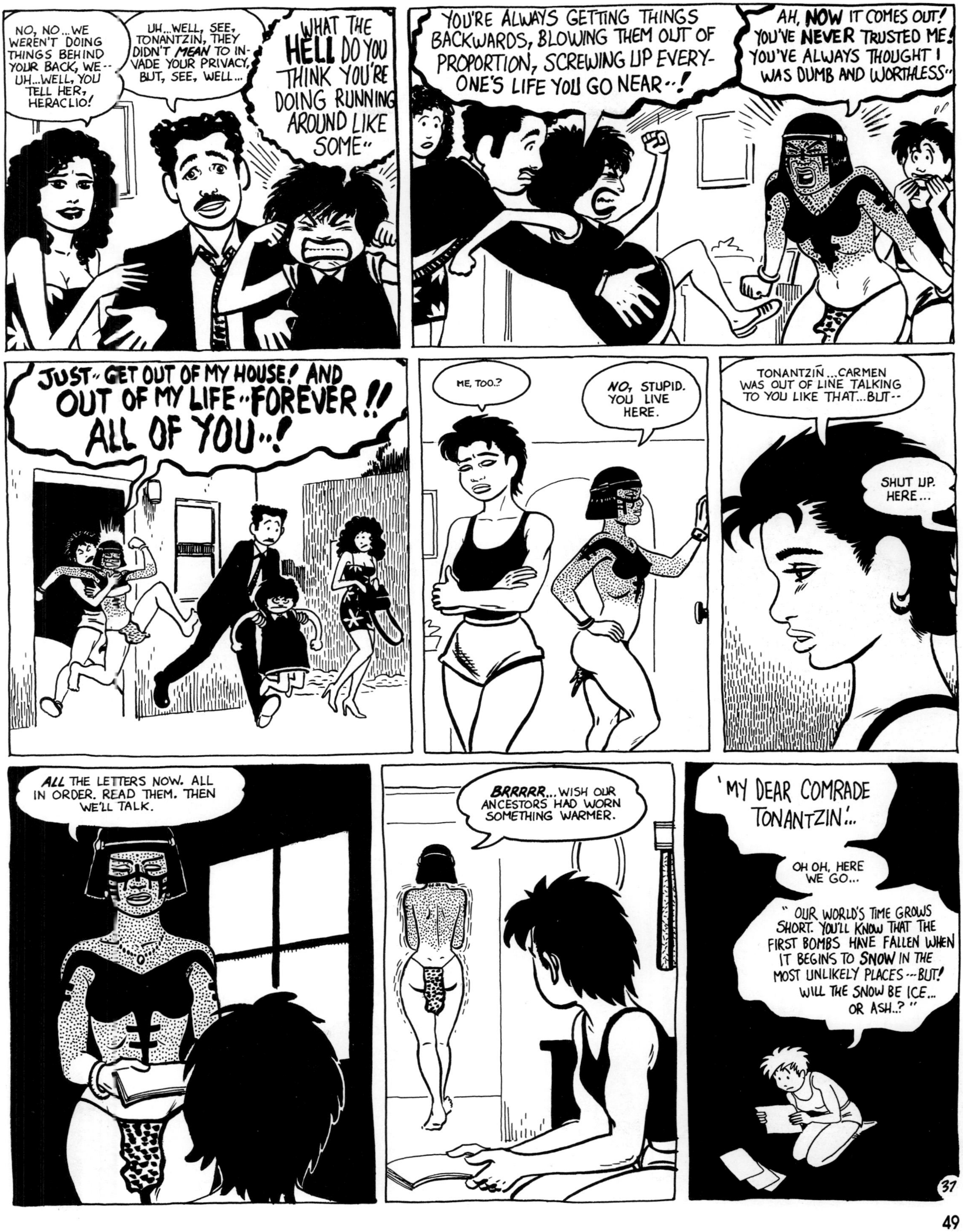
NO, NO...WE WEREN'T DOING THINGS BEHIND YOUR BACK, WE-- UH...WELL, YOU TELL HER, HERACLIO!
UH...WELL, SEE, TONANTZIN, THEY DIDN'T MEAN TO INVADE YOUR PRIVACY, BUT, SEE, WELL...
WHAT THE HELL DO YOU THINK YOU'RE DOING RUNNING AROUND LIKE SOME--
YOU'RE ALWAYS GETTING THINGS BACKWARDS, BLOWING THEM OUT OF PROPORTION, SCREWING UP EVERYONE'S LIFE YOU GO NEAR--!
AH, NOW IT COMES OUT! YOU'VE NEVER TRUSTED ME! YOU'VE ALWAYS THOUGHT I WAS DUMB AND WORTHLESS--
JUST-- GET OUT OF MY HOUSE! AND OUT OF MY LIFE--FOREVER!! ALL OF YOU--!
ME, TOO.?
NO, STUPID. YOU LIVE HERE.
TONANTZÍN...CARMEN WAS OUT OF LINE TALKING TO YOU LIKE THAT...BUT--
SHUT UP. HERE...
ALL THE LETTERS NOW. ALL IN ORDER. READ THEM. THEN WE'LL TALK.
BRRRRR...WISH OUR ANCESTORS HAD WORN SOMETHING WARMER.
'MY DEAR COMRADE TONANTZIN'...
OH OH, HERE WE GO...
" OUR WORLD'S TIME GROWS SHORT. YOU'LL KNOW THAT THE FIRST BOMBS HAVE FALLEN WHEN IT BEGINS TO SNOW IN THE MOST UNLIKELY PLACES---BUT! WILL THE SNOW BE ICE... OR ASH..? "
37

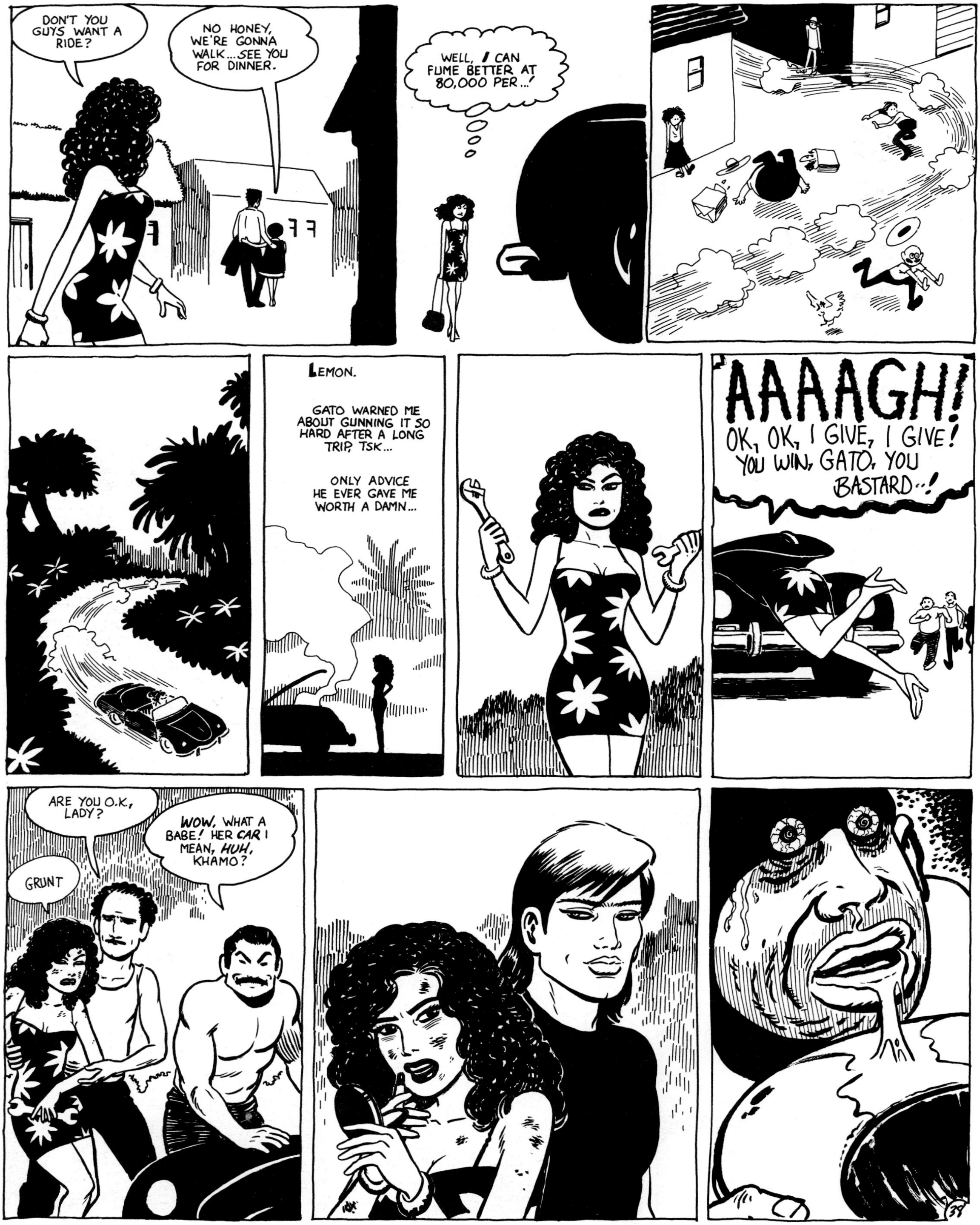
DON'T YOU GUYS WANT A RIDE?
NO HONEY, WE'RE GONNA WALK...SEE YOU FOR DINNER.
WELL, I CAN FUME BETTER AT 80,000 PER...!
LEMON.
GATO WARNED ME ABOUT GUNNING IT SO HARD AFTER A LONG TRIP, TSK...
ONLY ADVICE HE EVER GAVE ME WORTH A DAMN...
AAAAGH!
OK, OK, I GIVE, I GIVE! YOU WIN, GATO, YOU BASTARD..!
ARE YOU O.K., LADY?
GRUNT
WOW, WHAT A BABE! HER CAR I MEAN, HUH, KHAMO?

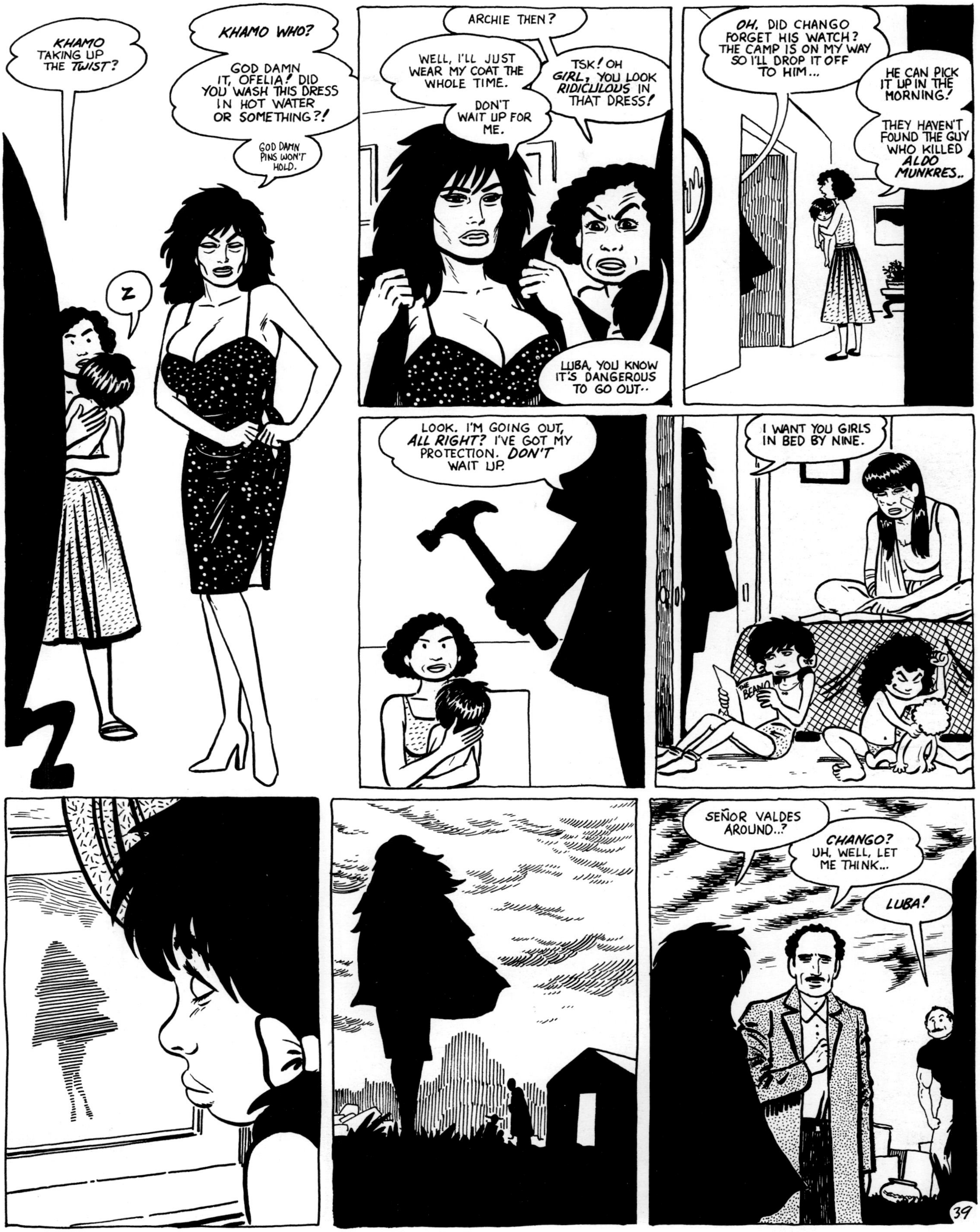
KHAMO TAKING UP THE TWIST?
KHAMO WHO?
GOD DAMN IT, OFELIA! DID YOU WASH THIS DRESS IN HOT WATER OR SOMETHING?!
GOD DAMN PINS WON'T HOLD.
Z
ARCHIE THEN?
WELL, I'LL JUST WEAR MY COAT THE WHOLE TIME.
DON'T WAIT UP FOR ME.
TSK! OH GIRL, YOU LOOK RIDICULOUS IN THAT DRESS!
LUBA, YOU KNOW IT'S DANGEROUS TO GO OUT..
OH, DID CHANGO FORGET HIS WATCH? THE CAMP IS ON MY WAY SO I'LL DROP IT OFF TO HIM...
HE CAN PICK IT UP IN THE MORNING!
THEY HAVEN'T FOUND THE GUY WHO KILLED ALDO MUNKRES..
LOOK. I'M GOING OUT, ALL RIGHT? I'VE GOT MY PROTECTION. DON'T WAIT UP.
I WANT YOU GIRLS IN BED BY NINE.
THE BEANO
SEÑOR VALDES AROUND..?
CHANGO? UH, WELL, LET ME THINK...
LUBA!
39

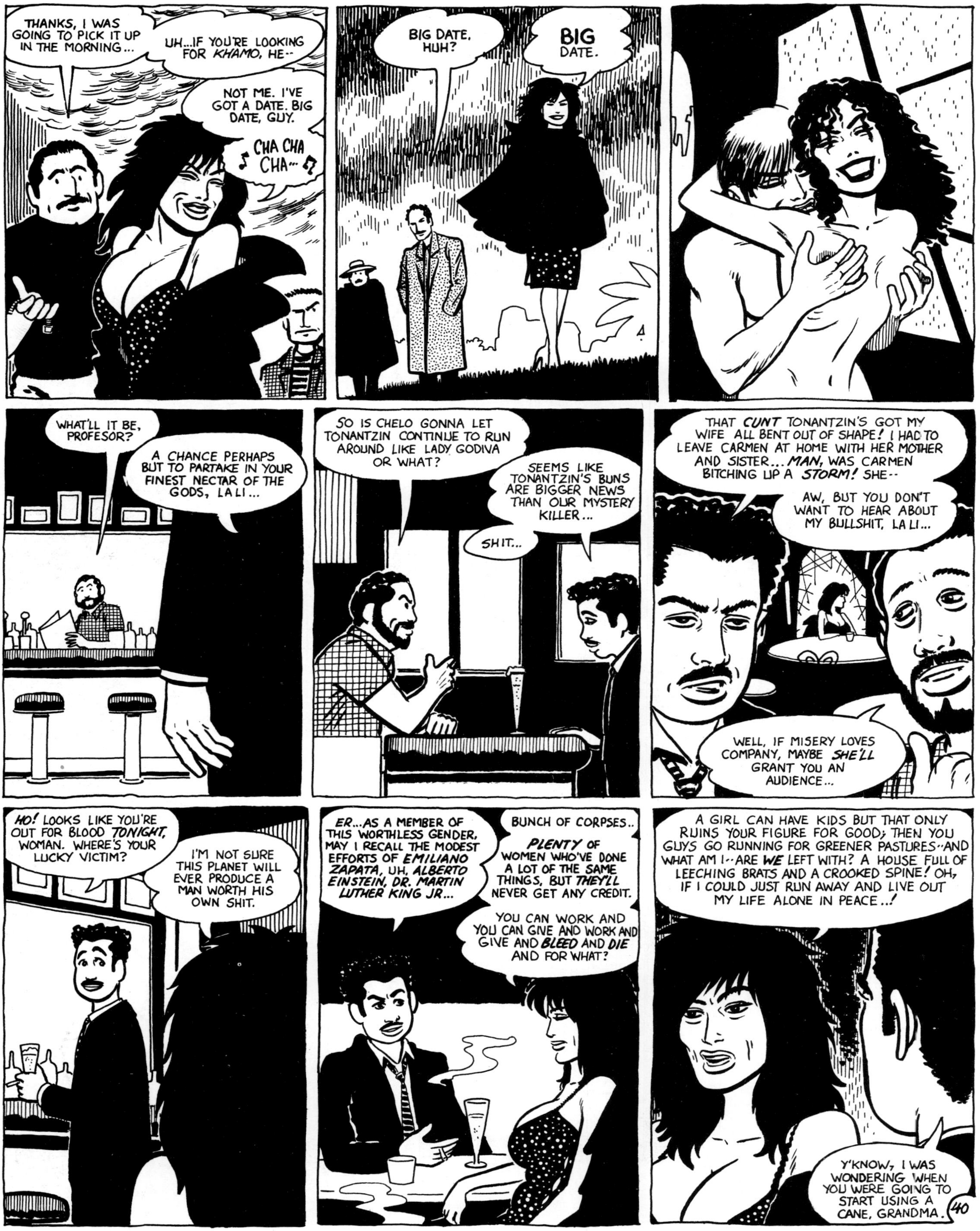

THANKS, I WAS GOING TO PICK IT UP IN THE MORNING...
UH...IF YOU'RE LOOKING FOR KHAMO, HE--
NOT ME. I'VE GOT A DATE. BIG DATE, GUY.
CHA CHA CHA...
BIG DATE, HUH?
BIG DATE.
WHAT'LL IT BE, PROFESOR?
A CHANCE PERHAPS BUT TO PARTAKE IN YOUR FINEST NECTAR OF THE GODS, LA LI...
SO IS CHELO GONNA LET TONANTZIN CONTINUE TO RUN AROUND LIKE LADY GODIVA OR WHAT?
SEEMS LIKE TONANTZIN'S BUNS ARE BIGGER NEWS THAN OUR MYSTERY KILLER...
SHIT...
THAT CUNT TONANTZIN'S GOT MY WIFE ALL BENT OUT OF SHAPE! I HAD TO LEAVE CARMEN AT HOME WITH HER MOTHER AND SISTER... MAN, WAS CARMEN BITCHING UP A STORM! SHE--
AW, BUT YOU DON'T WANT TO HEAR ABOUT MY BULLSHIT, LA LI...
WELL, IF MISERY LOVES COMPANY, MAYBE SHE'LL GRANT YOU AN AUDIENCE...
HO! LOOKS LIKE YOU'RE OUT FOR BLOOD TONIGHT, WOMAN. WHERE'S YOUR LUCKY VICTIM?
I'M NOT SURE THIS PLANET WILL EVER PRODUCE A MAN WORTH HIS OWN SHIT.
ER...AS A MEMBER OF THIS WORTHLESS GENDER, MAY I RECALL THE MODEST EFFORTS OF EMILIANO ZAPATA, UH, ALBERTO EINSTEIN, DR. MARTIN LUTHER KING JR...
BUNCH OF CORPSES..
PLENTY OF WOMEN WHO'VE DONE A LOT OF THE SAME THINGS, BUT THEY'LL NEVER GET ANY CREDIT.
YOU CAN WORK AND YOU CAN GIVE AND WORK AND GIVE AND BLEED AND DIE AND FOR WHAT?
A GIRL CAN HAVE KIDS BUT THAT ONLY RUINS YOUR FIGURE FOR GOOD; THEN YOU GUYS GO RUNNING FOR GREENER PASTURES--AND WHAT AM I--ARE WE LEFT WITH? A HOUSE FULL OF LEECHING BRATS AND A CROOKED SPINE! OH, IF I COULD JUST RUN AWAY AND LIVE OUT MY LIFE ALONE IN PEACE..!
Y'KNOW, I WAS WONDERING WHEN YOU WERE GOING TO START USING A CANE, GRANDMA.
40

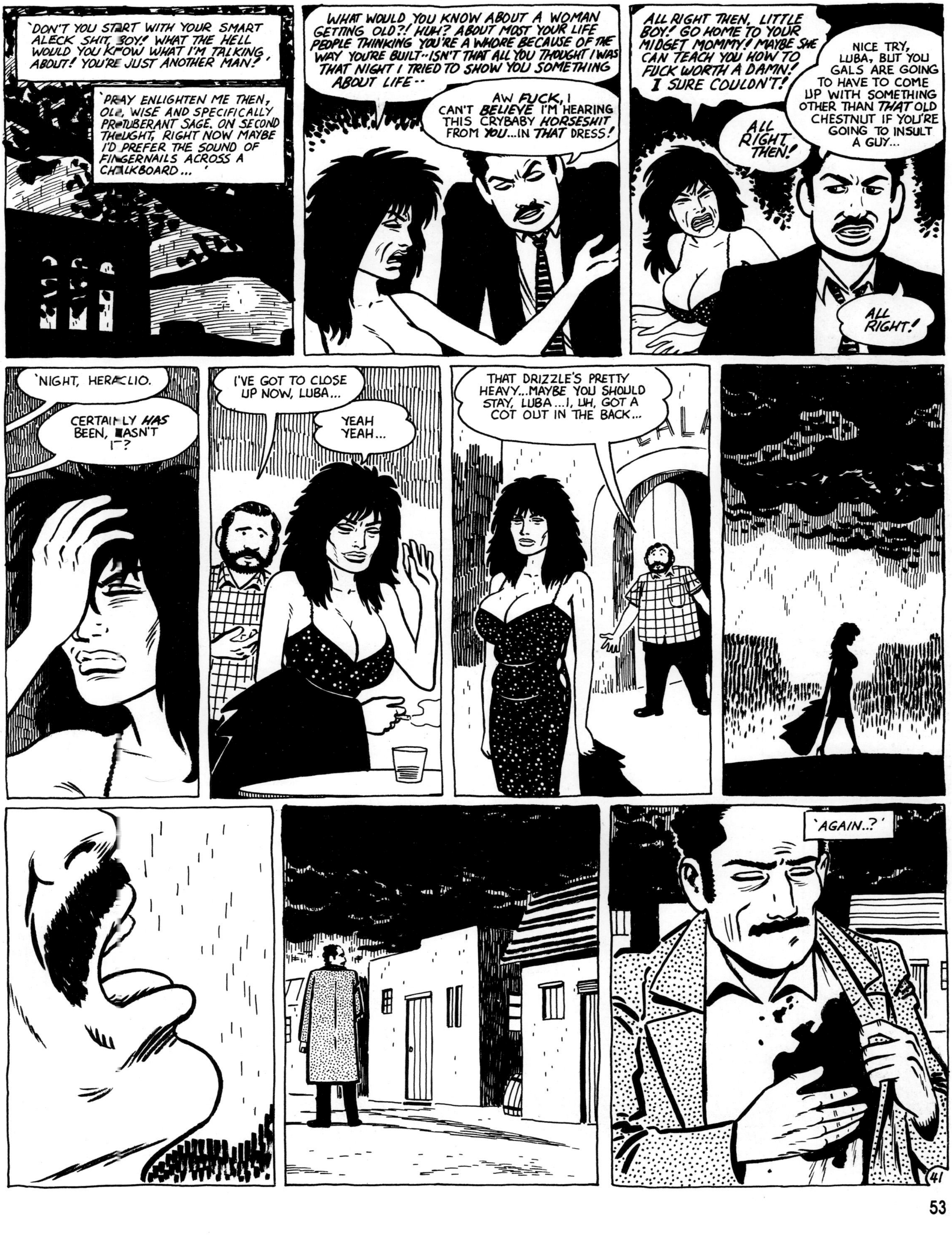
`DON'T YOU START WITH YOUR SMART ALECK SHIT, BOY! WHAT THE HELL WOULD YOU KNOW WHAT I'M TALKING ABOUT! YOU'RE JUST ANOTHER MAN!'
`PRAY ENLIGHTEN ME THEN, OLD, WISE AND SPECIFICALLY PROTUBERANT SAGE. ON SECOND THOUGHT, RIGHT NOW MAYBE I'D PREFER THE SOUND OF FINGERNAILS ACROSS A CHALKBOARD...'
WHAT WOULD YOU KNOW ABOUT A WOMAN GETTING OLD?! HUH? ABOUT MOST YOUR LIFE PEOPLE THINKING YOU'RE A WHORE BECAUSE OF THE WAY YOU'RE BUILT--ISN'T THAT ALL YOU THOUGHT I WAS THAT NIGHT I TRIED TO SHOW YOU SOMETHING ABOUT LIFE--
AW FUCK, I CAN'T BELIEVE I'M HEARING THIS CRYBABY HORSESHIT FROM YOU...IN THAT DRESS!
ALL RIGHT THEN, LITTLE BOY! GO HOME TO YOUR MIDGET MOMMY! MAYBE SHE CAN TEACH YOU HOW TO FUCK WORTH A DAMN! I SURE COULDN'T!
NICE TRY, LUBA, BUT YOU GALS ARE GOING TO HAVE TO COME UP WITH SOMETHING OTHER THAN THAT OLD CHESTNUT IF YOU'RE GOING TO INSULT A GUY...
ALL RIGHT, THEN!
ALL RIGHT!
`NIGHT, HERACLIO.
CERTAINLY HAS BEEN, HASN'T IT?
I'VE GOT TO CLOSE UP NOW, LUBA...
YEAH YEAH...
THAT DRIZZLE'S PRETTY HEAVY...MAYBE YOU SHOULD STAY, LUBA...I, UH, GOT A COT OUT IN THE BACK...
`AGAIN..?'
41

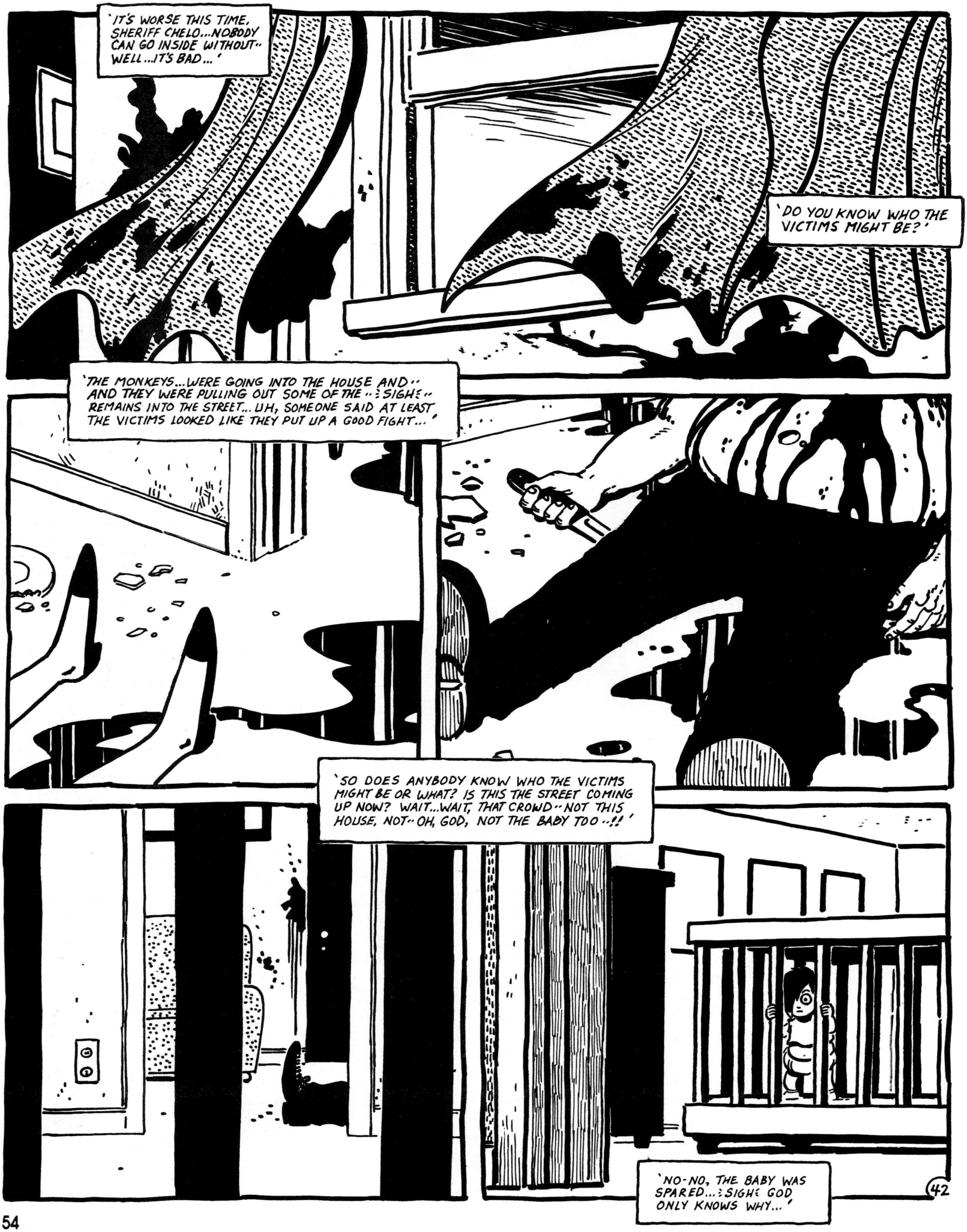
'IT'S WORSE THIS TIME, SHERIFF CHELO... NOBODY CAN GO INSIDE WITHOUT.. WELL... IT'S BAD...'
'DO YOU KNOW WHO THE VICTIMS MIGHT BE?'
'THE MONKEYS... WERE GOING INTO THE HOUSE AND.. AND THEY WERE PULLING OUT SOME OF THE .. :SIGH: .. REMAINS INTO THE STREET... UH, SOMEONE SAID AT LEAST THE VICTIMS LOOKED LIKE THEY PUT UP A GOOD FIGHT...'
'SO DOES ANYBODY KNOW WHO THE VICTIMS MIGHT BE OR WHAT? IS THIS THE STREET COMING UP NOW? WAIT... WAIT, THAT CROWD.. NOT THIS HOUSE, NOT.. OH, GOD, NOT THE BABY TOO..!!'
'NO-NO, THE BABY WAS SPARED... :SIGH: GOD ONLY KNOWS WHY...'
42

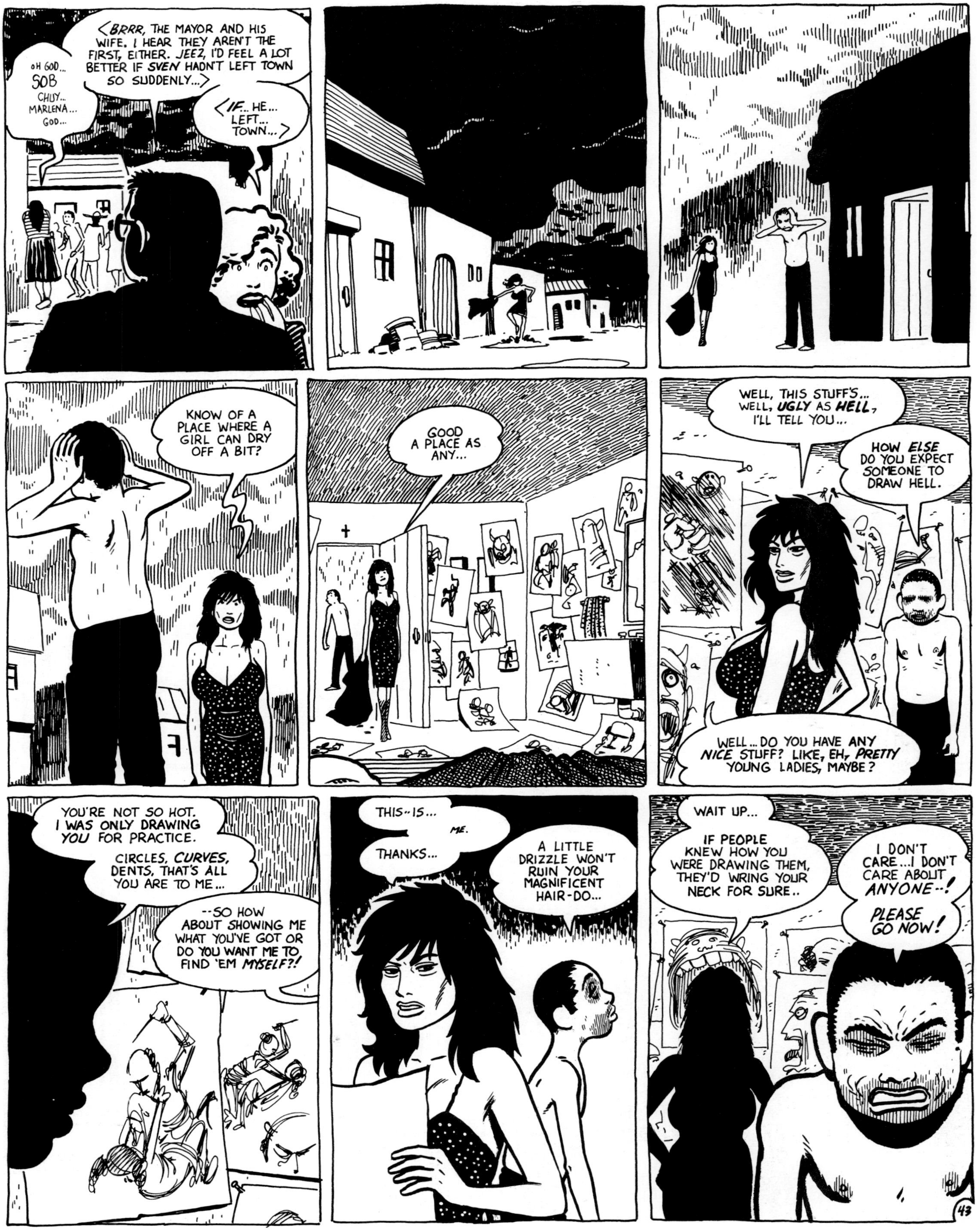
OH GOD... SOB CHUY... MARLENA... GOD...
<BRRR, THE MAYOR AND HIS WIFE. I HEAR THEY AREN'T THE FIRST, EITHER. JEEZ, I'D FEEL A LOT BETTER IF SVEN HADN'T LEFT TOWN SO SUDDENLY...>
<IF... HE... LEFT... TOWN...>
KNOW OF A PLACE WHERE A GIRL CAN DRY OFF A BIT?
GOOD A PLACE AS ANY...
WELL, THIS STUFF'S... WELL, UGLY AS HELL, I'LL TELL YOU...
HOW ELSE DO YOU EXPECT SOMEONE TO DRAW HELL.
WELL... DO YOU HAVE ANY NICE STUFF? LIKE, EH, PRETTY YOUNG LADIES, MAYBE?
YOU'RE NOT SO HOT. I WAS ONLY DRAWING YOU FOR PRACTICE.
CIRCLES, CURVES, DENTS, THAT'S ALL YOU ARE TO ME...
--SO HOW ABOUT SHOWING ME WHAT YOU'VE GOT OR DO YOU WANT ME TO FIND 'EM MYSELF?!
THIS-- IS... ME.
THANKS...
A LITTLE DRIZZLE WON'T RUIN YOUR MAGNIFICENT HAIR-DO...
WAIT UP...
IF PEOPLE KNEW HOW YOU WERE DRAWING THEM, THEY'D WRING YOUR NECK FOR SURE..
I DON'T CARE... I DON'T CARE ABOUT ANYONE--!
PLEASE GO NOW!
43

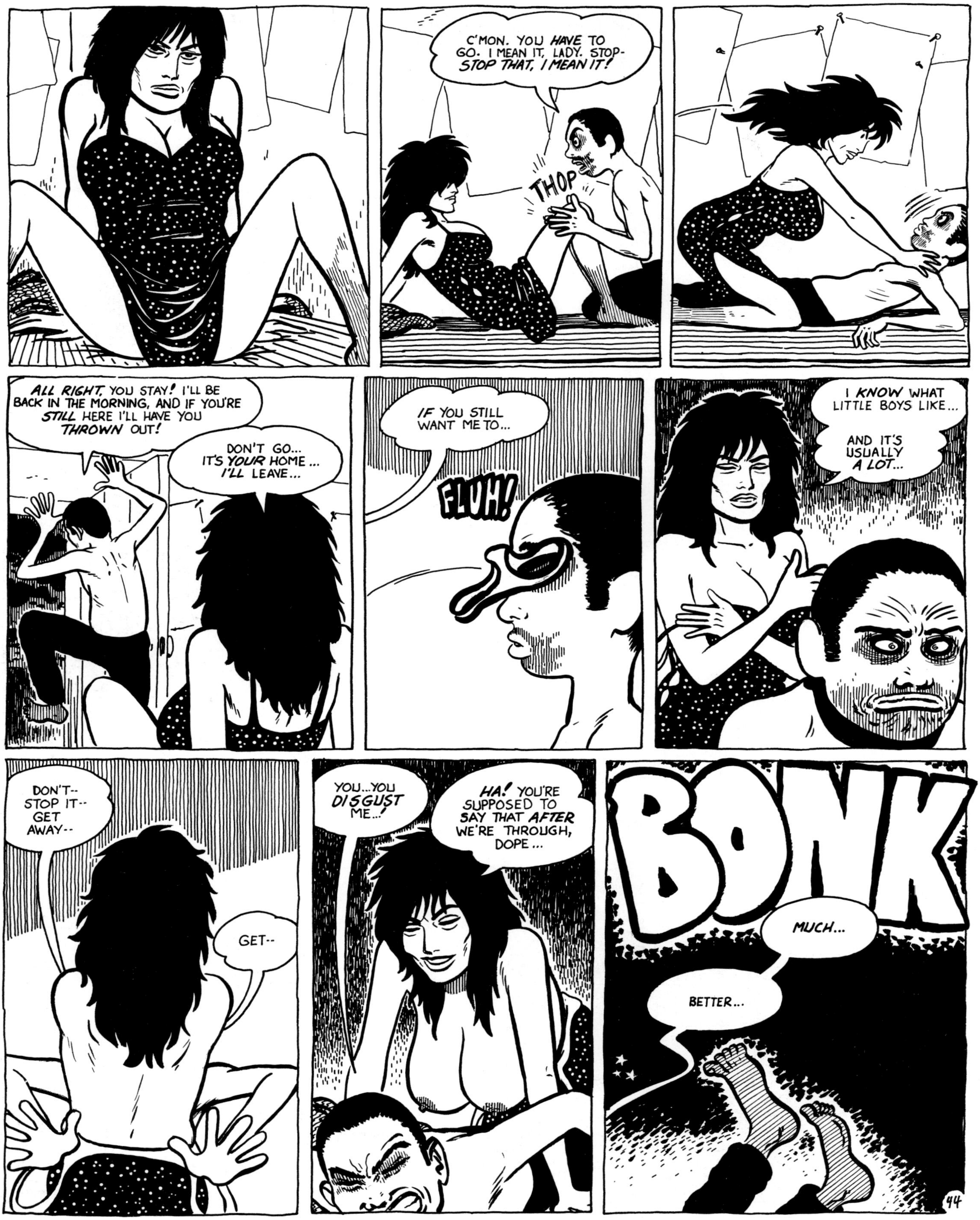
C'MON. YOU HAVE TO GO. I MEAN IT, LADY. STOP- STOP THAT, I MEAN IT!
THOP
ALL RIGHT, YOU STAY! I'LL BE BACK IN THE MORNING, AND IF YOU'RE STILL HERE I'LL HAVE YOU THROWN OUT!
DON'T GO... IT'S YOUR HOME... I'LL LEAVE...
IF YOU STILL WANT ME TO...
FLUH!
I KNOW WHAT LITTLE BOYS LIKE...
AND IT'S USUALLY A LOT...
DON'T-- STOP IT-- GET AWAY--
GET--
YOU...YOU DISGUST ME...!
HA! YOU'RE SUPPOSED TO SAY THAT AFTER WE'RE THROUGH, DOPE...
BONK
MUCH...
BETTER...
44

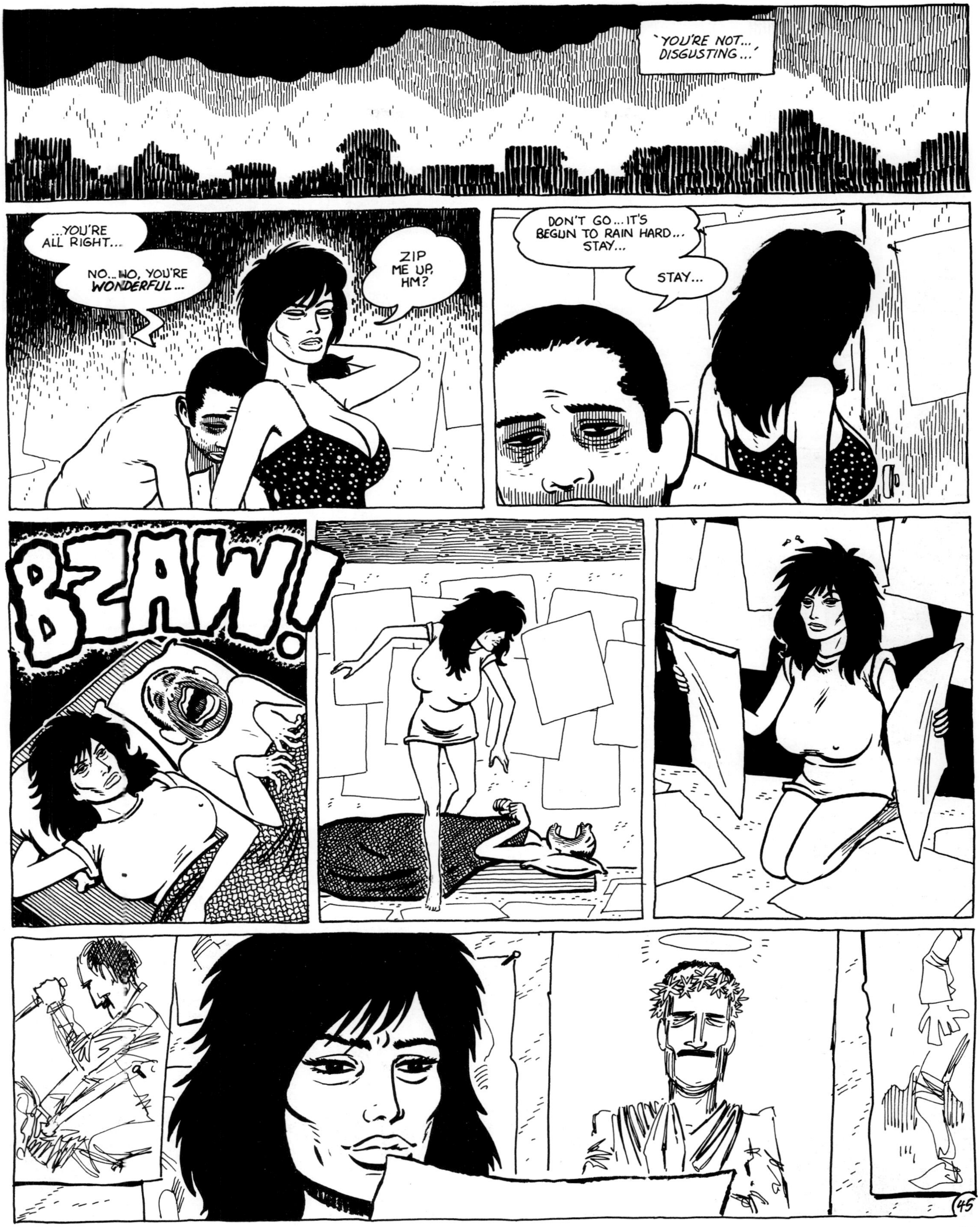
`YOU'RE NOT...,
DISGUSTING...'
...YOU'RE ALL RIGHT...
NO...NO, YOU'RE WONDERFUL...
ZIP ME UP, HM?
DON'T GO...IT'S BEGUN TO RAIN HARD... STAY...
STAY...
BZAW!
45

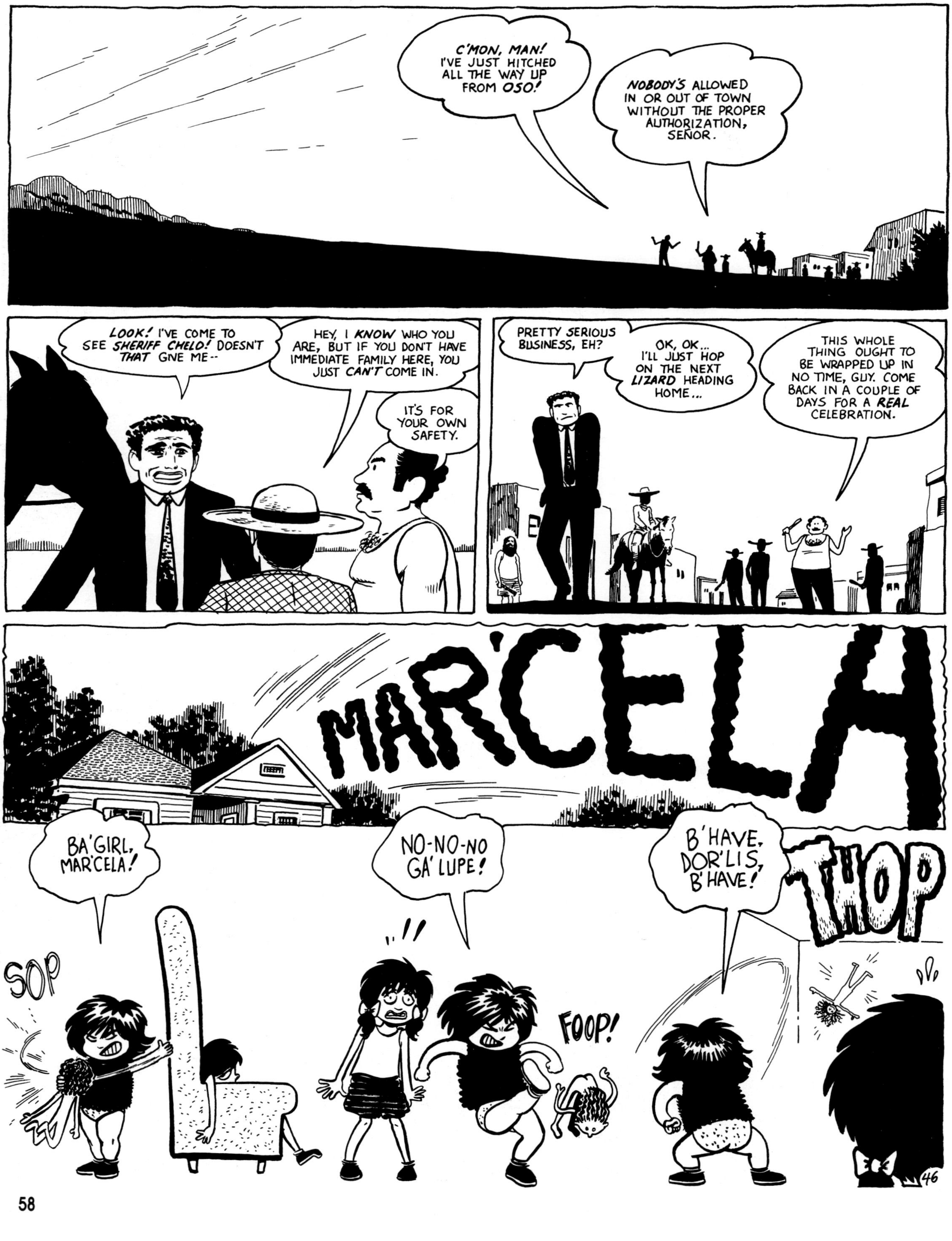
C'MON, MAN! I'VE JUST HITCHED ALL THE WAY UP FROM OSO!
NOBODY'S ALLOWED IN OR OUT OF TOWN WITHOUT THE PROPER AUTHORIZATION, SEÑOR.
LOOK! I'VE COME TO SEE SHERIFF CHELO! DOESN'T THAT GIVE ME--
HEY, I KNOW WHO YOU ARE, BUT IF YOU DON'T HAVE IMMEDIATE FAMILY HERE, YOU JUST CAN'T COME IN.
IT'S FOR YOUR OWN SAFETY.
PRETTY SERIOUS BUSINESS, EH?
OK, OK... I'LL JUST HOP ON THE NEXT LIZARD HEADING HOME...
THIS WHOLE THING OUGHT TO BE WRAPPED UP IN NO TIME, GUY. COME BACK IN A COUPLE OF DAYS FOR A REAL CELEBRATION.
MAR'CELA
BA'GIRL, MAR'CELA!
SOP
NO-NO-NO GA'LUPE!
FOOP!
B'HAVE, DOR'LIS, B'HAVE!
THOP
46

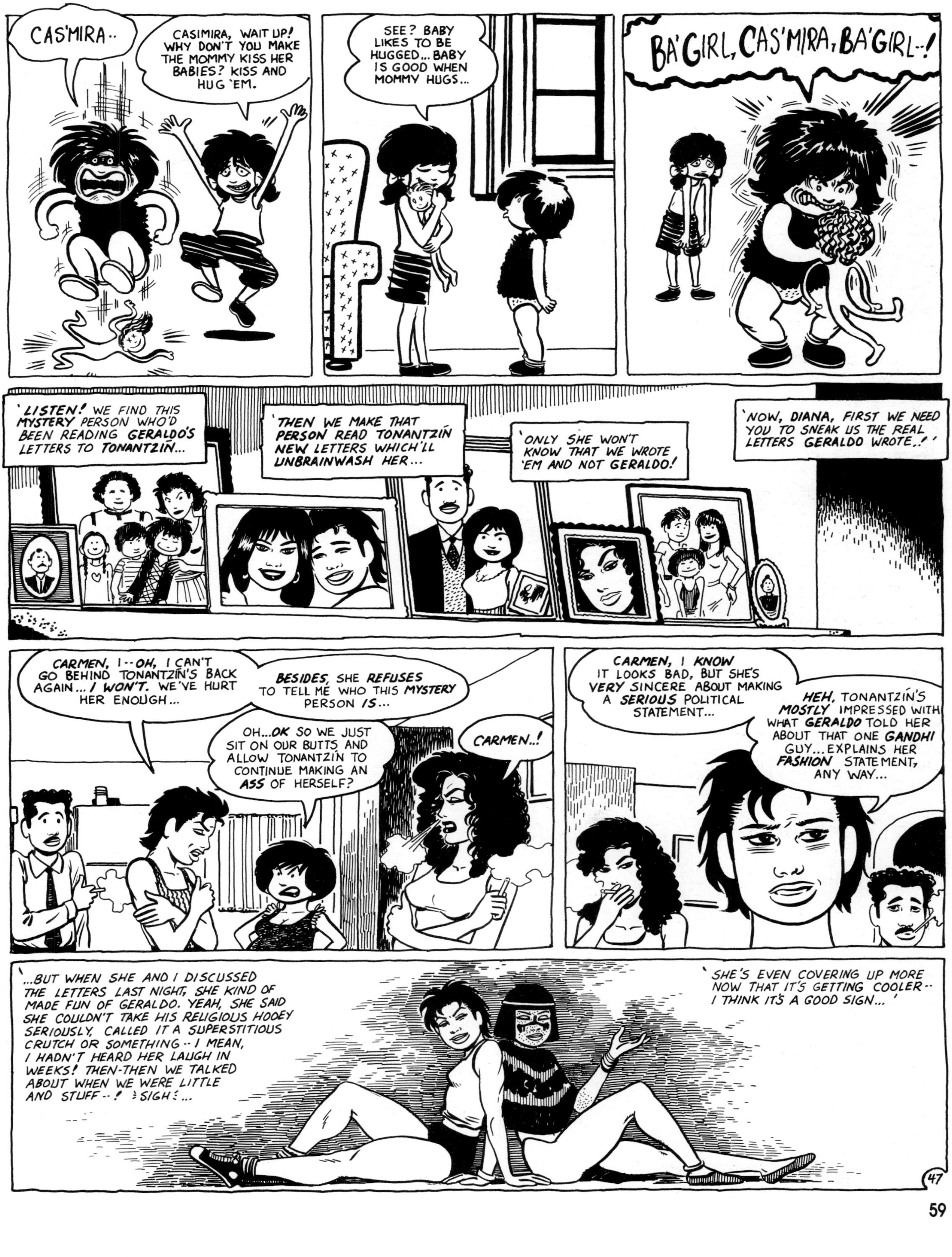
CAS'MIRA..
CASIMIRA, WAIT UP! WHY DON'T YOU MAKE THE MOMMY KISS HER BABIES? KISS AND HUG 'EM.
SEE? BABY LIKES TO BE HUGGED... BABY IS GOOD WHEN MOMMY HUGS...
BA'GIRL, CAS'MIRA, BA'GIRL..!
'LISTEN! WE FIND THIS MYSTERY PERSON WHO'D BEEN READING GERALDO'S LETTERS TO TONANTZIN...
'THEN WE MAKE THAT PERSON READ TONANTZIN NEW LETTERS WHICH'LL UNBRAINWASH HER...
'ONLY SHE WON'T KNOW THAT WE WROTE 'EM AND NOT GERALDO!
'NOW, DIANA, FIRST WE NEED YOU TO SNEAK US THE REAL LETTERS GERALDO WROTE..!'
CARMEN, I--OH, I CAN'T GO BEHIND TONANTZIN'S BACK AGAIN... I WON'T. WE'VE HURT HER ENOUGH...
BESIDES, SHE REFUSES TO TELL ME WHO THIS MYSTERY PERSON IS...
OH...OK SO WE JUST SIT ON OUR BUTTS AND ALLOW TONANTZIN TO CONTINUE MAKING AN ASS OF HERSELF?
CARMEN..!
CARMEN, I KNOW IT LOOKS BAD, BUT SHE'S VERY SINCERE ABOUT MAKING A SERIOUS POLITICAL STATEMENT...
HEH, TONANTZIN'S MOSTLY IMPRESSED WITH WHAT GERALDO TOLD HER ABOUT THAT ONE GANDHI GUY... EXPLAINS HER FASHION STATEMENT, ANY WAY...
'...BUT WHEN SHE AND I DISCUSSED THE LETTERS LAST NIGHT, SHE KIND OF MADE FUN OF GERALDO. YEAH, SHE SAID SHE COULDN'T TAKE HIS RELIGIOUS HOOEY SERIOUSLY, CALLED IT A SUPERSTITIOUS CRUTCH OR SOMETHING -- I MEAN, I HADN'T HEARD HER LAUGH IN WEEKS! THEN-THEN WE TALKED ABOUT WHEN WE WERE LITTLE AND STUFF --! ≥SIGH≤...
'SHE'S EVEN COVERING UP MORE NOW THAT IT'S GETTING COOLER-- I THINK IT'S A GOOD SIGN...'
47

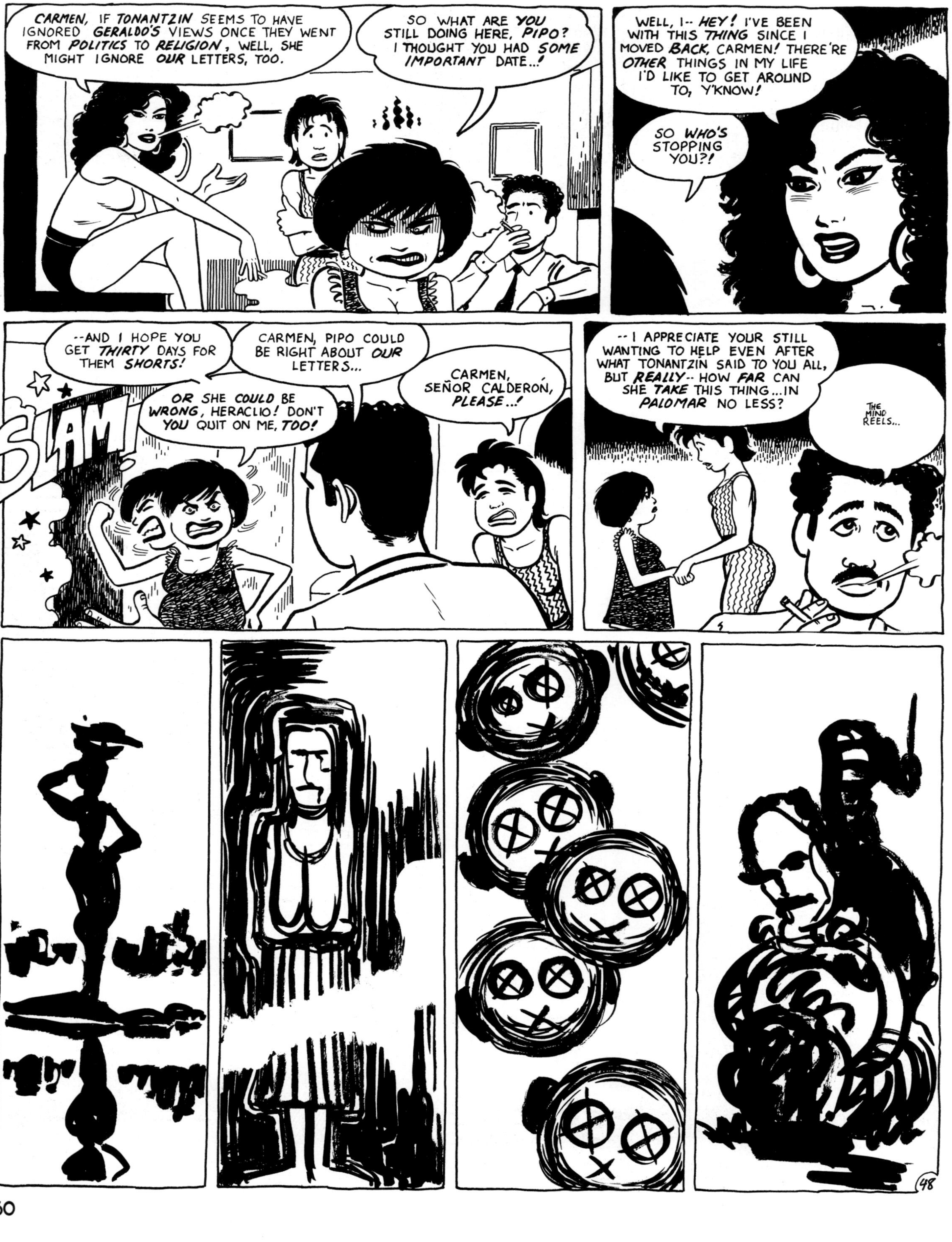
CARMEN, IF TONANTZIN SEEMS TO HAVE IGNORED GERALDO'S VIEWS ONCE THEY WENT FROM POLITICS TO RELIGION, WELL, SHE MIGHT IGNORE OUR LETTERS, TOO.
SO WHAT ARE YOU STILL DOING HERE, PIPO? I THOUGHT YOU HAD SOME IMPORTANT DATE...!
WELL, I-- HEY! I'VE BEEN WITH THIS THING SINCE I MOVED BACK, CARMEN! THERE'RE OTHER THINGS IN MY LIFE I'D LIKE TO GET AROUND TO, Y'KNOW!
SO WHO'S STOPPING YOU?!
--AND I HOPE YOU GET THIRTY DAYS FOR THEM SHORTS!
CARMEN, PIPO COULD BE RIGHT ABOUT OUR LETTERS...
SLAM!
OR SHE COULD BE WRONG, HERACLIO! DON'T YOU QUIT ON ME, TOO!
CARMEN, SEÑOR CALDERÓN, PLEASE...!
--I APPRECIATE YOUR STILL WANTING TO HELP EVEN AFTER WHAT TONANTZIN SAID TO YOU ALL, BUT REALLY-- HOW FAR CAN SHE TAKE THIS THING...IN PALOMAR NO LESS?
THE MIND REELS...
48

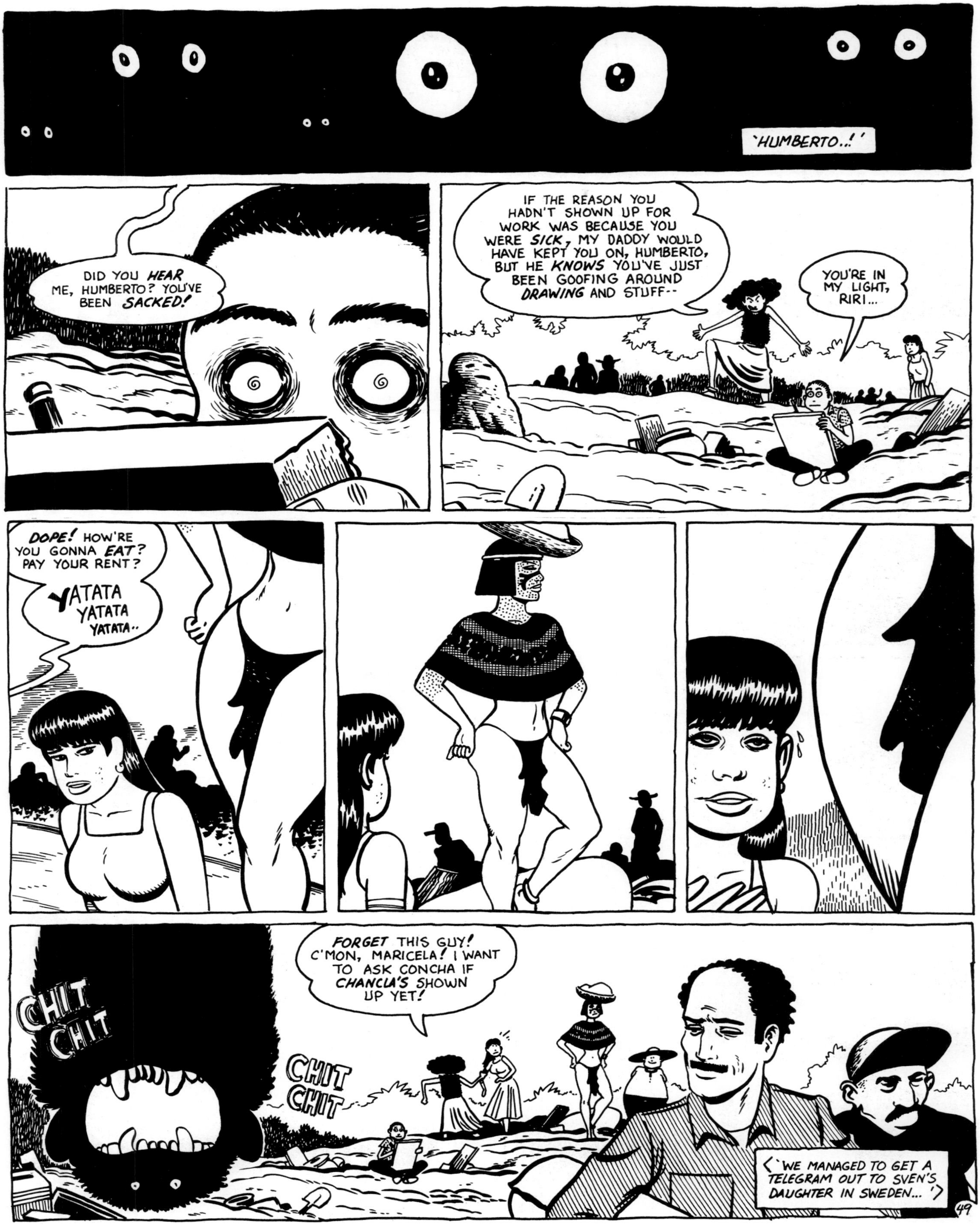

`HUMBERTO..!'
DID YOU HEAR ME, HUMBERTO? YOU'VE BEEN SACKED!
IF THE REASON YOU HADN'T SHOWN UP FOR WORK WAS BECAUSE YOU WERE SICK, MY DADDY WOULD HAVE KEPT YOU ON, HUMBERTO, BUT HE KNOWS YOU'VE JUST BEEN GOOFING AROUND DRAWING AND STUFF--
YOU'RE IN MY LIGHT, RIRI...
DOPE! HOW'RE YOU GONNA EAT? PAY YOUR RENT?
YATATA YATATA YATATA..
FORGET THIS GUY! C'MON, MARICELA! I WANT TO ASK CONCHA IF CHANCLA'S SHOWN UP YET!
CHIT CHIT
CHIT CHIT
<`WE MANAGED TO GET A TELEGRAM OUT TO SVEN'S DAUGHTER IN SWEDEN...'>
49

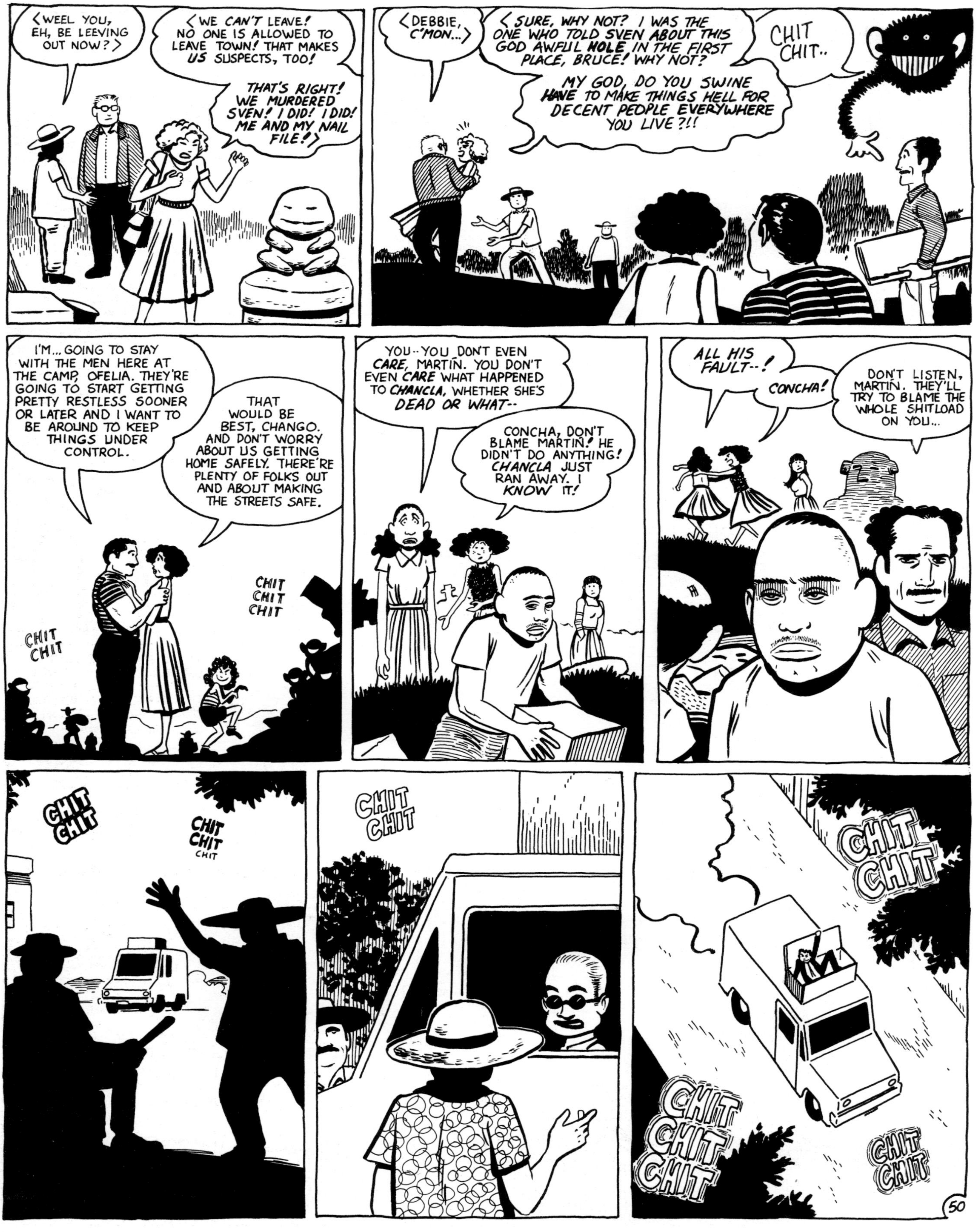
<WEEL YOU, EH, BE LEEVING OUT NOW?>
<WE CAN'T LEAVE! NO ONE IS ALLOWED TO LEAVE TOWN! THAT MAKES US SUSPECTS, TOO!
THAT'S RIGHT! WE MURDERED SVEN! I DID! I DID! ME AND MY NAIL FILE!>
<DEBBIE, C'MON...>
<SURE, WHY NOT? I WAS THE ONE WHO TOLD SVEN ABOUT THIS GOD AWFUL HOLE IN THE FIRST PLACE, BRUCE! WHY NOT?
MY GOD, DO YOU SWINE HAVE TO MAKE THINGS HELL FOR DECENT PEOPLE EVERYWHERE YOU LIVE?!!
CHIT CHIT..
I'M... GOING TO STAY WITH THE MEN HERE AT THE CAMP, OFELIA. THEY'RE GOING TO START GETTING PRETTY RESTLESS SOONER OR LATER AND I WANT TO BE AROUND TO KEEP THINGS UNDER CONTROL.
THAT WOULD BE BEST, CHANGO. AND DON'T WORRY ABOUT US GETTING HOME SAFELY. THERE'RE PLENTY OF FOLKS OUT AND ABOUT MAKING THE STREETS SAFE.
CHIT CHIT CHIT
CHIT CHIT
YOU-- YOU DON'T EVEN CARE, MARTIN. YOU DON'T EVEN CARE WHAT HAPPENED TO CHANCLA, WHETHER SHE'S DEAD OR WHAT--
CONCHA, DON'T BLAME MARTIN! HE DIDN'T DO ANYTHING! CHANCLA JUST RAN AWAY. I KNOW IT!
ALL HIS FAULT--!
CONCHA!
DON'T LISTEN, MARTIN. THEY'LL TRY TO BLAME THE WHOLE SHITLOAD ON YOU...
CHIT CHIT
CHIT CHIT CHIT
CHIT CHIT
CHIT CHIT
CHIT CHIT CHIT
CHIT CHIT
50

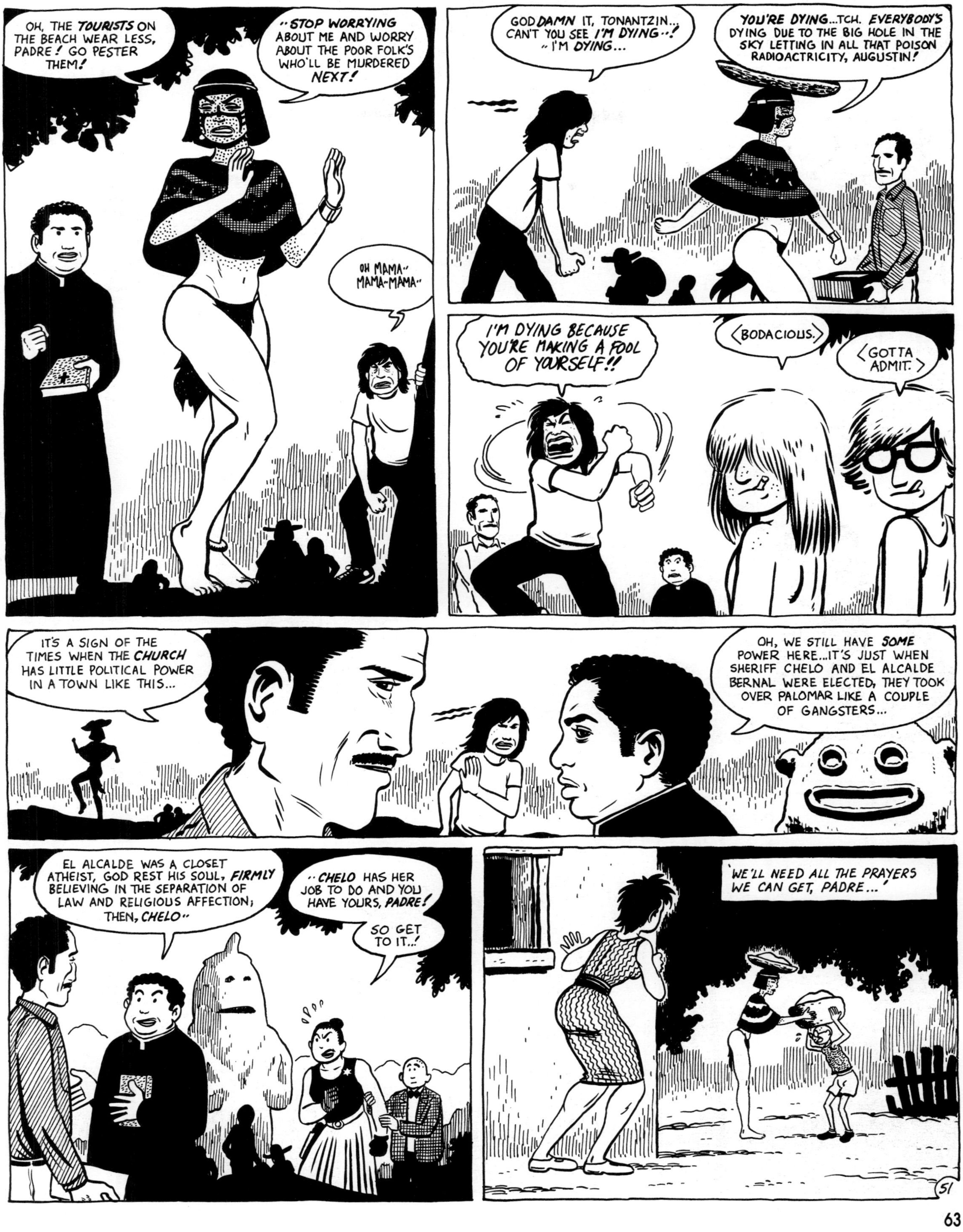

OH, THE TOURISTS ON THE BEACH WEAR LESS, PADRE! GO PESTER THEM!
..STOP WORRYING ABOUT ME AND WORRY ABOUT THE POOR FOLK'S WHO'LL BE MURDERED NEXT!
OH MAMA.. MAMA..MAMA..
GOD DAMN IT, TONANTZIN... CAN'T YOU SEE I'M DYING..! ..I'M DYING...
YOU'RE DYING...TCH. EVERYBODY'S DYING DUE TO THE BIG HOLE IN THE SKY LETTING IN ALL THAT POISON RADIOACTRICITY, AUGUSTIN!
I'M DYING BECAUSE YOU'RE MAKING A FOOL OF YOURSELF!!
⟨BODACIOUS.⟩
⟨GOTTA ADMIT.⟩
IT'S A SIGN OF THE TIMES WHEN THE CHURCH HAS LITTLE POLITICAL POWER IN A TOWN LIKE THIS...
OH, WE STILL HAVE SOME POWER HERE...IT'S JUST WHEN SHERIFF CHELO AND EL ALCALDE BERNAL WERE ELECTED, THEY TOOK OVER PALOMAR LIKE A COUPLE OF GANGSTERS...
EL ALCALDE WAS A CLOSET ATHEIST, GOD REST HIS SOUL, FIRMLY BELIEVING IN THE SEPARATION OF LAW AND RELIGIOUS AFFECTION; THEN, CHELO..
..CHELO HAS HER JOB TO DO AND YOU HAVE YOURS, PADRE!
SO GET TO IT..!
'WE'LL NEED ALL THE PRAYERS WE CAN GET, PADRE...'
51

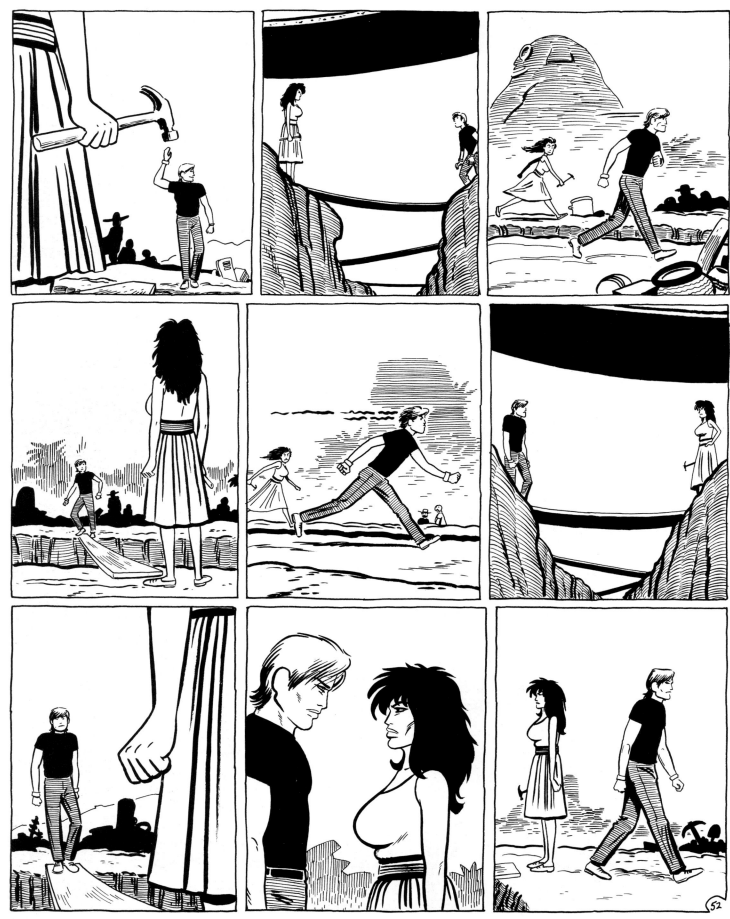

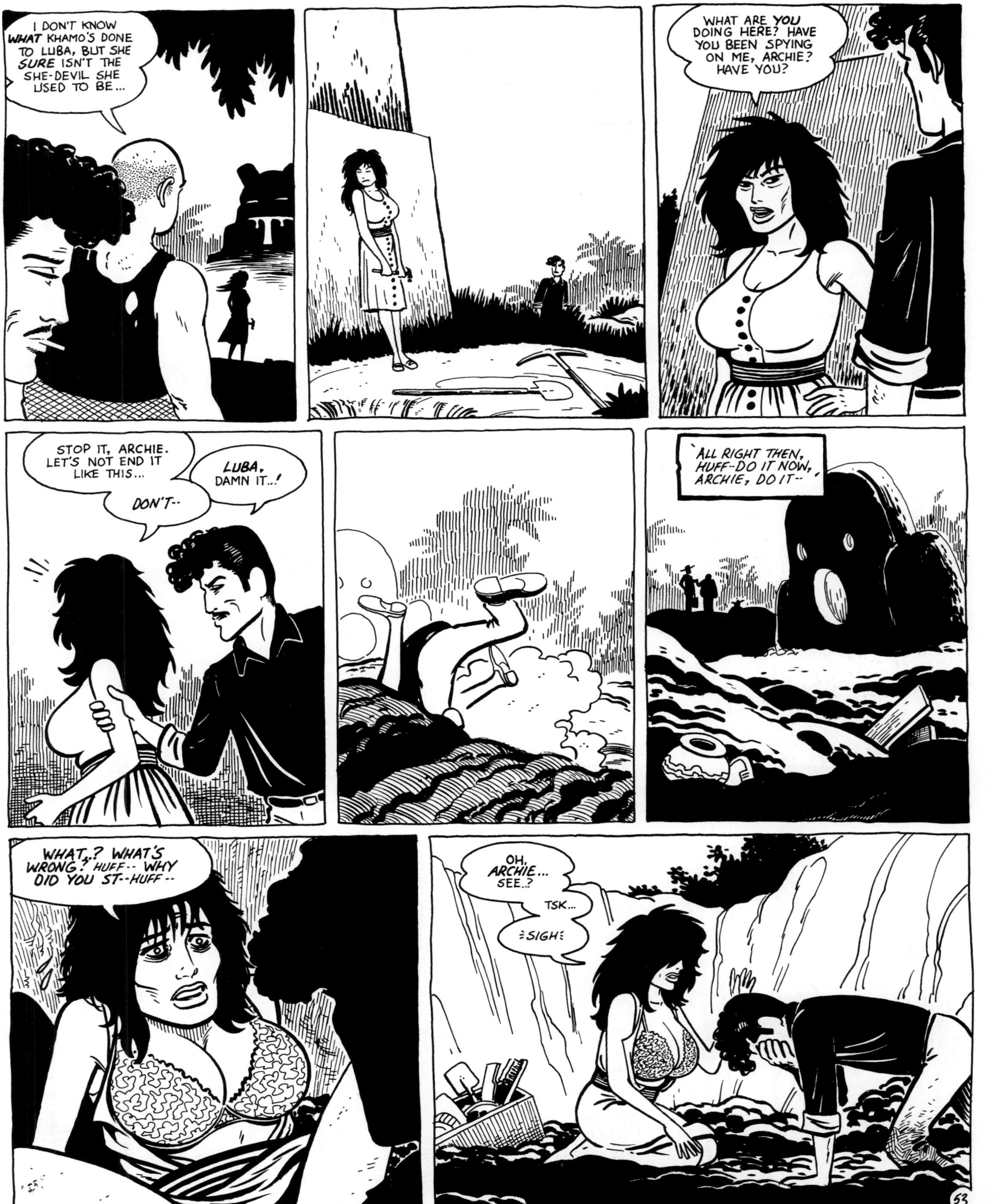
I DON'T KNOW WHAT KHAMO'S DONE TO LUBA, BUT SHE SURE ISN'T THE SHE-DEVIL SHE USED TO BE...
WHAT ARE YOU DOING HERE? HAVE YOU BEEN SPYING ON ME, ARCHIE? HAVE YOU?
STOP IT, ARCHIE. LET'S NOT END IT LIKE THIS...
DON'T--
LUBA, DAMN IT..!
'ALL RIGHT THEN, HUFF--DO IT NOW, ARCHIE, DO IT--'
WHAT..? WHAT'S WRONG? HUFF-- WHY DID YOU ST--HUFF--
OH, ARCHIE... SEE..?
TSK...
SIGH
53

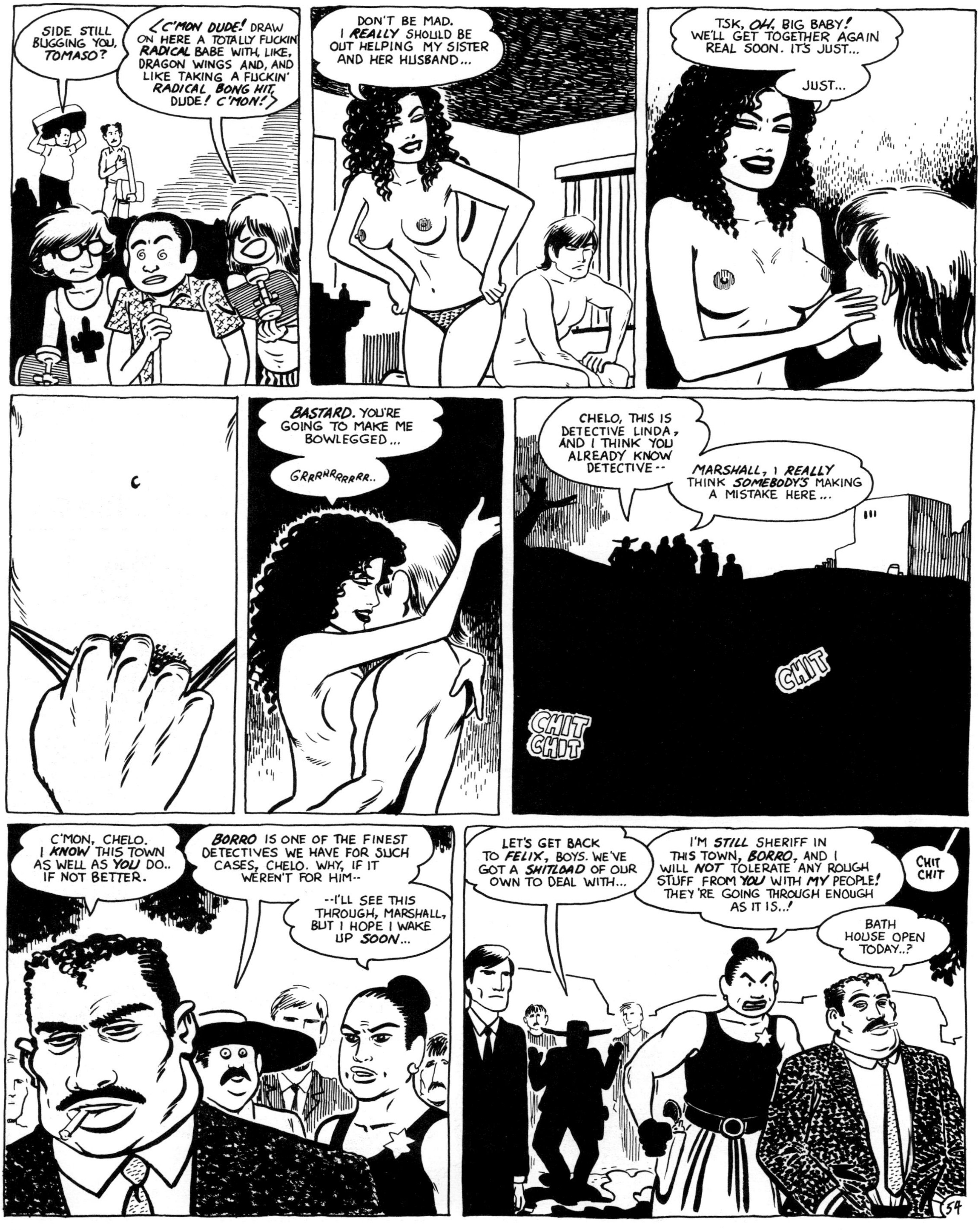
SIDE STILL BUGGING YOU, TOMASO?
<C'MON DUDE! DRAW ON HERE A TOTALLY FUCKIN' RADICAL BABE WITH, LIKE, DRAGON WINGS AND, AND LIKE TAKING A FUCKIN' RADICAL BONG HIT, DUDE! C'MON!>
DON'T BE MAD. I REALLY SHOULD BE OUT HELPING MY SISTER AND HER HUSBAND...
TSK, OH, BIG BABY! WE'LL GET TOGETHER AGAIN REAL SOON. IT'S JUST...
JUST...
C
BASTARD. YOU'RE GOING TO MAKE ME BOWLEGGED...
GRRRRRRRRR..
CHELO, THIS IS DETECTIVE LINDA, AND I THINK YOU ALREADY KNOW DETECTIVE--
MARSHALL, I REALLY THINK SOMEBODY'S MAKING A MISTAKE HERE...
CHIT
CHIT CHIT
C'MON, CHELO. I KNOW THIS TOWN AS WELL AS YOU DO.. IF NOT BETTER.
BORRO IS ONE OF THE FINEST DETECTIVES WE HAVE FOR SUCH CASES, CHELO. WHY, IF IT WEREN'T FOR HIM--
--I'LL SEE THIS THROUGH, MARSHALL, BUT I HOPE I WAKE UP SOON...
LET'S GET BACK TO FELIX, BOYS. WE'VE GOT A SHITLOAD OF OUR OWN TO DEAL WITH...
I'M STILL SHERIFF IN THIS TOWN, BORRO, AND I WILL NOT TOLERATE ANY ROUGH STUFF FROM YOU WITH MY PEOPLE! THEY'RE GOING THROUGH ENOUGH AS IT IS..!
CHIT CHIT
BATH HOUSE OPEN TODAY..?
54

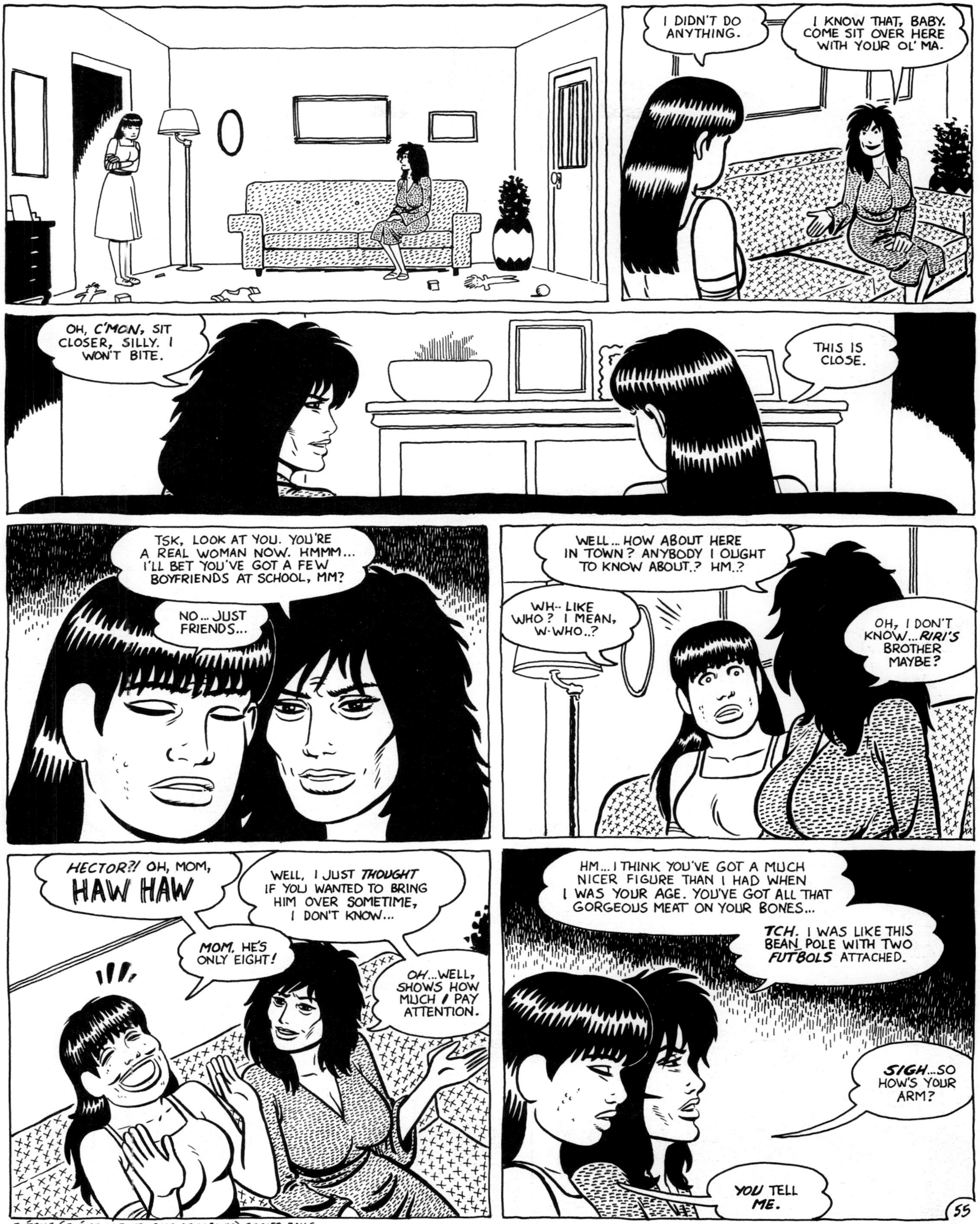
I DIDN'T DO ANYTHING.
I KNOW THAT, BABY. COME SIT OVER HERE WITH YOUR OL' MA.
OH, C'MON, SIT CLOSER, SILLY. I WON'T BITE.
THIS IS CLOSE.
TSK, LOOK AT YOU. YOU'RE A REAL WOMAN NOW. HMMM... I'LL BET YOU'VE GOT A FEW BOYFRIENDS AT SCHOOL, MM?
NO... JUST FRIENDS...
WELL... HOW ABOUT HERE IN TOWN? ANYBODY I OUGHT TO KNOW ABOUT.? HM.?
WH-- LIKE WHO? I MEAN, W-WHO..?
OH, I DON'T KNOW...RIRI'S BROTHER MAYBE?
HECTOR?! OH, MOM, HAW HAW
WELL, I JUST THOUGHT IF YOU WANTED TO BRING HIM OVER SOMETIME, I DON'T KNOW...
MOM, HE'S ONLY EIGHT!
OH...WELL, SHOWS HOW MUCH I PAY ATTENTION.
HM... I THINK YOU'VE GOT A MUCH NICER FIGURE THAN I HAD WHEN I WAS YOUR AGE. YOU'VE GOT ALL THAT GORGEOUS MEAT ON YOUR BONES...
TCH. I WAS LIKE THIS BEAN POLE WITH TWO FUTBOLS ATTACHED.
SIGH...SO HOW'S YOUR ARM?
YOU TELL ME.
55

FUTBOLS (FUT AS IN FLUTE, BOLS AS IN BOWLS) SOCCER BALLS

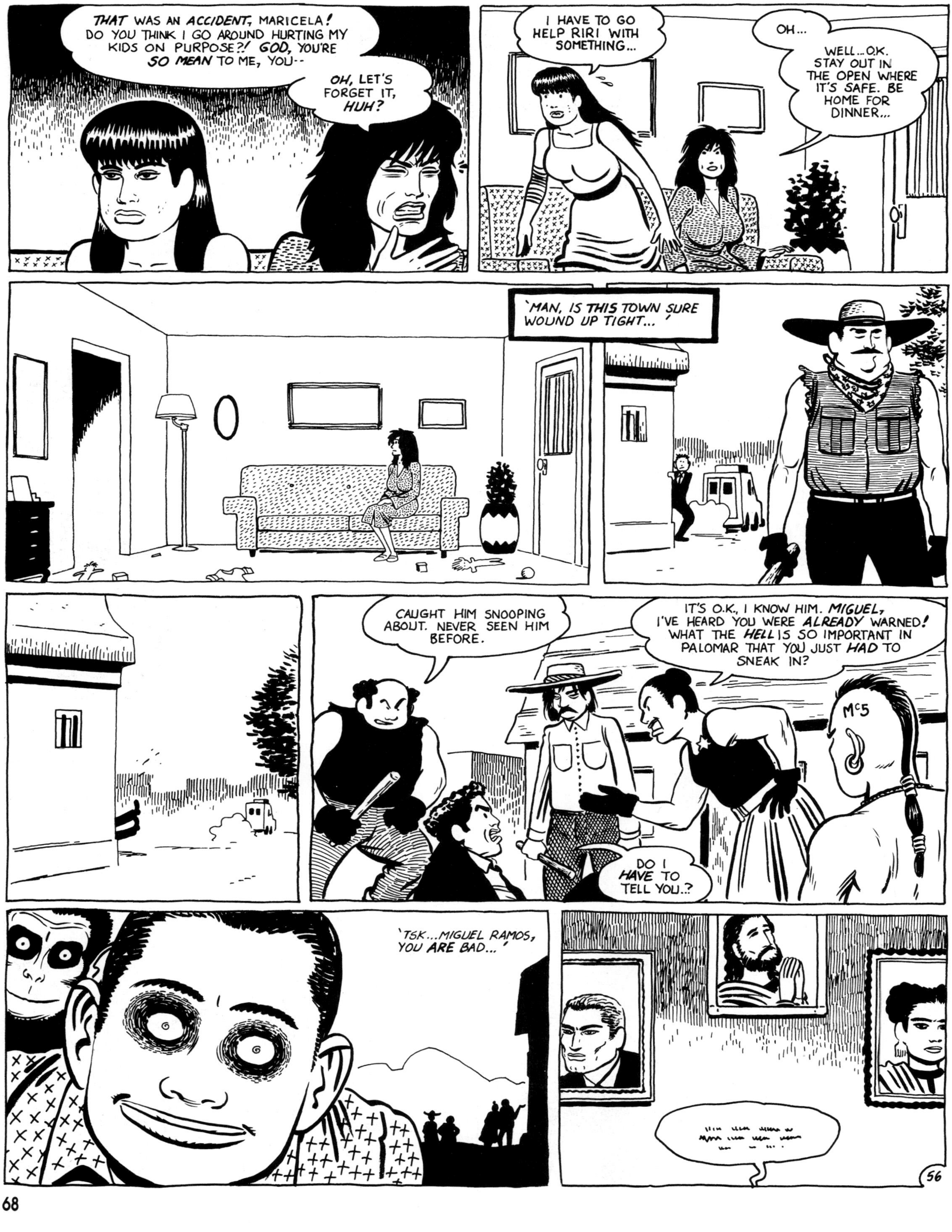
THAT WAS AN ACCIDENT, MARICELA! DO YOU THINK I GO AROUND HURTING MY KIDS ON PURPOSE?! GOD, YOU'RE SO MEAN TO ME, YOU--
OH, LET'S FORGET IT, HUH?
I HAVE TO GO HELP RIRI WITH SOMETHING...
OH...
WELL...O.K. STAY OUT IN THE OPEN WHERE IT'S SAFE. BE HOME FOR DINNER...
'MAN, IS THIS TOWN SURE WOUND UP TIGHT...'
CAUGHT HIM SNOOPING ABOUT. NEVER SEEN HIM BEFORE.
IT'S O.K., I KNOW HIM. MIGUEL, I'VE HEARD YOU WERE ALREADY WARNED! WHAT THE HELL IS SO IMPORTANT IN PALOMAR THAT YOU JUST HAD TO SNEAK IN?
M^c5
DO I HAVE TO TELL YOU..?
'TSK...MIGUEL RAMOS, YOU ARE BAD...'
56

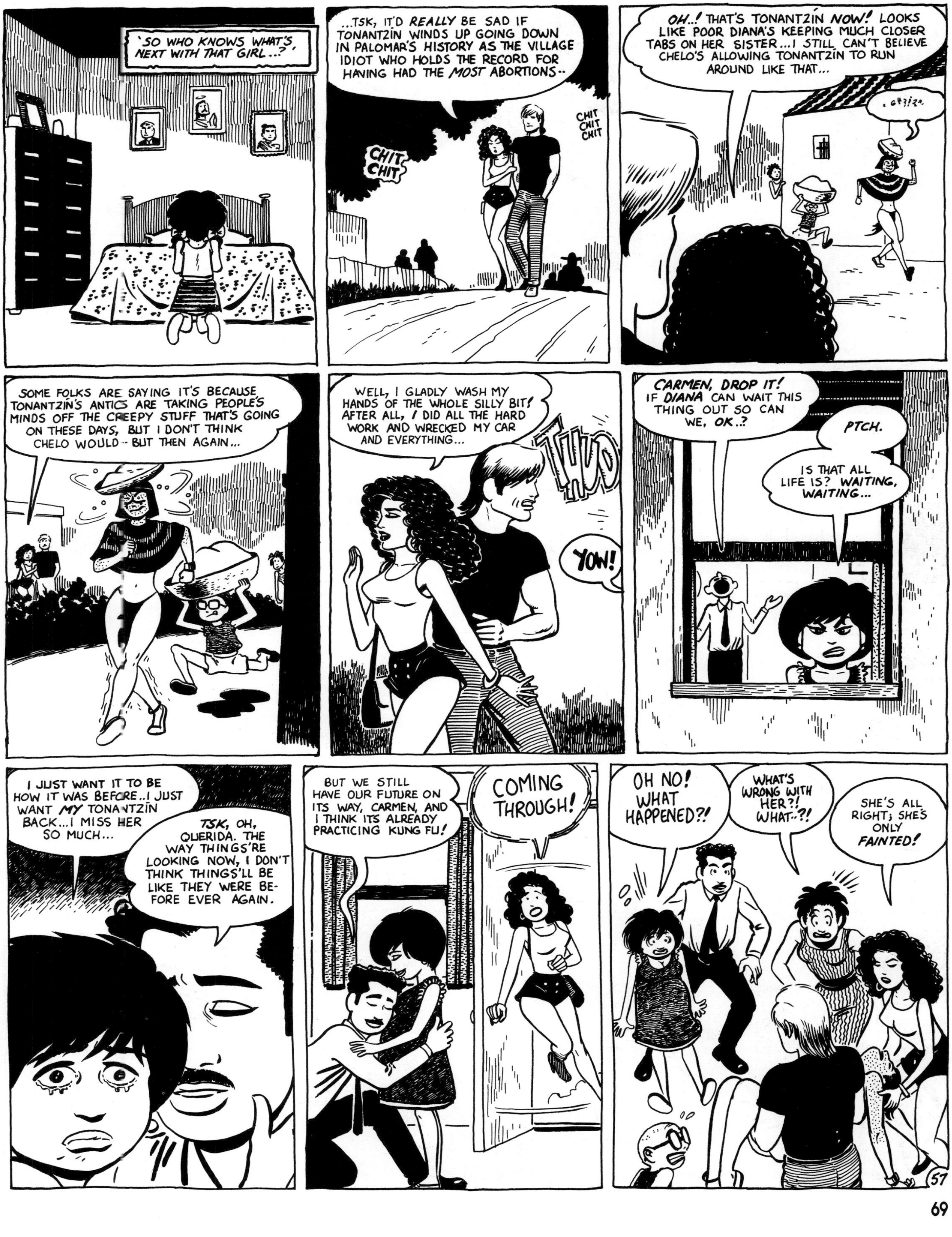
"SO WHO KNOWS WHAT'S NEXT WITH THAT GIRL..?"
...TSK, IT'D REALLY BE SAD IF TONANTZÍN WINDS UP GOING DOWN IN PALOMAR'S HISTORY AS THE VILLAGE IDIOT WHO HOLDS THE RECORD FOR HAVING HAD THE MOST ABORTIONS..
CHIT CHIT
CHIT CHIT CHIT
OH..! THAT'S TONANTZÍN NOW! LOOKS LIKE POOR DIANA'S KEEPING MUCH CLOSER TABS ON HER SISTER...I STILL CAN'T BELIEVE CHELO'S ALLOWING TONANTZÍN TO RUN AROUND LIKE THAT...
SOME FOLKS ARE SAYING IT'S BECAUSE TONANTZÍN'S ANTICS ARE TAKING PEOPLE'S MINDS OFF THE CREEPY STUFF THAT'S GOING ON THESE DAYS, BUT I DON'T THINK CHELO WOULD-- BUT THEN AGAIN...
WELL, I GLADLY WASH MY HANDS OF THE WHOLE SILLY BIT! AFTER ALL, I DID ALL THE HARD WORK AND WRECKED MY CAR AND EVERYTHING...
THUD
YOW!
CARMEN, DROP IT! IF DIANA CAN WAIT THIS THING OUT SO CAN WE, OK..?
PTCH.
IS THAT ALL LIFE IS? WAITING, WAITING...
I JUST WANT IT TO BE HOW IT WAS BEFORE..I JUST WANT MY TONANTZÍN BACK...I MISS HER SO MUCH...
TSK, OH, QUERIDA. THE WAY THINGS'RE LOOKING NOW, I DON'T THINK THINGS'LL BE LIKE THEY WERE BEFORE EVER AGAIN.
BUT WE STILL HAVE OUR FUTURE ON ITS WAY, CARMEN, AND I THINK ITS ALREADY PRACTICING KUNG FU!
COMING THROUGH!
OH NO! WHAT HAPPENED?!
WHAT'S WRONG WITH HER?! WHAT..?!
SHE'S ALL RIGHT; SHE'S ONLY FAINTED!
57

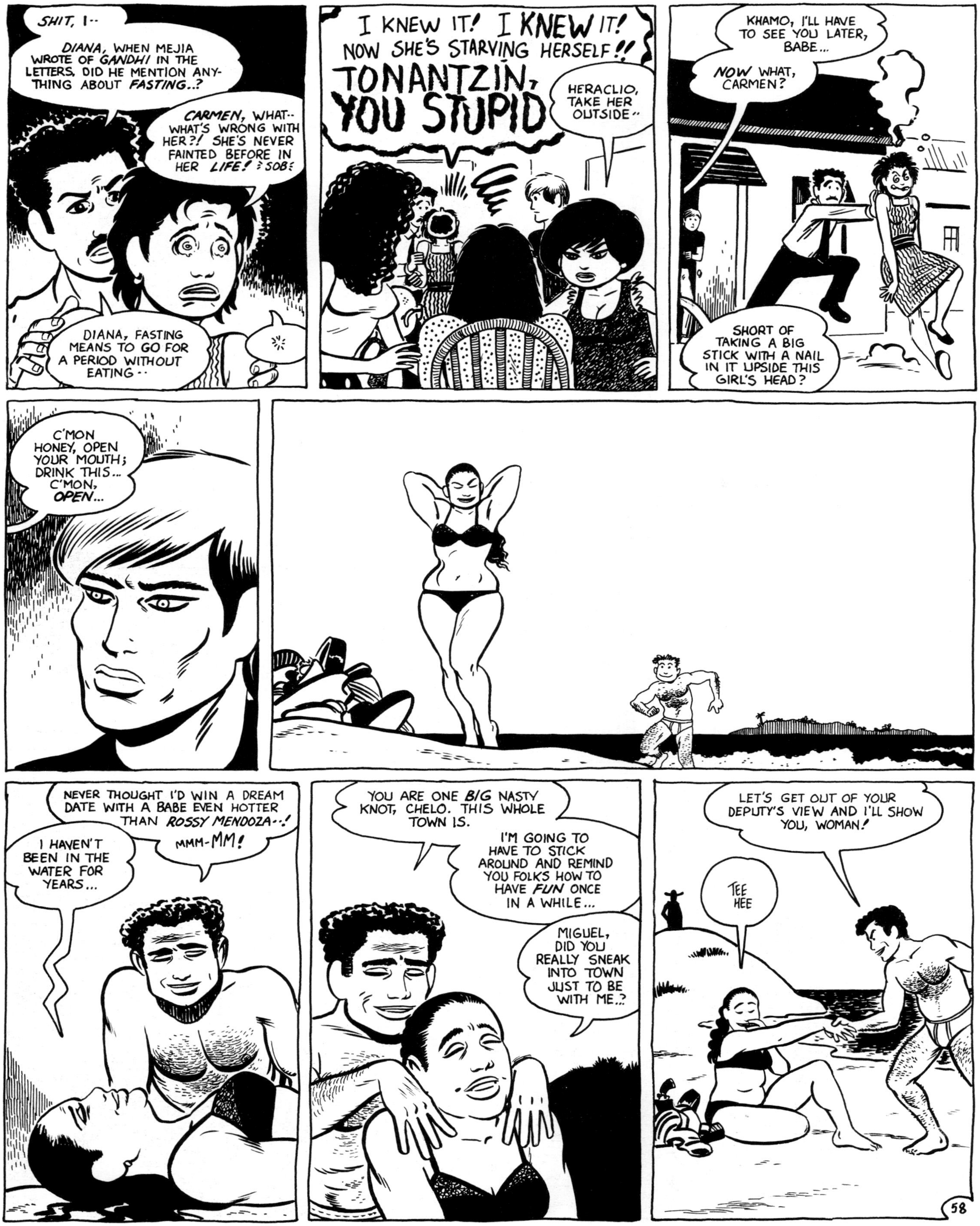
SHIT, I--
DIANA, WHEN MEJIA WROTE OF GANDHI IN THE LETTERS, DID HE MENTION ANYTHING ABOUT FASTING..?
CARMEN, WHAT--WHAT'S WRONG WITH HER?! SHE'S NEVER FAINTED BEFORE IN HER LIFE! ⁝SOB⁝
DIANA, FASTING MEANS TO GO FOR A PERIOD WITHOUT EATING--
I KNEW IT! I KNEW IT! NOW SHE'S STARVING HERSELF!!
TONANTZIN, YOU STUPID
HERACLIO, TAKE HER OUTSIDE--
KHAMO, I'LL HAVE TO SEE YOU LATER, BABE...
NOW WHAT, CARMEN?
SHORT OF TAKING A BIG STICK WITH A NAIL IN IT UPSIDE THIS GIRL'S HEAD?
C'MON HONEY, OPEN YOUR MOUTH; DRINK THIS... C'MON, OPEN...
NEVER THOUGHT I'D WIN A DREAM DATE WITH A BABE EVEN HOTTER THAN ROSSY MENDOZA--!
MMM-MM!
I HAVEN'T BEEN IN THE WATER FOR YEARS...
YOU ARE ONE BIG NASTY KNOT, CHELO. THIS WHOLE TOWN IS.
I'M GOING TO HAVE TO STICK AROUND AND REMIND YOU FOLKS HOW TO HAVE FUN ONCE IN A WHILE...
MIGUEL, DID YOU REALLY SNEAK INTO TOWN JUST TO BE WITH ME..?
LET'S GET OUT OF YOUR DEPUTY'S VIEW AND I'LL SHOW YOU, WOMAN!
TEE HEE
58

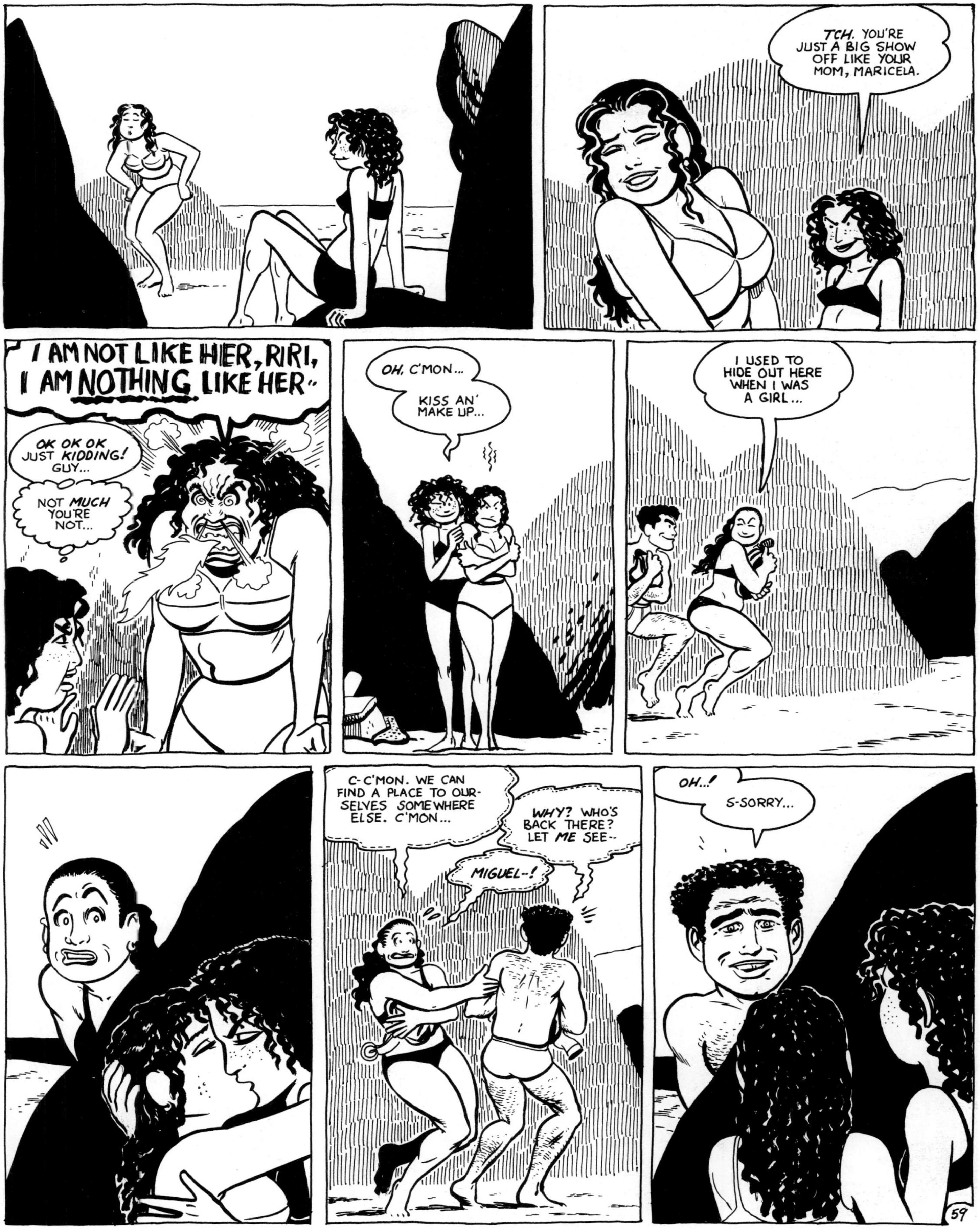
TCH. YOU'RE JUST A BIG SHOW OFF LIKE YOUR MOM, MARICELA.
I AM NOT LIKE HER, RIRI, I AM NOTHING LIKE HER
OK OK OK JUST KIDDING! GUY...
NOT MUCH YOU'RE NOT...
OH, C'MON...
KISS AN' MAKE UP...
I USED TO HIDE OUT HERE WHEN I WAS A GIRL...
C-C'MON. WE CAN FIND A PLACE TO OURSELVES SOMEWHERE ELSE. C'MON...
WHY? WHO'S BACK THERE? LET ME SEE--
MIGUEL--!
OH..!
S-SORRY...
59

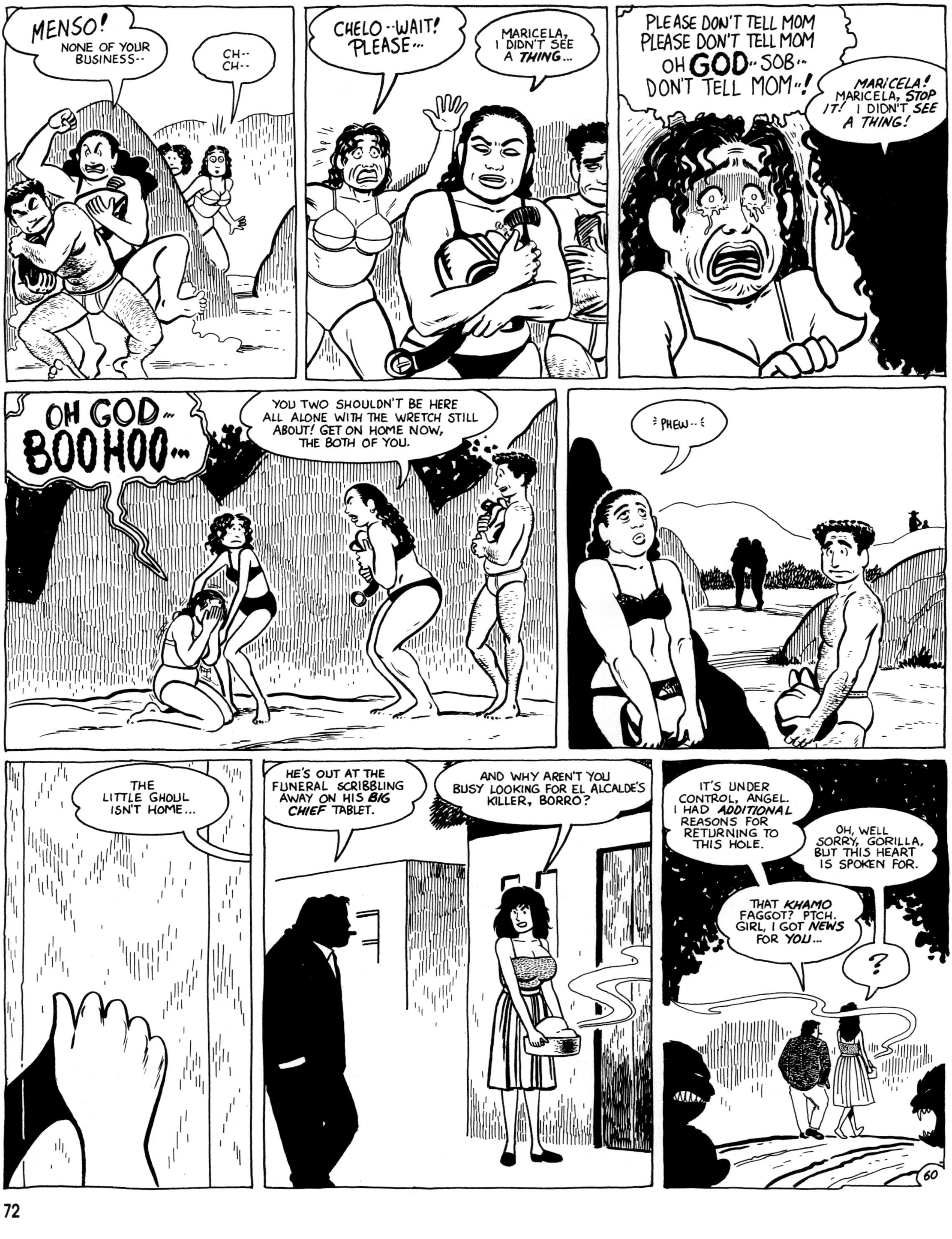
MENSO! NONE OF YOUR BUSINESS--
CH-- CH--
CHELO--WAIT! PLEASE...
MARICELA, I DIDN'T SEE A THING...
PLEASE DON'T TELL MOM PLEASE DON'T TELL MOM OH GOD--SOB-- DON'T TELL MOM--!
MARICELA! MARICELA, STOP IT! I DIDN'T SEE A THING!
OH GOD-- BOOHOO...
YOU TWO SHOULDN'T BE HERE ALL ALONE WITH THE WRETCH STILL ABOUT! GET ON HOME NOW, THE BOTH OF YOU.
PHEW--
THE LITTLE GHOUL ISN'T HOME...
HE'S OUT AT THE FUNERAL SCRIBBLING AWAY ON HIS BIG CHIEF TABLET.
AND WHY AREN'T YOU BUSY LOOKING FOR EL ALCALDE'S KILLER, BORRO?
IT'S UNDER CONTROL, ANGEL. I HAD ADDITIONAL REASONS FOR RETURNING TO THIS HOLE.
OH, WELL SORRY, GORILLA, BUT THIS HEART IS SPOKEN FOR.
THAT KHAMO FAGGOT? PTCH. GIRL, I GOT NEWS FOR YOU...
?
60

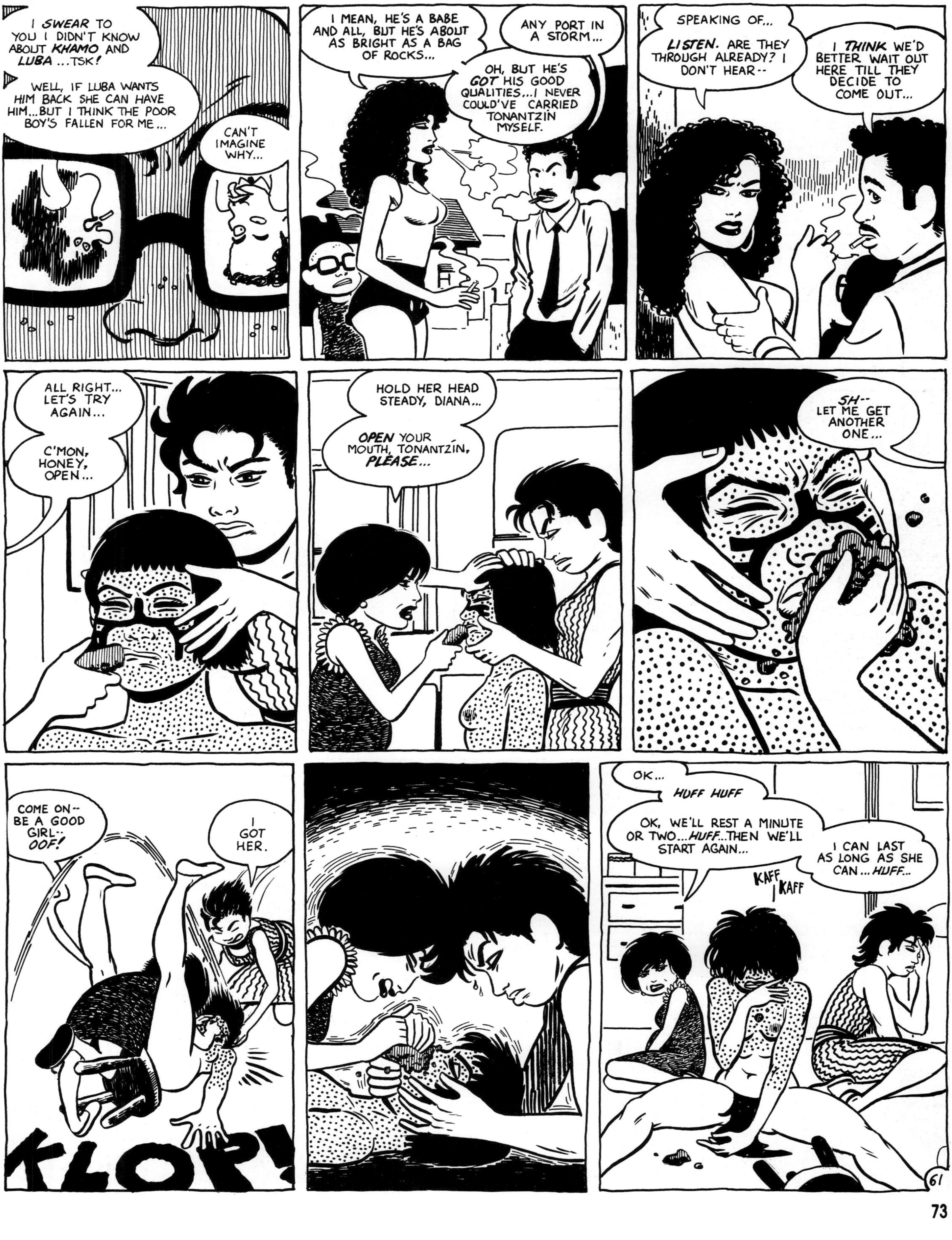
I SWEAR TO YOU I DIDN'T KNOW ABOUT KHAMO AND LUBA ...TSK!
WELL, IF LUBA WANTS HIM BACK SHE CAN HAVE HIM...BUT I THINK THE POOR BOY'S FALLEN FOR ME...
CAN'T IMAGINE WHY...
I MEAN, HE'S A BABE AND ALL, BUT HE'S ABOUT AS BRIGHT AS A BAG OF ROCKS...
ANY PORT IN A STORM...
OH, BUT HE'S GOT HIS GOOD QUALITIES...I NEVER COULD'VE CARRIED TONANTZIN MYSELF.
SPEAKING OF...
LISTEN. ARE THEY THROUGH ALREADY? I DON'T HEAR--
I THINK WE'D BETTER WAIT OUT HERE TILL THEY DECIDE TO COME OUT...
ALL RIGHT... LET'S TRY AGAIN...
C'MON, HONEY, OPEN...
HOLD HER HEAD STEADY, DIANA...
OPEN YOUR MOUTH, TONANTZÍN, PLEASE...
SH-- LET ME GET ANOTHER ONE...
COME ON-- BE A GOOD GIRL-- OOF!
I GOT HER.
KLOP!
OK...
HUFF HUFF
OK, WE'LL REST A MINUTE OR TWO...HUFF...THEN WE'LL START AGAIN...
KAFF KAFF
I CAN LAST AS LONG AS SHE CAN...HUFF...
61

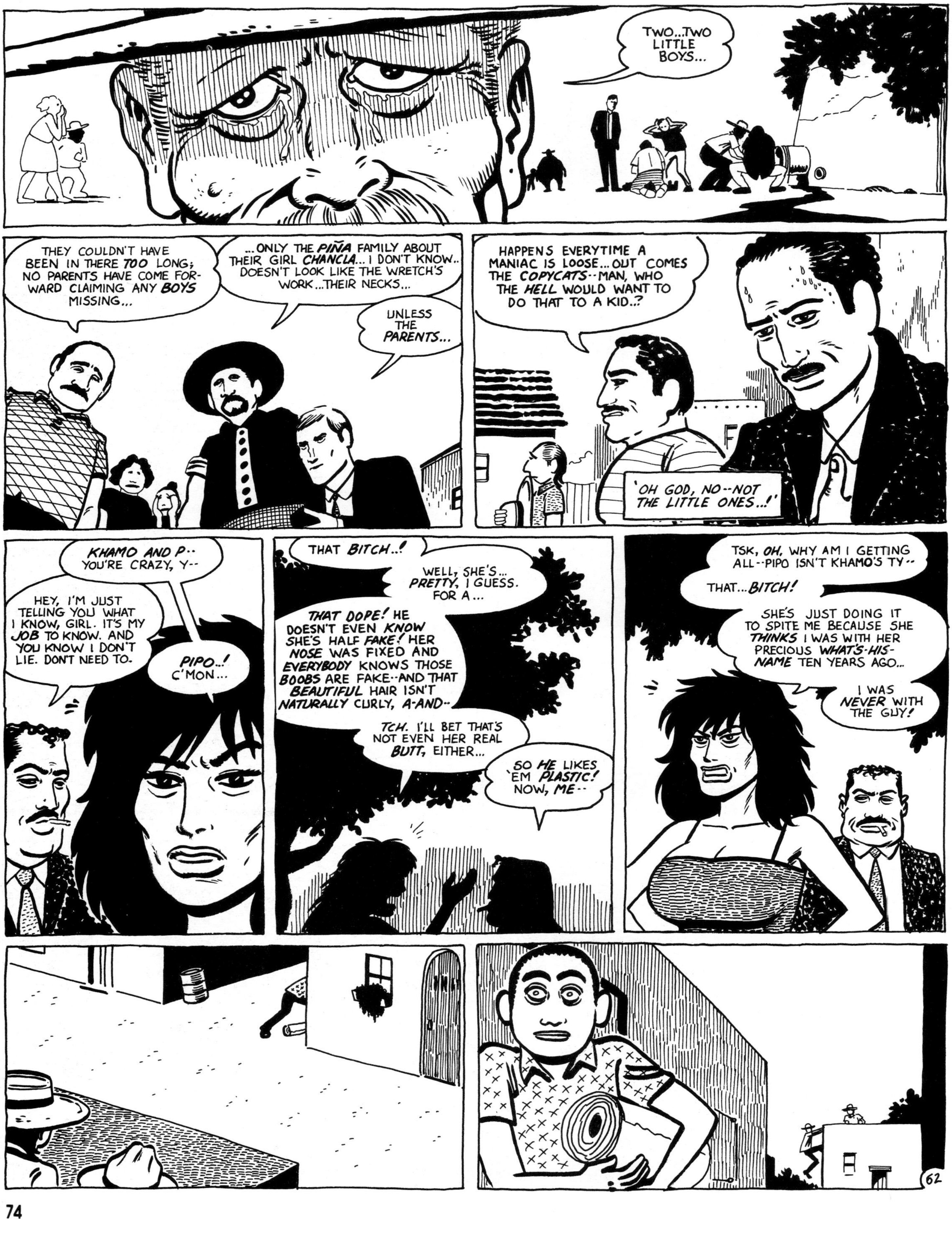
TWO...TWO LITTLE BOYS...
THEY COULDN'T HAVE BEEN IN THERE TOO LONG; NO PARENTS HAVE COME FORWARD CLAIMING ANY BOYS MISSING...
...ONLY THE PIÑA FAMILY ABOUT THEIR GIRL CHANCLA... I DON'T KNOW.. DOESN'T LOOK LIKE THE WRETCH'S WORK...THEIR NECKS...
UNLESS THE PARENTS...
HAPPENS EVERYTIME A MANIAC IS LOOSE...OUT COMES THE COPYCATS--MAN, WHO THE HELL WOULD WANT TO DO THAT TO A KID..?
'OH GOD, NO--NOT THE LITTLE ONES...!'
KHAMO AND P-- YOU'RE CRAZY, Y--
HEY, I'M JUST TELLING YOU WHAT I KNOW, GIRL. IT'S MY JOB TO KNOW. AND YOU KNOW I DON'T LIE. DON'T NEED TO.
PIPO..! C'MON...
THAT BITCH..!
WELL, SHE'S... PRETTY, I GUESS. FOR A...
THAT DOPE! HE DOESN'T EVEN KNOW SHE'S HALF FAKE! HER NOSE WAS FIXED AND EVERYBODY KNOWS THOSE BOOBS ARE FAKE--AND THAT BEAUTIFUL HAIR ISN'T NATURALLY CURLY, A-AND--
TCH. I'LL BET THAT'S NOT EVEN HER REAL BUTT, EITHER...
SO HE LIKES 'EM PLASTIC! NOW, ME--
TSK, OH, WHY AM I GETTING ALL--PIPO ISN'T KHAMO'S TY--
THAT...BITCH!
SHE'S JUST DOING IT TO SPITE ME BECAUSE SHE THINKS I WAS WITH HER PRECIOUS WHAT'S-HIS-NAME TEN YEARS AGO...
I WAS NEVER WITH THE GUY!
62

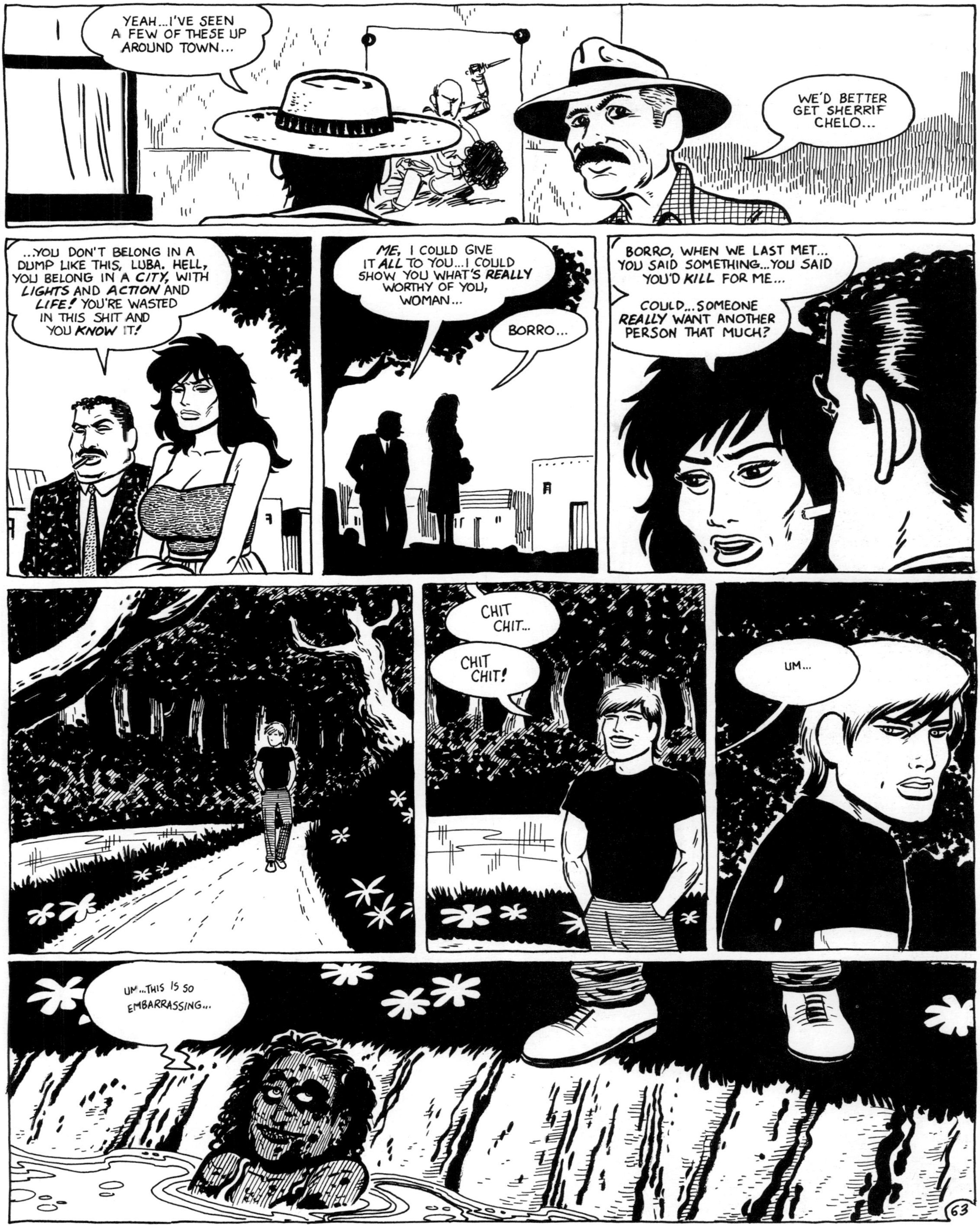
YEAH...I'VE SEEN A FEW OF THESE UP AROUND TOWN...
WE'D BETTER GET SHERRIF CHELO...
...YOU DON'T BELONG IN A DUMP LIKE THIS, LUBA. HELL, YOU BELONG IN A CITY, WITH LIGHTS AND ACTION AND LIFE! YOU'RE WASTED IN THIS SHIT AND YOU KNOW IT!
ME, I COULD GIVE IT ALL TO YOU...I COULD SHOW YOU WHAT'S REALLY WORTHY OF YOU, WOMAN...
BORRO...
BORRO, WHEN WE LAST MET... YOU SAID SOMETHING...YOU SAID YOU'D KILL FOR ME...
COULD...SOMEONE REALLY WANT ANOTHER PERSON THAT MUCH?
CHIT CHIT...
CHIT CHIT!
UM...
UM...THIS IS SO EMBARRASSING...
63

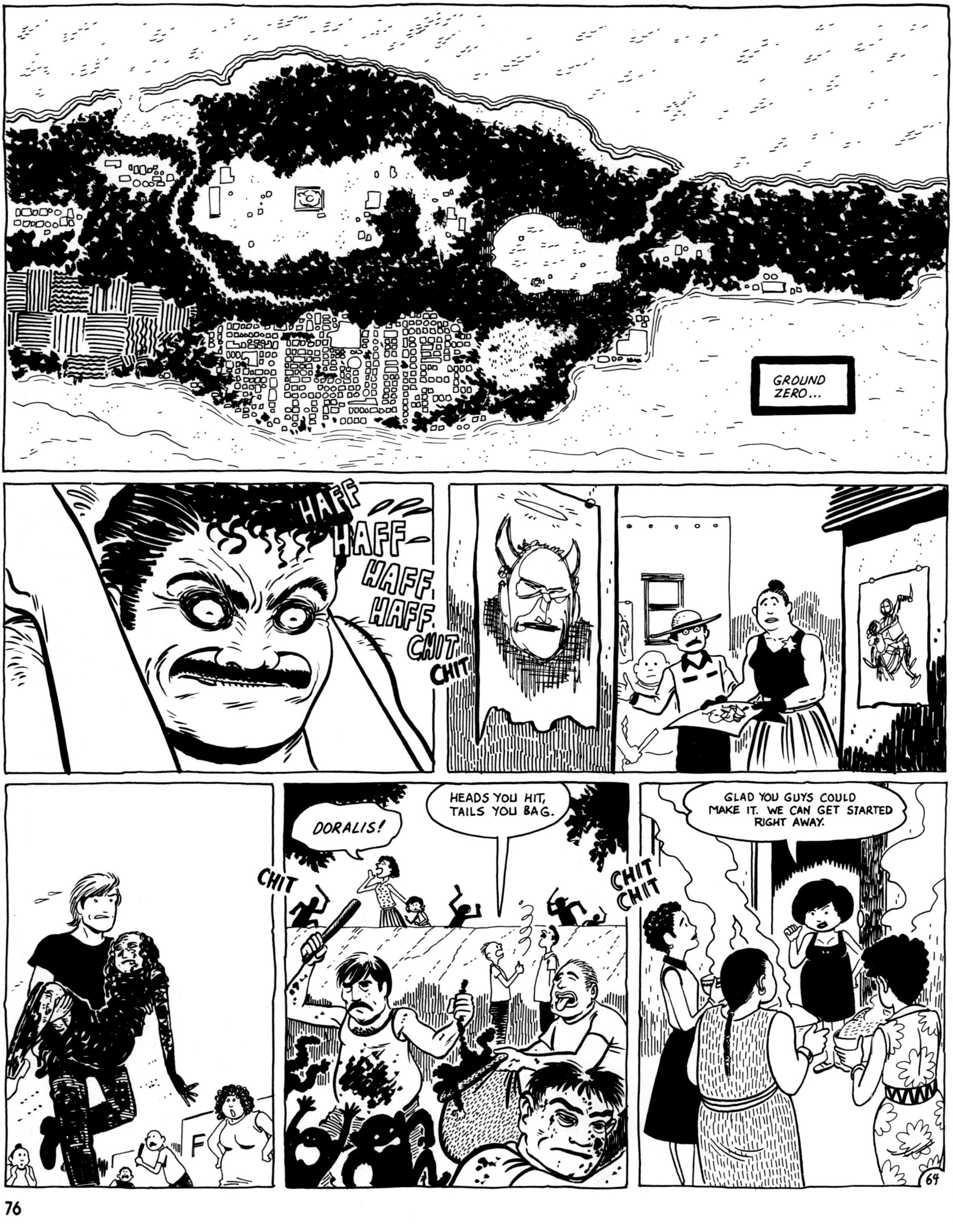
GROUND ZERO...
HAFF
HAFF
HAFF
HAFF
CHIT
CHIT
CHIT
DORALIS!
HEADS YOU HIT, TAILS YOU BAG.
CHIT CHIT
GLAD YOU GUYS COULD MAKE IT. WE CAN GET STARTED RIGHT AWAY.
64

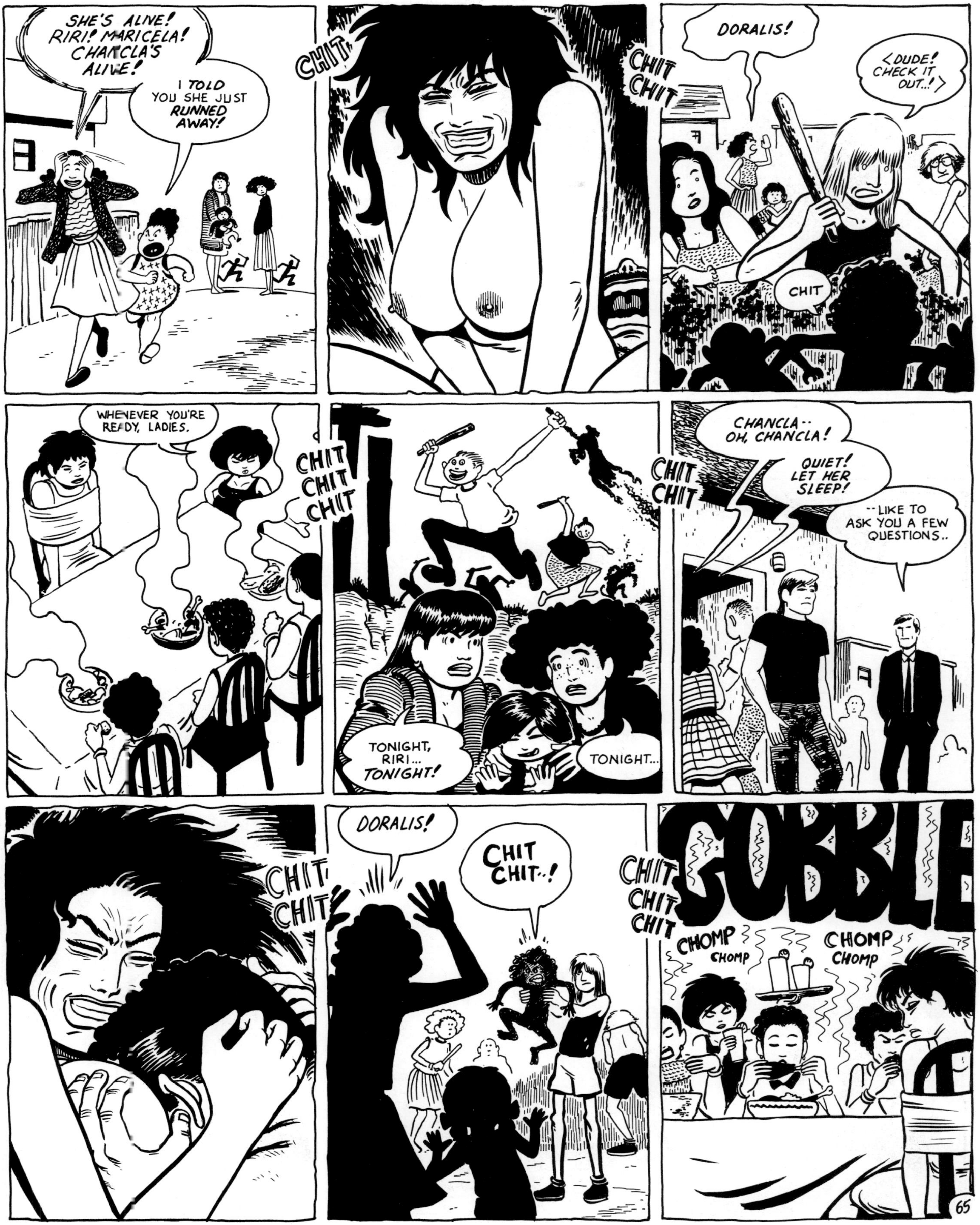
SHE'S ALIVE! RIRI! MARICELA! CHANCLA'S ALIVE!
I TOLD YOU SHE JUST RUNNED AWAY!
CHIT
CHIT CHIT
DORALIS!
<DUDE! CHECK IT OUT..!>
CHIT
WHENEVER YOU'RE READY, LADIES.
CHIT CHIT CHIT
TONIGHT, RIRI... TONIGHT!
TONIGHT...
CHIT CHIT
CHANCLA-- OH, CHANCLA!
QUIET! LET HER SLEEP!
--LIKE TO ASK YOU A FEW QUESTIONS..
CHIT CHIT
DORALIS!
CHIT CHIT..!
CHIT CHIT CHIT
GOBBLE
CHOMP CHOMP
CHOMP CHOMP
65

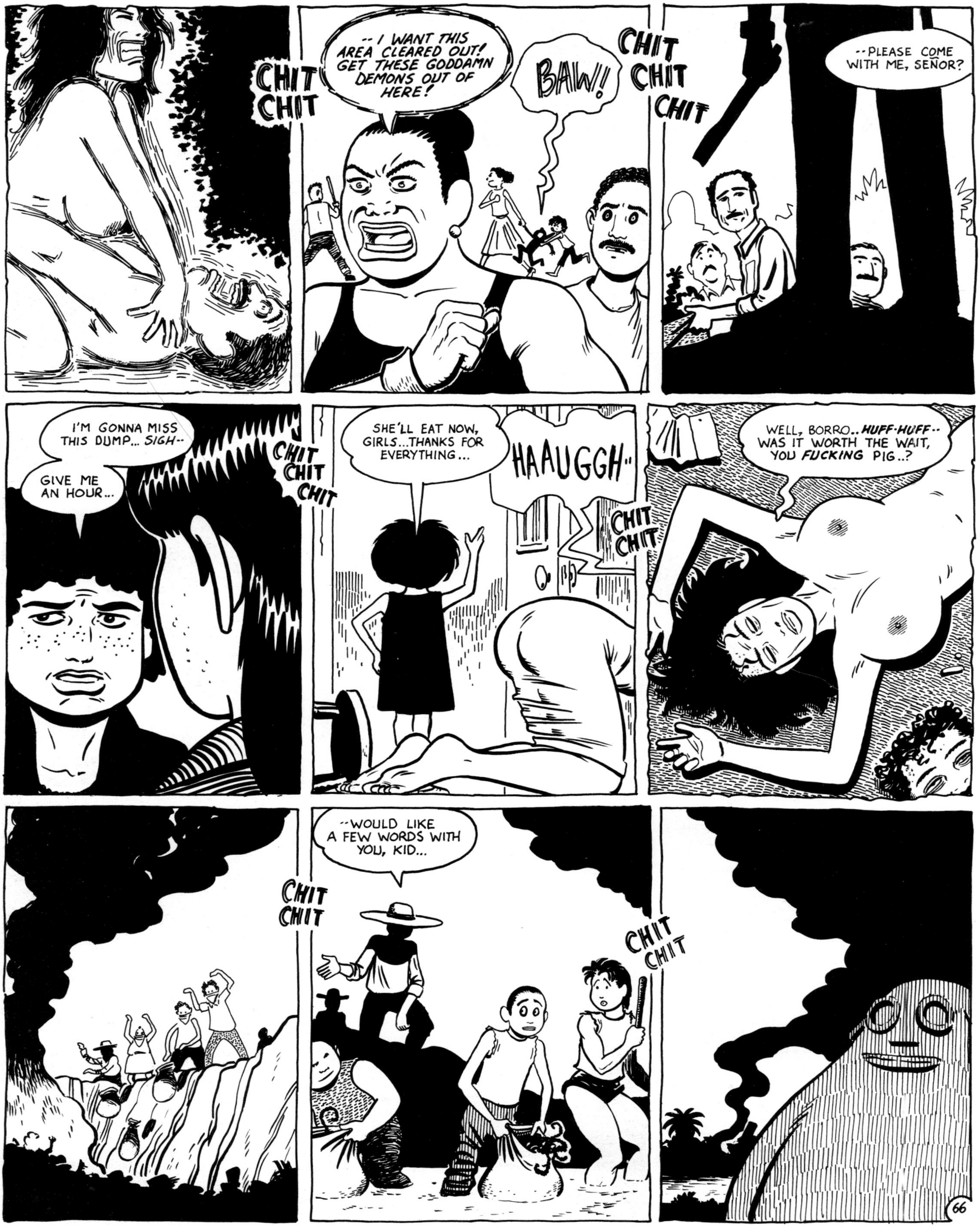
CHIT
CHIT
-- I WANT THIS AREA CLEARED OUT! GET THESE GODDAMN DEMONS OUT OF HERE!
BAW!
CHIT
CHIT
CHIT
--PLEASE COME WITH ME, SEÑOR?
I'M GONNA MISS THIS DUMP... SIGH--
GIVE ME AN HOUR...
CHIT
CHIT
CHIT
SHE'LL EAT NOW, GIRLS...THANKS FOR EVERYTHING...
HAAUGGH--
CHIT
CHIT
WELL, BORRO.. HUFF-HUFF-- WAS IT WORTH THE WAIT, YOU FUCKING PIG..?
CHIT
CHIT
--WOULD LIKE A FEW WORDS WITH YOU, KID...
CHIT
CHIT
66

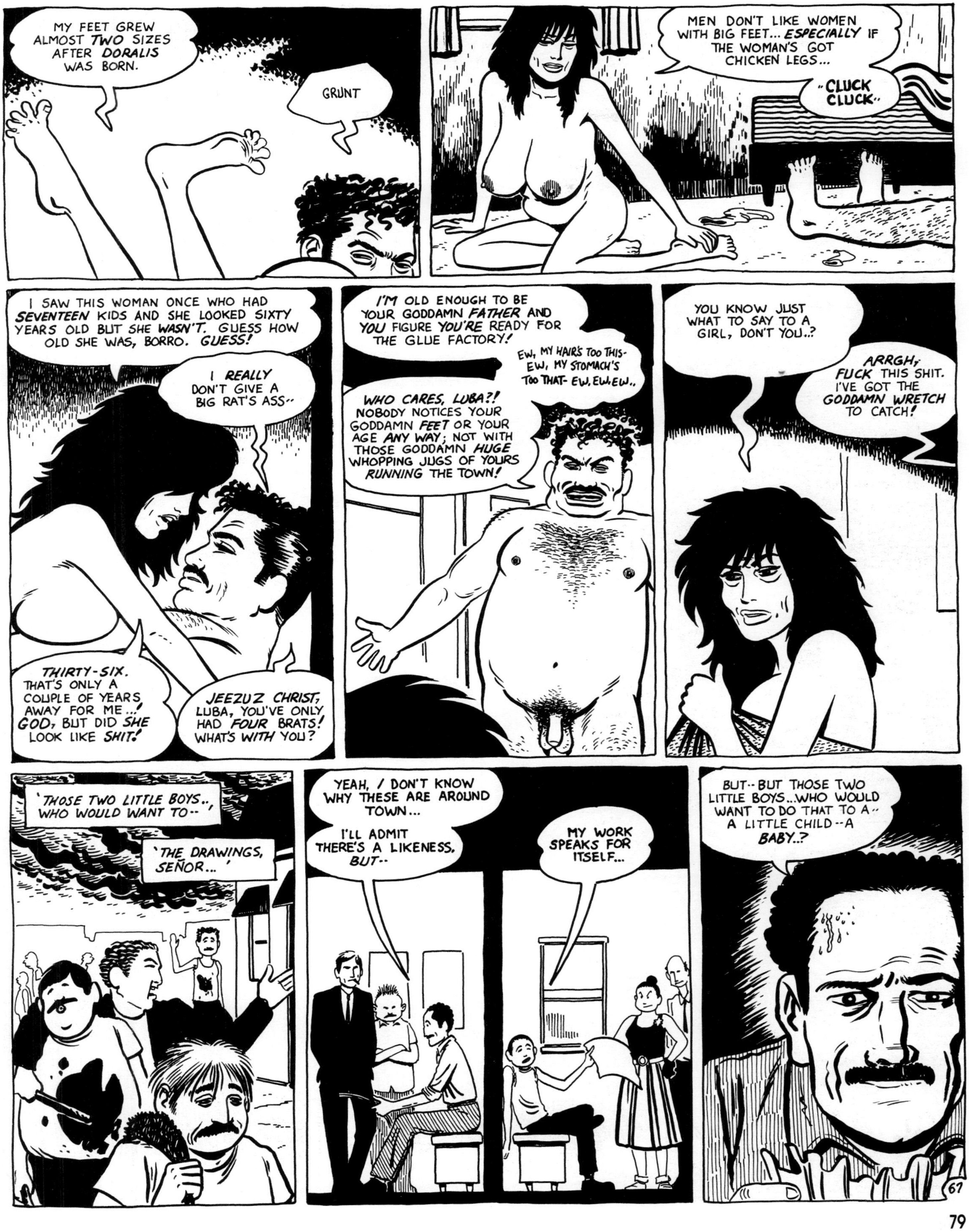
MY FEET GREW ALMOST TWO SIZES AFTER DORALIS WAS BORN.
GRUNT
MEN DON'T LIKE WOMEN WITH BIG FEET... ESPECIALLY IF THE WOMAN'S GOT CHICKEN LEGS...
"CLUCK CLUCK"
I SAW THIS WOMAN ONCE WHO HAD SEVENTEEN KIDS AND SHE LOOKED SIXTY YEARS OLD BUT SHE WASN'T. GUESS HOW OLD SHE WAS, BORRO. GUESS!
I REALLY DON'T GIVE A BIG RAT'S ASS--
THIRTY-SIX. THAT'S ONLY A COUPLE OF YEARS AWAY FOR ME...! GOD, BUT DID SHE LOOK LIKE SHIT!
JEEZUZ CHRIST, LUBA, YOU'VE ONLY HAD FOUR BRATS! WHAT'S WITH YOU?
I'M OLD ENOUGH TO BE YOUR GODDAMN FATHER AND YOU FIGURE YOU'RE READY FOR THE GLUE FACTORY!
EW, MY HAIR'S TOO THIS- EW, MY STOMACH'S TOO THAT- EW, EW, EW..
WHO CARES, LUBA?! NOBODY NOTICES YOUR GODDAMN FEET OR YOUR AGE ANY WAY; NOT WITH THOSE GODDAMN HUGE WHOPPING JUGS OF YOURS RUNNING THE TOWN!
YOU KNOW JUST WHAT TO SAY TO A GIRL, DON'T YOU..?
ARRGH, FUCK THIS SHIT. I'VE GOT THE GODDAMN WRETCH TO CATCH!
'THOSE TWO LITTLE BOYS.., WHO WOULD WANT TO--'
'THE DRAWINGS, SEÑOR...'
YEAH, I DON'T KNOW WHY THESE ARE AROUND TOWN...
I'LL ADMIT THERE'S A LIKENESS, BUT--
MY WORK SPEAKS FOR ITSELF...
BUT--BUT THOSE TWO LITTLE BOYS...WHO WOULD WANT TO DO THAT TO A-- A LITTLE CHILD--A BABY..?
67

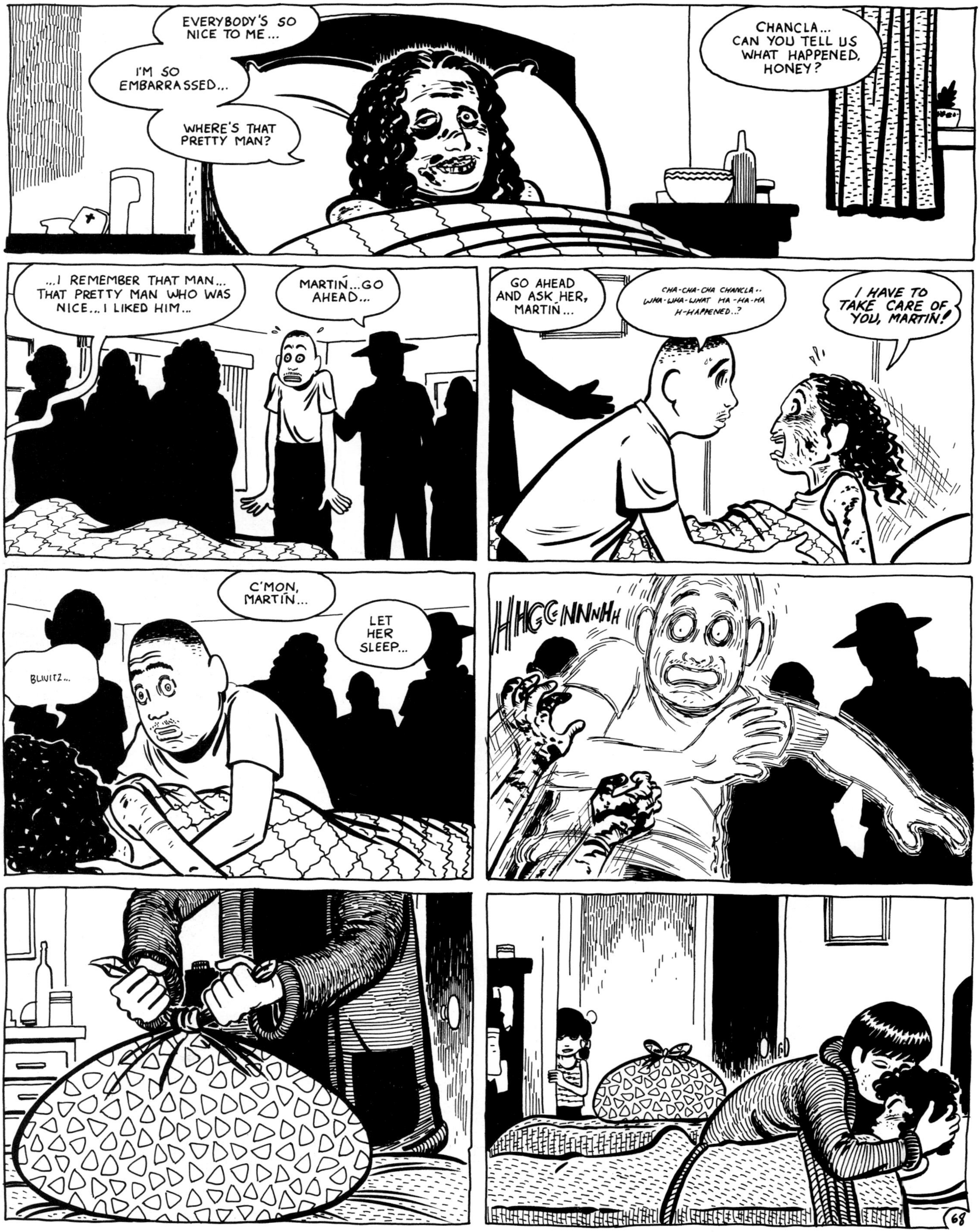
EVERYBODY'S SO NICE TO ME...
I'M SO EMBARRASSED...
WHERE'S THAT PRETTY MAN?
CHANCLA... CAN YOU TELL US WHAT HAPPENED, HONEY?
...I REMEMBER THAT MAN... THAT PRETTY MAN WHO WAS NICE... I LIKED HIM...
MARTÍN...GO AHEAD...
GO AHEAD AND ASK HER, MARTÍN...
CHA-CHA-CHA CHANCLA.. WHA-WHA-WHAT HA-HA-HA H-HAPPENED..?
I HAVE TO TAKE CARE OF YOU, MARTÍN!
C'MON, MARTÍN...
LET HER SLEEP...
BLIVITZ...
HHGGNNNHH
68

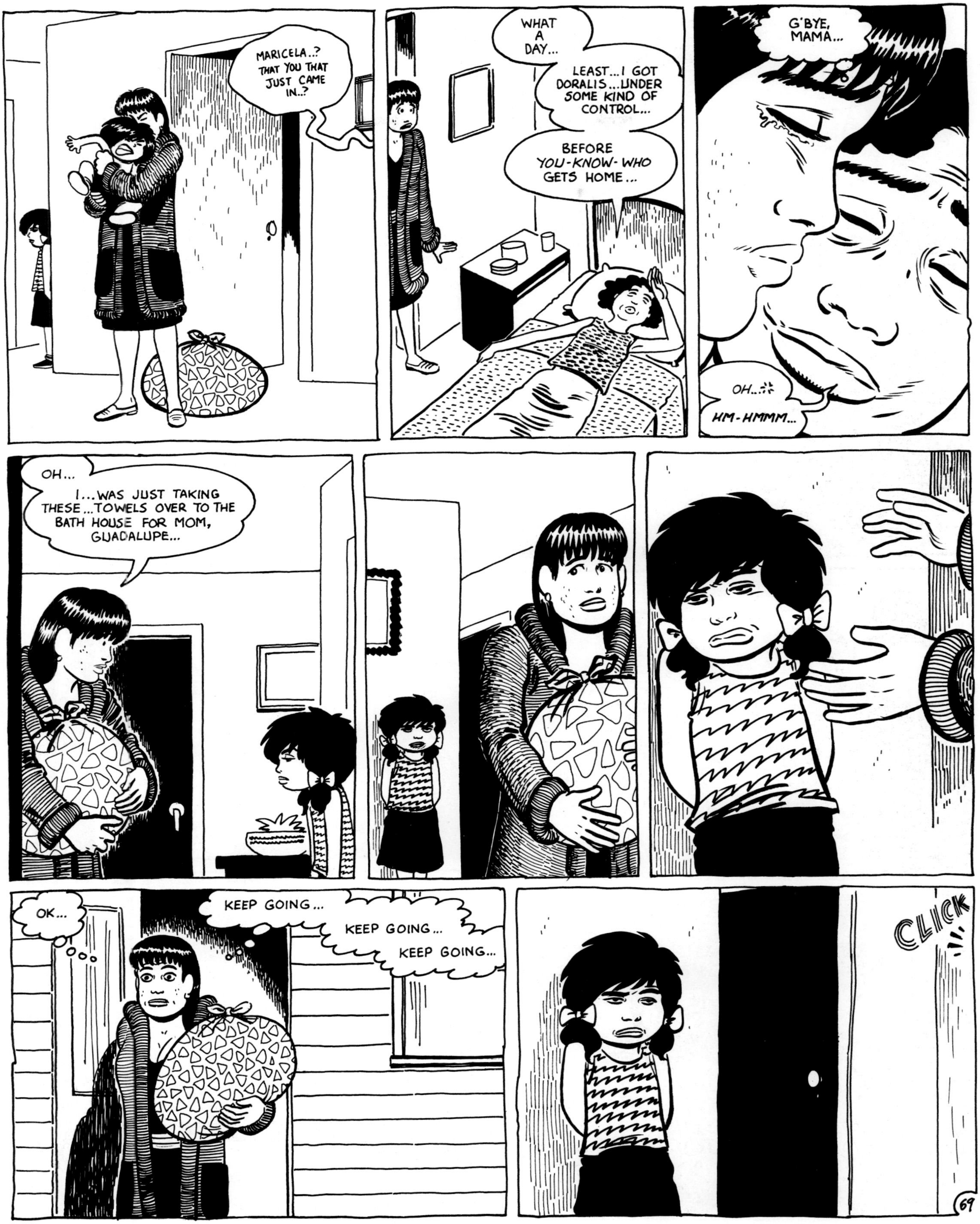
MARICELA..? THAT YOU THAT JUST CAME IN..?
WHAT A DAY...
LEAST...I GOT DORALIS...UNDER SOME KIND OF CONTROL...
BEFORE YOU-KNOW-WHO GETS HOME...
G'BYE, MAMA...
OH...
HM-HMMM...
OH...
I...WAS JUST TAKING THESE...TOWELS OVER TO THE BATH HOUSE FOR MOM, GUADALUPE...
OK...
KEEP GOING...
KEEP GOING...
KEEP GOING...
CLICK
69

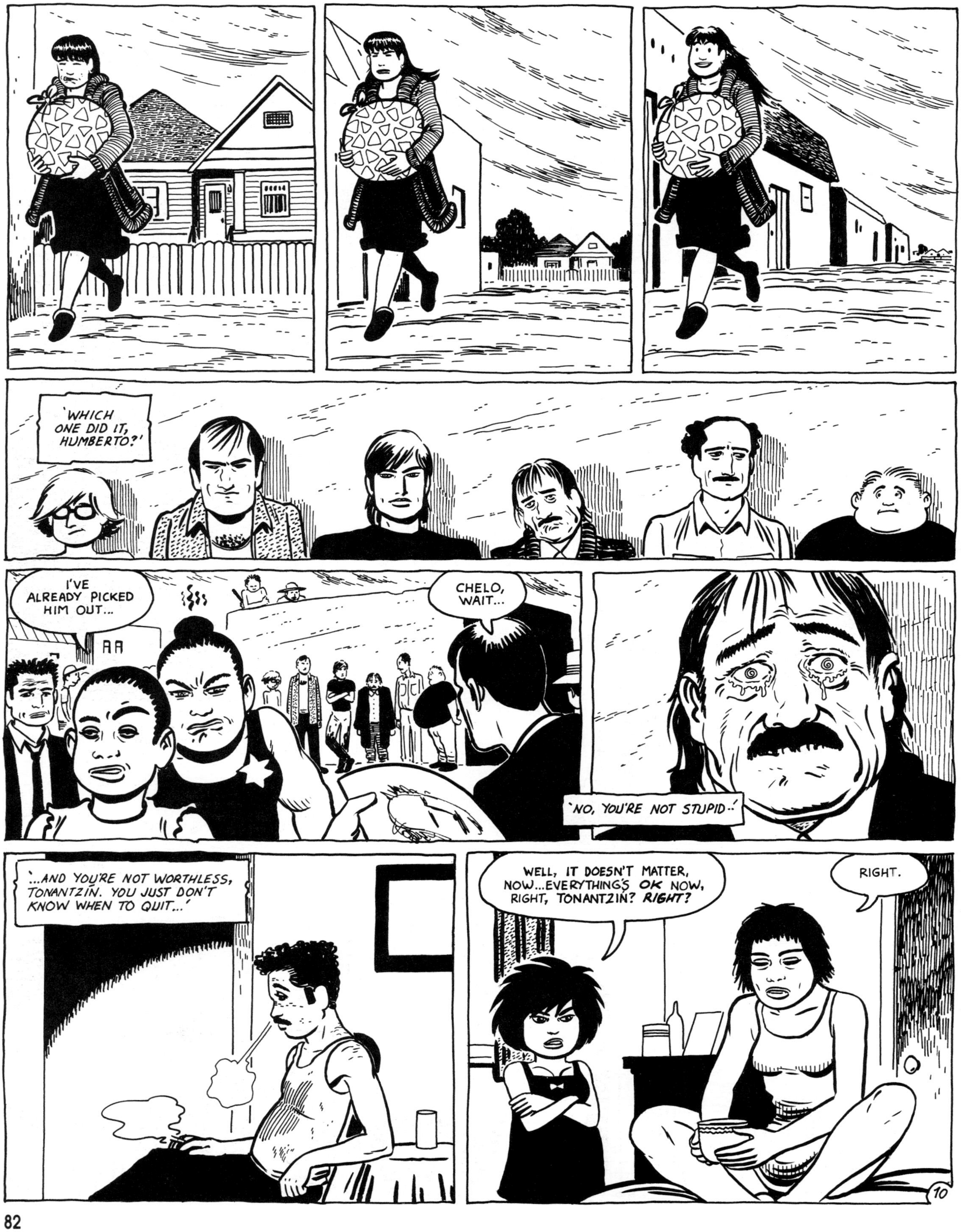
'WHICH ONE DID IT, HUMBERTO?'
I'VE ALREADY PICKED HIM OUT...
CHELO, WAIT...
'NO, YOU'RE NOT STUPID-'
'...AND YOU'RE NOT WORTHLESS, TONANTZIN. YOU JUST DON'T KNOW WHEN TO QUIT...'
WELL, IT DOESN'T MATTER, NOW...EVERYTHING'S **OK** NOW, RIGHT, TONANTZIN? ***RIGHT?***
RIGHT.
10

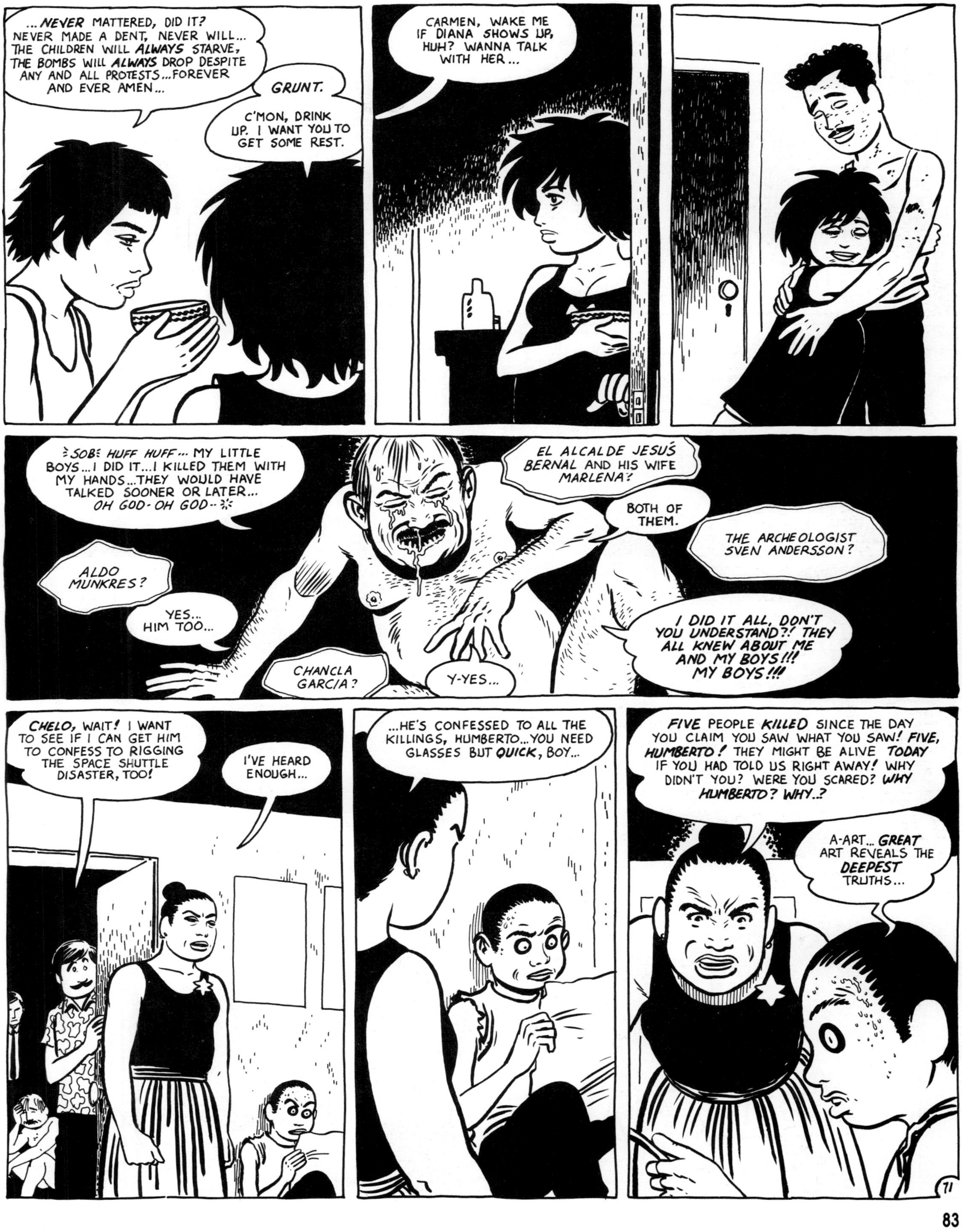

...NEVER MATTERED, DID IT? NEVER MADE A DENT, NEVER WILL... THE CHILDREN WILL ALWAYS STARVE, THE BOMBS WILL ALWAYS DROP DESPITE ANY AND ALL PROTESTS...FOREVER AND EVER AMEN...
GRUNT.
C'MON, DRINK UP. I WANT YOU TO GET SOME REST.
CARMEN, WAKE ME IF DIANA SHOWS UP, HUH? WANNA TALK WITH HER...
SOB HUFF HUFF... MY LITTLE BOYS...I DID IT...I KILLED THEM WITH MY HANDS...THEY WOULD HAVE TALKED SOONER OR LATER... OH GOD-OH GOD..*
EL ALCALDE JESÚS BERNAL AND HIS WIFE MARLENA?
BOTH OF THEM.
THE ARCHEOLOGIST SVEN ANDERSSON?
ALDO MUNKRES?
YES... HIM TOO...
CHANCLA GARCIA?
Y-YES...
I DID IT ALL, DON'T YOU UNDERSTAND?! THEY ALL KNEW ABOUT ME AND MY BOYS!!! MY BOYS!!!
CHELO, WAIT! I WANT TO SEE IF I CAN GET HIM TO CONFESS TO RIGGING THE SPACE SHUTTLE DISASTER, TOO!
I'VE HEARD ENOUGH...
...HE'S CONFESSED TO ALL THE KILLINGS, HUMBERTO...YOU NEED GLASSES BUT QUICK, BOY...
FIVE PEOPLE KILLED SINCE THE DAY YOU CLAIM YOU SAW WHAT YOU SAW! FIVE, HUMBERTO! THEY MIGHT BE ALIVE TODAY IF YOU HAD TOLD US RIGHT AWAY! WHY DIDN'T YOU? WERE YOU SCARED? WHY HUMBERTO? WHY..?
A-ART... GREAT ART REVEALS THE DEEPEST TRUTHS...
71

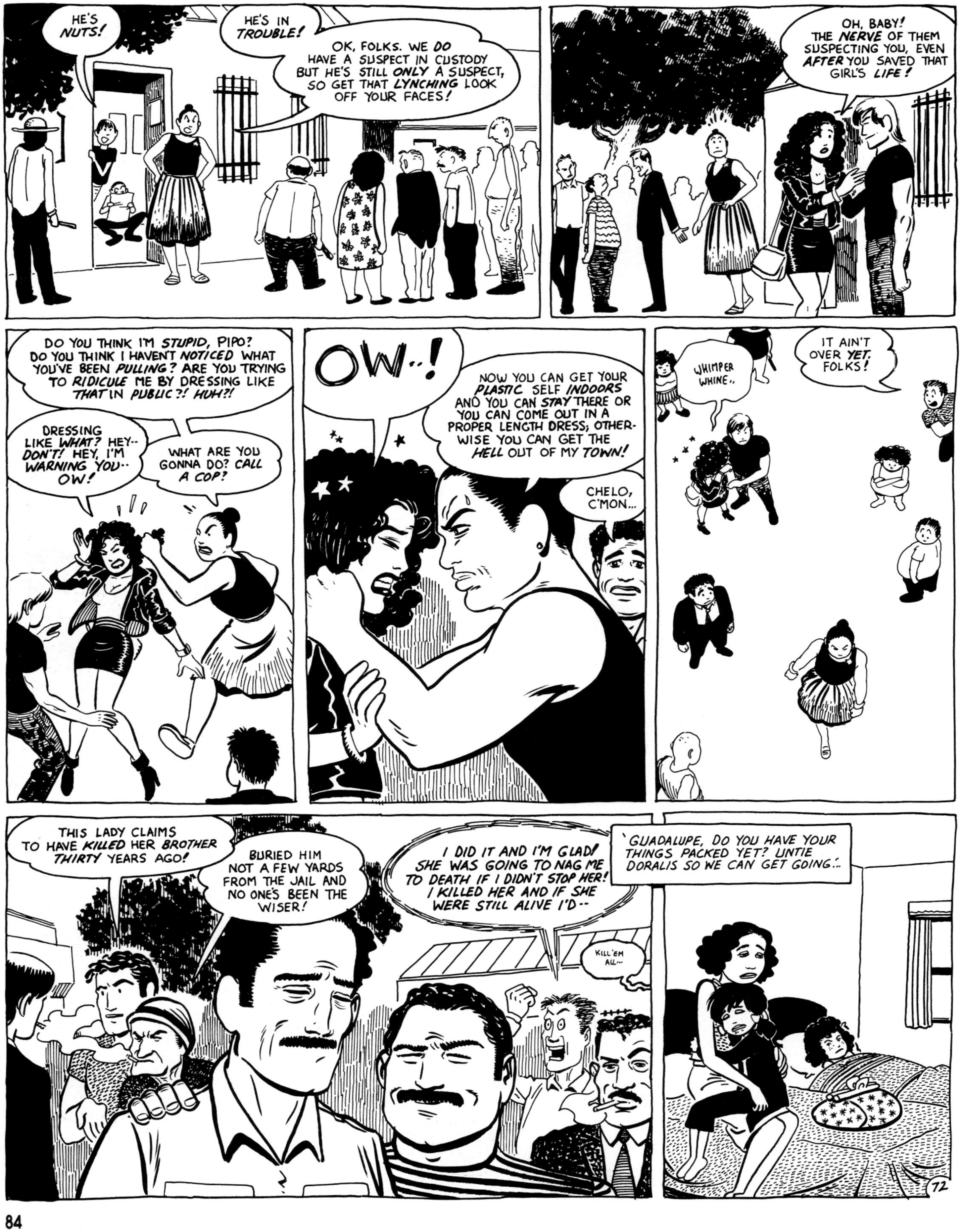
HE'S NUTS!
HE'S IN TROUBLE!
OK, FOLKS. WE DO HAVE A SUSPECT IN CUSTODY BUT HE'S STILL ONLY A SUSPECT, SO GET THAT LYNCHING LOOK OFF YOUR FACES!
OH, BABY! THE NERVE OF THEM SUSPECTING YOU, EVEN AFTER YOU SAVED THAT GIRL'S LIFE!
DO YOU THINK I'M STUPID, PIPO? DO YOU THINK I HAVEN'T NOTICED WHAT YOU'VE BEEN PULLING? ARE YOU TRYING TO RIDICULE ME BY DRESSING LIKE THAT IN PUBLIC?! HUH?!
DRESSING LIKE WHAT? HEY-- DON'T! HEY, I'M WARNING YOU-- OW!
WHAT ARE YOU GONNA DO? CALL A COP?
OW..!
NOW YOU CAN GET YOUR PLASTIC SELF INDOORS AND YOU CAN STAY THERE OR YOU CAN COME OUT IN A PROPER LENGTH DRESS; OTHERWISE YOU CAN GET THE HELL OUT OF MY TOWN!
CHELO, C'MON...
WHIMPER WHINE..
IT AIN'T OVER YET, FOLKS!
THIS LADY CLAIMS TO HAVE KILLED HER BROTHER THIRTY YEARS AGO!
BURIED HIM NOT A FEW YARDS FROM THE JAIL AND NO ONE'S BEEN THE WISER!
I DID IT AND I'M GLAD! SHE WAS GOING TO NAG ME TO DEATH IF I DIDN'T STOP HER! I KILLED HER AND IF SHE WERE STILL ALIVE I'D--
KILL 'EM ALL...
"GUADALUPE, DO YOU HAVE YOUR THINGS PACKED YET? UNTIE DORALIS SO WE CAN GET GOING."
72

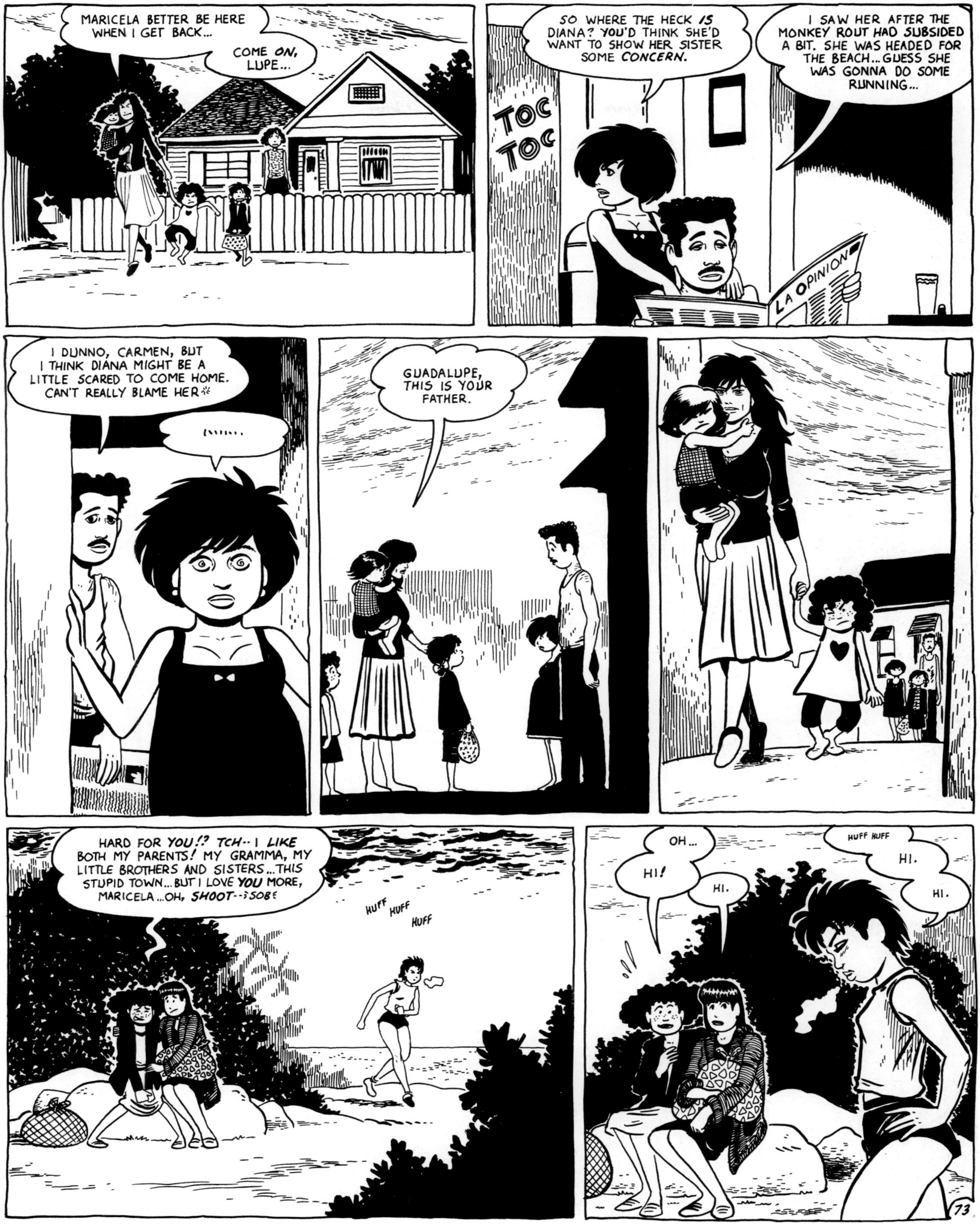
MARICELA BETTER BE HERE WHEN I GET BACK...
COME ON, LUPE...
SO WHERE THE HECK IS DIANA? YOU'D THINK SHE'D WANT TO SHOW HER SISTER SOME CONCERN.
TOC TOC
I SAW HER AFTER THE MONKEY ROUT HAD SUBSIDED A BIT. SHE WAS HEADED FOR THE BEACH...GUESS SHE WAS GONNA DO SOME RUNNING...
LA OPINION
I DUNNO, CARMEN, BUT I THINK DIANA MIGHT BE A LITTLE SCARED TO COME HOME. CAN'T REALLY BLAME HER
GUADALUPE, THIS IS YOUR FATHER.
HARD FOR YOU!? TCH·· I LIKE BOTH MY PARENTS! MY GRAMMA, MY LITTLE BROTHERS AND SISTERS...THIS STUPID TOWN...BUT I LOVE YOU MORE, MARICELA...OH, SHOOT··SOB
HUFF HUFF HUFF
OH...
HI!
HI.
HUFF HUFF
HI.
HI.
73

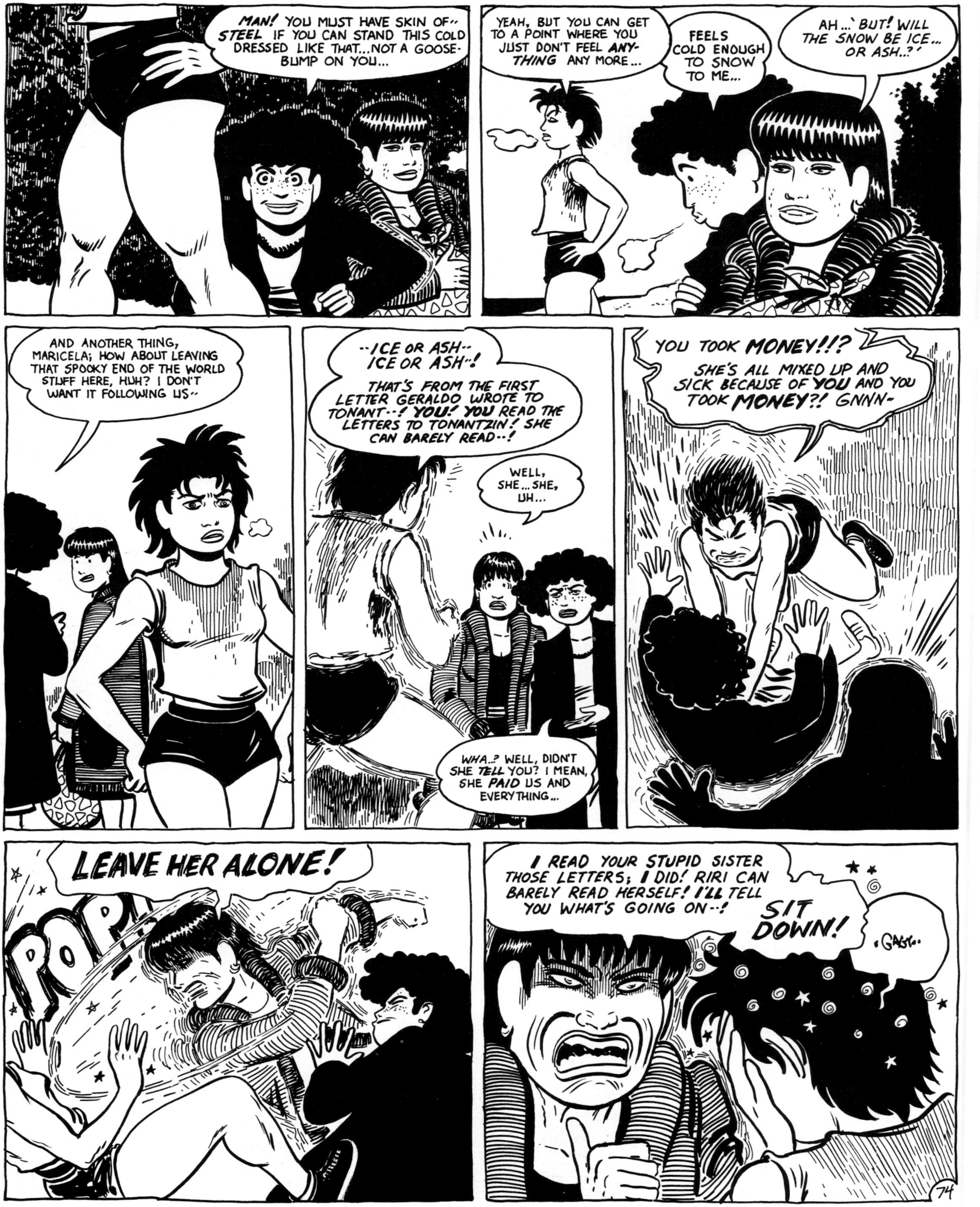
MAN! YOU MUST HAVE SKIN OF.. STEEL IF YOU CAN STAND THIS COLD DRESSED LIKE THAT...NOT A GOOSE-BUMP ON YOU...
YEAH, BUT YOU CAN GET TO A POINT WHERE YOU JUST DON'T FEEL ANY-THING ANY MORE...
FEELS COLD ENOUGH TO SNOW TO ME...
AH...`BUT! WILL THE SNOW BE ICE... OR ASH..?'
AND ANOTHER THING, MARICELA; HOW ABOUT LEAVING THAT SPOOKY END OF THE WORLD STUFF HERE, HUH? I DON'T WANT IT FOLLOWING US..
..ICE OR ASH.. ICE OR ASH..!
THAT'S FROM THE FIRST LETTER GERALDO WROTE TO TONANT..! YOU! YOU READ THE LETTERS TO TONANTZIN! SHE CAN BARELY READ..!
WELL, SHE...SHE, UH...
WHA..? WELL, DIDN'T SHE TELL YOU? I MEAN, SHE PAID US AND EVERYTHING...
YOU TOOK MONEY!!?
SHE'S ALL MIXED UP AND SICK BECAUSE OF YOU AND YOU TOOK MONEY?! GNNN-
LEAVE HER ALONE!
POP
I READ YOUR STUPID SISTER THOSE LETTERS; I DID! RIRI CAN BARELY READ HERSELF! I'LL TELL YOU WHAT'S GOING ON..!
SIT DOWN!
74

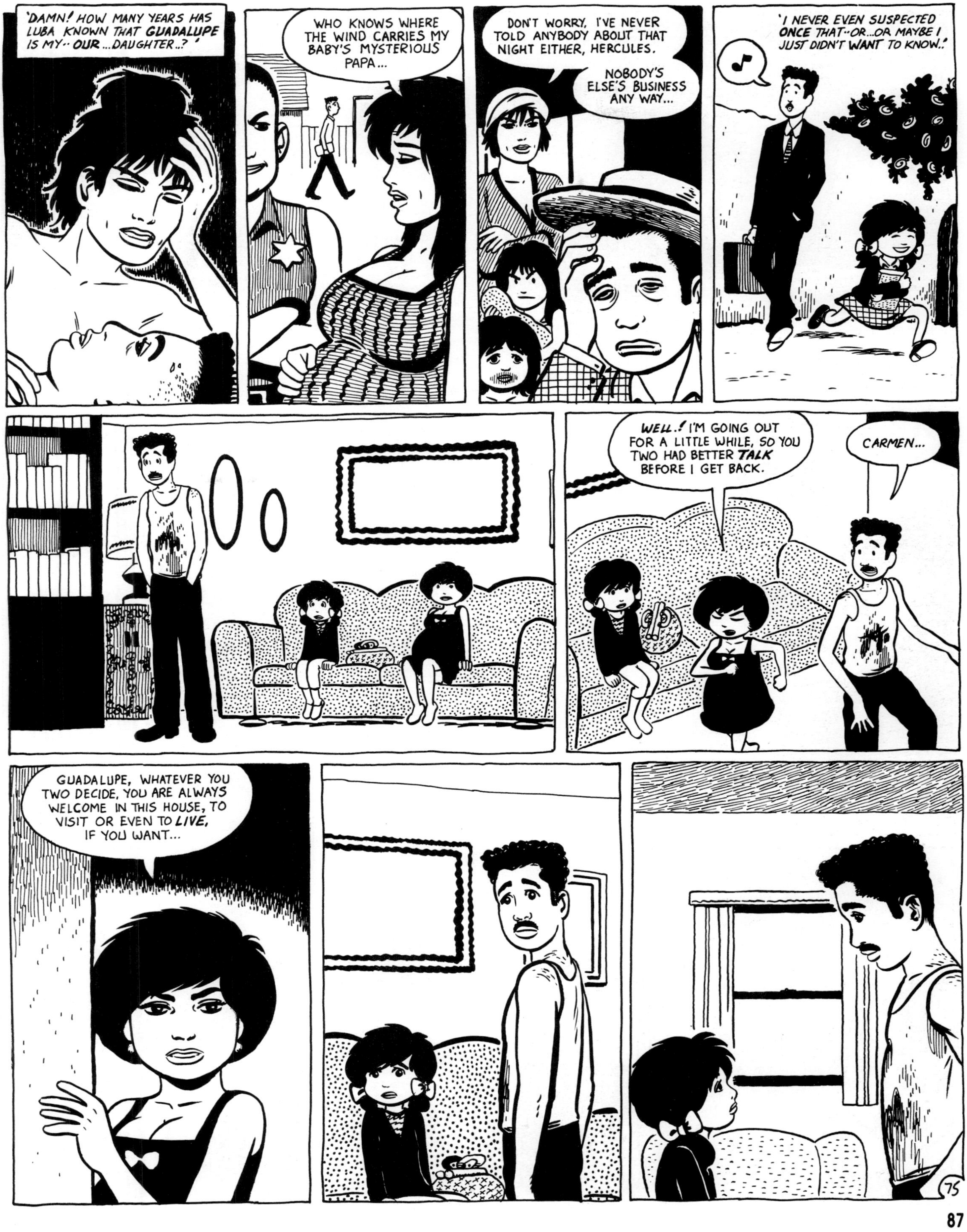
'DAMN! HOW MANY YEARS HAS LUBA KNOWN THAT GUADALUPE IS MY·· OUR ...DAUGHTER..? '
WHO KNOWS WHERE THE WIND CARRIES MY BABY'S MYSTERIOUS PAPA...
DON'T WORRY, I'VE NEVER TOLD ANYBODY ABOUT THAT NIGHT EITHER, HERCULES.
NOBODY'S ELSE'S BUSINESS ANY WAY...
'I NEVER EVEN SUSPECTED ONCE THAT··OR...OR MAYBE I JUST DIDN'T WANT TO KNOW.'
♪
WELL.! I'M GOING OUT FOR A LITTLE WHILE, SO YOU TWO HAD BETTER TALK BEFORE I GET BACK.
CARMEN...
GUADALUPE, WHATEVER YOU TWO DECIDE, YOU ARE ALWAYS WELCOME IN THIS HOUSE, TO VISIT OR EVEN TO LIVE, IF YOU WANT...
75

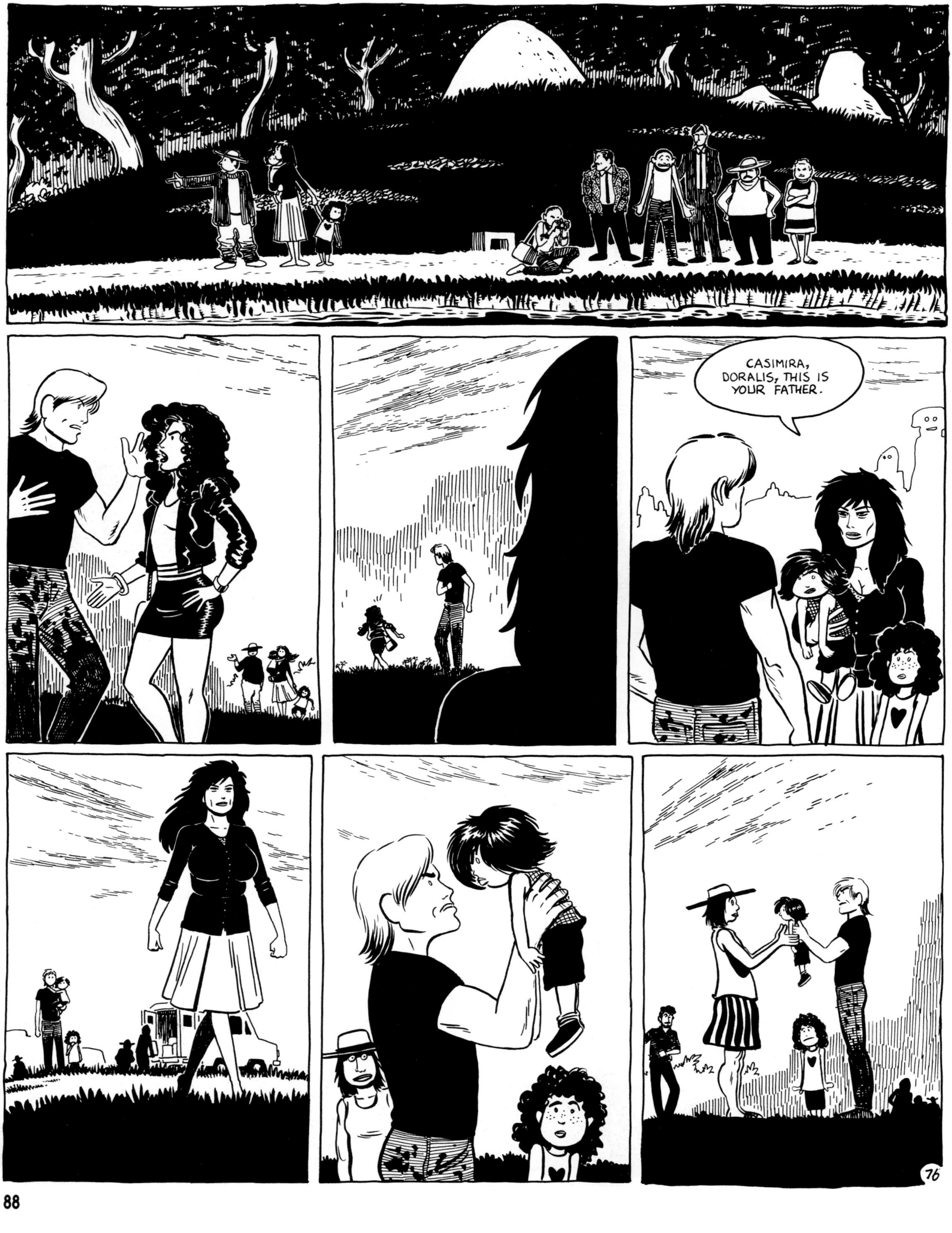
CASIMIRA, DORALIS, THIS IS YOUR FATHER.
76

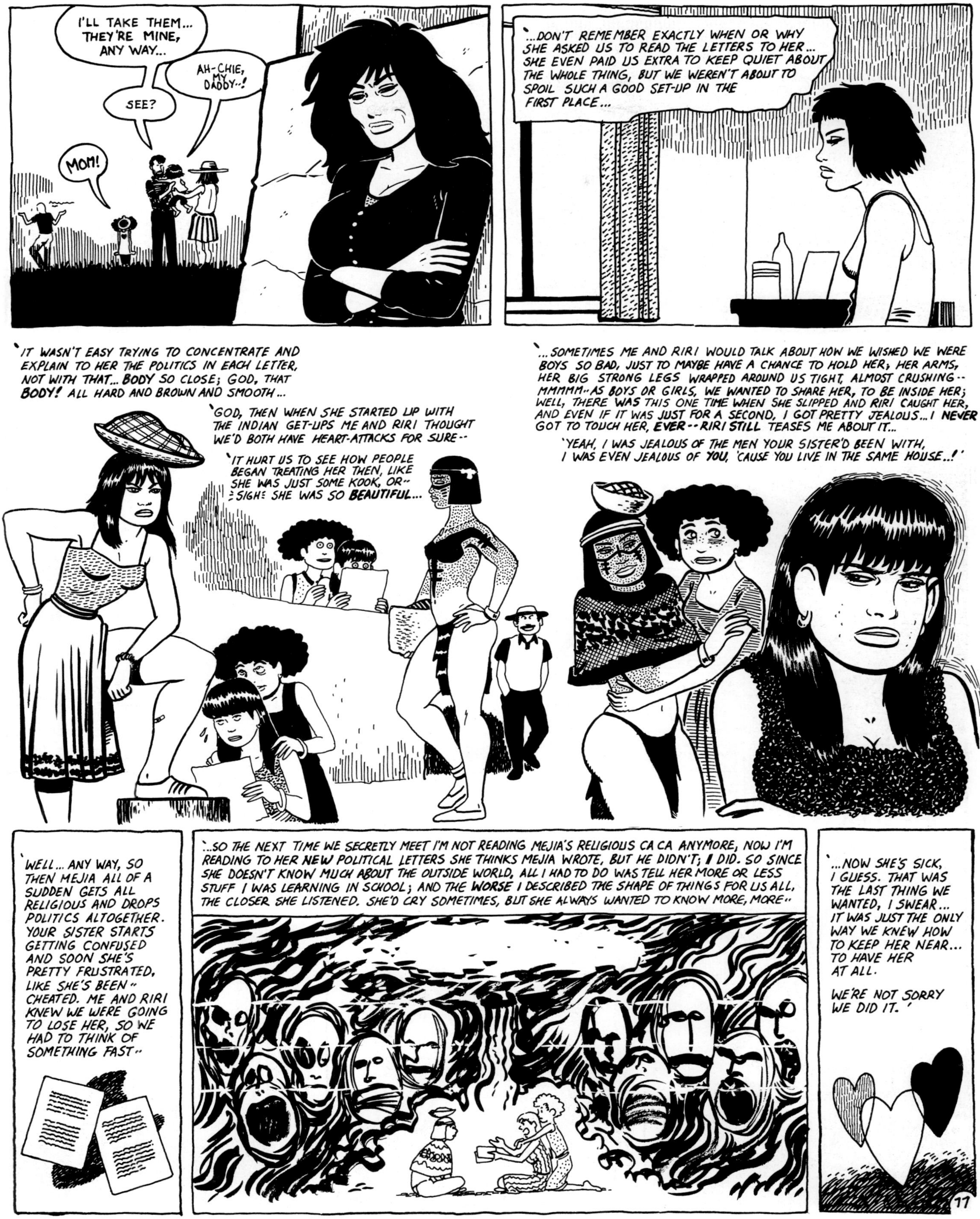
I'LL TAKE THEM... THEY'RE MINE, ANY WAY...
SEE?
AH-CHIE, MY DADDY..!
MOM!
'...DON'T REMEMBER EXACTLY WHEN OR WHY SHE ASKED US TO READ THE LETTERS TO HER... SHE EVEN PAID US EXTRA TO KEEP QUIET ABOUT THE WHOLE THING, BUT WE WEREN'T ABOUT TO SPOIL SUCH A GOOD SET-UP IN THE FIRST PLACE...
'IT WASN'T EASY TRYING TO CONCENTRATE AND EXPLAIN TO HER THE POLITICS IN EACH LETTER, NOT WITH THAT... BODY SO CLOSE; GOD, THAT BODY! ALL HARD AND BROWN AND SMOOTH...
'GOD, THEN WHEN SHE STARTED UP WITH THE INDIAN GET-UPS ME AND RIRI THOUGHT WE'D BOTH HAVE HEART-ATTACKS FOR SURE--
'IT HURT US TO SEE HOW PEOPLE BEGAN TREATING HER THEN, LIKE SHE WAS JUST SOME KOOK, OR-- =SIGH= SHE WAS SO BEAUTIFUL...
'...SOMETIMES ME AND RIRI WOULD TALK ABOUT HOW WE WISHED WE WERE BOYS SO BAD, JUST TO MAYBE HAVE A CHANCE TO HOLD HER, HER ARMS, HER BIG STRONG LEGS WRAPPED AROUND US TIGHT, ALMOST CRUSHING-- MMMMM--AS BOYS OR GIRLS, WE WANTED TO SHARE HER, TO BE INSIDE HER; WELL, THERE WAS THIS ONE TIME WHEN SHE SLIPPED AND RIRI CAUGHT HER, AND EVEN IF IT WAS JUST FOR A SECOND, I GOT PRETTY JEALOUS... I NEVER GOT TO TOUCH HER, EVER--RIRI STILL TEASES ME ABOUT IT...
'YEAH, I WAS JEALOUS OF THE MEN YOUR SISTER'D BEEN WITH, I WAS EVEN JEALOUS OF YOU, 'CAUSE YOU LIVE IN THE SAME HOUSE..!'
'WELL... ANY WAY, SO THEN MEJIA ALL OF A SUDDEN GETS ALL RELIGIOUS AND DROPS POLITICS ALTOGETHER. YOUR SISTER STARTS GETTING CONFUSED AND SOON SHE'S PRETTY FRUSTRATED, LIKE SHE'S BEEN-- CHEATED. ME AND RIRI KNEW WE WERE GOING TO LOSE HER, SO WE HAD TO THINK OF SOMETHING FAST--
'...SO THE NEXT TIME WE SECRETLY MEET I'M NOT READING MEJIA'S RELIGIOUS CA CA ANYMORE, NOW I'M READING TO HER NEW POLITICAL LETTERS SHE THINKS MEJIA WROTE, BUT HE DIDN'T; I DID. SO SINCE SHE DOESN'T KNOW MUCH ABOUT THE OUTSIDE WORLD, ALL I HAD TO DO WAS TELL HER MORE OR LESS STUFF I WAS LEARNING IN SCHOOL; AND THE WORSE I DESCRIBED THE SHAPE OF THINGS FOR US ALL, THE CLOSER SHE LISTENED. SHE'D CRY SOMETIMES, BUT SHE ALWAYS WANTED TO KNOW MORE, MORE--
'...NOW SHE'S SICK, I GUESS. THAT WAS THE LAST THING WE WANTED, I SWEAR... IT WAS JUST THE ONLY WAY WE KNEW HOW TO KEEP HER NEAR... TO HAVE HER AT ALL.
WE'RE NOT SORRY WE DID IT.'
17

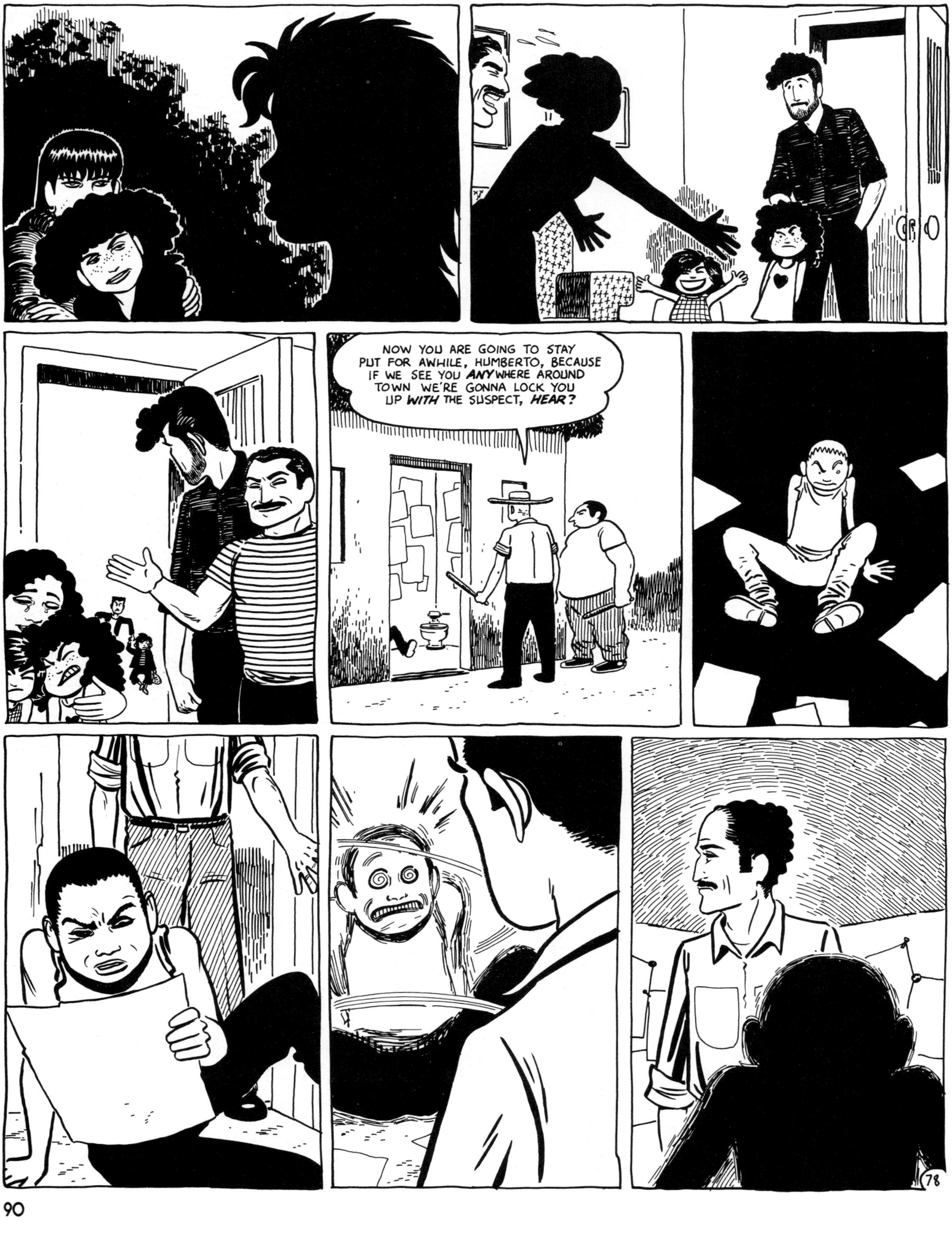
NOW YOU ARE GOING TO STAY PUT FOR AWHILE, HUMBERTO, BECAUSE IF WE SEE YOU **ANY**WHERE AROUND TOWN WE'RE GONNA LOCK YOU UP **WITH** THE SUSPECT, **HEAR?**
78

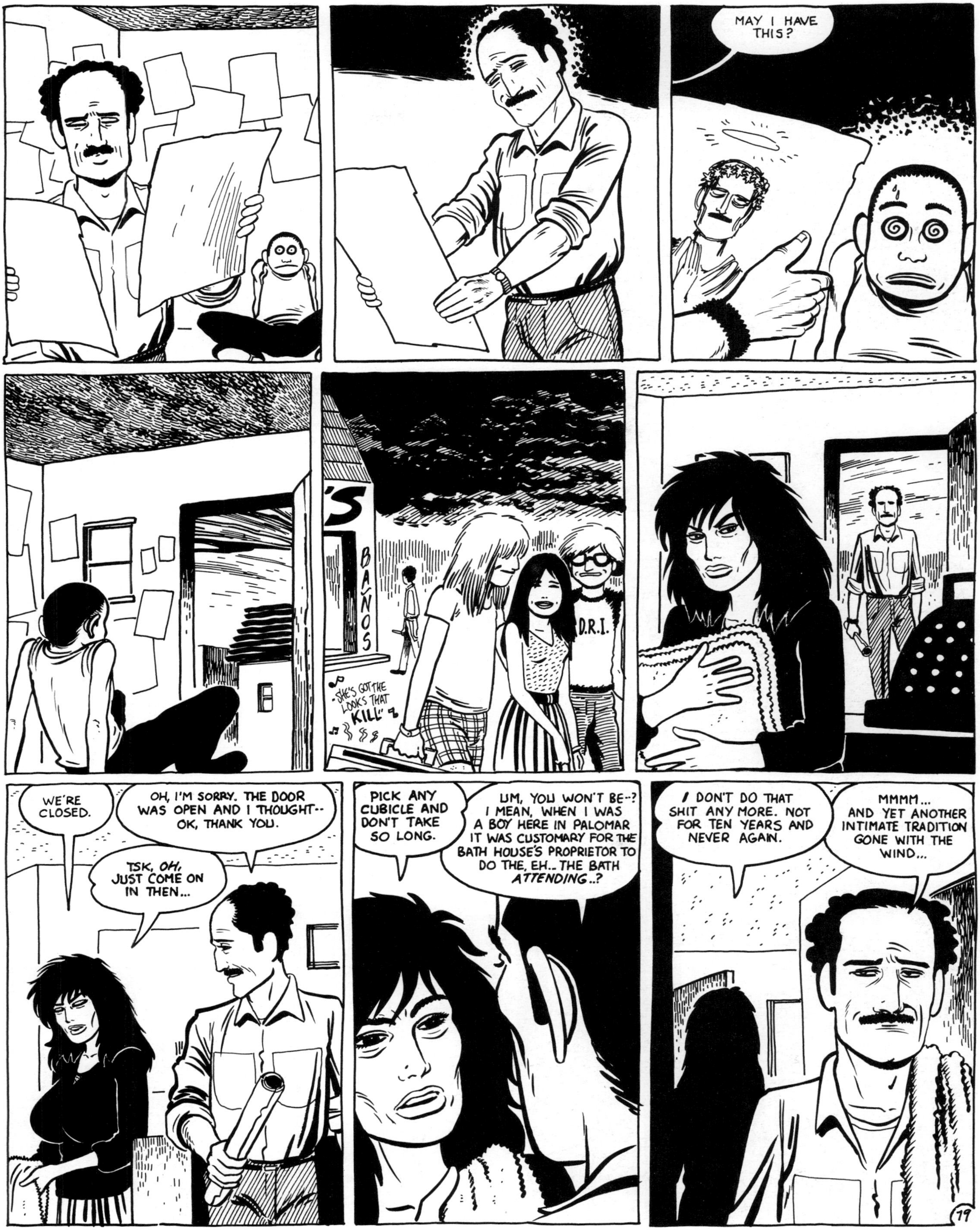
MAY I HAVE THIS?
'S
BAÑOS
♪ "SHE'S GOT THE LOOKS THAT KILL" ♪
D.R.I.
WE'RE CLOSED.
OH, I'M SORRY. THE DOOR WAS OPEN AND I THOUGHT-- OK, THANK YOU.
TSK, OH, JUST COME ON IN THEN...
PICK ANY CUBICLE AND DON'T TAKE SO LONG.
UM, YOU WON'T BE--? I MEAN, WHEN I WAS A BOY HERE IN PALOMAR IT WAS CUSTOMARY FOR THE BATH HOUSE'S PROPRIETOR TO DO THE, EH... THE BATH ATTENDING..?
I DON'T DO THAT SHIT ANY MORE. NOT FOR TEN YEARS AND NEVER AGAIN.
MMMM... AND YET ANOTHER INTIMATE TRADITION GONE WITH THE WIND...
79

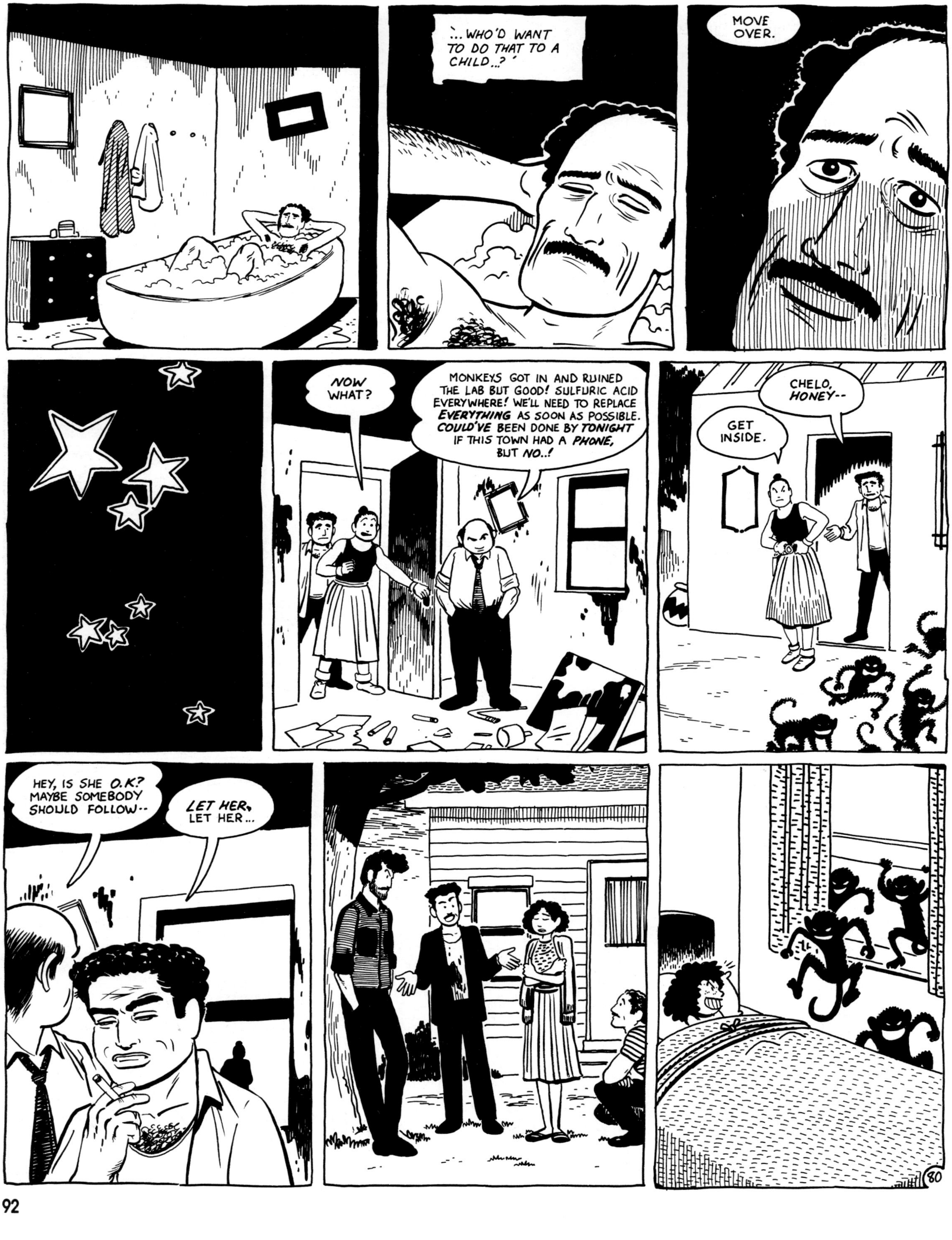
"...WHO'D WANT TO DO THAT TO A CHILD..?"
MOVE OVER.
NOW WHAT?
MONKEYS GOT IN AND RUINED THE LAB BUT GOOD! SULFURIC ACID EVERYWHERE! WE'LL NEED TO REPLACE *EVERYTHING* AS SOON AS POSSIBLE. *COULD'VE* BEEN DONE BY *TONIGHT* IF THIS TOWN HAD A *PHONE*, BUT *NO..!*
CHELO, *HONEY--*
GET INSIDE.
HEY, IS SHE *O.K?* MAYBE SOMEBODY SHOULD FOLLOW--
LET HER, LET HER...
80

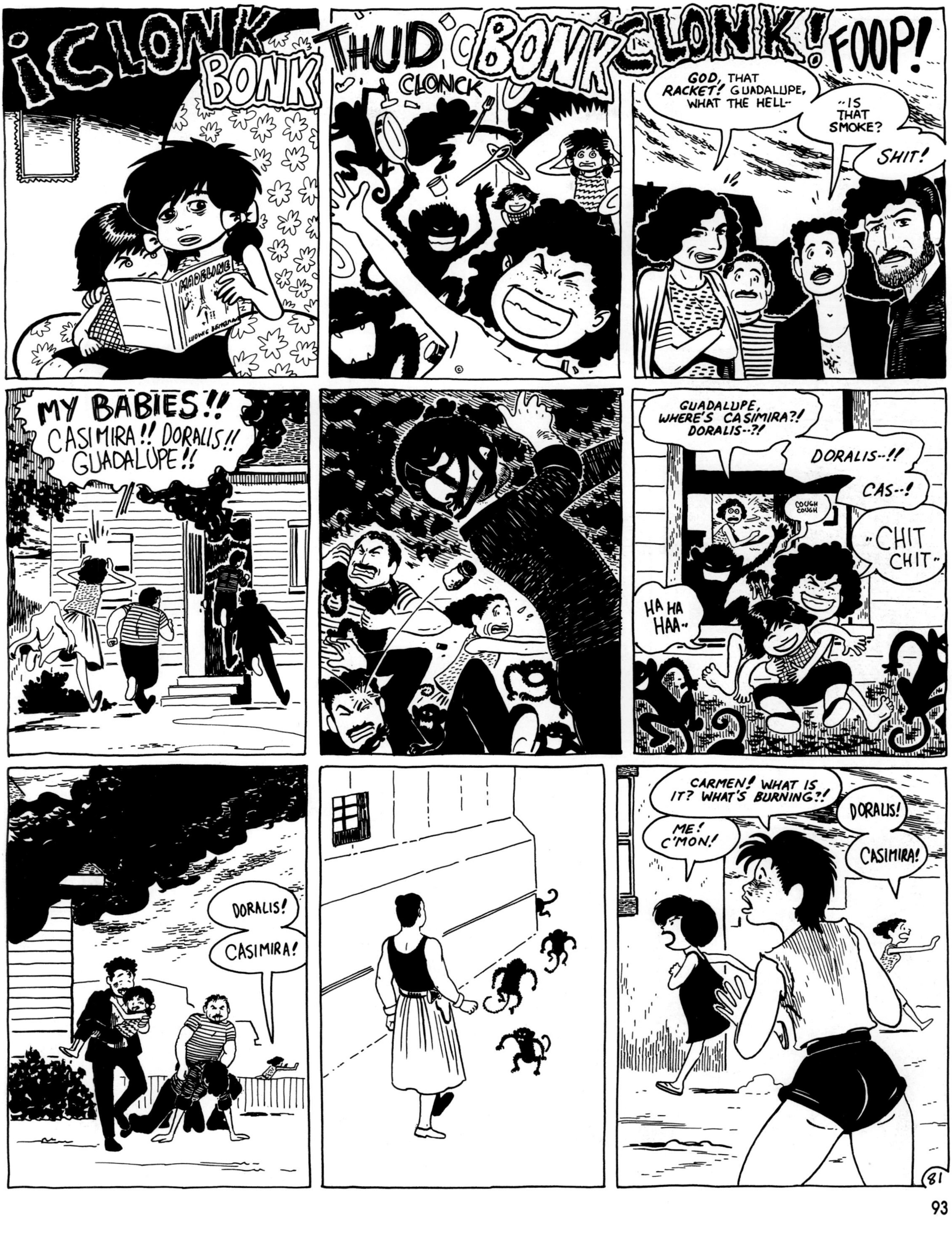
¡CLONK
BONK
THUD
BONK
CLONK!
FOOP!
CLONICK
GOD, THAT RACKET! GUADALUPE, WHAT THE HELL--
--IS THAT SMOKE?
SHIT!
MY BABIES!!
CASIMIRA!! DORALIS!! GUADALUPE!!
GUADALUPE, WHERE'S CASIMIRA?! DORALIS--?!
DORALIS--!!
CAS--!
COUGH COUGH
"CHIT CHIT"
HA HA HAA..
DORALIS!
CASIMIRA!
CARMEN! WHAT IS IT? WHAT'S BURNING?!
ME! C'MON!
DORALIS!
CASIMIRA!
81

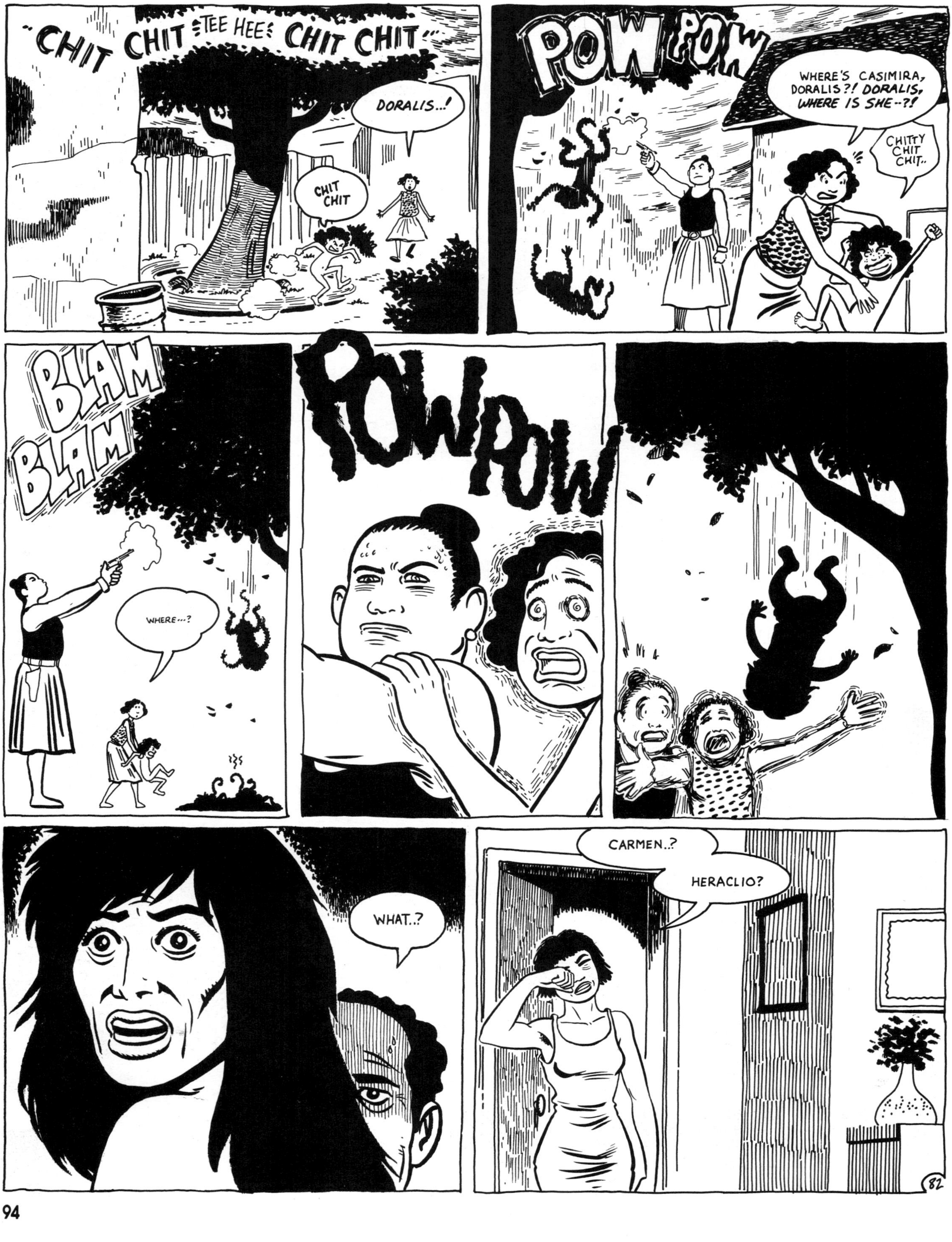
CHIT CHIT TEE HEE CHIT CHIT
DORALIS..!
CHIT CHIT
POW POW
WHERE'S CASIMIRA, DORALIS?! DORALIS, WHERE IS SHE--?!
CHITTY CHIT CHIT..
BLAM BLAM
WHERE...?
POW POW
CARMEN..?
HERACLIO?
WHAT..?
82

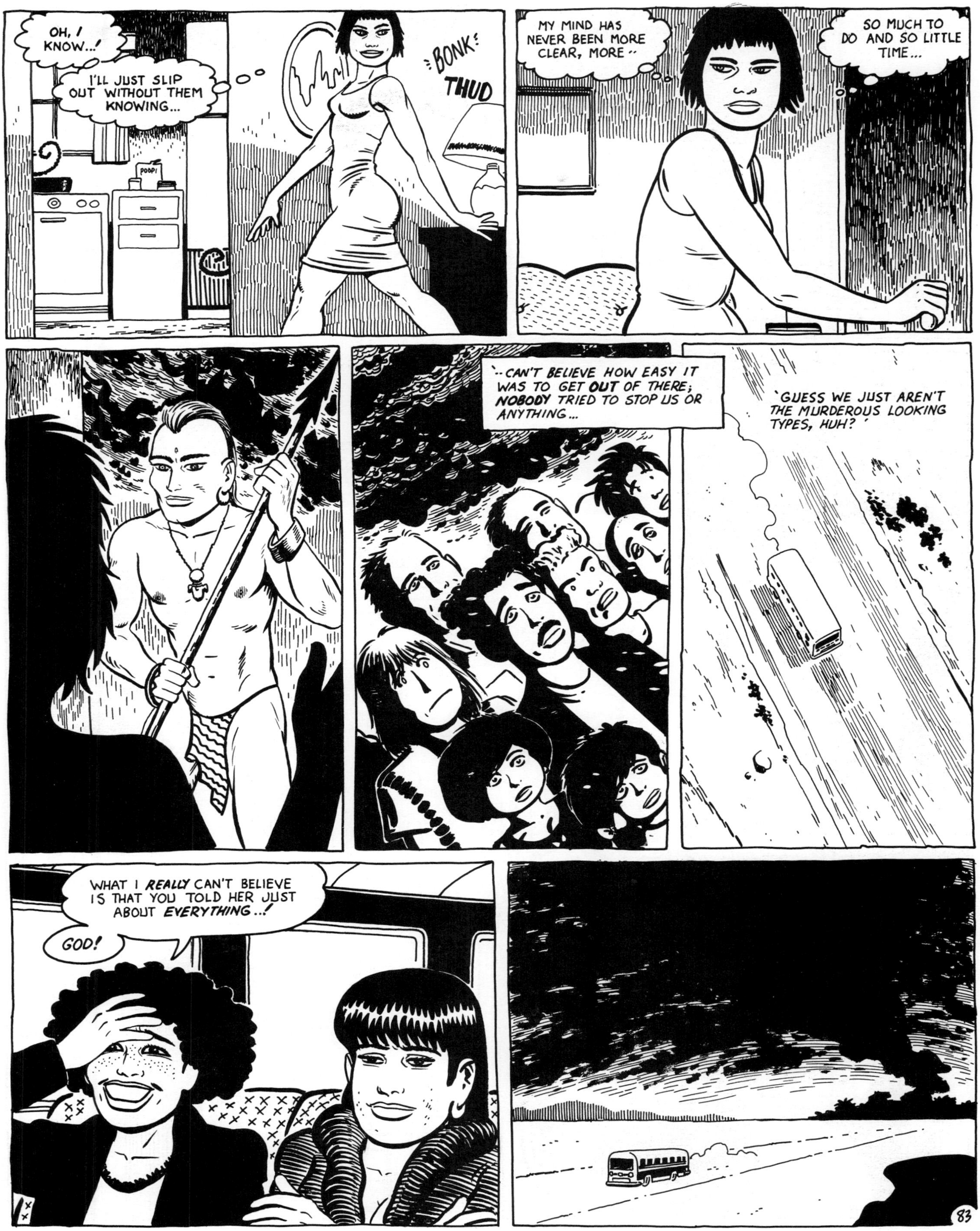

OH, I KNOW...!
I'LL JUST SLIP OUT WITHOUT THEM KNOWING...
POOP!
BONK
THUD
MY MIND HAS NEVER BEEN MORE CLEAR, MORE --
SO MUCH TO DO AND SO LITTLE TIME...
`--CAN'T BELIEVE HOW EASY IT WAS TO GET OUT OF THERE; NOBODY TRIED TO STOP US OR ANYTHING...
`GUESS WE JUST AREN'T THE MURDEROUS LOOKING TYPES, HUH? '
WHAT I REALLY CAN'T BELIEVE IS THAT YOU TOLD HER JUST ABOUT EVERYTHING...!
GOD!
83

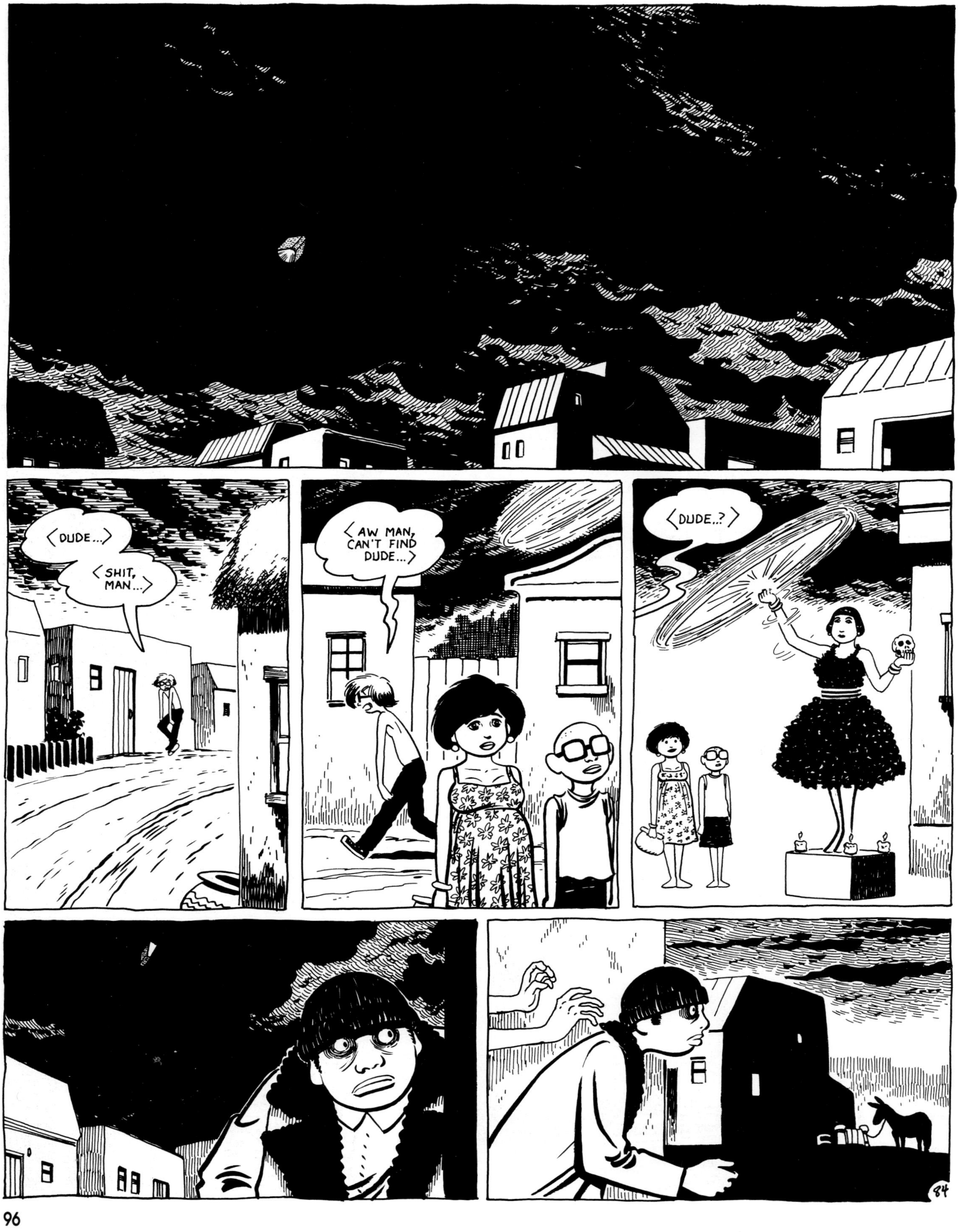
⟨DUDE...⟩
⟨SHIT, MAN...⟩
⟨AW MAN, CAN'T FIND DUDE...⟩
⟨DUDE..?⟩
84

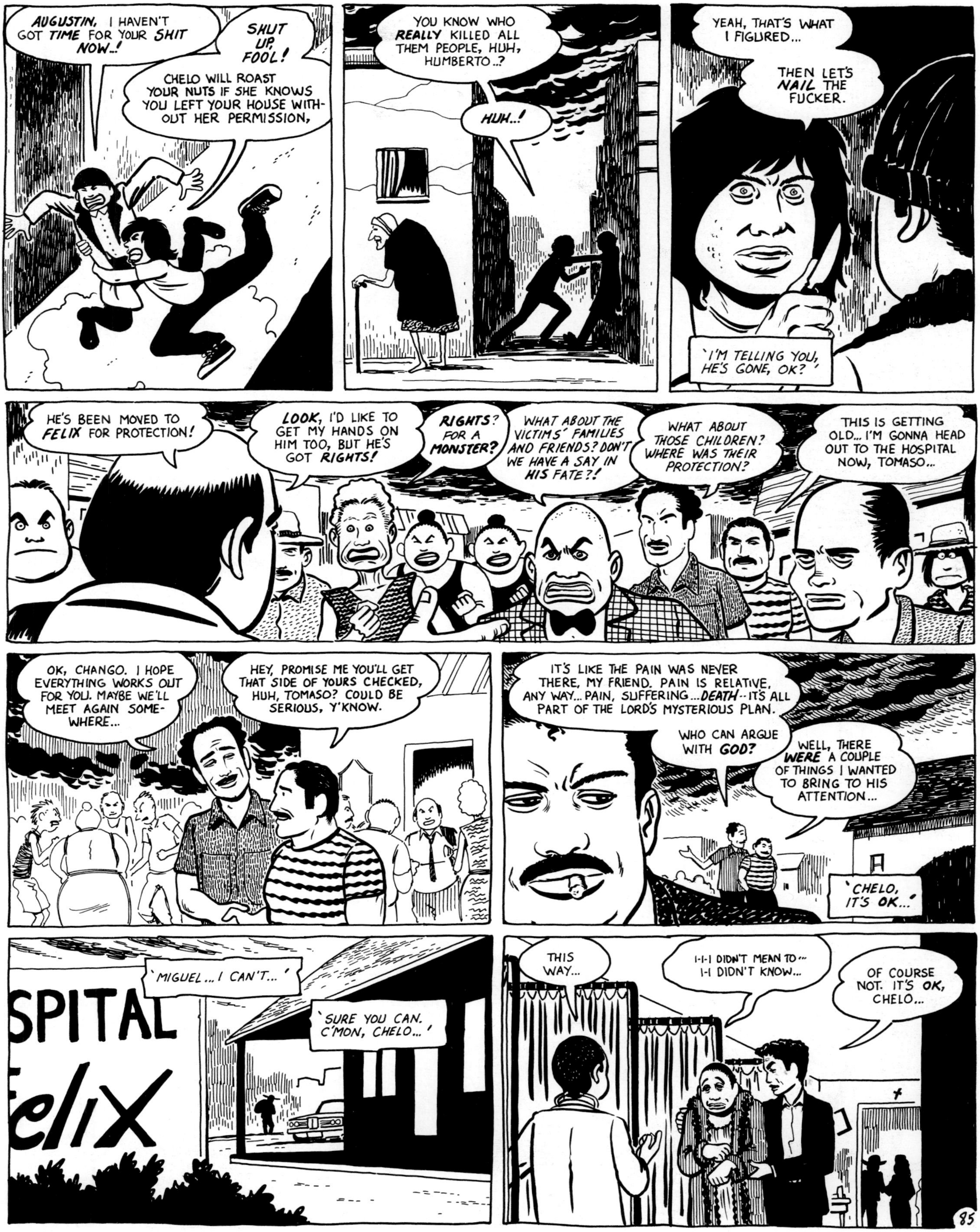
AUGUSTIN, I HAVEN'T GOT TIME FOR YOUR SHIT NOW..!
SHUT UP, FOOL!
CHELO WILL ROAST YOUR NUTS IF SHE KNOWS YOU LEFT YOUR HOUSE WITHOUT HER PERMISSION,
YOU KNOW WHO REALLY KILLED ALL THEM PEOPLE, HUH, HUMBERTO..?
HUH..!
YEAH, THAT'S WHAT I FIGURED...
THEN LET'S NAIL THE FUCKER.
'I'M TELLING YOU, HE'S GONE, OK?'
HE'S BEEN MOVED TO FELIX FOR PROTECTION!
LOOK, I'D LIKE TO GET MY HANDS ON HIM TOO, BUT HE'S GOT RIGHTS!
RIGHTS? FOR A MONSTER?
WHAT ABOUT THE VICTIMS' FAMILIES AND FRIENDS? DON'T WE HAVE A SAY IN HIS FATE?!
WHAT ABOUT THOSE CHILDREN? WHERE WAS THEIR PROTECTION?
THIS IS GETTING OLD... I'M GONNA HEAD OUT TO THE HOSPITAL NOW, TOMASO...
OK, CHANGO. I HOPE EVERYTHING WORKS OUT FOR YOU. MAYBE WE'LL MEET AGAIN SOMEWHERE...
HEY, PROMISE ME YOU'LL GET THAT SIDE OF YOURS CHECKED, HUH, TOMASO? COULD BE SERIOUS, Y'KNOW.
IT'S LIKE THE PAIN WAS NEVER THERE, MY FRIEND. PAIN IS RELATIVE, ANY WAY... PAIN, SUFFERING... DEATH-- IT'S ALL PART OF THE LORD'S MYSTERIOUS PLAN.
WHO CAN ARGUE WITH GOD?
WELL, THERE WERE A COUPLE OF THINGS I WANTED TO BRING TO HIS ATTENTION...
'CHELO, IT'S OK...'
'MIGUEL... I CAN'T...'
SPITAL
FelIX
'SURE YOU CAN. C'MON, CHELO...'
THIS WAY...
I-I-I DIDN'T MEAN TO--
I-I DIDN'T KNOW...
OF COURSE NOT. IT'S OK, CHELO...
85

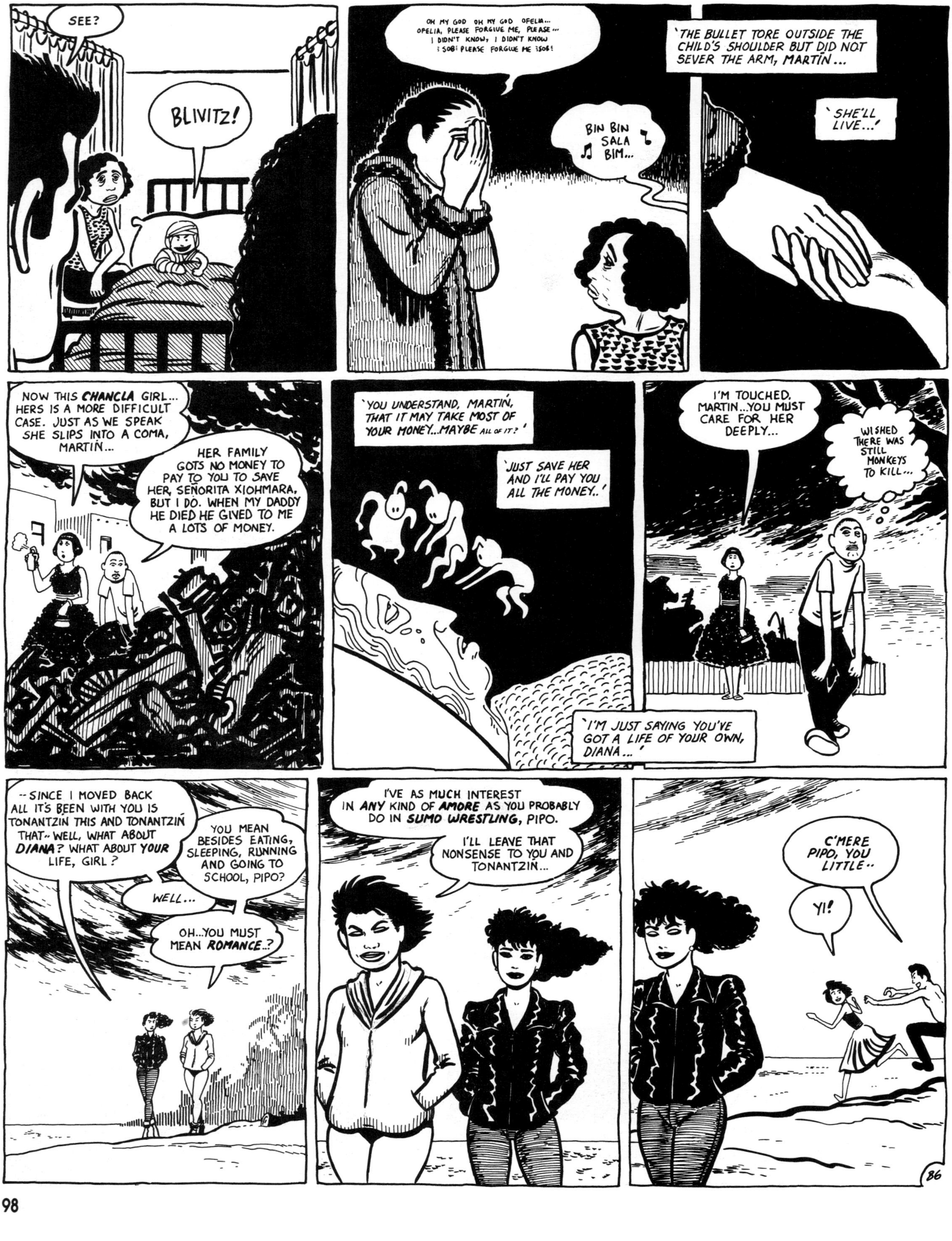
SEE?
BLIVITZ!
OH MY GOD OH MY GOD OFELIA... OFELIA, PLEASE FORGIVE ME, PLEASE... I DIDN'T KNOW, I DIDN'T KNOW :SOB: PLEASE FORGIVE ME :SOB:
BIN BIN SALA BIM...
'THE BULLET TORE OUTSIDE THE CHILD'S SHOULDER BUT DID NOT SEVER THE ARM, MARTÍN...
'SHE'LL LIVE...'
NOW THIS CHANCLA GIRL... HERS IS A MORE DIFFICULT CASE. JUST AS WE SPEAK SHE SLIPS INTO A COMA, MARTÍN...
HER FAMILY GOTS NO MONEY TO PAY TO YOU TO SAVE HER, SEÑORITA XIOHMARA, BUT I DO. WHEN MY DADDY HE DIED HE GIVED TO ME A LOTS OF MONEY.
'YOU UNDERSTAND, MARTÍN, THAT IT MAY TAKE MOST OF YOUR MONEY...MAYBE ALL OF IT?'
'JUST SAVE HER AND I'LL PAY YOU ALL THE MONEY..'
I'M TOUCHED, MARTIN...YOU MUST CARE FOR HER DEEPLY...
WISHED THERE WAS STILL MONKEYS TO KILL...
'I'M JUST SAYING YOU'VE GOT A LIFE OF YOUR OWN, DIANA...'
--SINCE I MOVED BACK ALL IT'S BEEN WITH YOU IS TONANTZIN THIS AND TONANTZIN THAT-- WELL, WHAT ABOUT DIANA? WHAT ABOUT YOUR LIFE, GIRL?
YOU MEAN BESIDES EATING, SLEEPING, RUNNING AND GOING TO SCHOOL, PIPO?
WELL...
OH...YOU MUST MEAN ROMANCE..?
I'VE AS MUCH INTEREST IN ANY KIND OF AMORE AS YOU PROBABLY DO IN SUMO WRESTLING, PIPO.
I'LL LEAVE THAT NONSENSE TO YOU AND TONANTZIN...
C'MERE PIPO, YOU LITTLE--
YI!
86

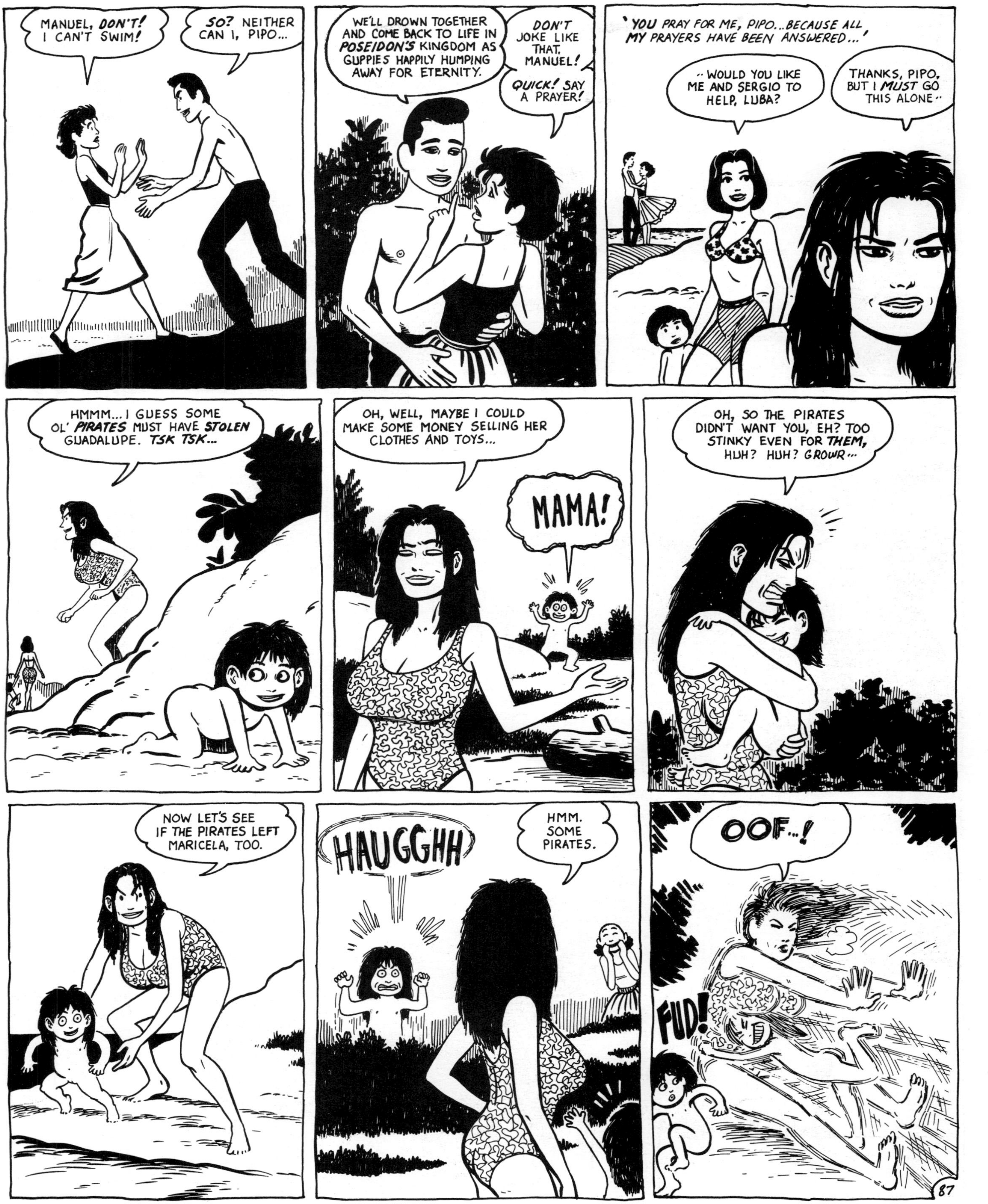

MANUEL, DON'T! I CAN'T SWIM!
SO? NEITHER CAN I, PIPO...
WE'LL DROWN TOGETHER AND COME BACK TO LIFE IN POSEIDON'S KINGDOM AS GUPPIES HAPPILY HUMPING AWAY FOR ETERNITY.
DON'T JOKE LIKE THAT, MANUEL!
QUICK! SAY A PRAYER!
'YOU PRAY FOR ME, PIPO...BECAUSE ALL MY PRAYERS HAVE BEEN ANSWERED...'
..WOULD YOU LIKE ME AND SERGIO TO HELP, LUBA?
THANKS, PIPO, BUT I MUST GO THIS ALONE..
HMMM...I GUESS SOME OL' PIRATES MUST HAVE STOLEN GUADALUPE. TSK TSK...
OH, WELL, MAYBE I COULD MAKE SOME MONEY SELLING HER CLOTHES AND TOYS...
MAMA!
OH, SO THE PIRATES DIDN'T WANT YOU, EH? TOO STINKY EVEN FOR THEM, HUH? HUH? GROWR...
NOW LET'S SEE IF THE PIRATES LEFT MARICELA, TOO.
HAUGGHH
HMM. SOME PIRATES.
OOF..!
FUD!
87

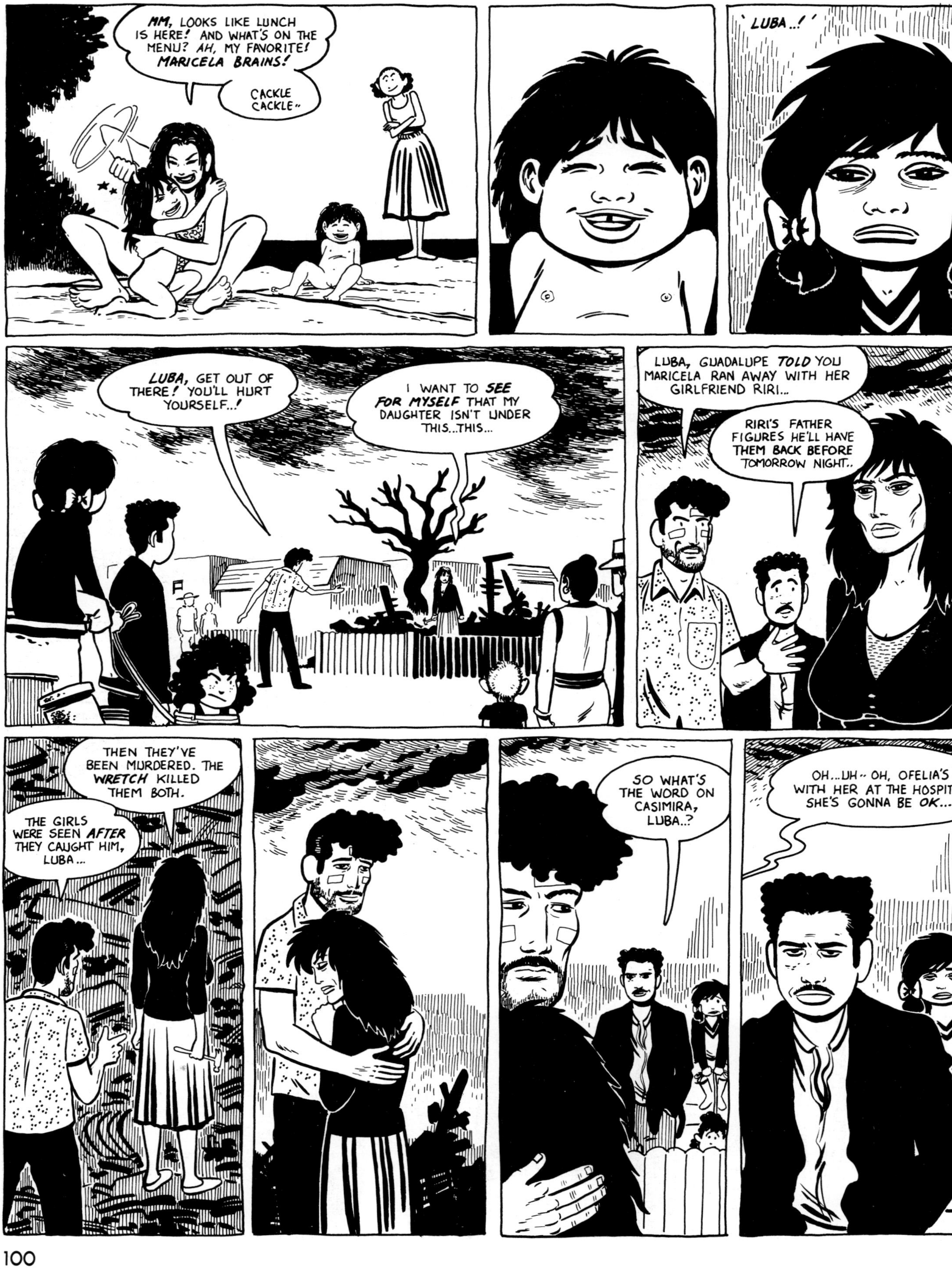
MM, LOOKS LIKE LUNCH IS HERE! AND WHAT'S ON THE MENU? AH, MY FAVORITE! MARICELA BRAINS!
CACKLE CACKLE..
LUBA..!
LUBA, GET OUT OF THERE! YOU'LL HURT YOURSELF..!
I WANT TO SEE FOR MYSELF THAT MY DAUGHTER ISN'T UNDER THIS...THIS...
LUBA, GUADALUPE TOLD YOU MARICELA RAN AWAY WITH HER GIRLFRIEND RIRI...
RIRI'S FATHER FIGURES HE'LL HAVE THEM BACK BEFORE TOMORROW NIGHT..
THE GIRLS WERE SEEN AFTER THEY CAUGHT HIM, LUBA...
THEN THEY'VE BEEN MURDERED. THE WRETCH KILLED THEM BOTH.
SO WHAT'S THE WORD ON CASIMIRA, LUBA..?
OH...UH.. OH, OFELIA'S WITH HER AT THE HOSPITAL... SHE'S GONNA BE OK...
88

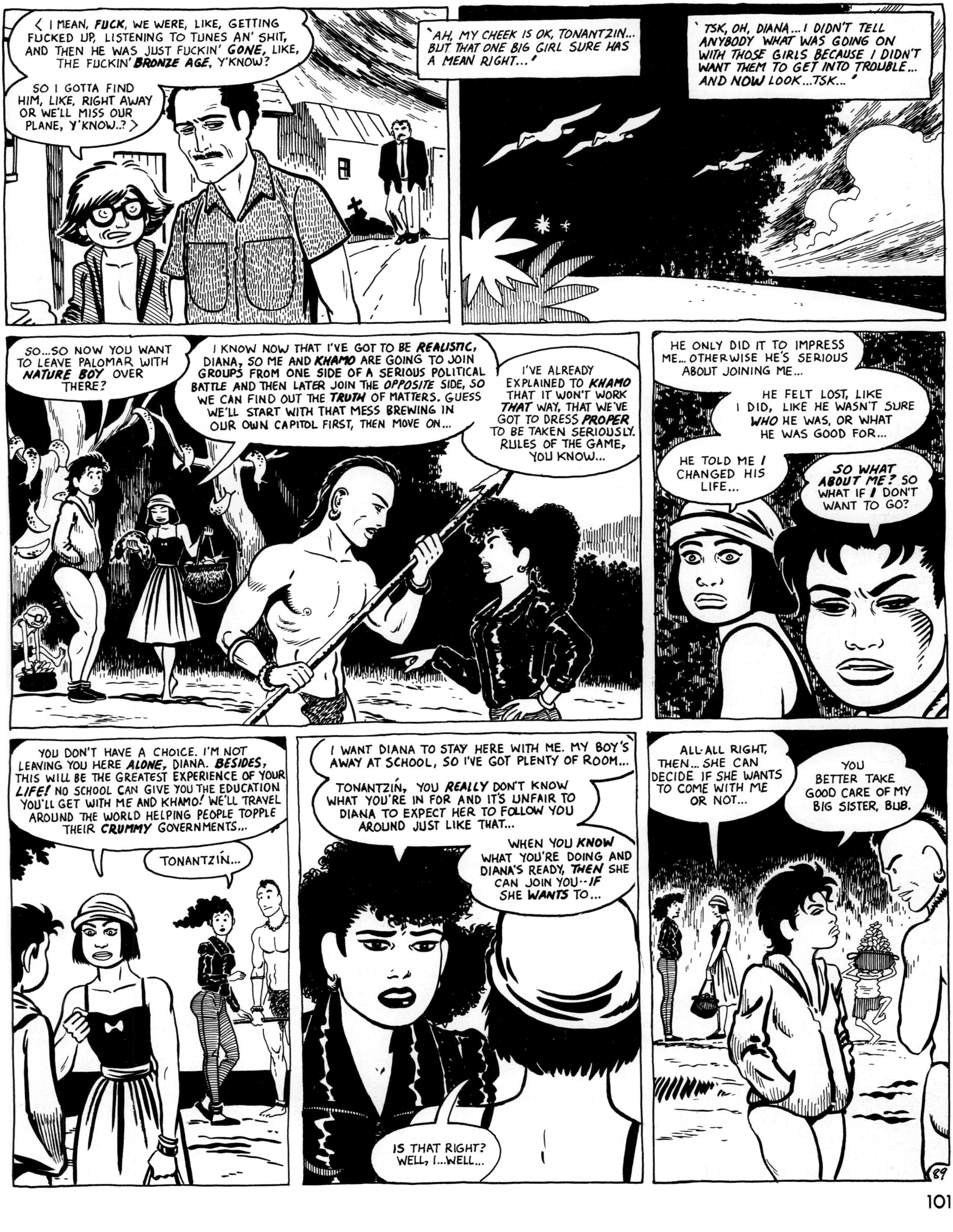
< I MEAN, FUCK, WE WERE, LIKE, GETTING FUCKED UP, LISTENING TO TUNES AN' SHIT, AND THEN HE WAS JUST FUCKIN' GONE, LIKE, THE FUCKIN' BRONZE AGE, Y'KNOW?
SO I GOTTA FIND HIM, LIKE, RIGHT AWAY OR WE'LL MISS OUR PLANE, Y'KNOW..? >
'AH, MY CHEEK IS OK, TONANTZIN... BUT THAT ONE BIG GIRL SURE HAS A MEAN RIGHT...'
'TSK, OH, DIANA... I DIDN'T TELL ANYBODY WHAT WAS GOING ON WITH THOSE GIRLS BECAUSE I DIDN'T WANT THEM TO GET INTO TROUBLE... AND NOW LOOK... TSK...'
SO... SO NOW YOU WANT TO LEAVE PALOMAR WITH NATURE BOY OVER THERE?
I KNOW NOW THAT I'VE GOT TO BE REALISTIC, DIANA, SO ME AND KHAMO ARE GOING TO JOIN GROUPS FROM ONE SIDE OF A SERIOUS POLITICAL BATTLE AND THEN LATER JOIN THE OPPOSITE SIDE, SO WE CAN FIND OUT THE TRUTH OF MATTERS. GUESS WE'LL START WITH THAT MESS BREWING IN OUR OWN CAPITOL FIRST, THEN MOVE ON...
I'VE ALREADY EXPLAINED TO KHAMO THAT IT WON'T WORK THAT WAY, THAT WE'VE GOT TO DRESS PROPER TO BE TAKEN SERIOUSLY. RULES OF THE GAME, YOU KNOW...
HE ONLY DID IT TO IMPRESS ME... OTHERWISE HE'S SERIOUS ABOUT JOINING ME...
HE FELT LOST, LIKE I DID, LIKE HE WASN'T SURE WHO HE WAS, OR WHAT HE WAS GOOD FOR...
HE TOLD ME I CHANGED HIS LIFE...
SO WHAT ABOUT ME? SO WHAT IF I DON'T WANT TO GO?
YOU DON'T HAVE A CHOICE. I'M NOT LEAVING YOU HERE ALONE, DIANA. BESIDES, THIS WILL BE THE GREATEST EXPERIENCE OF YOUR LIFE! NO SCHOOL CAN GIVE YOU THE EDUCATION YOU'LL GET WITH ME AND KHAMO! WE'LL TRAVEL AROUND THE WORLD HELPING PEOPLE TOPPLE THEIR CRUMMY GOVERNMENTS...
TONANTZÍN...
I WANT DIANA TO STAY HERE WITH ME. MY BOY'S AWAY AT SCHOOL, SO I'VE GOT PLENTY OF ROOM...
TONANTZÍN, YOU REALLY DON'T KNOW WHAT YOU'RE IN FOR AND IT'S UNFAIR TO DIANA TO EXPECT HER TO FOLLOW YOU AROUND JUST LIKE THAT...
WHEN YOU KNOW WHAT YOU'RE DOING AND DIANA'S READY, THEN SHE CAN JOIN YOU--IF SHE WANTS TO...
IS THAT RIGHT? WELL, I...WELL...
ALL-ALL RIGHT, THEN... SHE CAN DECIDE IF SHE WANTS TO COME WITH ME OR NOT...
YOU BETTER TAKE GOOD CARE OF MY BIG SISTER, BUB.
89

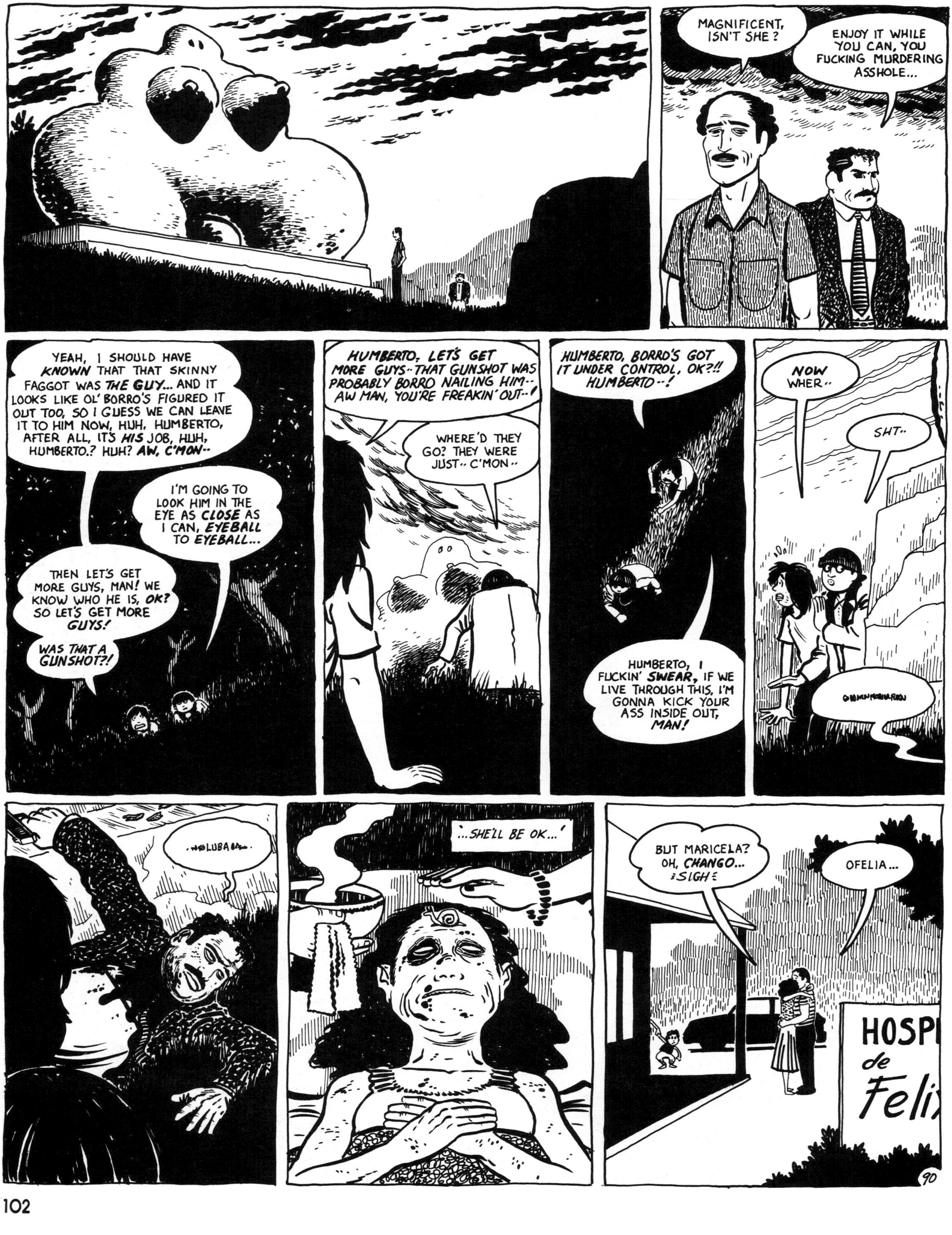
MAGNIFICENT, ISN'T SHE?
ENJOY IT WHILE YOU CAN, YOU FUCKING MURDERING ASSHOLE...
YEAH, I SHOULD HAVE KNOWN THAT THAT SKINNY FAGGOT WAS THE GUY... AND IT LOOKS LIKE OL' BORRO'S FIGURED IT OUT TOO, SO I GUESS WE CAN LEAVE IT TO HIM NOW, HUH, HUMBERTO, AFTER ALL, IT'S HIS JOB, HUH, HUMBERTO.? HUH? AW, C'MON--
I'M GOING TO LOOK HIM IN THE EYE AS CLOSE AS I CAN, EYEBALL TO EYEBALL...
THEN LET'S GET MORE GUYS, MAN! WE KNOW WHO HE IS, OK? SO LET'S GET MORE GUYS!
WAS THAT A GUNSHOT?!
HUMBERTO, LET'S GET MORE GUYS--THAT GUNSHOT WAS PROBABLY BORRO NAILING HIM-- AW MAN, YOU'RE FREAKIN' OUT--!
WHERE'D THEY GO? THEY WERE JUST-- C'MON--
HUMBERTO, BORRO'S GOT IT UNDER CONTROL, OK?!! HUMBERTO--!
HUMBERTO, I FUCKIN' SWEAR, IF WE LIVE THROUGH THIS, I'M GONNA KICK YOUR ASS INSIDE OUT, MAN!
NOW WHER--
SHT--
...SHE'LL BE OK...
BUT MARICELA? OH, CHANGO... SIGH
OFELIA...
HOSP
de
Felix
90

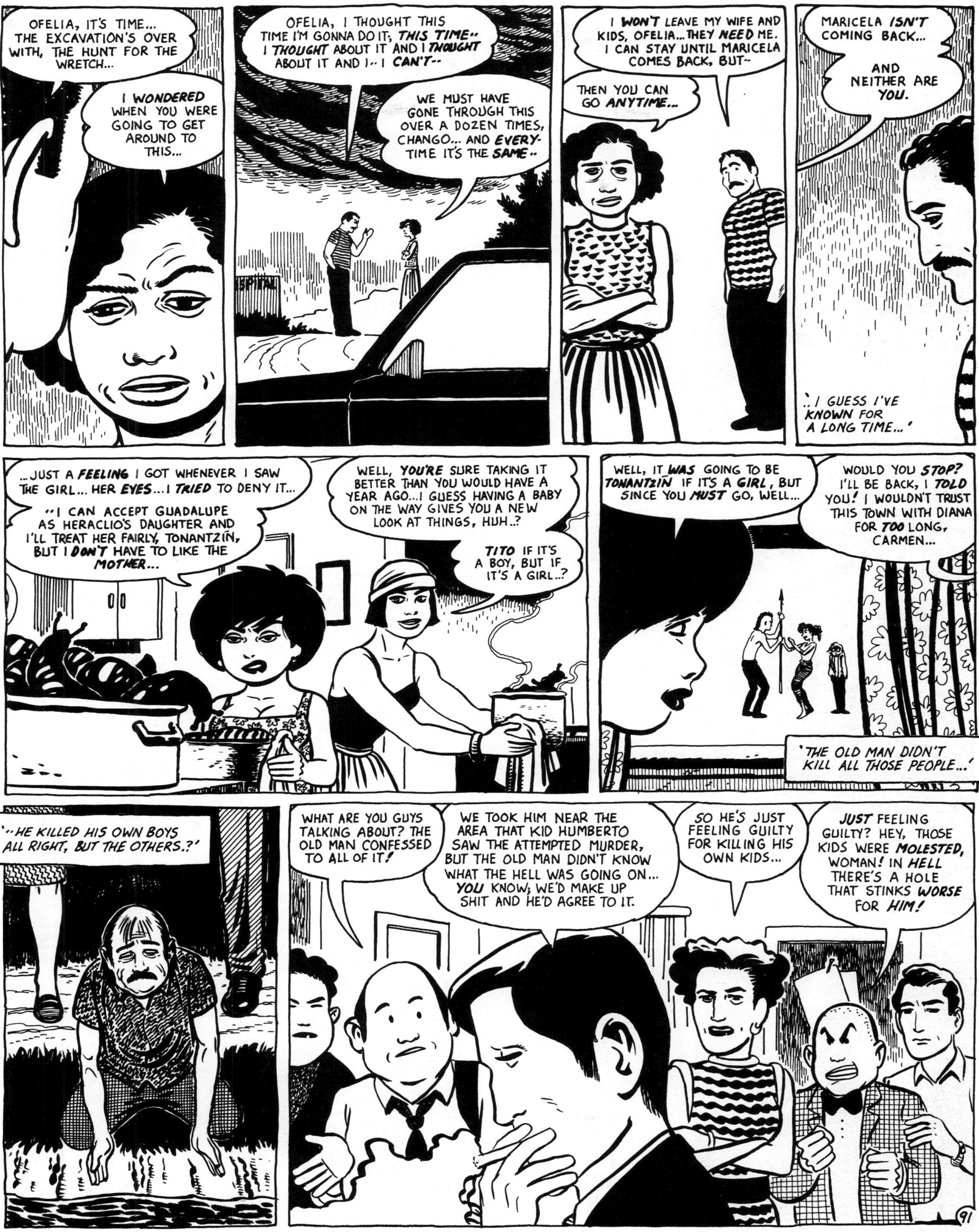

OFELIA, IT'S TIME... THE EXCAVATION'S OVER WITH, THE HUNT FOR THE WRETCH...
I WONDERED WHEN YOU WERE GOING TO GET AROUND TO THIS...
OFELIA, I THOUGHT THIS TIME I'M GONNA DO IT; THIS TIME.. I THOUGHT ABOUT IT AND I THOUGHT ABOUT IT AND I.. I CAN'T--
WE MUST HAVE GONE THROUGH THIS OVER A DOZEN TIMES, CHANGO... AND EVERY-TIME IT'S THE SAME..
I WON'T LEAVE MY WIFE AND KIDS, OFELIA... THEY NEED ME. I CAN STAY UNTIL MARICELA COMES BACK, BUT--
THEN YOU CAN GO ANYTIME...
MARICELA ISN'T COMING BACK...
AND NEITHER ARE YOU.
'.. I GUESS I'VE KNOWN FOR A LONG TIME...'
...JUST A FEELING I GOT WHENEVER I SAW THE GIRL... HER EYES... I TRIED TO DENY IT...
..I CAN ACCEPT GUADALUPE AS HERACLIO'S DAUGHTER AND I'LL TREAT HER FAIRLY, TONANTZÍN, BUT I DON'T HAVE TO LIKE THE MOTHER...
WELL, YOU'RE SURE TAKING IT BETTER THAN YOU WOULD HAVE A YEAR AGO... I GUESS HAVING A BABY ON THE WAY GIVES YOU A NEW LOOK AT THINGS, HUH..?
TITO IF IT'S A BOY, BUT IF IT'S A GIRL..?
WELL, IT WAS GOING TO BE TONANTZÍN IF IT'S A GIRL, BUT SINCE YOU MUST GO, WELL...
WOULD YOU STOP? I'LL BE BACK, I TOLD YOU! I WOULDN'T TRUST THIS TOWN WITH DIANA FOR TOO LONG, CARMEN...
'THE OLD MAN DIDN'T KILL ALL THOSE PEOPLE...'
'...HE KILLED HIS OWN BOYS ALL RIGHT, BUT THE OTHERS..?'
WHAT ARE YOU GUYS TALKING ABOUT? THE OLD MAN CONFESSED TO ALL OF IT!
WE TOOK HIM NEAR THE AREA THAT KID HUMBERTO SAW THE ATTEMPTED MURDER, BUT THE OLD MAN DIDN'T KNOW WHAT THE HELL WAS GOING ON... YOU KNOW; WE'D MAKE UP SHIT AND HE'D AGREE TO IT.
SO HE'S JUST FEELING GUILTY FOR KILLING HIS OWN KIDS...
JUST FEELING GUILTY? HEY, THOSE KIDS WERE MOLESTED, WOMAN! IN HELL THERE'S A HOLE THAT STINKS WORSE FOR HIM!
'91

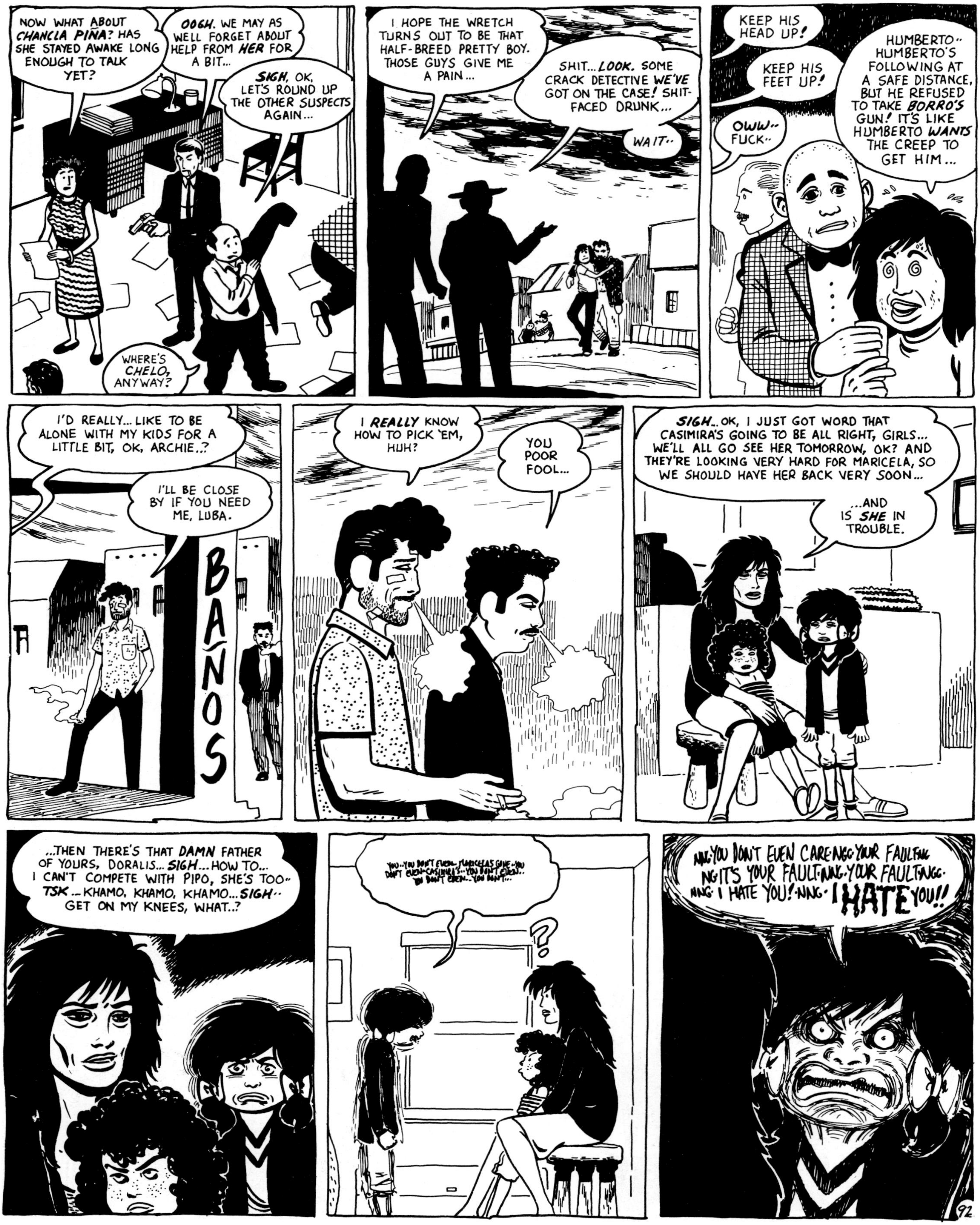
NOW WHAT ABOUT CHANCLA PIÑA? HAS SHE STAYED AWAKE LONG ENOUGH TO TALK YET?
OOGH. WE MAY AS WELL FORGET ABOUT HELP FROM HER FOR A BIT...
SIGH, OK, LET'S ROUND UP THE OTHER SUSPECTS AGAIN...
WHERE'S CHELO, ANYWAY?
I HOPE THE WRETCH TURNS OUT TO BE THAT HALF-BREED PRETTY BOY. THOSE GUYS GIVE ME A PAIN...
SHIT... LOOK. SOME CRACK DETECTIVE WE'VE GOT ON THE CASE! SHIT-FACED DRUNK...
WAIT..
KEEP HIS HEAD UP!
KEEP HIS FEET UP!
OWW.. FUCK..
HUMBERTO.. HUMBERTO'S FOLLOWING AT A SAFE DISTANCE, BUT HE REFUSED TO TAKE BORRO'S GUN! IT'S LIKE HUMBERTO WANTS THE CREEP TO GET HIM...
I'D REALLY... LIKE TO BE ALONE WITH MY KIDS FOR A LITTLE BIT, OK, ARCHIE..?
I'LL BE CLOSE BY IF YOU NEED ME, LUBA.
BAÑOS
I REALLY KNOW HOW TO PICK 'EM, HUH?
YOU POOR FOOL...
SIGH.. OK, I JUST GOT WORD THAT CASIMIRA'S GOING TO BE ALL RIGHT, GIRLS... WE'LL ALL GO SEE HER TOMORROW, OK? AND THEY'RE LOOKING VERY HARD FOR MARICELA, SO WE SHOULD HAVE HER BACK VERY SOON...
...AND IS SHE IN TROUBLE.
...THEN THERE'S THAT DAMN FATHER OF YOURS, DORALIS... SIGH... HOW TO... I CAN'T COMPETE WITH PIPO, SHE'S TOO.. TSK .. KHAMO, KHAMO, KHAMO... SIGH.. GET ON MY KNEES, WHAT..?
YOU.. YOU DON'T EVEN.. MARICELA'S GONE.. YOU DON'T EVEN.. CASIMIRA'S.. YOU DON'T EVEN.. YOU DON'T EVEN.. YOU DON'T...
?
NNG. YOU DON'T EVEN CARE. NGG. YOUR FAULT. NG. NG. IT'S YOUR FAULT. NNG. YOUR FAULT. NGG. NNG. I HATE YOU! NNG. I HATE YOU!!

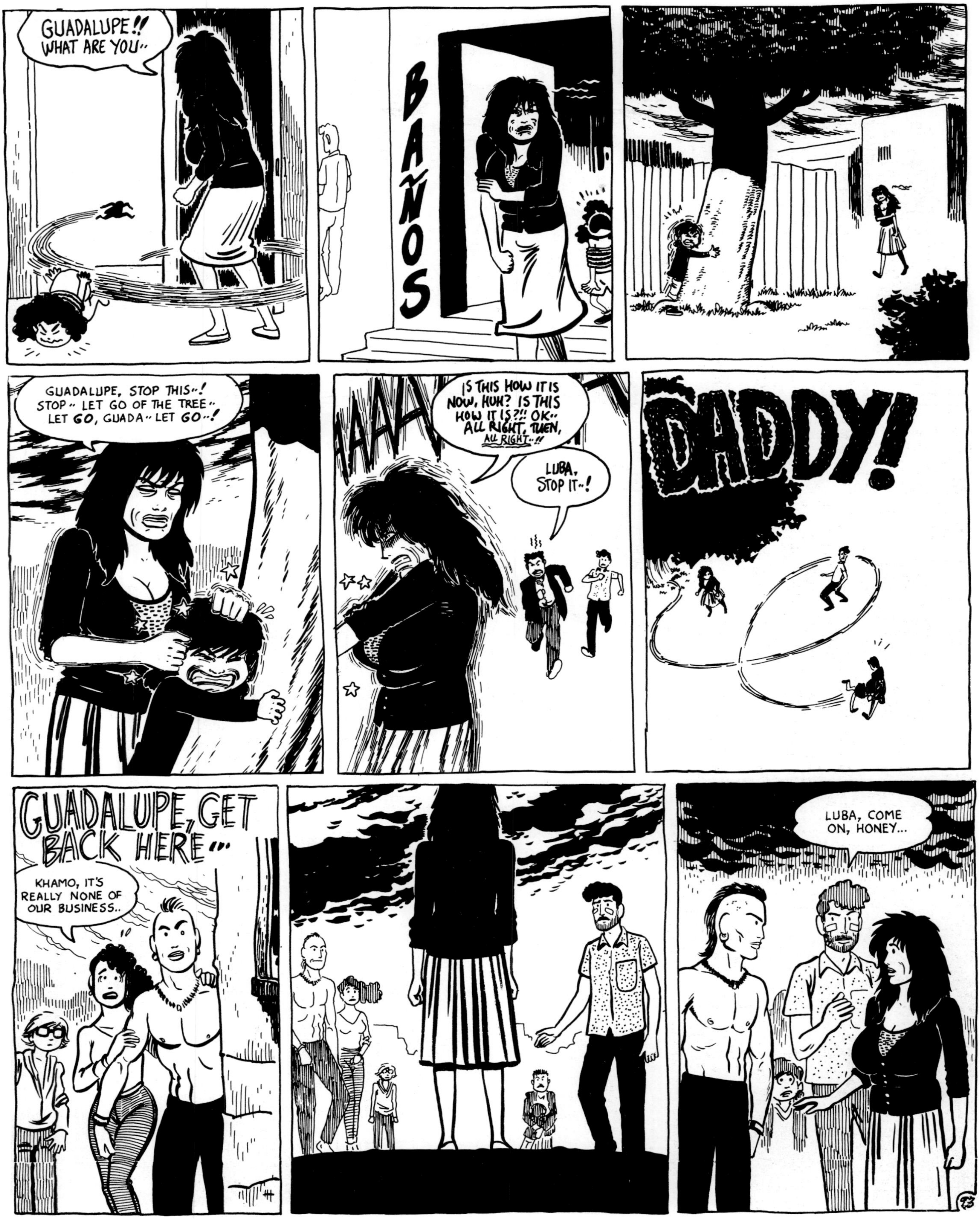
GUADALUPE!! WHAT ARE YOU..
BAÑOS
GUADALUPE, STOP THIS..! STOP.. LET GO OF THE TREE.. LET GO, GUADA.. LET GO..!
AAAAA
IS THIS HOW IT IS NOW, HUH? IS THIS HOW IT IS?!! OK.. ALL RIGHT, TUEN, ALL RIGHT..!!
LUBA, STOP IT..!
DADDY!
GUADALUPE, GET BACK HERE...
KHAMO, IT'S REALLY NONE OF OUR BUSINESS..
LUBA, COME ON, HONEY...

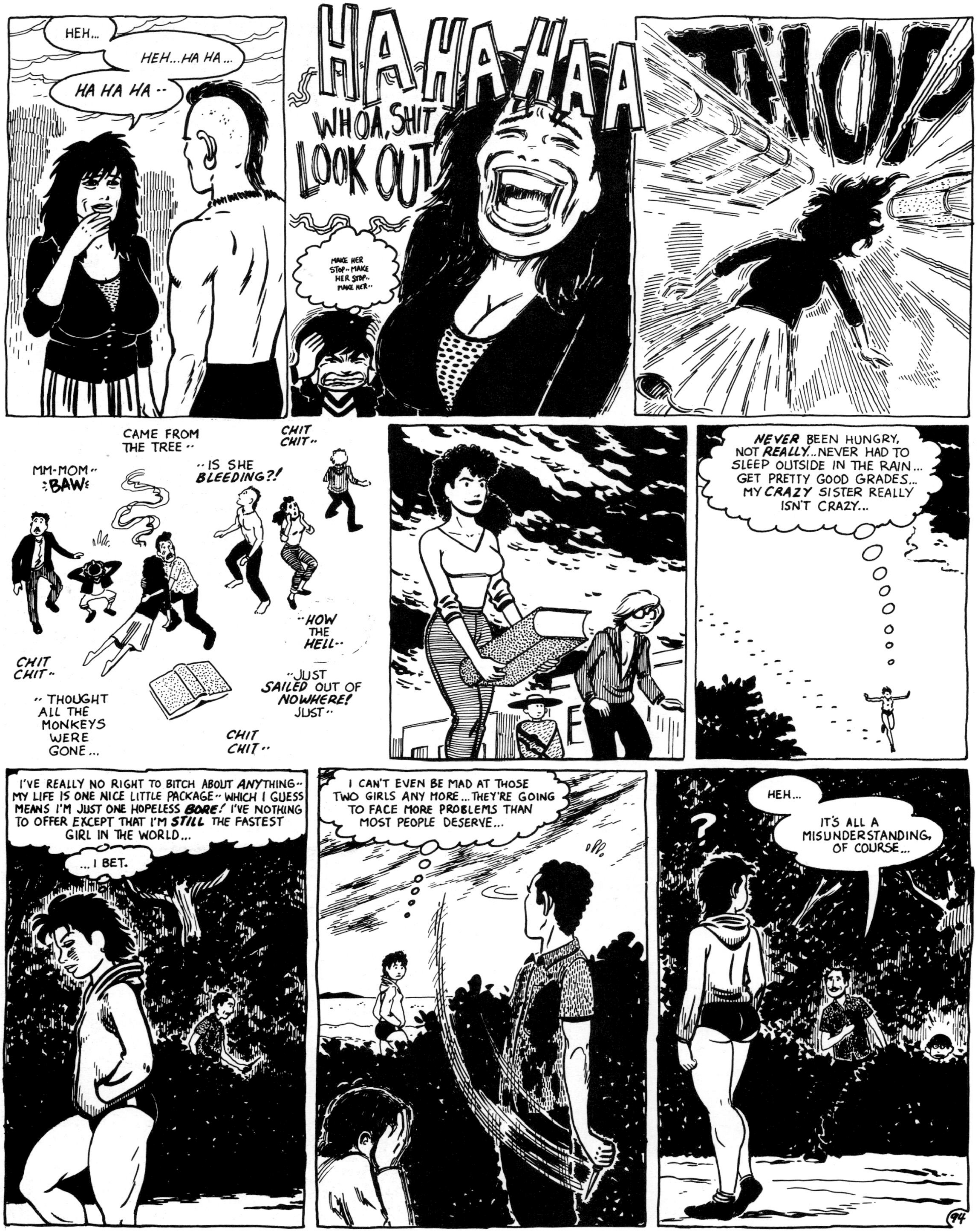
HEH...
HEH... HA HA...
HA HA HA..
HAHAHAHAA
WHOA, SHIT LOOK OUT
MAKE HER STOP.. MAKE HER STOP.. MAKE HER..
THOP
CAME FROM THE TREE..
CHIT CHIT..
MM-MOM.. BAW
..IS SHE BLEEDING?!
..HOW THE HELL..
CHIT CHIT..
..JUST SAILED OUT OF NOWHERE! JUST..
..THOUGHT ALL THE MONKEYS WERE GONE...
CHIT CHIT..
NEVER BEEN HUNGRY, NOT REALLY... NEVER HAD TO SLEEP OUTSIDE IN THE RAIN... GET PRETTY GOOD GRADES... MY CRAZY SISTER REALLY ISN'T CRAZY...
I'VE REALLY NO RIGHT TO BITCH ABOUT ANYTHING.. MY LIFE IS ONE NICE LITTLE PACKAGE.. WHICH I GUESS MEANS I'M JUST ONE HOPELESS BORE! I'VE NOTHING TO OFFER EXCEPT THAT I'M STILL THE FASTEST GIRL IN THE WORLD...
... I BET.
I CAN'T EVEN BE MAD AT THOSE TWO GIRLS ANY MORE... THEY'RE GOING TO FACE MORE PROBLEMS THAN MOST PEOPLE DESERVE...
?
HEH...
IT'S ALL A MISUNDERSTANDING, OF COURSE...
'94

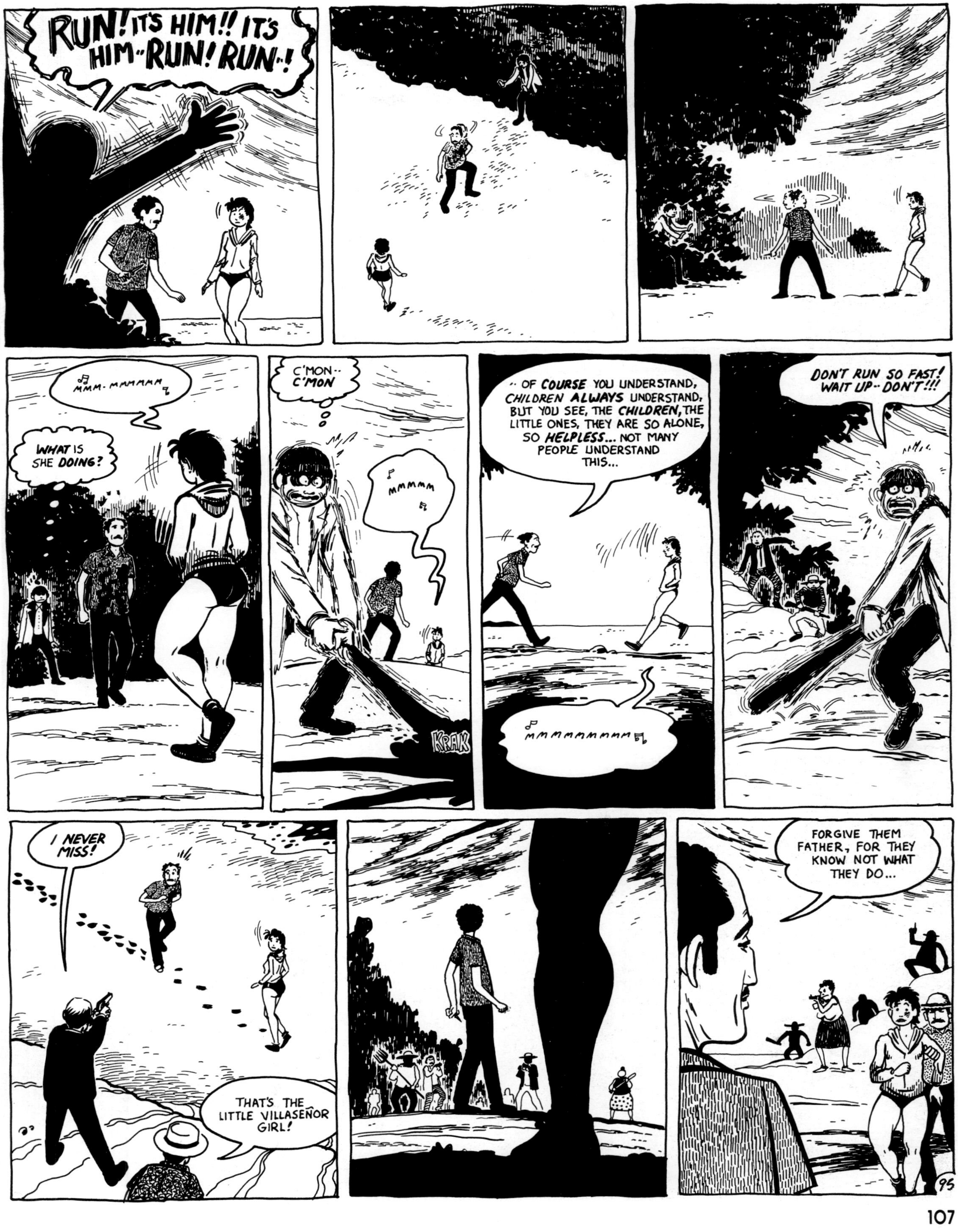
RUN! IT'S HIM!! IT'S HIM.. RUN! RUN..!
♫ MMM-MMMMMM ♫
WHAT IS SHE DOING?
C'MON.. C'MON
♪ MMMMM ♫
KRAK
.. OF COURSE YOU UNDERSTAND, CHILDREN ALWAYS UNDERSTAND, BUT YOU SEE, THE CHILDREN, THE LITTLE ONES, THEY ARE SO ALONE, SO HELPLESS... NOT MANY PEOPLE UNDERSTAND THIS...
♪ MMMMMMMMMM ♫
DON'T RUN SO FAST! WAIT UP.. DON'T!!!
I NEVER MISS!
THAT'S THE LITTLE VILLASEÑOR GIRL!
FORGIVE THEM FATHER, FOR THEY KNOW NOT WHAT THEY DO...
95

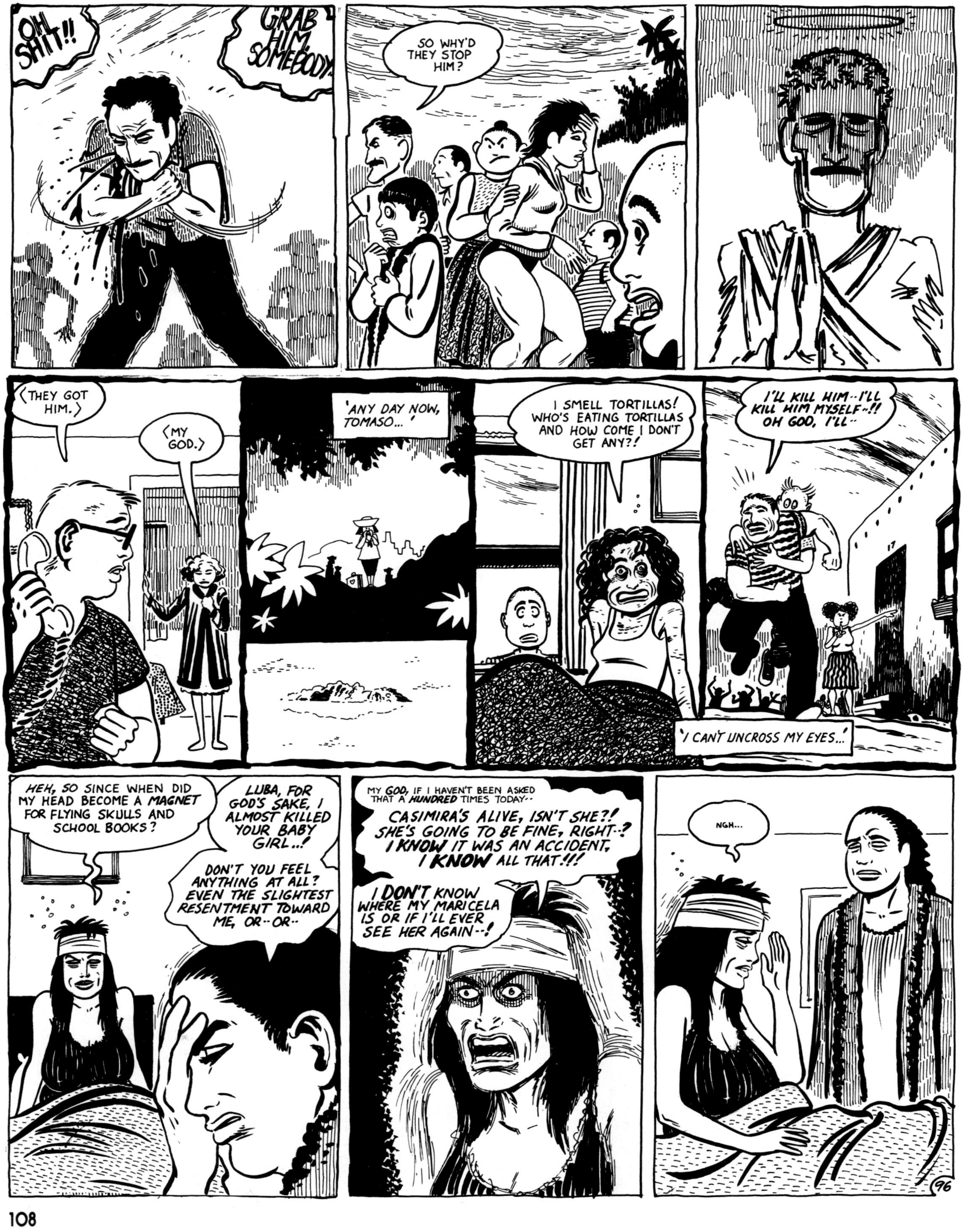
OH SHIT!!
GRAB HIM, SOMEBODY!
SO WHY'D THEY STOP HIM?
<THEY GOT HIM.>
<MY GOD.>
'ANY DAY NOW, TOMASO...'
I SMELL TORTILLAS! WHO'S EATING TORTILLAS AND HOW COME I DON'T GET ANY?!
I'LL KILL HIM--I'LL KILL HIM MYSELF--!! OH GOD, I'LL--
'I CAN'T UNCROSS MY EYES...'
HEH, SO SINCE WHEN DID MY HEAD BECOME A MAGNET FOR FLYING SKULLS AND SCHOOL BOOKS?
LUBA, FOR GOD'S SAKE, I ALMOST KILLED YOUR BABY GIRL..!
DON'T YOU FEEL ANYTHING AT ALL? EVEN THE SLIGHTEST RESENTMENT TOWARD ME, OR--OR--
MY GOD, IF I HAVEN'T BEEN ASKED THAT A HUNDRED TIMES TODAY--
CASIMIRA'S ALIVE, ISN'T SHE?! SHE'S GOING TO BE FINE, RIGHT--? I KNOW IT WAS AN ACCIDENT, I KNOW ALL THAT!!!
I DON'T KNOW WHERE MY MARICELA IS OR IF I'LL EVER SEE HER AGAIN--!
NGH...
96

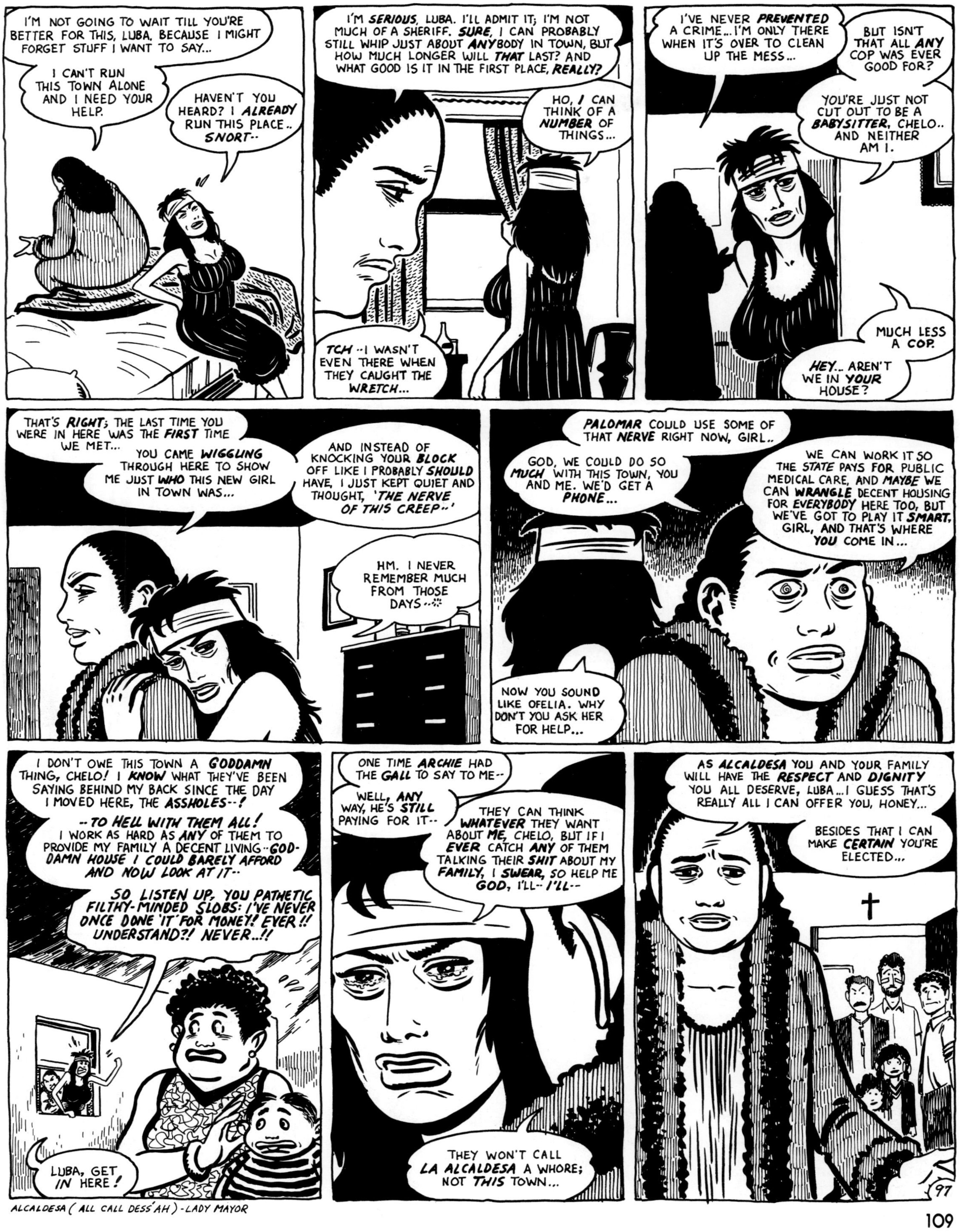
I'M NOT GOING TO WAIT TILL YOU'RE BETTER FOR THIS, LUBA, BECAUSE I MIGHT FORGET STUFF I WANT TO SAY...
I CAN'T RUN THIS TOWN ALONE AND I NEED YOUR HELP.
HAVEN'T YOU HEARD? I ALREADY RUN THIS PLACE.. SNORT--
I'M SERIOUS, LUBA. I'LL ADMIT IT; I'M NOT MUCH OF A SHERIFF. SURE, I CAN PROBABLY STILL WHIP JUST ABOUT ANYBODY IN TOWN, BUT HOW MUCH LONGER WILL THAT LAST? AND WHAT GOOD IS IT IN THE FIRST PLACE, REALLY?
HO, I CAN THINK OF A NUMBER OF THINGS...
TCH --I WASN'T EVEN THERE WHEN THEY CAUGHT THE WRETCH...
I'VE NEVER PREVENTED A CRIME... I'M ONLY THERE WHEN IT'S OVER TO CLEAN UP THE MESS...
BUT ISN'T THAT ALL ANY COP WAS EVER GOOD FOR?
YOU'RE JUST NOT CUT OUT TO BE A BABYSITTER, CHELO.. AND NEITHER AM I.
MUCH LESS A COP.
HEY... AREN'T WE IN YOUR HOUSE?
THAT'S RIGHT; THE LAST TIME YOU WERE IN HERE WAS THE FIRST TIME WE MET...
YOU CAME WIGGLING THROUGH HERE TO SHOW ME JUST WHO THIS NEW GIRL IN TOWN WAS...
AND INSTEAD OF KNOCKING YOUR BLOCK OFF LIKE I PROBABLY SHOULD HAVE, I JUST KEPT QUIET AND THOUGHT, 'THE NERVE OF THIS CREEP--'
HM. I NEVER REMEMBER MUCH FROM THOSE DAYS--
PALOMAR COULD USE SOME OF THAT NERVE RIGHT NOW, GIRL..
GOD, WE COULD DO SO MUCH WITH THIS TOWN, YOU AND ME. WE'D GET A PHONE...
WE CAN WORK IT SO THE STATE PAYS FOR PUBLIC MEDICAL CARE, AND MAYBE WE CAN WRANGLE DECENT HOUSING FOR EVERYBODY HERE TOO, BUT WE'VE GOT TO PLAY IT SMART, GIRL, AND THAT'S WHERE YOU COME IN...
NOW YOU SOUND LIKE OFELIA. WHY DON'T YOU ASK HER FOR HELP...
I DON'T OWE THIS TOWN A GODDAMN THING, CHELO! I KNOW WHAT THEY'VE BEEN SAYING BEHIND MY BACK SINCE THE DAY I MOVED HERE, THE ASSHOLES--!
--TO HELL WITH THEM ALL! I WORK AS HARD AS ANY OF THEM TO PROVIDE MY FAMILY A DECENT LIVING--GOD-DAMN HOUSE I COULD BARELY AFFORD AND NOW LOOK AT IT--
SO LISTEN UP, YOU PATHETIC FILTHY-MINDED SLOBS: I'VE NEVER ONCE DONE 'IT' FOR MONEY! EVER!! UNDERSTAND?! NEVER..!!
LUBA, GET IN HERE!
ONE TIME ARCHIE HAD THE GALL TO SAY TO ME--
WELL, ANY WAY, HE'S STILL PAYING FOR IT--
THEY CAN THINK WHATEVER THEY WANT ABOUT ME, CHELO, BUT IF I EVER CATCH ANY OF THEM TALKING THEIR SHIT ABOUT MY FAMILY, I SWEAR, SO HELP ME GOD, I'LL-- I'LL--
THEY WON'T CALL LA ALCALDESA A WHORE; NOT THIS TOWN...
AS ALCALDESA YOU AND YOUR FAMILY WILL HAVE THE RESPECT AND DIGNITY YOU ALL DESERVE, LUBA... I GUESS THAT'S REALLY ALL I CAN OFFER YOU, HONEY...
BESIDES THAT I CAN MAKE CERTAIN YOU'RE ELECTED...
97

ALCALDESA (ALL CALL DESS'AH) - LADY MAYOR

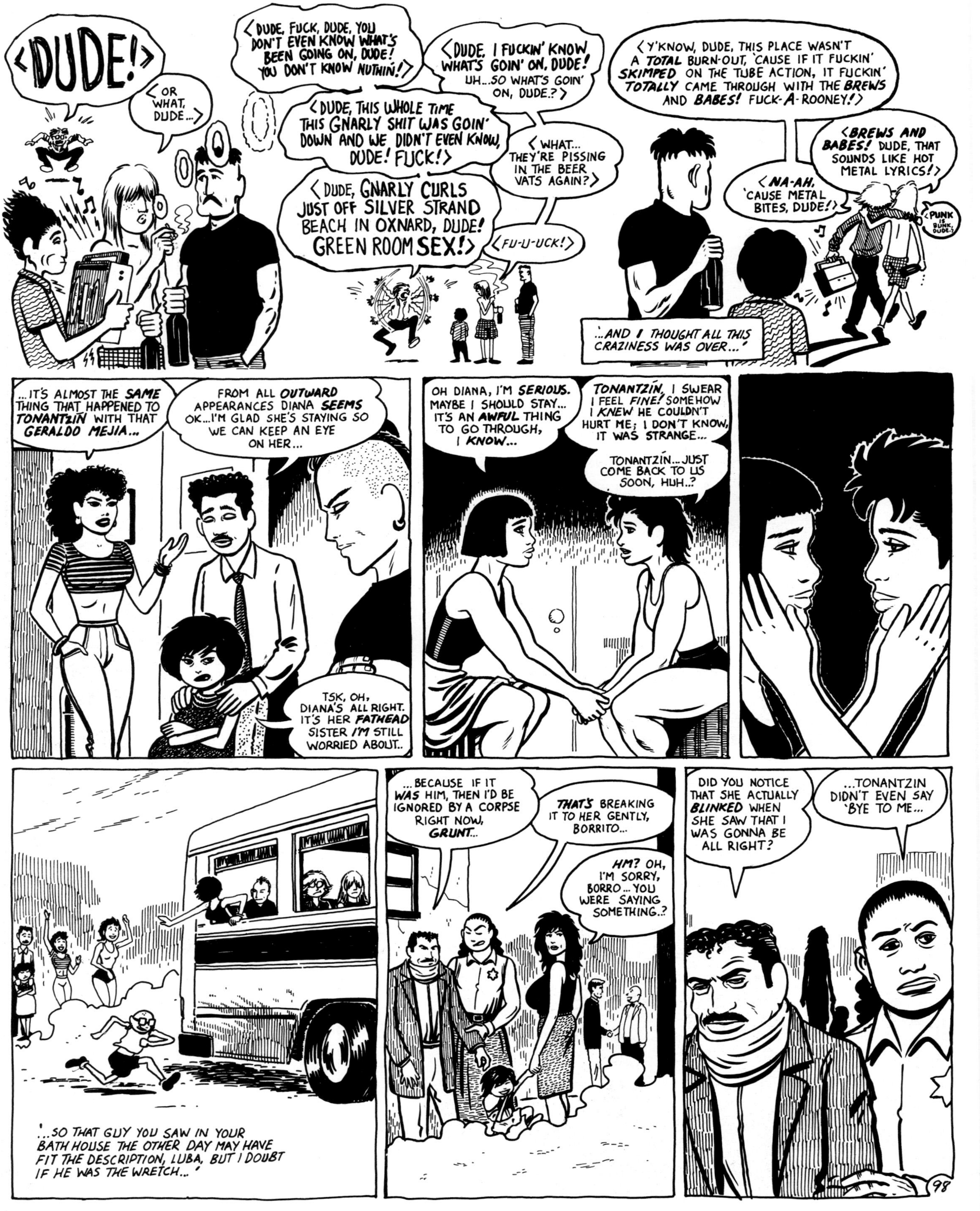

<DUDE!>
<OR WHAT, DUDE...>
<DUDE, FUCK, DUDE, YOU DON'T EVEN KNOW WHAT'S BEEN GOING ON, DUDE! YOU DON'T KNOW NUTHIN'!>
<DUDE, I FUCKIN' KNOW WHAT'S GOIN' ON, DUDE! UH...SO WHAT'S GOIN' ON, DUDE.?>
<DUDE, THIS WHOLE TIME THIS GNARLY SHIT WAS GOIN' DOWN AND WE DIDN'T EVEN KNOW, DUDE! FUCK!>
<WHAT... THEY'RE PISSING IN THE BEER VATS AGAIN?>
<DUDE, GNARLY CURLS JUST OFF SILVER STRAND BEACH IN OXNARD, DUDE! GREEN ROOM SEX!>
<FU-U-UCK!>
<Y'KNOW, DUDE, THIS PLACE WASN'T A TOTAL BURN-OUT, 'CAUSE IF IT FUCKIN' SKIMPED ON THE TUBE ACTION, IT FUCKIN' TOTALLY CAME THROUGH WITH THE BREWS AND BABES! FUCK-A-ROONEY!>
<BREWS AND BABES! DUDE, THAT SOUNDS LIKE HOT METAL LYRICS!>
<NA-AH. 'CAUSE METAL BITES, DUDE!>
<PUNK IS BUNK, DUDE.>
'...AND I THOUGHT ALL THIS CRAZINESS WAS OVER...'
...IT'S ALMOST THE SAME THING THAT HAPPENED TO TONANTZÍN WITH THAT GERALDO MEJIA...
FROM ALL OUTWARD APPEARANCES DIANA SEEMS OK...I'M GLAD SHE'S STAYING SO WE CAN KEEP AN EYE ON HER...
TSK, OH, DIANA'S ALL RIGHT. IT'S HER FATHEAD SISTER I'M STILL WORRIED ABOUT..
OH DIANA, I'M SERIOUS. MAYBE I SHOULD STAY... IT'S AN AWFUL THING TO GO THROUGH, I KNOW...
TONANTZÍN, I SWEAR I FEEL FINE! SOMEHOW I KNEW HE COULDN'T HURT ME; I DON'T KNOW, IT WAS STRANGE...
TONANTZÍN... JUST COME BACK TO US SOON, HUH..?
'...SO THAT GUY YOU SAW IN YOUR BATH HOUSE THE OTHER DAY MAY HAVE FIT THE DESCRIPTION, LUBA, BUT I DOUBT IF HE WAS THE WRETCH...'
...BECAUSE IF IT WAS HIM, THEN I'D BE IGNORED BY A CORPSE RIGHT NOW, GRUNT..
THAT'S BREAKING IT TO HER GENTLY, BORRITO...
HM? OH, I'M SORRY, BORRO... YOU WERE SAYING SOMETHING..?
DID YOU NOTICE THAT SHE ACTUALLY BLINKED WHEN SHE SAW THAT I WAS GONNA BE ALL RIGHT?
...TONANTZIN DIDN'T EVEN SAY 'BYE TO ME...
98

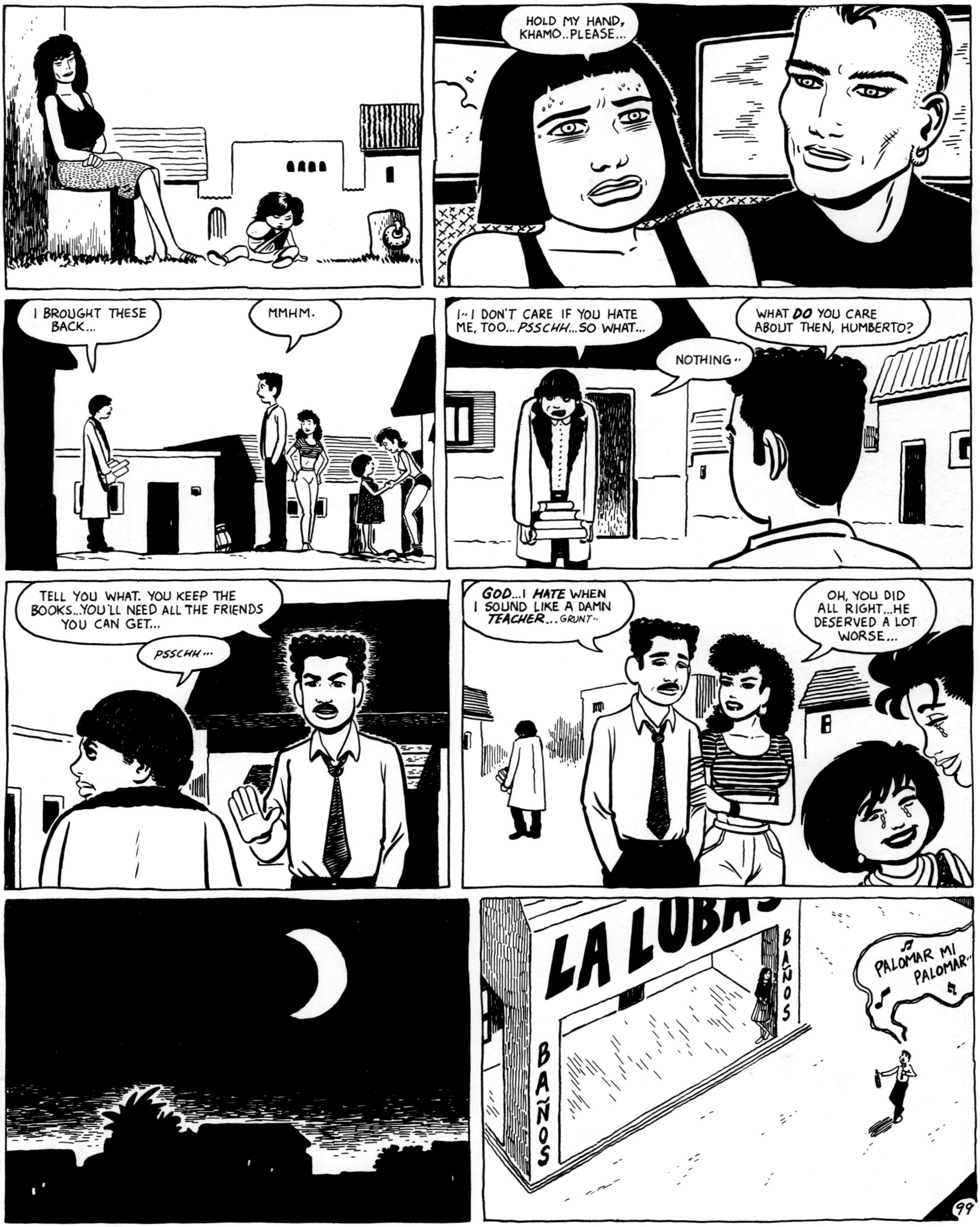
HOLD MY HAND, KHAMO..PLEASE...
I BROUGHT THESE BACK...
MMHM.
I-- I DON'T CARE IF YOU HATE ME, TOO... PSSCHH...SO WHAT...
WHAT DO YOU CARE ABOUT THEN, HUMBERTO?
NOTHING--
TELL YOU WHAT. YOU KEEP THE BOOKS...YOU'LL NEED ALL THE FRIENDS YOU CAN GET...
PSSCHH...
GOD...I HATE WHEN I SOUND LIKE A DAMN TEACHER... GRUNT--
OH, YOU DID ALL RIGHT...HE DESERVED A LOT WORSE...
LA LOBA'S
BAÑOS
BAÑOS
PALOMAR MI PALOMAR--
99

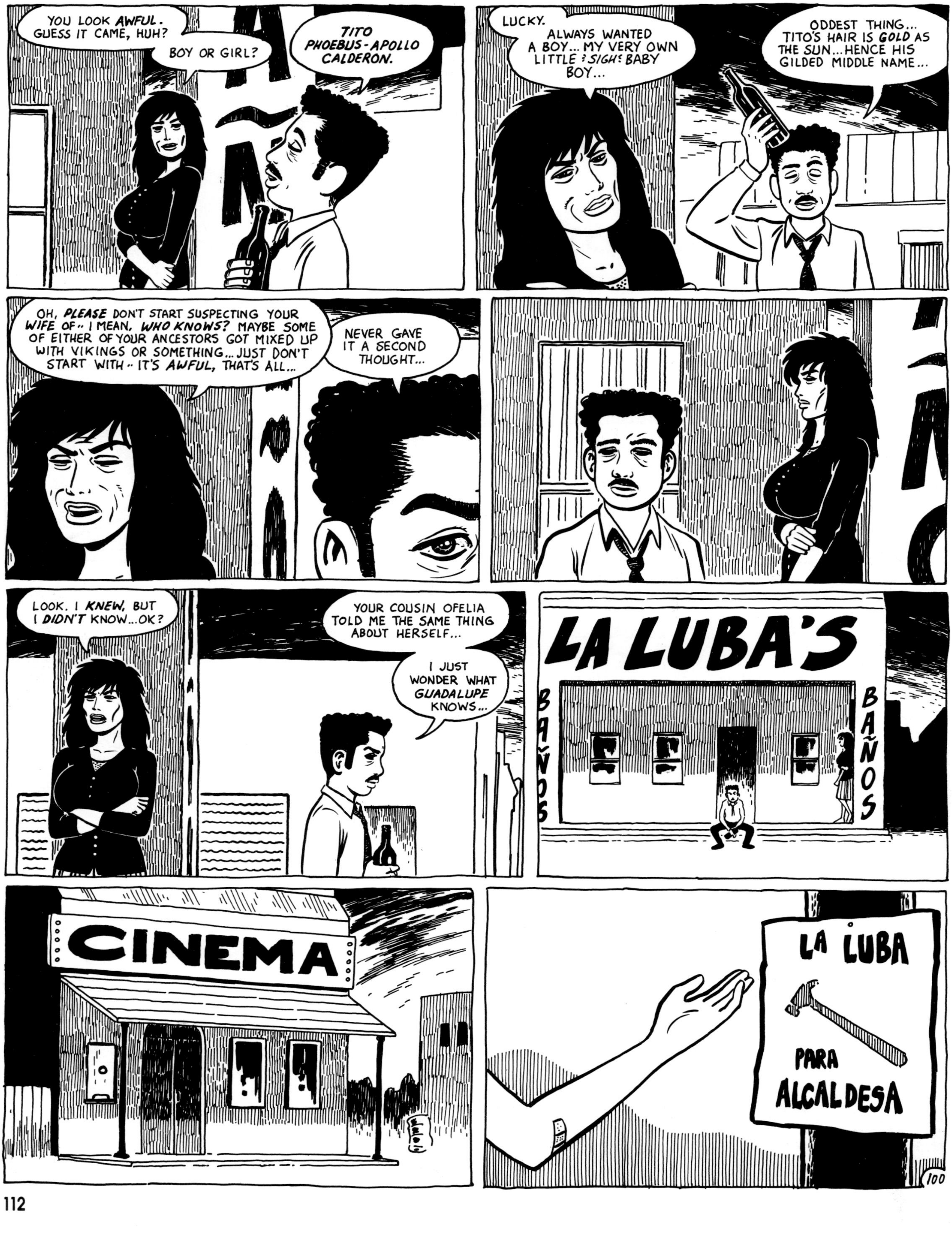
YOU LOOK AWFUL. GUESS IT CAME, HUH?
BOY OR GIRL?
TITO PHOEBUS-APOLLO CALDERON.
LUCKY.
ALWAYS WANTED A BOY... MY VERY OWN LITTLE ⁑SIGH⁑ BABY BOY...
ODDEST THING... TITO'S HAIR IS GOLD AS THE SUN... HENCE HIS GILDED MIDDLE NAME...
OH, PLEASE DON'T START SUSPECTING YOUR WIFE OF -- I MEAN, WHO KNOWS? MAYBE SOME OF EITHER OF YOUR ANCESTORS GOT MIXED UP WITH VIKINGS OR SOMETHING... JUST DON'T START WITH -- IT'S AWFUL, THAT'S ALL...
NEVER GAVE IT A SECOND THOUGHT...
LOOK. I KNEW, BUT I DIDN'T KNOW... OK?
YOUR COUSIN OFELIA TOLD ME THE SAME THING ABOUT HERSELF...
I JUST WONDER WHAT GUADALUPE KNOWS...
LA LUBA'S
BAÑOS
BAÑOS
CINEMA
LA LUBA
PARA
ALCALDESA
100

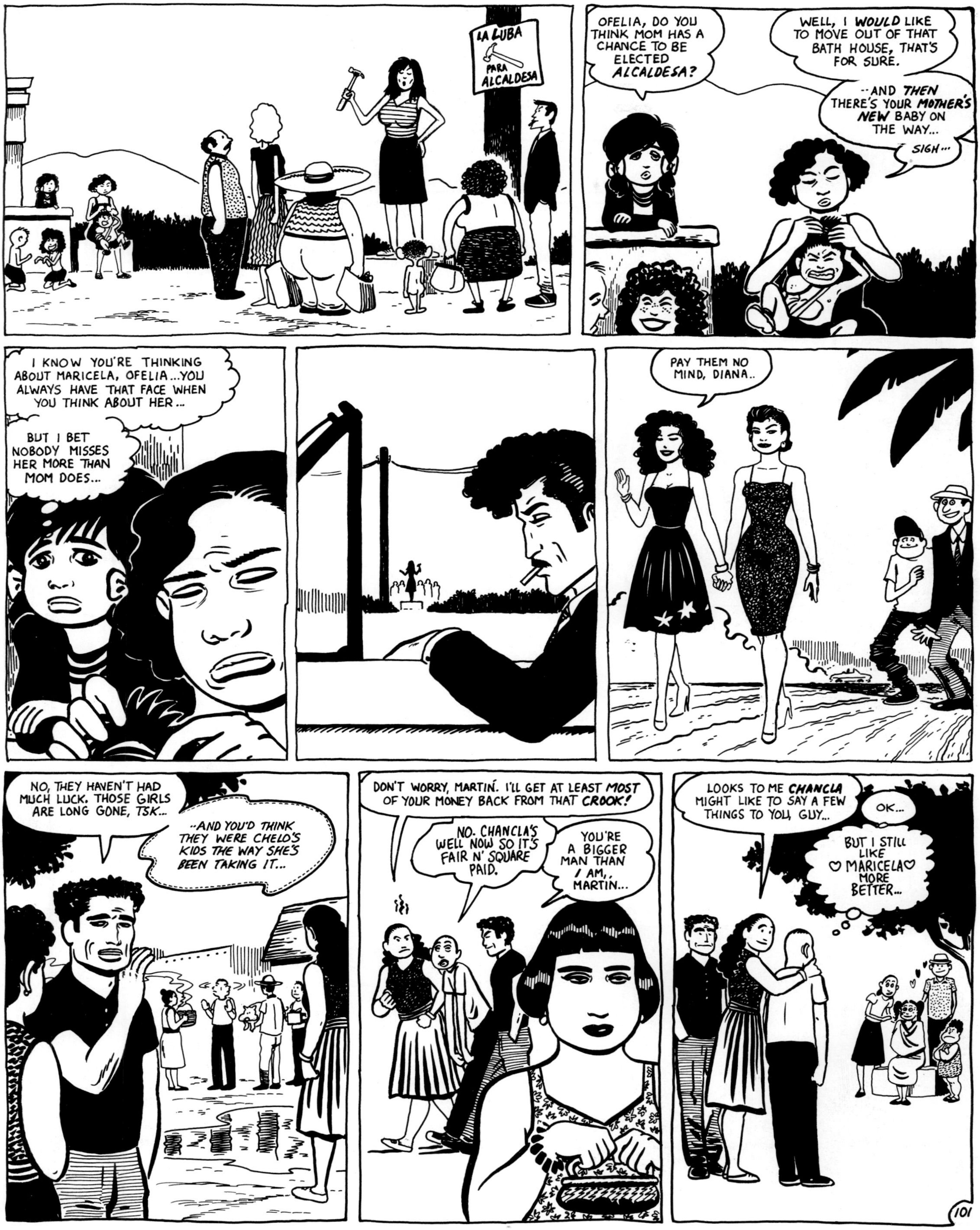
LA LUBA PARA ALCALDESA
OFELIA, DO YOU THINK MOM HAS A CHANCE TO BE ELECTED ALCALDESA?
WELL, I WOULD LIKE TO MOVE OUT OF THAT BATH HOUSE, THAT'S FOR SURE.
--AND THEN THERE'S YOUR MOTHER'S NEW BABY ON THE WAY...
SIGH...
I KNOW YOU'RE THINKING ABOUT MARICELA, OFELIA...YOU ALWAYS HAVE THAT FACE WHEN YOU THINK ABOUT HER...
BUT I BET NOBODY MISSES HER MORE THAN MOM DOES...
PAY THEM NO MIND, DIANA..
NO, THEY HAVEN'T HAD MUCH LUCK. THOSE GIRLS ARE LONG GONE, TSK...
--AND YOU'D THINK THEY WERE CHELO'S KIDS THE WAY SHE'S BEEN TAKING IT...
DON'T WORRY, MARTÍN. I'LL GET AT LEAST MOST OF YOUR MONEY BACK FROM THAT CROOK!
NO. CHANCLA'S WELL NOW SO IT'S FAIR N' SQUARE PAID.
YOU'RE A BIGGER MAN THAN I AM, MARTIN...
LOOKS TO ME CHANCLA MIGHT LIKE TO SAY A FEW THINGS TO YOU, GUY...
OK...
BUT I STILL LIKE ♡MARICELA♡ MORE BETTER...
101

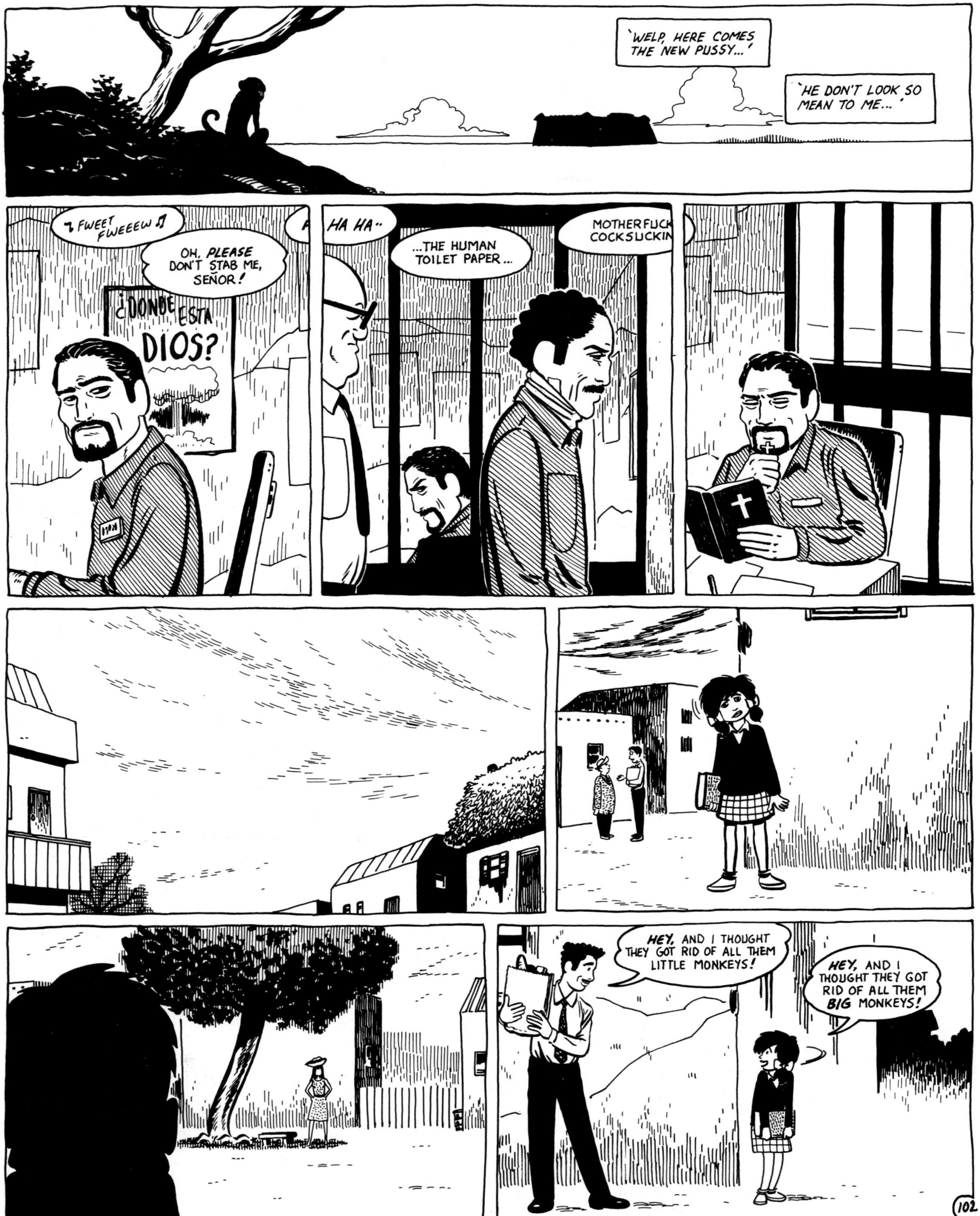

`WELP, HERE COMES THE NEW PUSSY...'
`HE DON'T LOOK SO MEAN TO ME...'
FWEET FWEEEW
OH, PLEASE DON'T STAB ME, SEÑOR!
¿DONDE ESTA DIOS?
HA HA
...THE HUMAN TOILET PAPER...
MOTHERFUCK COCKSUCKIN
HEY, AND I THOUGHT THEY GOT RID OF ALL THEM LITTLE MONKEYS!
HEY, AND I THOUGHT THEY GOT RID OF ALL THEM BIG MONKEYS!
102

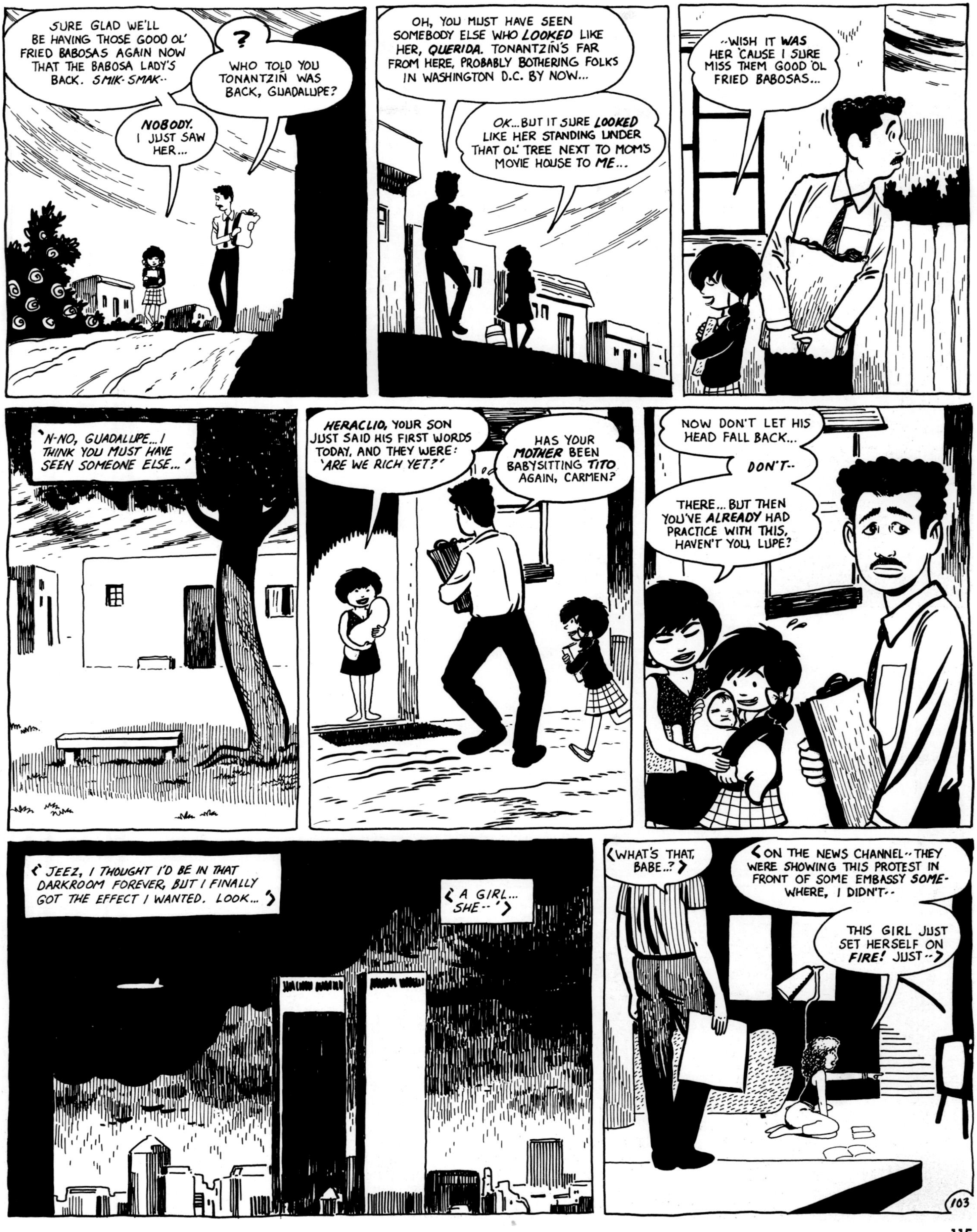
SURE GLAD WE'LL BE HAVING THOSE GOOD OL' FRIED BABOSAS AGAIN NOW THAT THE BABOSA LADY'S BACK. SMIK-SMAK··
?
WHO TOLD YOU TONANTZIN WAS BACK, GUADALUPE?
NOBODY. I JUST SAW HER...
OH, YOU MUST HAVE SEEN SOMEBODY ELSE WHO LOOKED LIKE HER, QUERIDA. TONANTZIN'S FAR FROM HERE, PROBABLY BOTHERING FOLKS IN WASHINGTON D.C. BY NOW...
OK... BUT IT SURE LOOKED LIKE HER STANDING UNDER THAT OL' TREE NEXT TO MOM'S MOVIE HOUSE TO ME...
··WISH IT WAS HER 'CAUSE I SURE MISS THEM GOOD 'OL FRIED BABOSAS...
'N-NO, GUADALUPE... I THINK YOU MUST HAVE SEEN SOMEONE ELSE...'
HERACLIO, YOUR SON JUST SAID HIS FIRST WORDS TODAY, AND THEY WERE: 'ARE WE RICH YET?'
HAS YOUR MOTHER BEEN BABYSITTING TITO AGAIN, CARMEN?
NOW DON'T LET HIS HEAD FALL BACK...
DON'T··
THERE... BUT THEN YOU'VE ALREADY HAD PRACTICE WITH THIS, HAVEN'T YOU, LUPE?
<'JEEZ, I THOUGHT I'D BE IN THAT DARKROOM FOREVER, BUT I FINALLY GOT THE EFFECT I WANTED. LOOK...'>
<'A GIRL... SHE··'>
<WHAT'S THAT, BABE..?>
<ON THE NEWS CHANNEL·· THEY WERE SHOWING THIS PROTEST IN FRONT OF SOME EMBASSY SOMEWHERE, I DIDN'T··
THIS GIRL JUST SET HERSELF ON FIRE! JUST··>
103

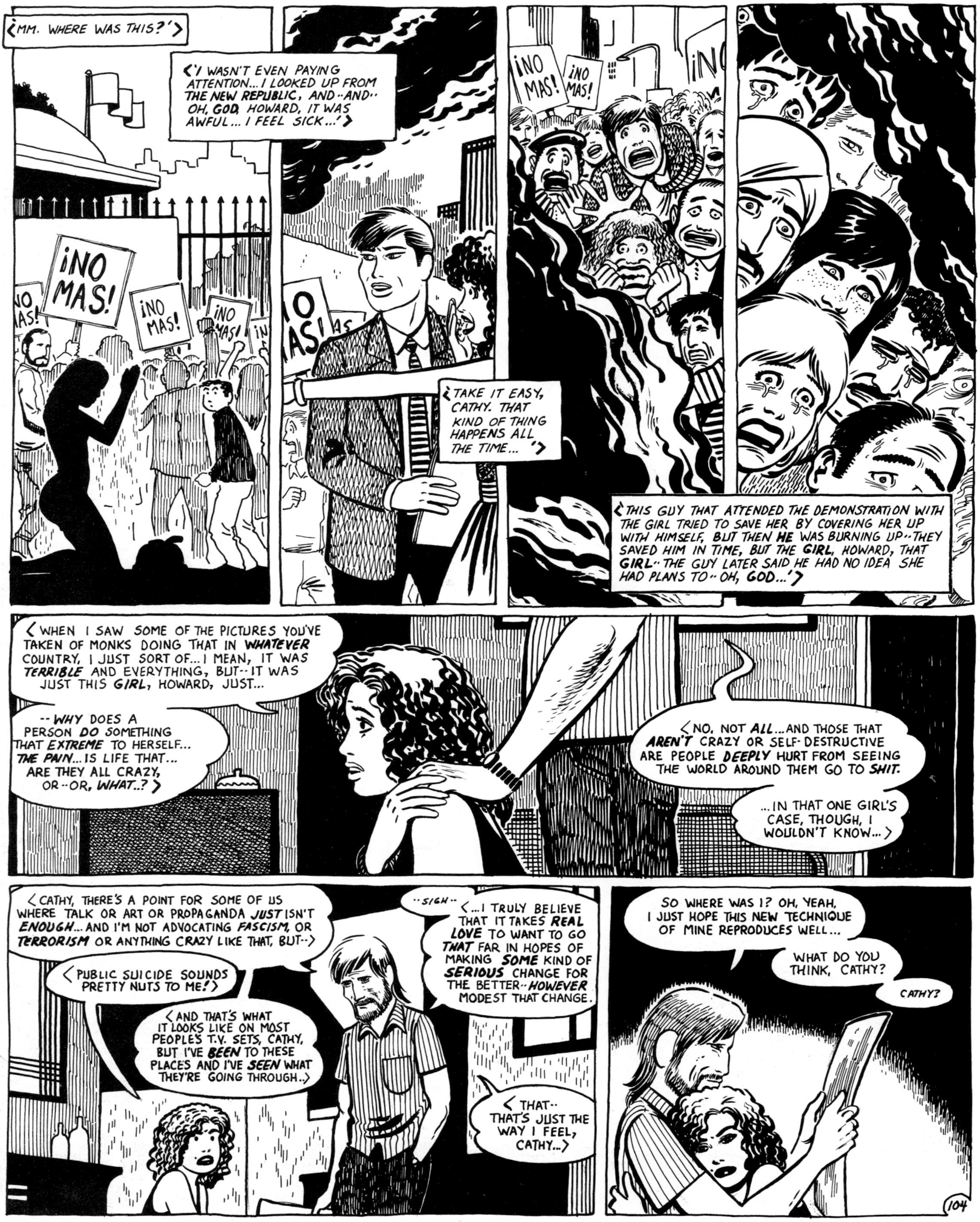
¿MM. WHERE WAS THIS?'>
<'I WASN'T EVEN PAYING ATTENTION... I LOOKED UP FROM THE NEW REPUBLIC, AND--AND-- OH, GOD, HOWARD, IT WAS AWFUL... I FEEL SICK...'>
¡NO MAS!
¿TAKE IT EASY, CATHY. THAT KIND OF THING HAPPENS ALL THE TIME...'>
¿THIS GUY THAT ATTENDED THE DEMONSTRATION WITH THE GIRL TRIED TO SAVE HER BY COVERING HER UP WITH HIMSELF, BUT THEN HE WAS BURNING UP--THEY SAVED HIM IN TIME, BUT THE GIRL, HOWARD, THAT GIRL-- THE GUY LATER SAID HE HAD NO IDEA SHE HAD PLANS TO--OH, GOD...'>
<WHEN I SAW SOME OF THE PICTURES YOU'VE TAKEN OF MONKS DOING THAT IN WHATEVER COUNTRY, I JUST SORT OF... I MEAN, IT WAS TERRIBLE AND EVERYTHING, BUT--IT WAS JUST THIS GIRL, HOWARD, JUST...
--WHY DOES A PERSON DO SOMETHING THAT EXTREME TO HERSELF... THE PAIN... IS LIFE THAT... ARE THEY ALL CRAZY, OR--OR, WHAT..?>
<NO, NOT ALL... AND THOSE THAT AREN'T CRAZY OR SELF-DESTRUCTIVE ARE PEOPLE DEEPLY HURT FROM SEEING THE WORLD AROUND THEM GO TO SHIT.
...IN THAT ONE GIRL'S CASE, THOUGH, I WOULDN'T KNOW...>
<CATHY, THERE'S A POINT FOR SOME OF US WHERE TALK OR ART OR PROPAGANDA JUST ISN'T ENOUGH... AND I'M NOT ADVOCATING FASCISM, OR TERRORISM OR ANYTHING CRAZY LIKE THAT, BUT-->
<PUBLIC SUICIDE SOUNDS PRETTY NUTS TO ME!>
<AND THAT'S WHAT IT LOOKS LIKE ON MOST PEOPLE'S T.V. SETS, CATHY, BUT I'VE BEEN TO THESE PLACES AND I'VE SEEN WHAT THEY'RE GOING THROUGH..>
--SIGH--
<...I TRULY BELIEVE THAT IT TAKES REAL LOVE TO WANT TO GO THAT FAR IN HOPES OF MAKING SOME KIND OF SERIOUS CHANGE FOR THE BETTER--HOWEVER MODEST THAT CHANGE.
<THAT-- THAT'S JUST THE WAY I FEEL, CATHY...>
SO WHERE WAS I? OH, YEAH, I JUST HOPE THIS NEW TECHNIQUE OF MINE REPRODUCES WELL...
WHAT DO YOU THINK, CATHY?
CATHY?
104

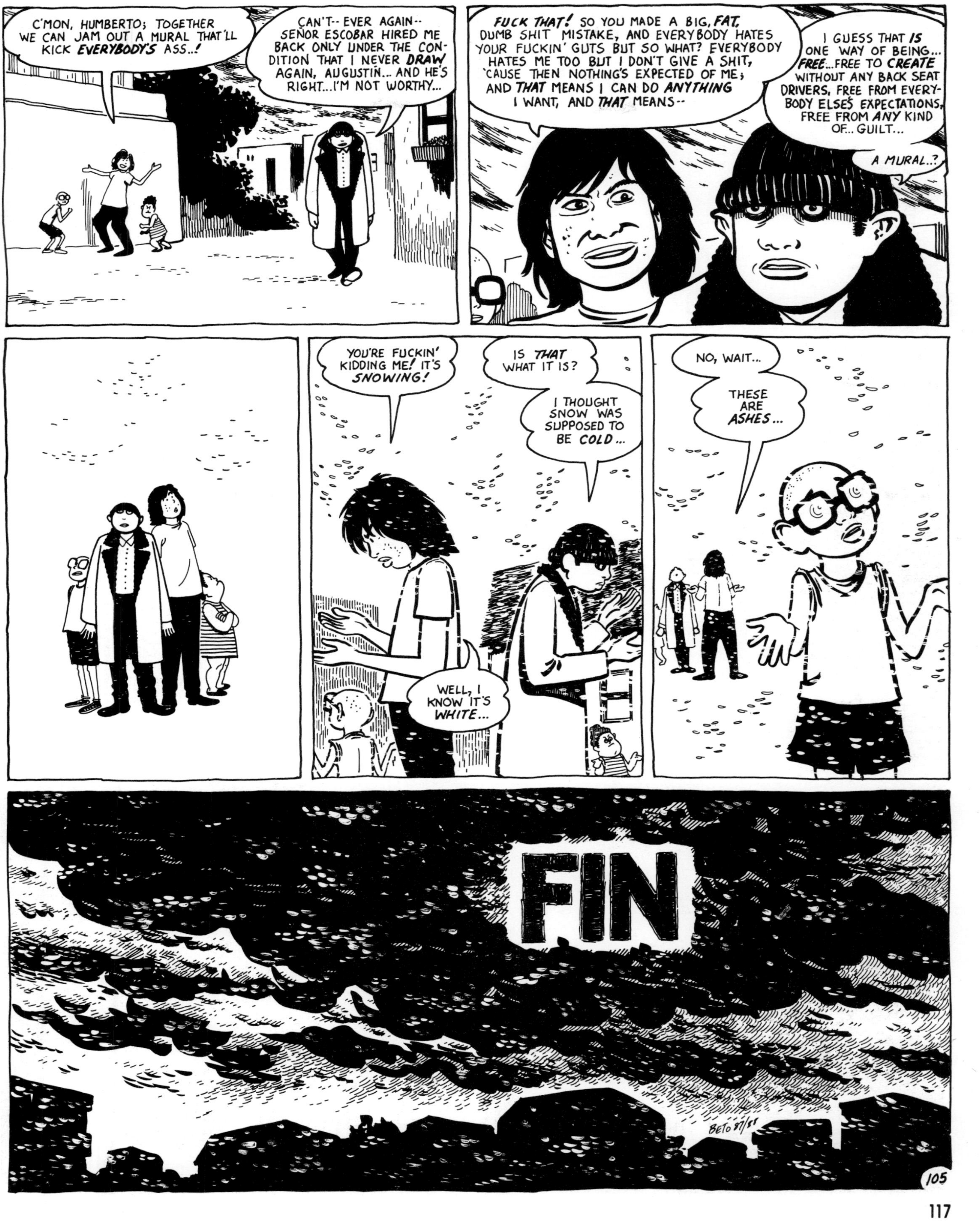
C'MON, HUMBERTO; TOGETHER WE CAN JAM OUT A MURAL THAT'LL KICK EVERYBODY'S ASS..!
CAN'T-- EVER AGAIN-- SEÑOR ESCOBAR HIRED ME BACK ONLY UNDER THE CONDITION THAT I NEVER DRAW AGAIN, AUGUSTIN... AND HE'S RIGHT... I'M NOT WORTHY...
FUCK THAT! SO YOU MADE A BIG, FAT, DUMB SHIT MISTAKE, AND EVERYBODY HATES YOUR FUCKIN' GUTS BUT SO WHAT? EVERYBODY HATES ME TOO BUT I DON'T GIVE A SHIT, 'CAUSE THEN NOTHING'S EXPECTED OF ME; AND THAT MEANS I CAN DO ANYTHING I WANT, AND THAT MEANS--
I GUESS THAT IS ONE WAY OF BEING... FREE... FREE TO CREATE WITHOUT ANY BACK SEAT DRIVERS, FREE FROM EVERYBODY ELSE'S EXPECTATIONS, FREE FROM ANY KIND OF... GUILT...
A MURAL..?
YOU'RE FUCKIN' KIDDING ME! IT'S SNOWING!
IS THAT WHAT IT IS?
I THOUGHT SNOW WAS SUPPOSED TO BE COLD...
WELL, I KNOW IT'S WHITE...
NO, WAIT...
THESE ARE ASHES...
FIN
BETO 87/88
105

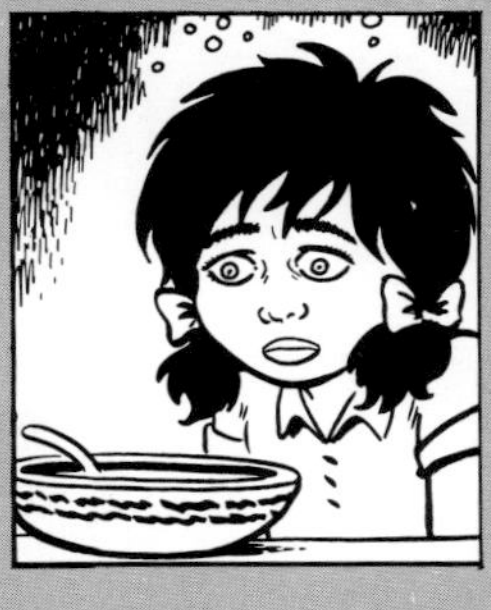

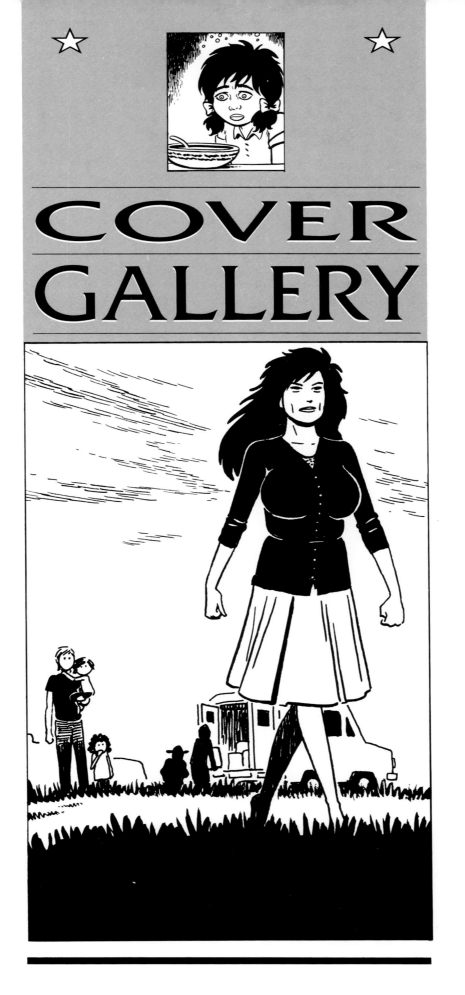

COVER GALLERY

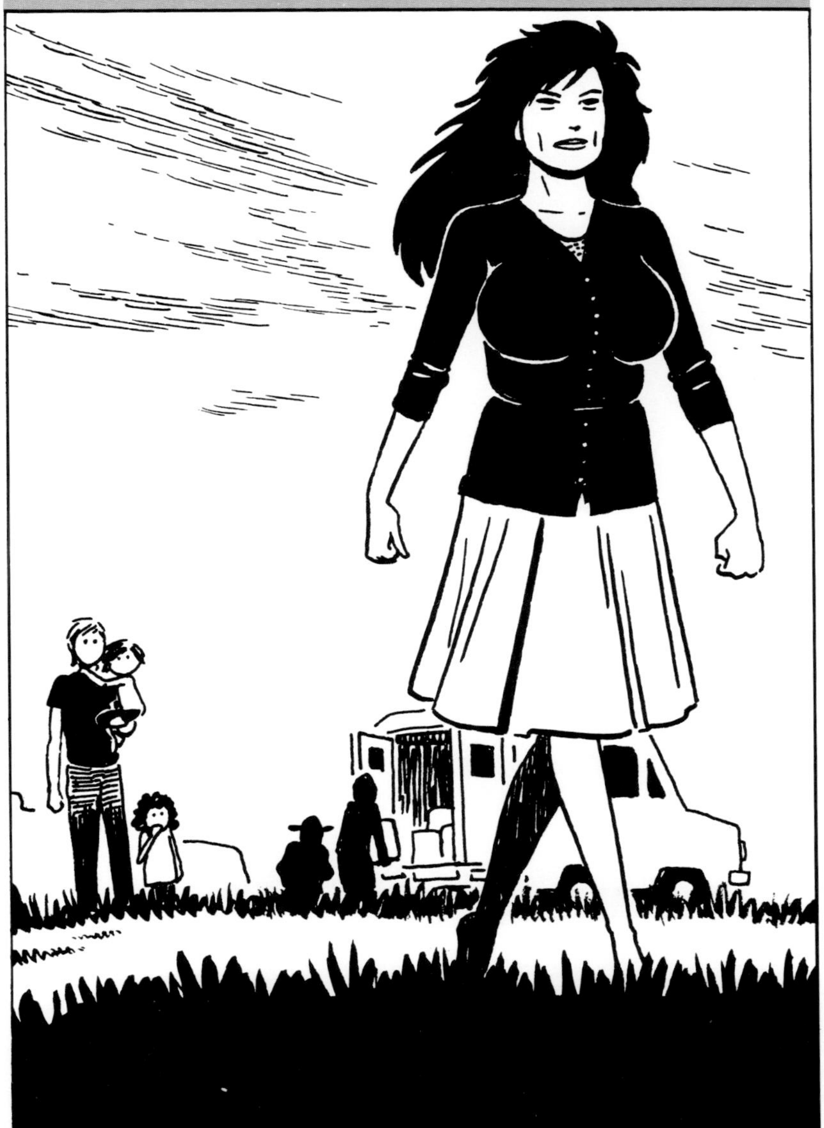

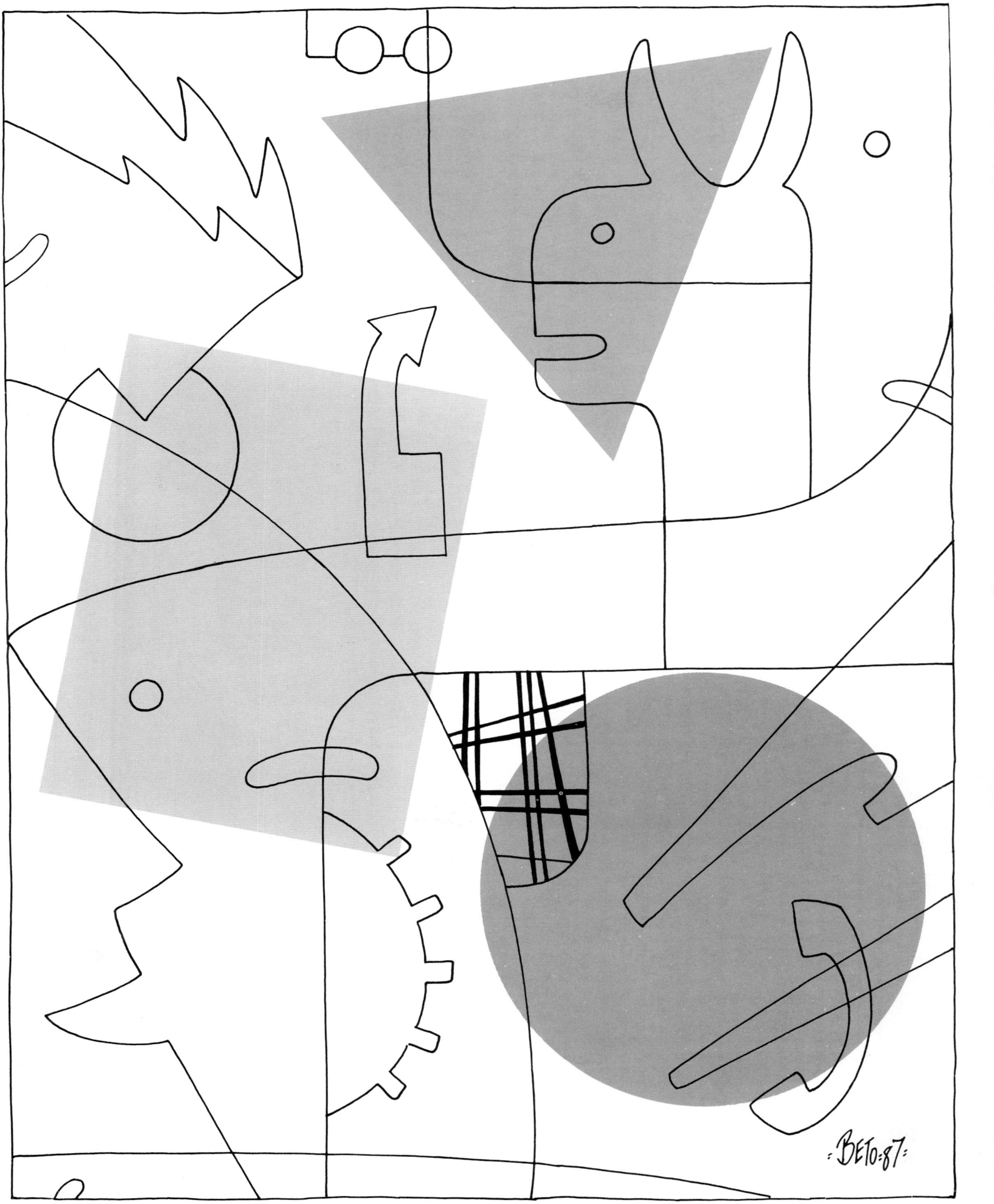
BETO 87

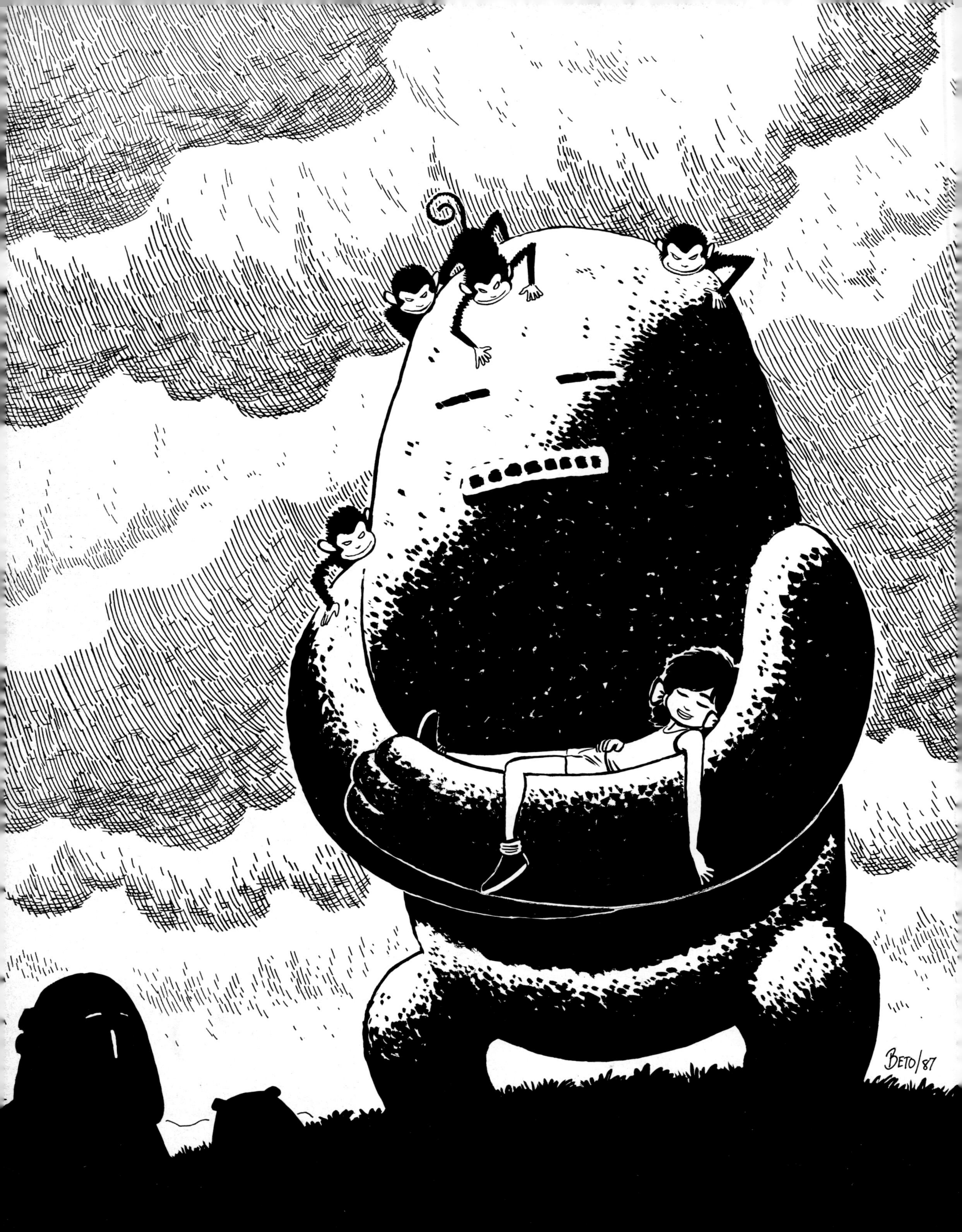
BETO/87

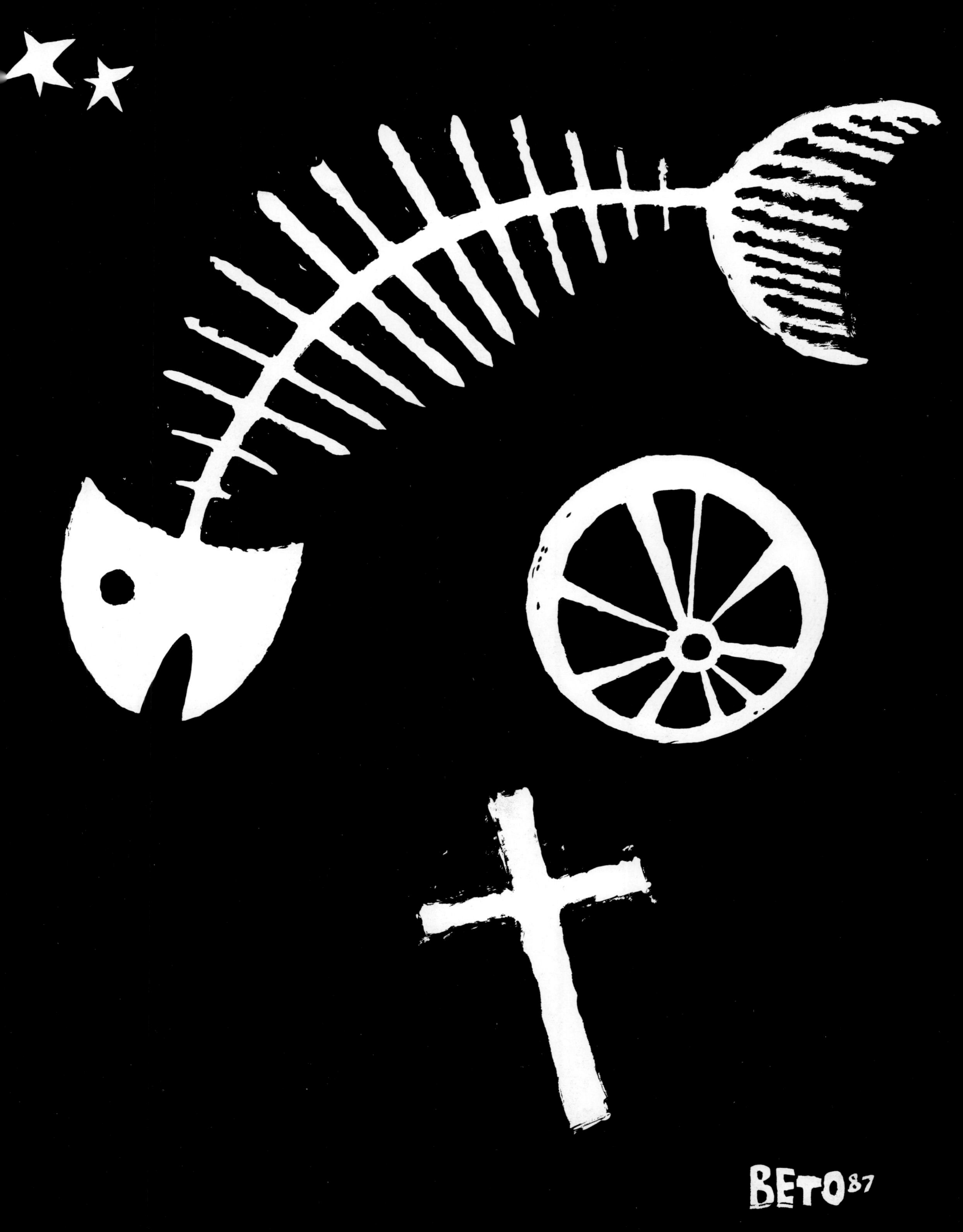
BETO 87

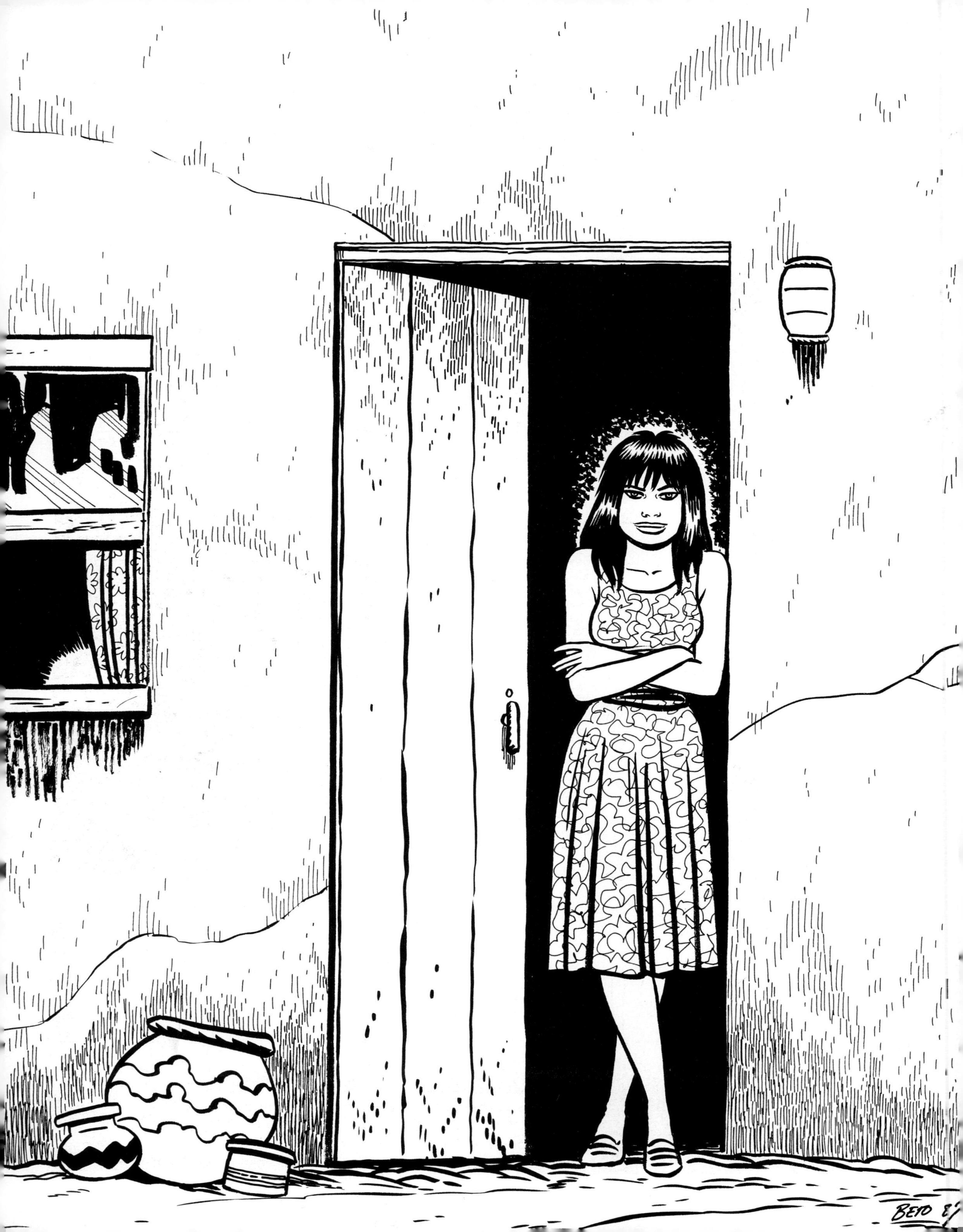
BETO

PART 2

HUMAN

DIASTROPHISM

BETO-87

IN PART ONE: LUBA'S OLD FLAME KHAMO HAS COME TO PALOMAR. A LETTER TO TONANTZÍN FROM GERALDO MEJIA (WHO'S IN PRISON) HAS DIANA, CARMEN AND PIPO CONVINCED THAT IT'S MEJIA'S FAULT TONANTZÍN'S LOSING HER MARBLES.

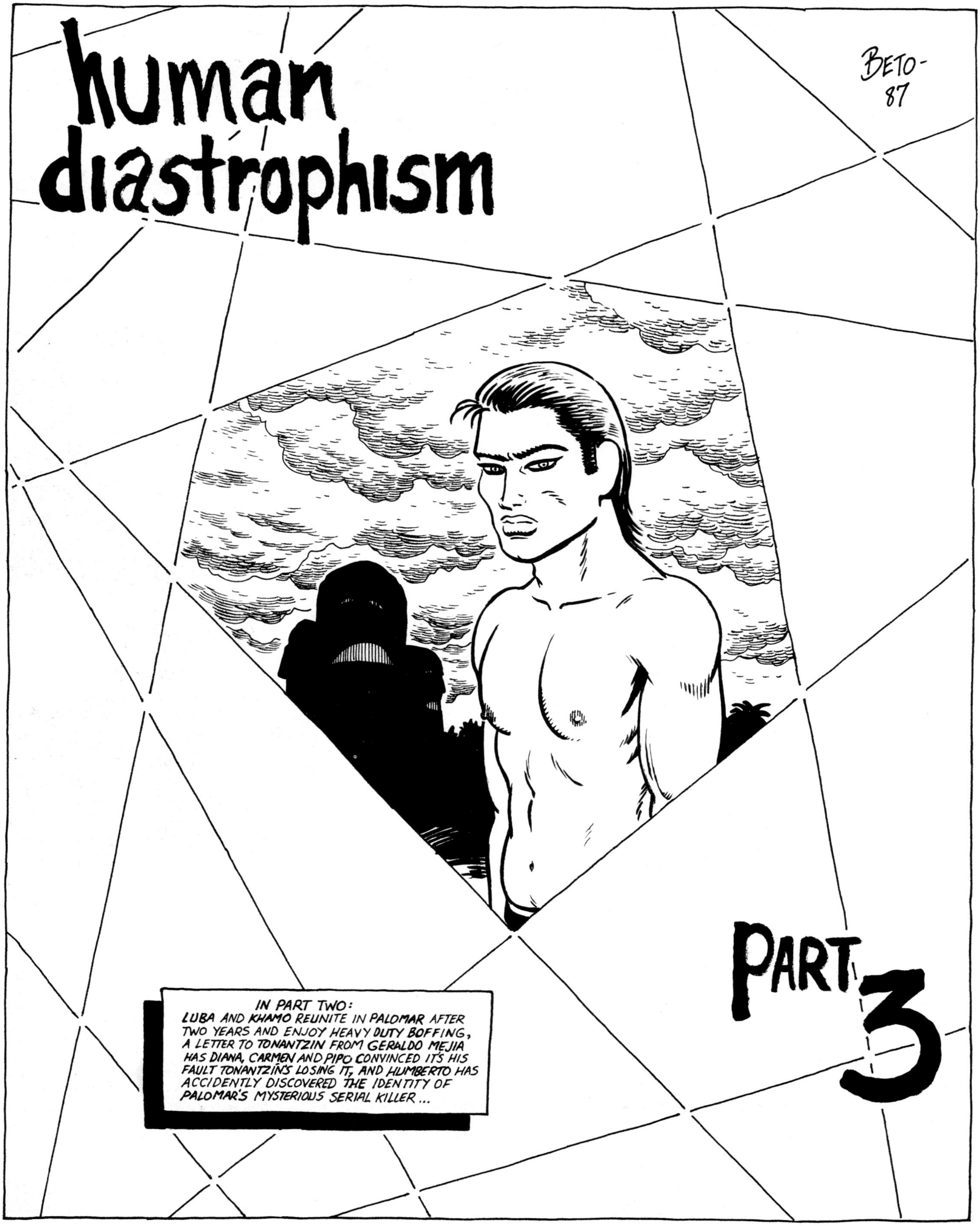
human diastrophism
BETO-87
IN PART TWO:
LUBA AND KHAMO REUNITE IN PALOMAR AFTER TWO YEARS AND ENJOY HEAVY DUTY BOFFING, A LETTER TO TONANTZIN FROM GERALDO MEJIA HAS DIANA, CARMEN AND PIPO CONVINCED IT'S HIS FAULT TONANTZÍN'S LOSING IT, AND HUMBERTO HAS ACCIDENTLY DISCOVERED THE IDENTITY OF PALOMAR'S MYSTERIOUS SERIAL KILLER...
PART 3

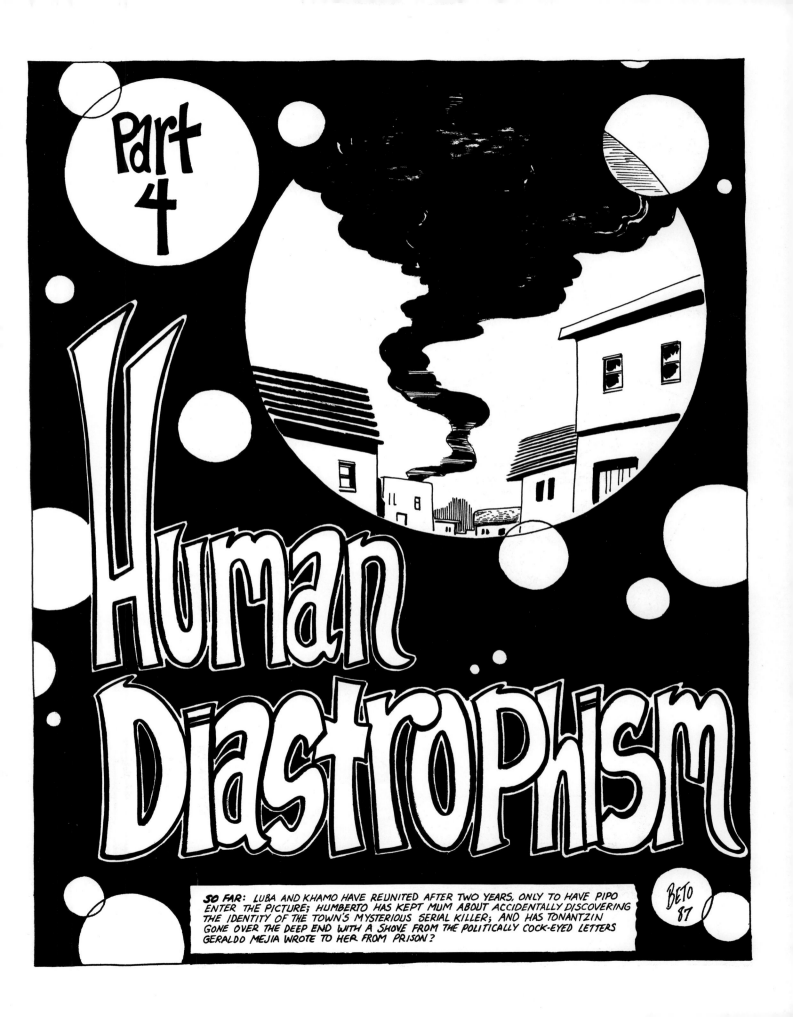

Part 4

Human Diastrophism

BETO 87

SO FAR: LUBA AND KHAMO HAVE REUNITED AFTER TWO YEARS, ONLY TO HAVE PIPO ENTER THE PICTURE; HUMBERTO HAS KEPT MUM ABOUT ACCIDENTALLY DISCOVERING THE IDENTITY OF THE TOWN'S MYSTERIOUS SERIAL KILLER; AND HAS TONANTZIN GONE OVER THE DEEP END WITH A SHOVE FROM THE POLITICALLY COCK-EYED LETTERS GERALDO MEJIA WROTE TO HER FROM PRISON?

...PART FIVE...

hū·man diaś·trō·fiz·ĕm

A. BELONGING TO, OR HAVING THE QUALITIES OF, MAN OR MANKIND.

N. THE ACTION OF FORCES THAT DEFORM THE EARTH'S CRUST AND SO PRODUCE CONTINENTS, MOUNTAINS, ETC...

SO FAR...

LUBA: HER OLD FLAME KHAMO HAS COME TO PALOMAR.
PIPO: SHE PLUS KHAMO EQUALS **BOFF CITY.**
HUMBERTO: ONLY HE KNOWS THE IDENTITY OF THE SERIAL KILLER... OR DOES HE?
BORRO: HE'S RETURNED TO CATCH THIS MYSTERY KILLER AND WANTS ANOTHER CHANCE AT LUBA.
TONANTZIN: SHE HAS BECOME POLITICIZED DUE TO LETTERS SENT TO HER FROM EX-LOVER/NOW CONVICT GERALDO MEJIA. HER CONCERN OVER THE CONDITION OF THE WORLD HAS LED HER TO FASTING.

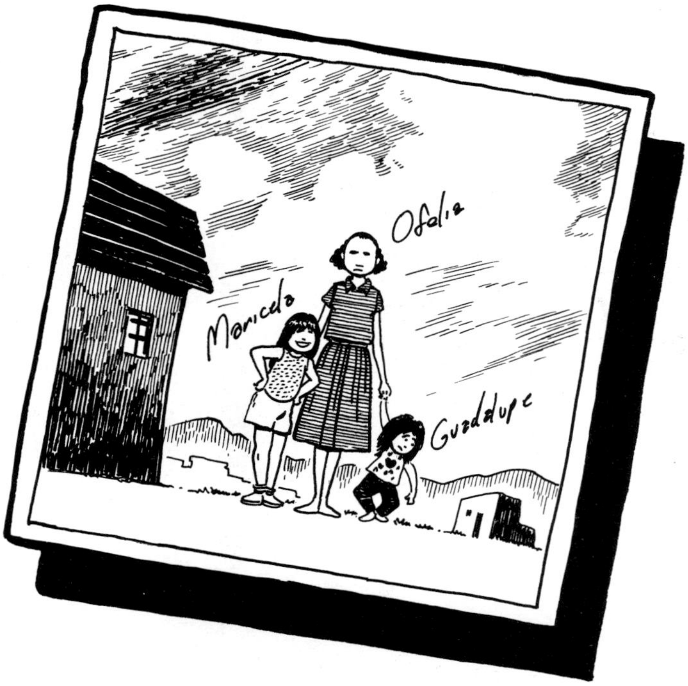
Ofelia
Maricela
Guadalupe

BETO '87

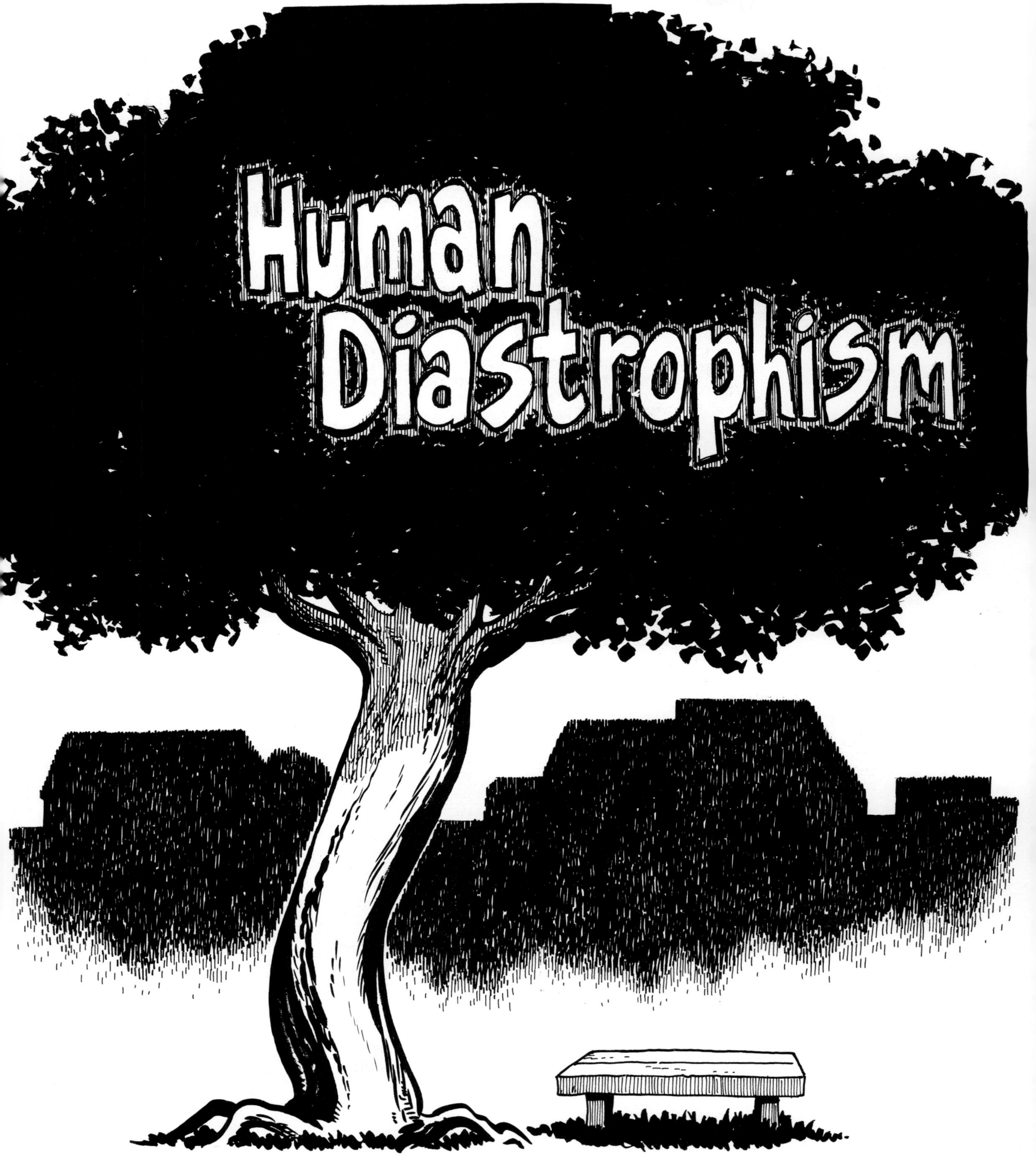
Human Diastrophism

.. PINTOR'S TREE ..
IT IS BELIEVED BY SOME THAT THE GHOSTS OF PINTOR SALCEDO AND OTHERS MANIFEST THEMSELVES BY THIS TREE FROM TIME TO TIME...

BETO/ 87.88

IF YOU ENJOYED THIS BOOK...

Fantagraphics Books has also published the following books by Los Bros. Hernandez.

Love and Rockets Books 1-7 ($12.95 each). In the same format as the tome currently clutched in your hands, these volumes combined reprint the entirety of the first 26 issues of the **Love and Rockets** comic –plus a selection of new stories as well.

Love and Rockets: Short Stories and **The Lost Women** ($10.95 each) Two compact volumes (6" x 9"), each reprinting over 130 pages of Jaime Hernandez's strips–including the "Locas/Mechanics" series and "Rocky." Introductions by Carter Scholz and Brad Holland.

Heartbreak Soup and Other Stories and **The Reticent Heart** ($10.95 each) In the same format as the Jaime Hernandez solo books, the first two installments of Gilbert Hernandez's Palomar saga–plus "Errata Stigmata," and more. Introductions by Alan Moore and Harvey Pekar.

The Love and Rockets Sketchbook ($19.95) Not just a sketchbook (although there's hundreds of roughs and finished drawings from the Bros. in here too), but a collection of pre-L&R comics and illustrations, including SF strips by Gilbert and Mario Hernandez, and a very early "Mechanics" yarn by Jaime Hernandez. 180 pages, oversize format.

Love and Rockets Calendars 1989 and **1990** ($9.95) Many brand new full-page illustrations by Gilbert and Jaime Hernandez (plus a few dozen small ones), as well as an eclectic collection of dates to remember.

*Each of these can be had by mail for $1.00 postage and handling from Fantagraphics Books, 7563 Lake City Way, Seattle, WA 98115. You can also subscribe to **Love and Rockets** for six issues ($15.00)–or just send us a postcard to get our catalogue of new & classic comics work by R. Crumb, Jules Feiffer, Berni Wrightson, Vaughn Bode, Stan Sakai, Frank Frazetta, Hal Foster, E.C. Segar, Kaz, Peter Bagge, Winsor McCay, and many others.*